Earth Governance

NEW HORIZONS IN ENVIRONMENTAL AND ENERGY LAW

Series Editors: Kurt Deketelaere, *Professor of Law, University of Leuven, Belgium and University of Dundee, Scotland* and Zen Makuch, *Reader in Law, Barrister, Imperial College, London, UK*

Environmental law – including the pressing considerations of energy law and climate change – is an increasingly important area of legal research and practice. Given the growing interdependence of global society and the significant steps being made towards environmental protection and energy efficiency, there are few people untouched by environmental and energy lawmaking processes.

At the same time, environmental and energy law is at a crossroads. The command and control methodology that evolved in the 1960s and 1970s for air, land and water protection may have reached the limit of its environmental protection achievements. New life needs to be injected into our environmental protection regimes – perhaps through the concept of sustainability in its environmental, economic and social forms. The same goes for energy policy and law, where liberalization, environmental protection and security of supply are at the centre of attention. This important series seeks to press forward the boundaries of environmental and energy law through innovative research into environmental and energy law, doctrine and case law. Adopting a wide interpretation of environmental and energy law, it includes contributions from both leading and emerging international scholars.

Titles in the series include:

Energy for the 21st Century
Opportunities and Challenges for Liquefied Natural Gas (LNG)
Susan L. Sakmar

Emissions Trading Design
A Critical Overview
Stefan E. Weishaar

EU Environmental Legislation
Legal Perspectives on Regulatory Strategies
Edited by Marjan Peeters and Rosa Uylenburg

Polar Oceans Governance in an Era of Environmental Change
Edited by Tim Stephens and David L. VanderZwaag

The Fragmentation of Global Climate Governance
Consequences and Management of Regime Interactions
Harro van Asselt

Renewable Energy Law in the EU
Legal Perspectives on Bottom-up Approaches
Edited by Marjan Peeters and Thomas Schomerus

Environmental Enforcement Networks
Concepts, Implementation and Effectiveness
Edited by Michael Faure, Peter De Smedt and An Stas

Regulation of the Upstream Petroleum Sector
A Comparative Study of Licensing and Concession Systems
Edited by Tina Hunter

Regional Environmental Law
Transregional Comparative Lessons in Pursuit of Sustainable Development
Edited by Werner Scholtz and Jonathan Verschuuren

Earth Governance
Trusteeship of the Global Commons
Klaus Bosselmann

Earth Governance

Trusteeship of the Global Commons

Klaus Bosselmann

Director, New Zealand Centre for Environmental Law, University of Auckland, New Zealand

NEW HORIZONS IN ENVIRONMENTAL AND ENERGY LAW

Edward Elgar
PUBLISHING

Cheltenham, UK • Northampton, MA, USA

Published by
Edward Elgar Publishing Limited
The Lypiatts
15 Lansdown Road
Cheltenham
Glos GL50 2JA
UK

Edward Elgar Publishing, Inc.
William Pratt House
9 Dewey Court
Northampton
Massachusetts 01060
USA

A catalogue record for this book
is available from the British Library

Library of Congress Control Number: 2015933454

This book is available electronically in the Elgaronline
Law subject collection
DOI 10.4337/9781783477821

MIX
Paper from responsible sources
FSC® C013056

ISBN 978 1 78347 781 4 (cased)
ISBN 978 1 78347 782 1 (eBook)

Typeset by Servis Filmsetting Ltd, Stockport, Cheshire
Printed and bound in Great Britain by T.J. International Ltd, Padstow

To
Johannes, Christian and Olivia (of the next generation)
and Greta (of the generation thereafter)

Contents

Preface

Twenty years ago, the Commission on Global Governance published its Report *Our Global Neighbourhood*.[1] It was written at a time when the world began to realize the need for remodelling international law and governance. Most problems such as climate change, poverty or free market ideology are global, but none of them can be solved in an outdated system of inter-state governance based on an outdated idea of sovereignty:

> Sovereignty has been the cornerstone of the inter-state system. In an increasingly interdependent world, however, the notions of territoriality, independence, and non-intervention have lost some of their meaning. In certain areas, sovereignty must be exercised collectively, particularly in relation to the global commons.[2]

To this end, the report recommended reforming the United Nations, in particular: 'The Trusteeship Council should be given a new mandate over the global commons in the context of concern for the security of the planet.'

Essentially, the report called for a shift from state-centered governance to what can be described as earth-centered governance, assuming the interrelatedness of earth as a whole. At the core of this shift is the concern for the global commons, that is, the oceans, the atmosphere, the entire biosphere. We are rapidly losing the global commons and in the process we may also lose local commons such as livelihoods, knowledge, the cultural sphere. By definition, commons are for all and cannot be owned privately. They are the stuff that make up communities and societies – and ultimately 'the security of the planet'.

This book examines our prospects 20 years after the Global Governance Report. Since then, there have been high-powered global summits, numerous initiatives for more effective governance and many proposals for saving the commons. In this way, progress has been made.

On the other hand, the world has gone backwards and some would

---

[1] Commission on Global Governance, *Our Global Neighbourhood* (OUP, 1995).

[2] Ibid.

say it is all too late now: runaway climate change, exploding biodiversity loss and collapsing ecosystems, but also poverty, disintegrating societies, over-indebted countries and governments barely able to manage the crisis. Active and formative politics seem a distant prospect today. In fact, corporate power has grown so strong that most politicians seem to have adopted a corporate mentality. Money dominates everything: some have too much of it, many too little and financial logic dictates what governments can or cannot do. The problems of the 1990s have amounted to a single challenge, that is, keeping up the civilizationary project. Who would have foreseen that the power of the people ('democracy') could be superseded by corporate power ('corporatism') in such a short space of time?

Something dramatic has to happen if we are to continue the civilizationary project. Many say that the most pressing issue right now is to preserve and restore democracy, but this alone is not enough: we need to develop a sense of commonality across nations, a sense of 'we-are-all-in-this-together'. People in diverse countries and cultures need to learn to speak with one voice, that is, the voice of global citizens. The global citizenship perspective is the most significant step towards earth governance. Its emergence means that nation-states are bound to eventually convert from competing to cooperating members of a global community. Such a conversion will not be initiated by states as they tend to concern themselves purely with their own territories and constituencies.

This dynamic will change, however, as constituencies become aware of their mutual interdependencies. Arguably, this has been happening through the emergence of global civil society since the 1990s.[3] As people realize how much their individual and collective lives are influenced by global forces beyond their control or the control of their governments, they demand more effective forms of governance. Correspondingly, states may see it in their enlightened self-interest to offer mutually beneficial cooperation to other states.

This creates a new dynamic in international relations. That states are 'absolute' or 'exclusive' in their sovereignty has probably always been a myth, but any such attributes must give way to more realistic ones such as 'relative', 'cooperative', 'collective', 'responsible' or 'smart', in order to describe effective sovereignty. This is particularly true with respect to the global environment. In no other segment of global governance are we seeing the need for 'sovereign' states to cooperate for a common goal.

---

[3] As an indication, Google brings up nearly 100 million references to the emergence of global civil society, with numerous publications focusing on the challenge of making global institutions effective and accountable.

Climate change is just one example of the dilemma that states, in their current configuration, find themselves in. Caught between the habit of economic nationalism and the desire for environmental globalism, they appear paralysed and incapable of creating effective climate regimes. The paralysis is caused by a mismatch between legal accountability (to own constituencies) and moral responsibility (towards all constituencies). It is conceivable that the gap between legality and morality can be closed over time, but it won't happen without fundamentally redefining the roles and functions of the state.

The dynamics of change are there, but have not yet resulted in new forms and institutions of governance, although the breakthrough may happen sooner rather than later, as this book is going to argue. The core argument is for a shift from state-centred governance to governance centred around the earth as an integrated, interconnected whole. Earth governance gives priority to the protection of what all humanity has in common, in particular the global commons and the interest in preserving them. This implies an ethic of stewardship or trusteeship, an ethic that expresses itself in the attitude of decision-makers and in the way institutions are being changed or created.

The urgency of this ethic was the motivation behind the book, but also the rich tradition of the commons that all cultures and jurisdictions can draw from. In fact, until the emergence of modern property rights during the eighteenth century, the commons represented the dominant form of entitlement. Collective entitlements to the commons had priority over individual entitlements such as lease, user rights or private property. Considering the wealth of experience that most legal cultures have with governing the commons, the case for trusteeship of the global commons is indeed compelling.

The book's eight chapters aim to make this case. The first chapter describes some ecological, economic and political tipping points that the world is facing. The second chapter then introduces earth governance as a new framework for both national and global policies. Chapters 3 and 4 examine the global commons with their two components of the 'commons' (including their ongoing enclosure) and their global, transnational nature. Chapters 5 and 6 explore trusteeship as an established concept of law and governance. As will be shown, governance institutions such as the state have recognizable trusteeship functions that are now becoming crucial for securing the planet. Arguably, existing legal underpinnings allow and oblige the state to act as an environmental trustee – both internally (under domestic law) and externally (under international law). The final two chapters of the book focus on trusteeship institutions at international level. The United Nations has its own tradition of trusteeship concepts to draw from, which is entirely predicated by the corresponding trusteeship traditions of its member states. From this perspective, new institutions such as a fiduciary World Environment Organization or a UN Environmental Trusteeship Council are feasible and desirable.

The overall objective is to demonstrate that the integrity of the earth's ecological systems now depends on institutional reform, but not on any institutional reform. Only an ethic of stewardship and trusteeship will create institutions, policies and laws powerful enough to reclaim and protect the global commons.

A number of colleagues and research students have helped to bring this book project, which started in 2011, to a successful close. I am grateful for ideas and support from Prue Taylor, Lucy Stroud, Michael Schröter, Ron Engel, Peter Burdon, Peter Sand and David Bollier. My colleagues at the New Zealand Centre for Environmental Law have been supportive in many ways, possibly more than they can imagine. Special thanks are due to Sarah Lawrence, Phillipa Norman, Grace Abbott and Sam Johnston for their invaluable research assistance and to Ben Booth and Laura Mann from Edward Elgar for their enthusiasm and patience.

Klaus Bosselmann
April 2015, Waiheke Island

1. World at a tipping point

> The liberty of a democracy is not safe if the people tolerate the growth of private power to a point where it becomes stronger than their democratic state itself. That, in its essence, is fascism – ownership of government by an individual, by a group, or by any other controlling private power. Among us today a concentration of private power without equal in history is growing.
>
> Franklin D. Roosevelt

1. INTRODUCTION

The global ecological crisis, on the one hand, and responses from nation-states to deal with it, on the other, are in complete disconnect. States and governments seem mere bystanders, unable, perhaps unwilling, to reclaim the commons and revert the forces of human self-destruction. They no longer govern. Rather, our democratically elected governments are caught up in crisis management with no signs of vision and direction. Are we seeing the end of functioning democracies on a global scale?

The critique of the democratic deficit of international law and governance is not new,[1] but it has never gathered more intuitive plausibility than now in an age of global warming. The impacts of climate change are all around us. Although the knowledge of an emerging ecological crisis is at least 40 years old, political leaders and the state-centred structure of international governance appear incapable of responding to it in an effective way: there is not only a democratic deficit but an ecological deficit as well.

The democratic and ecological deficits of international politics could have common ground though.[2] At international level the nations' representatives conventionally find themselves in a bargaining situation and

---

[1] See, for example, Steven Wheatley, *The Democratic Legitimacy of International Law* (Hart Publishing, 2010).

[2] See Vandana Shiva, 'The Greening of the Global Reach', in Wolfgang Sachs (ed.), *Global Ecology: A New Arena of Political Conflict* (Zed Books, London 1993): 155; Walter F. Barber and Robert V. Bartlett, *Global Democracy and Sustainable Jurisprudence: Deliberative Environmental Law* (The MIT Press, Cambridge/London 2009): 5; 'Earth Convention' (Democracy Convention, 2013): http://democracyconvention.org/focus-area/earth-democracy.

entangled in a situation of anarchy between states. National interests trump any sense of the common good. Such a rational choice perspective can hardly be democratic as it neither reflects a global nor a local perspective. At a global level, we are confronted with egos unable to see their collective destiny. From a local perspective, nations and their representatives rarely connect with the affected people, especially if they live in different countries. The ever-increasing gap between the rich North and the poor South is a direct result of the failure of state-centred governance.[3]

The antithesis of state-centred governance is earth-centred governance, or earth governance for short. If we start our thinking about and around global governance from the perspective of earth, we see the whole first, not its parts. The needs of earth and all her inhabitants stand right before us. They define the ends of action for which we must find the means. In this pursuit, states are means, not ends in themselves. It is wrong to believe that states define the means and ends of global governance. They can only ever be instruments (means) of people (earth's inhabitants) who ultimately define the purpose (ends) of human action. Earth governance describes a new starting point, a new goal and new ways to get there.

Essentially, earth governance is the epitome of people taking responsibility for the lives of all beings. A strong expression of this sense of responsibility can be found in the Earth Charter. The Earth Charter provides an ethical framework for global governance, a new covenant between humans and nature. In part IV, 'Democracy, Nonviolence, and Peace', it states four principles aiming at a democratic culture for sustainable governance:[4]

1. to strengthen democracy at all levels (including transparency, accountability, participation and access to justice);
2. to integrate the required capabilities for a sustainable way of living in a process of lifelong learning;
3. to treat all living beings with respect and consideration;
4. to promote a culture of tolerance, nonviolence, and peace.[5]

---

[3] Klaus Bosselmann, 'Towards Multilevel Governance for Sustainability: Trends and Challenges', in *Contested Futures: Sustainability, Governance and International Human Rights* (Europe – New Zealand Research Series Paper, 2010): 1, 11, 26.

[4] See also Klaus Bosselmann, J. Ronald Engel and Prue Taylor, *Governance for Sustainability: Issues, Challenges, Successes* (IUCN Environmental Policy and Law Paper No. 70, 2008).

[5] For further democratic implications of the Earth Charter, see J. Ronald Engel, 'The Earth Charter as a New Covenant for Democracy', in Klaus Bosselmann and J. Ronald Engel (eds), *The Earth Charter: A Framework for Global Governance* (KIT Publishing, Leiden 2010): 29–40.

The current ecological crisis has been scientifically examined and politically discussed for over 40 years.[6] Several international meetings have taken place and some of them have resulted in soft law documents such as agreements, conventions, treaties, etc. So far, only one global treaty actually sets out targets and timetables, that is, the Kyoto Protocol.[7] Although the Kyoto Protocol is flawed both in content and execution, it represents the first international attempt at practical action to tackle one serious threat of the ecological crisis (global warming). Nothing comparable can be said about the international regime for biodiversity protection that lacks any specific rules and enforcement mechanisms. The widely perceived failure of international environmental agreements defies a notable consensus between scientists and politicians that humanity is quickly facing – or already experiencing – ecological tipping points.[8]

It looks as if the worsening of the ecological crisis is accompanied by an ever more obvious failure of the system of international governance. The ability of the entire world population to control ('govern') itself seems at stake now. The question of whether the world is at a tipping point might be rhetorical, but should alert us to an entirely new dimension of the human experience. If it is true that we are about to undermine our own conditions of survival, we must ask what the role of the human species is in the grand scheme of things. Perhaps there is no answer to this question, but common sense would suggest we try harder. If the current system of governance is insufficient, we should have the courage to explore and demand a new or much improved system. In the end, states are mere vehicles of governance, probably overrated and certainly not without alternatives. A multilayered, transnational system of democratic governance based on constitutional principles (such as those expressed in the Earth Charter) may still involve states, but is not dependent on them. It can't be, as any democratic system is accountable only to the *demos*, neither to states nor corporations nor any other legal constructs.

---

[6] The concern of humanity being in a somehow unhealthy relationship with nature is much older, though. For a history of sustainable thinking in Europe, see Ulrich Grober, *Sustainability: A Cultural History* (Green Books, Cambridge 2012).

[7] The Montreal Protocol (1989) to ban CFCs worldwide could also be mentioned, however the availability of substances to substitute CFCs allowed this treaty to merely codify what economically posed no real challenge; see, for example, Barber and Bartlett (note 2): 97.

[8] Johan Rockström et al., 'A Safe Operating Space for Humanity' (2006) *Nature*, 461, 472; WWF, 'Living Planet Report 2010' (2010): http://assets.wwf.org.uk/downloads/wwf_lpr2010_lr_1_.pdf.

2. ECOLOGICAL TIPPING POINTS

Numerous commentators have argued that the planet is now at an ecological tipping point. A 'tipping point', with respect to the environment, is the point at which the environmental damage wrought upon the earth will cause ecosystems to shift from one state to another, at which time it will be difficult or impossible to return it to the former conditions which have been previously relied upon.[9] While no one can predict with precise accuracy *exactly* how close ecosystems are to their tipping points, and how much additional pressure might bring them about, or whether they have already been tipped into another state, what is known is that the present state and trends concerning the environment are creating a perilously dangerous situation.[10]

The effect that humans are having upon the earth has been vividly illustrated by the renowned environmentalist David Suzuki in his book, *The Legacy*. Suzuki traces the evolution of human life in order to show that until the recent past (relative to a long timescale) the environment of the earth has remained fairly stable. As Suzuki notes, the 'hockey stick' graph of our population explosion (100,000 years to reach a billion, and a mere 200 years to multiply that figure by 6.9), viewed in conjunction with other negative environmental impacts such as carbon emissions, deforestation and biodiversity loss, which all follow the same curvature, paints a frightening picture for our future.[11] Indeed, with overall unsustainable consumption continuing, the global demand for resources now exceeds the biological capacity of the earth to renew those resources by some 25 percent.[12] This has meant that '[f]or the first time in the 3.8 billion years that life has existed on Earth one species – humanity – is altering the biological, physical and chemical features of the planet on a geological scale'.[13]

---

[9] Secretariat of the Convention on Biological Diversity, 'Global Biodiversity Outlook 3' (Montreal 2010): 11.

[10] For example, the Fifth Assessment Report of the Intergovernmental Panel on Climate Change describes some of the current risks as follows: 'With increasing warming, some physical systems or ecosystems may be at risk of abrupt and irreversible changes (. . .) warm-water coral reefs and Arctic ecosystems are already experiencing irreversible regime shifts (. . .).' (IPCC, *Climate Change 2014: Impacts, Adaptation, and Vulnerability. Summary for Policymakers*, Working Group II, at 12; http://www.ipcc.ch/pdf/assessment-report/ar5/wg2/ar5_wgII_spm_en.pdf.

[11] David Suzuki, *The Legacy* (Allen & Unwin, Crows Nest, NSW 2010): 20.

[12] Wolfgang Sachs, Tilman Santarius and Patrick Carniller, *Fair Future: Resource Conflicts, Security and Global Justice: A Report of the Wuppertal Institute for Climate and Energy* (Zed Books, London 2005): 26.

[13] This is often referred to as the shift from the relatively stable Holocene period of the last 10,000 years to the unstable and much more hazardous Anthropocene

When viewed in this light, it becomes clear that humanity's effect on the earth is not a marginal phenomenon, but literally an earth-changing event with massive implications. The following will give a brief (and not exhaustive) survey of some of the major ecological problems which we find ourselves confronted with as we move into the second decade of the twenty-first century. The ecological crisis finds perhaps its most vivid illustration in the issue of global warming, which has garnered considerable public attention. The issue has been highlighted by numerous prominent scientists and environmentalists and is to date the only environmental issue that has resulted in comprehensive international action.[14] The scientific evidence affirming global warming is now unequivocal, as was shown by the 2007 Intergovernmental Panel on Climate Change (IPCC), which found that global warming was evident from observations in global average air and ocean temperatures, widespread melting of snow and ice, and rising global average sea level.[15] This observed increase in temperature was considered 'very likely' (90 percent certainty) to have been induced by human causes.[16] The 2014 IPCC report rates this as 'extremely likely' (95–100 percent certainty).[17]

It is important to note that climate change is not merely a future risk, but a phenomenon which is affecting millions of lives already. In fact, a report issued by the Global Humanitarian Forum found that climate change affects 325 million people each year.[18] As the problem escalates, the number of those seriously affected by climate change is expected to more than double within 20 years.[19]

---

period where humans have had a profound impact upon the earth. David T. Suzuki, Amanda McConnell and Adrienne Mason, *The Sacred Balance: Rediscovering Our Place in Nature* (Allen & Unwin, Crows Nest, NSW 1997): 11; Paul Crutzen and Eugene Stoermer, The 'Anthropocene' 41 (2000) *Global Change Newsletter* 17–18.

[14] *Kyoto Protocol to the United Nations Framework Convention on Climate Change* FCCC/CP/1997/7/Add 1 (1997).

[15] S. Solomon, D. Qin, M. Manning, Z. Chen, M. Marquis, K.B. Averyt, M. Tignor and H.L. Miller (eds), *Climate Change 2007: The Physical Science Basis Contribution of Working Group I to the Fourth Assessment Report of the Intergovernmental Panel on Climate Change* (Cambridge University Press, Cambridge 2007): 8. See also Naomi Oreskes, 'Beyond the Ivory Tower: The Scientific Consensus on Climate Change' (2004) 306 (5702) *Science* 22, which found that out of over 9000 journal abstracts analysed dealing with climate change none refuted the argument that global warming is occurring.

[16] Ibid.: 17.

[17] Fifth Assessment Report (note 10) at 15.

[18] 'Human Impact Report: Climate Change – The Anatomy of a Silent Crisis' (Global Humanitarian Forum, 2009): 19.

[19] Ibid.

While global warming has been the ecological problem which has garnered the most attention, the empirical evidence illustrates that there has been a rapid deterioration of ecological conditions in almost all biospheres. Indeed, the different biospheres that have been endangered by human action are truly daunting. For example, soil erosion is another area of ecology which, while not having drawn much widespread attention, is in a dire state. As one expert specializing in soil conditions has remarked, '[l]and degradation and desertification may be regarded as the silent crisis of the world, a genuine threat to the future of humankind'.[20] Given the evidence, such remarks do not overstate the case; it is estimated that, overall, soil is being lost from land areas 10–40 times faster than the rate of soil renewal, thereby imperiling future human food, security and environmental quality.[21] This is a trend which, in conjunction with the cumulative effects of global climate change, is expected to get exponentially worse.[22] Furthermore, the worsening state of soil erosion will in turn increase the effects of global warming, thus creating a vicious cycle.[23]

Another area of major ecological concern is dwindling biodiversity. The Global Biodiversity Outlook Report has provided a reminder of just how serious the problem is. This report found that species which have been assessed for extinction risk are, on average, moving closer to extinction. For example, nearly a quarter of all plant species are estimated to be threatened with extinction, while trends of some 3,000 wild populations of species show a consistent decline in average species abundance of nearly 50 percent between 1970 and 2010; inland water species have declined by 50 percent, while marine and terrestrial species have both declined by around 35 percent.[24]

Furthermore, loss of biodiversity is a phenomenon which will assuredly worsen with climate change. Indeed, studies are finding that the climate change that has occurred thus far is already having a marked impact upon animal and plant populations, and it is expected that the synergism of rapid temperature rise and other stresses, in particular habitat destruction, will

---

[20] Andres Arnald quoted in Stephen Leahy, 'Peak Soil: The Silent Global Crisis' (2008) 23 (1) *Earth Island Journal* 58.

[21] David Pimentel, 'Soil Erosion: a Food and Environmental Threat' (2006) 8 (1) *Environment Development and Sustainability* 119.

[22] M.A. Nearing, F.F. Pruski and M.R. O' Neal, 'Expected Climate Change Impacts on Soil Erosion Rates: A Review' (2004) 59 *Journal of Soil and Water Conservation* 45.

[23] R. Lal, 'Soil Carbon Sequestrian Impacts on Global Climate Change and Food Security' (2004) 304 (5677) *Science* 1623.

[24] Secretariat of the Convention on Biological Diversity (note 9): 9.

ultimately result in numerous extirpations and possibly extinctions.[25] This flow-on effect of climate change is particularly problematic as the contribution of biodiverse ecosystems to human societies promises to become all the more important as environmental change accelerates. This is because biodiverse ecosystems tend to be more resilient and can therefore better cope with an increasingly unpredictable world.[26] A final area of concern briefly to be noted here is the issue of deforestation. Deforestation, mainly through conversion of forests to agricultural land, continues at an alarmingly high rate: the loss of primary forest since 2000 has been estimated at 6 million hectares annually.[27] In addition, forests and other natural habitats are being increasingly fragmented, affecting their ability to maintain biodiversity and deliver ecosystem goods and services. As is well known, deforestation is also a leading cause of our current climate crisis.

What we can say about these ecological issues is that they are not readily separable, but rather are interlinked with each ecological dynamic feeding into another, ultimately leading to a downward spiral of ecological disintegration. Thus, we can see the immense fragility of ecosystems and the perilousness of the ecological situation with which we are faced. While there are still some gaps in scientific knowledge (indeed, when we are dealing with such complex ecosystems we could hardly expect it to be otherwise), current scientific evidence is converging on consensus: we are facing a massive ecological crisis. It is clear that this 'hockey graph' cannot continue indefinitely; the earth can only sustain this trend for so long. Indeed, if continued unabated, it can well be argued that the end result of this dramatic human impact on the earth will be that we follow a path to our own extinction. While as Suzuki points out there is nothing unique about a species becoming extinct – 99.9999 percent of species that have ever existed are now extinct – humans, unlike other species, are in a unique position in that we alone have the ability to change the future by what we do today.[28]

But will it not all be too late? The evidence of planetary ecological decline caused by humans is overwhelming. Furthermore, leaders in government and business are not denying the evidence. Only in extreme cases

---

[25] Terry Root et al., 'Fingerprints of Global Warming on Wild Animals and Plants' (2005) 421 *Nature* 57.

[26] Rob Roggema, *Adaptation to Climate Change: A Spatial Challenge* (Springer, Berlin 2009): 232.

[27] 'State of the World's Forests' (Food and Agriculture Organization of the United States, 2007): 64.

[28] David Suzuki, *David Suzuki: The Autobiography* (Greystone Books, Vancouver, BC 2007): 398.

do we see fundamentalists – in politics, religion or business – talking down climate change or biodiversity loss as a threat to humanity. The problem is not lack of awareness, but lack of action. We allow the ecological decline to take its course without any attempt at stopping it. The defining problem of Western civilization seems to be its incapacity to act, despite knowing what is going on and what will happen next. Unlike previous civilizations such as the Roman or Mayan empires which collapsed as a result of ignorance, current Western civilization has sophisticated technological means to predict the consequences of its actions. Just how much we know is staggering, but even more astonishing is our inability to act upon what we know.

Perhaps the most striking example of inertia is that precisely at a time when the transition to renewable energy becomes realistic and palpable, the world production of greenhouse gases is on the increase. Indeed, energy transition is often seen as an opportunity to get even more oil, gas and coal out of the ground, no matter how costly (fracking, deep-seabed mining, large-scale open mining). The motives behind such behaviour resemble hysteria and paranoia.

In classical physics, as formulated by Isaac Newton, the law of inertia states that an object will stay at rest or stay in motion unless acted on by external forces. In human life, inertia describes the resistance to motion or action either for physical or for psychological reasons. Most of us occasionally experience a lack of initiative or traits of remaining inactive despite a strongly felt need to do something that needs to be done. This can lead to some strange behaviour: just to put off working on a project that we see as daunting, we go to great lengths to find excuses for doing more of the same or something different, as long as we are not 'forced' into actually beginning the project. The more we are locked into this kind of inertia, the more it becomes paradoxical in the sense of being self-contradictory and counterproductive. The paradox of inertia then is a state of paralysis where a situation worsens through deliberate avoidance.

In normal life, the paradox of inertia is often broken when a critical incident occurs: the classic learning-by-mistake experience; an unexpected marriage breakdown after years of not wanting to see the writing on the wall; a heart attack that puts someone on track for a healthier life only after years of avoiding nutritious food and exercise; or the lung cancer that finally causes the addict smoker to quit and pursue the 'good life'.

It may well be that, collectively, we will have to wait for the critical incident – the collapse of civilization – before being ready for change. Obviously, we won't know until it is too late. The paradox of inertia is well worth exploring further though. Arguably, it can also be broken by fully understanding what is going on and actually wanting to do what needs to be done.

3. POLITICAL TIPPING POINTS

One paradox we can observe is the process of ever increasing numbers of democracies while simultaneously seeing a general decline in democracy.

The last few decades have seen a remarkable turn towards democracy. Qualitative data show that 120 sovereign states out of 192 are democratic, embracing 58 percent of the world's population.[29] This turn to democracy has led one political philosopher to declare that 'democracy is the only regime most living humans now deem worthy of serious consideration, exploration, clarification, articulation, exportation, importation, and finally faith'.[30] Yet alongside democratization has been the advent of globalization which has had a marked impact on the ability of states, and the citizens they represent, to exercise control over their financial, social and environmental affairs. The globalization process has meant that the sheer scale of 'contemporary social and economic change appears to outstrip the capacity of national governments or citizens to control contest or resist that change. Thus the limits of national politics are forcefully suggested by globalization'.[31] Citizens in countries as diverse as Brazil to Tanzania, to Samoa or Greece, feel that they are being swept up in a tide of change over which they have little control and often no voice.

The declining power of states to regulate their affairs can, in large part, be attributed to the spread of neo-liberal economics. This is because neoliberal economic policies such as free trade and the liberalization of markets, while held to be the key to nation-state independence through increased prosperity, in reality serve to usurp power from governments. A striking example of how free-trade agreements have the potential to restrict the sovereignty of governments can be found in the proposed Transatlantic Trade and Investment Partnership (TTIP) between North America and Europe[32] and the proposed Transpacific Trade Partnership (TPP) between

---

[29] Danille Archibugi, 'Demos and Cosmopolis' (2002) 13 *New Left Review* 27.

[30] Patrick J. Deneen, *Democratic Faith* (Princeton University Press, Princeton, NJ 2005): xvi.

[31] David Held, *Global Transformations: Politics, Economics and Culture* (Stanford University Press, Stanford, CA 1999): 1.

[32] John Hilary (ed.), *The Transatlantic Trade and Investment Partnership (TTIP): A Charter for Deregulation, an Attack on Jobs, an End to Democracy*

North America, South East Asia and Oceania.[33] The key proposals in each of these agreements would guarantee foreign investors the right to comment on proposed new laws that affect their operations, thereby giving foreign companies more say over regulations than the voters in the countries in which the companies reside. Furthermore, these proposals would result in foreign corporations having the power to take governments to international arbitration, in order to claim compensation for implementing regulations that have reduced the value of their investment. Such agreements 'deliberately close off the ideological and legal space for governments to give priority to social needs and the common good over "trade" commitments or even to respond to a disabling political crisis. States are relegated to a self-limiting and "enabling" role vis-a-vis capital'.[34]

More generally, the sovereignty of governments has been reduced by vast privatization schemes, which have resulted in the private sector performing the services that had previously been the prerogative of the state. Privatization of public services leaves a government's hands tied and makes putting into effect policies that may have a negative effect on the market all but impossible. As nation-states have scurried to fulfil the vagaries of the market, any other concerns, such as inequality or deleterious environmental impacts, are marginalized. In effect, this has resulted in much power being wrested from the public majority to be held in very few hands. Thus, neoliberal economics has diminished the capacity of democracy to function according to the dictates of the public. Commenting on the democratic nature of the neoliberal age, Jane Kelsey asserts 'a sterile spectator-style of democracy where the responsibility to govern is entrusted to political leaders and "voices of the market". Citizens are informed of decisions, often *ex post-facto*, but not actively involved in making them'.[35]

Furthermore, under the current system those who are facing the worst impacts of environmental degradation rarely have a voice over the practices which are jeopardising their present and even more so their futures. The fact that those who have been forced to suffer the brunt of

---

(Rosa Luxemburg Stiftung, Brussels 2014): http://rosalux-europa.info/userfiles/file/TTIP_EN.pdf.

[33] Jane Kelsey (ed.), *No Ordinary Deal: Unmasking the Transpacific Partnership Free Trade Agreement* (Allen & Unwin, Sydney 2010).

[34] Jane Kelsey, *Serving Whose Interests? The Political Economy of Trade in Services Agreements* (Routledge, London 2008): 319; see also Jane Kelsey, *The FIRE Economy* (Bridget Williams Books, Wellington, NZ 2015).

[35] Ibid.

our declining environment are also marginalized politically is no mere coincidence. Rather, with the globalization of neo-liberal economics, wealthy states have often been able to export some of the worst environmental effects to the developing world.[36] Accordingly, the green political challenge raised by the ecological crisis involves the double challenge of not only finding ways of reducing ecological and social risks wherever possible, but also finding ways of minimizing the unfair externalization and displacement of risks onto innocent third parties in space and time.[37]

The impact of neo-liberal policies has been illustrated by the last economic crisis. As is well known, in 2008 the global financial system came to the brink of collapse due to the housing bubble, subprime mortgages, securitization, a lack of government regulation and oversight and greed. The stock markets, which were at or near their all-time peaks in late 2007, came tumbling down, with the DOW Jones Industrial Average falling to a 12-year low by early 2009.[38] The result was an economic recession which rivalled that of the Great Depression.[39] The impact of this economic collapse was particularly hard felt in countries such as Iceland, which had grown rich through the types of investments that collapsed, but even more so in countries such as Greece, Portugal and Spain, which were forced into strangling austerity measures by the Eurozone's rich countries.

This economic meltdown has been illustrative of the fact that neo-liberal economic policies have undoubtedly failed. The reactive character of bailing out measures – unaccompanied by regulatory reforms – demonstrated that governments are at the mercy of financial institutions rather than controlling them.[40] As citizens saw their governments rescue the financial giants who created the very disasters for which they were now paying, they began to wonder who actually benefits from the current economic system. More and more people feel that something has gone

---

[36] See Wolfgang Sachs, *Planet Dialectics: Explorations in Environment and Development* (Zed Books, London 1992).

[37] Robin Eckersley, 'Deliberative Democracy, Ecological Representation, and Risk: Towards a Democracy of the Affected', in Graham Smith (ed.), *Democratic Innovation, Deliberation, Representation and Association* (Routledge, London 2000).

[38] Peter A. McKay, 'DOW is Off 7, 401.24 Points from its Record High in '07', *The Wall Street Journal* (3 March 2009): http://online.wsj.com/article/SB123599406229708501.html.

[39] 'Riots Rock Greece as Thousands Take to the Streets', *Huffington Post* (3 November 2010): http://www.huffingtonpost.com/2010/03/11/riots-rock-greece-as-thou_n_495203.html.

[40] Klaus Bosselmann, 'Values for Governing Ourselves: the Earth Charter' (2011) 4 *Indigo* 112.

dreadfully awry with our economic system and that the status quo cannot continue for much longer.[41]

The economic crisis has thus become more than a matter of economics; it is merging into a social and political crisis as citizens experience a serious disconnect between themselves and those who represent them.

From this vantage point, neoliberal economics can be seen as a root cause not only of the recent economic crisis, but of the ecological and political crises as well. Indeed, as the effects of the ecological damage which we have wrought upon our planet becomes more and more palpable, neo-liberal economics is increasingly out of sync with the interests of the majority of the world's citizens. The price of continuing the status quo is therefore escalating and if there is to be any hope of addressing the crises with which we find ourselves confronted, we need an approach to politics which is mindful not only of the dictates of the market, but of environmental and social concerns as well.[42] Needs of the market and needs of society are not the same and must be carefully separated.[43] The fact that governments have increasingly neglected this separation points to a crisis of democracy. Quite obviously, it is not in the interest of the 'demos' if governments allow markets to determine the direction, scope and content of public policies. Democratic process 'requires that citizens decide all issues that are politically decidable'.[44]

While the democratic control of national governments is being hollowed out by the globalization of neo-liberal economics, the international arena also operates in an undemocratic fashion, perhaps most glaringly illustrated by the existence of the Security Council, and the vastly unequal power exercised by states within the UN. Within this power paradigm, states in the developing world are marginalized and their concerns sidelined, and as states continue to act according to the dictates of their own self-interest and are primarily motivated by economic and security concerns, prospects for consensus on ecological issues are undermined. International climate change negotiations provide an all too vivid

---

[41] See Roger Boyes, 'World Agenda: Riots in Iceland, Latvia and Bulgaria are a Sign of Things to Come', *Times Online* (21 January 2009): 21: http://www.timesonline.co.uk/tol/news/world/europe/article5559773.ece.

[42] Halina Ward, 'One World: Democracy and Sustainable Development' (Presentation to Salzburg Global Seminar Boar Weekend, Salzburg, June 2009).

[43] Klaus Bosselmann, Peter Brown and Brendan Mackey, 'Enabling Flourishing Earth: Challenges for the Green Economy, Opportunities for Global Governance' (2012) 21 (1) *Review of European Community and International Environmental Law* 20–38.

[44] Wheatley (note 1): 2.

illustration of states' unwillingness to make sacrifices for the common good. Yet the processes of globalization and the fact that we all share only one world mean that the strengthening of the international arena in a democratic fashion is not only desirable, but simply necessary. As Falkman has noted, '[n]ow the lines between national and international policy have begun to blur. What is in the national interest when truly seen, merges naturally into the international interest'.[45] In particular, the common interest of our shared environment on which we all depend makes an internationally coordinated response essential.

As these crises have shown, governments and big businesses acting on their own are unable to respond to the issues of the twenty-first century. Current institutions based on the concerns of nations acting in their own self-interest are insufficient to accommodate more democratic forms of decision-making. Therefore, we are in need of a new approach to governance both at the domestic and international levels. The following sections are concerned with exploring institutions of governance that are firmly grounded in the principles of sustainability, democracy and good governance.

4. SOCIETIES' RESPONSES SO FAR

Considering the deepening and seemingly unstoppable ecological crisis, we may well ask whether human society behaves in an irrational or unreasonable manner. 'Irrational' here is used for a society that ignores scientifically proven risks to its own flourishing and continued existence. 'Unreasonable' characterizes a society that is responding to identified risks, but in an inappropriate manner.

Can society act irrationally? On a personal level, we would consider someone who persistently ignores his or her condition, say their rapidly deteriorating health, to be irrational. But what if a whole group of people or society in general behaves in such a manner? What if we let ourselves and our governments conduct business-as-usual knowing that only major change would protect us from demise? We could consider irrational behaviour of society here, but this presupposes actual and sufficiently clear knowledge that is being ignored. More often than not, we hear that environmental problems are difficult to quantify. Unlike markets that are measured on a daily basis and with great detail, environmental conditions

---

[45] K. Falkman (ed.), *To Speak for the World: Speeches and Statements by Dag Hammarskjold* (Atlantis, Stockholm 2005): 143.

can only be estimated. This is partly due to an actual lack of available data, but also due to the principle problem of not clearly knowing what to look for. When is an ecosystem healthy or what exactly would it take to restore deteriorating ecosystems to the level of health required by society? There are a lot of unknowns and intangibles here, including the fact that we are notoriously slow at detecting environmental problems, and where they are detected their hard-hitting consequences may only be felt when it is too late.

The solution that most Western societies have given themselves to respond to inevitable environmental uncertainties is the precautionary approach. Better safe than sorry. Yet, while variations of the precautionary principle are part and parcel of modern environmental policy and law, they are not entrenched constitutionally or otherwise, so are ineffective.[46] The many shortcomings of the precautionary principle are ultimately due to the fact that environmental policy and law themselves are not 'entrenched' and at the centre of society's attention. Rather, they operate at the periphery and are unrelated to the overarching concern for economic growth.[47] This automatically makes empirical data about the state of the environment less urgent and less relevant than data about the state of the economy. Given such imbalances, deeply embedded in society, it is difficult for politicians to take leadership of and give priority to, not to mention act upon, environmental concerns.

Seeing the economy as more important than the environment may in itself be irrational, but this does not mean that society acts irrationally. The reason for this is the diversity of viewpoints and values that exist despite society's perceived fixation with economics. Diversity of viewpoints is also the reason why societies as a whole are less likely to experience complete inertia, as described earlier. While power elites in government and business may well suffer from the paradox of inertia – and being in the hands of these power elites means that we all suffer – the diversity of viewpoints remains our greatest resource.

It is crucial therefore to realize the potential for change. Like any change, social and political change is determined by the dynamics of active and passive forces. If active forces ('activists') find sufficient resonance amongst other members of society and those in power, then change will occur. The actual chances of this occurring for activists depends on many

---

[46] Klaus Bosselmann, *The Principle of Sustainability: Transforming Law and Governance* (Ashgate, Farnham 2008): 60, 87–88.

[47] Klaus Bosselmann, *When Two Worlds Collide: Society and Ecology* (RSVP, Auckland 1995): 125–126.

factors, but more than anything on their ability to communicate in a way that resonates with others. The chance to get the environmental message across is good, precisely because it is a rational and urgent message. What could hinder this, however, is a lack of effective communication channels. This goes to the core of modern liberal democracies. To what extent are they capable of maintaining effective communication channels?

An open, democratic process of debate is not only useful, it becomes an indispensable prerequisite for initiating the kind of social change required for long-term sustainability. How else could the various levels and sectors of society embrace such structural change? One option of course is ruling by decree, as typically in dictatorial regimes. In theory, democratic process can be seen as inferior to dictatorial leadership. In practice, this is not likely to happen as the knowledge required for society to be successful is unlikely to reside with a small elite group of leaders. At least, history has proven this not to be the case. In complex systems such as social organizations, it is more promising to build upon a multitude of contributors to knowledge when reaching decisions. This makes knowledge and subsequent decision-making more robust than acting upon shaky or assumed evidence. In addition, open, participatory democracies create active citizens (who in turn create more openness and participation).

In conclusion, a society can only be called irrational if it won't start processes of pondering the political implications drawn from the empirical ecological data. In this sense, the current processes of discussing ways to respond to the ecological crisis at local, national and international level can hardly be described as irrational. We do have debate and plenty of it. The amounts of political and legal documents produced as a result of debates demonstrate that there has been an involvement of societies in the empirically gained data on our ecological situation. The question, however, remains of whether this involvement has led to anything tangible. As the ecological debate has been taking place for more than 40 years[48] and as the threatening aspects of the ecological crisis are clear to see for everyone, it must be asked whether humanity's response has in fact been adequate and reasonable.

Acting unreasonably is less harmful than acting irrationally. As mentioned, reasonableness refers to the question of whether the actions that are taken or envisaged are sufficient to solve the problem. If we assume – optimistically or not – that societies are acting in a rational fashion, then we need to further ask what it takes to reach a solution to a

---

[48] Assuming a beginning at the 1972 Stockholm Conference on the Human Environment.

perceived problem. Modern societies have institutional arrangements for solving environmental problems. No government without some kind of ministerial portfolio for the environment; no international legal document without mentioning the importance of protecting the environment; and no supranational institution can claim credibility without giving the environment some special emphasis.

Yet, the ecological crisis continues to worsen as if none of those governmental activities and commitments ever occurred. This situation draws the effectiveness of governance in all its existing forms into question. The way we have been responding to the challenge is in need of a review. Our current practice or 'covenant of reason'[49] seems in need of an overhaul. Is this covenant appropriate for the dimensions we are facing as a result of the ecological crisis? And is it at all reasonable to stick with traditional patterns of problem-solving that appear to drive us deeper and deeper into the crisis?

5. FAILURE OF LIBERAL DEMOCRACIES?

The suspicion about our current ways of tackling the ecological crisis just not being appropriate, especially at international level, is growing strongly in the literature.[50] The current international system emerged in response to some of the most devastating wars humankind has encountered so far. It can be traced back politically to the Westphalian settlement (1648) and philosophically to Hugo Grotius. A second important cornerstone is, of course, the institutional structure of international law and governance following World War II, that is, the UN system. Throughout its existence, however, supra- and international law has maintained the notion of the sovereignty of nation-states. And with it, international diplomacy has followed the liberal perception of trade and exchange as the first means for bridging cultural gaps, promoting prosperity and achieving peace. In the vein of fostering a culture of perpetual peace, as envisaged by Immanuel Kant (1795), the prime focus was on economics. The set-up of the treaties of Rome (1957) creating the European Communities is a striking example of Europe's way of seeking unity through economic harmonization.

If peaceful relations between nation-states have been the ambition of

---

[49] Isaac Levi, *The Covenant of Reason: Rationality and the Commitments of Thought* (Cambridge University Press, Cambridge 1997); the notion and concept of a 'covenant' have great importance for understanding human relationships, as we will discuss later.

[50] For example, Barber and Bartlett (note 2): 63.

international law, and more recently of supranational law, they were largely determined by economic interests. Military threats to nations and their societies can perhaps be addressed in this way. Wars between European countries and their allies around the globe are less likely today than they have ever been. But what about ecological threats? They affect countries in a more profound way than military threats, not least as the 'enemy' is not 'out there', but within and everywhere. Economic forces won't help as long as they do nothing to address their own ecological dimensions.

The situation we find ourselves confronted with today is unprecedented. It was never considered before in the history of international law. Although steps have been taken to advance the international system in some institutional and legal manner as mentioned, such advances have been modest and totally insufficient. The foundations, principles, structures and processes of international law have hardly been affected.[51] The principle of the sovereignty of nation-states as stipulated in Art. 2 of the UN Charter, for example, sets limits to the extent of responsibilities that the individual member state has for global affairs.[52] Characteristically, environmental measures are essentially seen as domestic affairs preventing any interference by other states.[53] Facing the ever-increasing threats of the ecological crisis might be less a problem of what states *eo ipso* are willing to do, but more of a problem of the way they have been designed. They are considered to be autonomous ('sovereign') and resting on autonomously acting citizens. The liberal tradition of modern democracies emphasizes individualism over collectivism and individual interests over common interests. From such a perspective, the natural environment appears separate and remote.

One theoretical approach suitable for illustrating this phenomenon

---

[51] An overview of the established institutions is provided by Linda A. Malone and Scott Pasternack, *Defending the Environment: Civil Society Strategies to Enforce International Environmental Law* (Island Press, Washington, DC 2006): 17; Marvin S. Soroos, 'Global Institutions and the Environment: An Evolutionary Perspective', in Regina S. Axelrod, Stacy D. Van Deveer and David Leonard Downie (eds), *The Global Environment: Institutions, Law, and Policy*, 3rd edn (CQ Press, Thousand Oaks, CA 2011): 24.

[52] 'Nothing contained in the present Charter shall authorize the United Nations to intervene in matters which are essentially within the domestic jurisdiction of any state (. . .)' (Art. 2, para. 7, Charter of the United Nations).

[53] Such limitation even applies within the European Union; see Jürgen Neyer and Michael Schröter, 'Deliberative Europe and the Rejected Constitution', in Erik Eriksen, Christian Joerges and Florian Rödl (eds), *Law and Democracy in the Post-National-Union* (Arena-Report, Oslo 2006): 61–90.

is system theory as developed by Niklas Luhmann.[54] To him, society is defined by its functional difference to its natural environment. This difference is characterized by communication as the mode by which society operates. Thus, society can be understood as the encompassing system of meaningful communication.[55] A social system interacts with other social systems in an evolutionary process of creating higher complexity. Systems define their boundaries supported by binary codes such as, for example, 'profit/cost' for the economic system or 'rights/non-rights' for the legal system. Through these binary codes, systems constitute themselves inside a process of communicative self-reference, also called *autopoiesis*.[56] As a consequence, Luhmann considers society as an operationally closed system of communication only able to deal with itself. For the ecological system this means that *autopoietic* systems of society have a tendency to ignore or underestimate ecological problems because they are not able, by definition, to communicate with their natural environment. As systems are capable of communicating with each other only through translation and resonance, the process of adopting ecological awareness and knowledge is complex and slow.[57]

While Western liberal democracies may not be well suited for acknowledging ecological challenges, this does not mean that they are incapable of learning. It does mean, however, that international decision-making of states is cumbersome and typically follows a process of negotiation. At the international level, an air of bargaining like independent merchants prevails. This makes conversations in the spirit of humanity awkwardly 'foreign'. The bargaining atmosphere, akin to rational choice and economic rationality, fosters tendencies of shortsighted and selfish results, usually aiming at the lowest common denominator. The binary code of this international system therefore appears as: 'affecting my sovereign interest/not affecting it'. This explains why international systems are

---

[54] Niklas Luhmann, *The Differentiation of Society* (1982); Benjamin Richardson, 'Trends in North America and Europe', in Klaus Bosselmann, David Grinlinton and Prue Taylor (eds), *Environmental Law for a Sustainable Society* 2nd edn (NZCEL Monograph Series, 2013): 47–66.

[55] Niklas Luhmann, *Social Systems* (Stanford University Press, Stanford, CA 1995).

[56] Niklas Luhmann, *Ecological Communication* (1986); see also Günther Teubner, *Recht als Autopoetisches System* (1989) and Benjamin Richardson, 'Trends in North America and Europe', in Klaus Bosselmann, David Grinlinton and Prue Taylor (eds), *Environmental Law for a Sustainable Society* 2nd edn (NZCEL Monograph Series, 2013): 47, 51.

[57] Klaus Bosselmann, *When Two Worlds Collide: Society and Ecology* (RSVP, Auckland 1995): 153.

inherently hostile to the idea and needs of participative, transparent and accountable communication, hence the lack of democratic culture and an almost complete absence of the needs of the poor, the natural environment and future generations.

The most fashionable way to communicate the challenges of the ecological crisis is by perceiving them as risks[58] and, more often than not, perceiving them as economic risks. The normative perspective that serves as a criterion for the risk-measuring process is the precautionary principle.[59] It therefore does not surprise us that the precautionary principle was mainly developed in reaction to situations of crisis, especially in reaction to food contaminations and irreversible environmental damage.[60] Although the precautionary principle is supposed to give law a character of risk prevention, its legislative implementation occurred mostly in reaction to major events such as terrorist acts, sudden diseases, nuclear accidents, tsunamis or floods and droughts. This questions the popular reasoning behind the principle often expressed as 'better safe than sorry' (in German: *Vorsorgeist besser als Nachsorge*, literally: precaution is better than aftercare). If the precautionary principle were taken seriously and applied to actually prevent further environmental deterioration, it would be understood as a rule of fundamental self-constraint that 'place(s) the burden of proof on those who argue that a proposed activity will not cause significant harm'.[61]

Defined in this way, the precautionary approach would challenge the assumption of a self-evident prerogative of economic prosperity or social well-being. The problem here is not terminology, but the concepts associated with it. In the prevailing paradigm of economic rationality, prosperity equals growth at all cost, and social well-being or distributive justice are metaphors for access to natural resources no matter how detrimental to the environment. The precautionary approach would challenge, for example, the rationale of the system of international trade under the World Trade Organization (WTO) that considers scientifically proven

---

[58] That is why some sociologists describe modern societies as risk societies – see Ulrich Beck, *Risikogesellschaft* (Suhrkamp, Frankfurt 1986).

[59] For example, Björn M. Funke, 'The Precautionary Principle', in Klaus Bosselmann and Ron Engel (eds), *The Earth Charter: A Framework for Global Governance* (KIT Publishing, Leiden 2010): 191; Birger Arndt, *Das Vorsorgeprinzip im EU-Recht* (Mohr Siebeck, Tuebingen 2009).

[60] Michael W. Schröter, 'Lebensmittelrechtliche Vorsorge als Rechtsprinzip – nationale, europäische und welthandelsrechtliche Aspekte', ZERP-Diskussionspapier 4 (University of Bremen, Bremen 2002).

[61] Principle 6 (b) of the Earth Charter.

risks as relevant purely to human health concerns and only as a matter of risk management (e.g. Art. 5, WTO Agreement on the Application on Sanitary and Phytosanitary Measures). Effectively, such logic places the burden of proof on those who argue that precautionary measures will not cause significant harm to free trade.

Taking this logic to the challenges of the ecological crisis, we encounter two problems. One is the reactionary character of the precautionary principle: it applies only in response to already quantified, widely recognized risks. The other problem is that it overestimates the reliability of science. No environmental scientist can ever provide evidence beyond reasonable doubt; the nature of the beast would simply not allow for such certainty. As a consequence, evidence of risk based on best-available science must suffice to trigger precautionary measures. Fundamentally, we should ask whether we have more trust in the wisdom of precaution or economic cost–benefit analysis.

The debate around global warming gives a warning example. The scientific discovery of human-induced impacts on our climate is over 100 years old.[62] But, because the system of earth climate is highly complex, the all-encompassing scientific evidence of temporal scales and physical impacts of climate change is still missing, despite consistently growing evidence that climate change is anthropogenic, real and happening now. For more than two decades now, the remaining uncertainties have prevented states from taking definite action. Instead of following a precautionary approach, states have allowed global temperatures to increase to a level where it becomes virtually impossible to reverse current trends to a scientifically acceptable level of 350 carbon dioxide parts per million increase of 1 degree Celsius in average temperatures. We may now be forced into crisis management, trying to cope with impacts, rather than formulating proactive, precautionary measures.

In sum, it is reasonable to suggest that our current ways of problem-solving, although somehow rational, are unreasonable. The predominant rationality seems incapable of responding in a way that can be considered reasonable and effective. This rationality can also be described as the economic rationality of liberal democracies. In the following, we will therefore briefly examine how liberal democracies produce political decisions.

Modern Western-style democracies rely on the political ideology of liberalism. This implies, among other things, the ideas of equality and

---

[62] Compare: 'Fourth Assessment Report, Chapter 1' (2007) IPCC: http://www.ipcc.ch/pdf/assessment-report/ar4/wg1/ar4-wg1-chapter1.pdf (accessed November 2010).

rule of law. It also alludes to a democratic culture where political power is executed on behalf of the people, perceived as the cumulative will of individuals as the consequence of free and equal elections. That is why some political philosophers consider democracy and liberalism as essentially intertwined.[63] But there is also a negative aspect of liberalism that continues to feature in the political discourse, that is, the association of liberalism with economic rationality emphasizing individualism and greed over collective responsibilities.[64] The economic side of liberalism is considered by some to be its very heart, because liberalism aims primarily at self-realization through individual property: freedom becomes a genuine materialistic idea.[65] As a consequence, liberalism mutates into the opposite of its original purpose: instead of creating free, just and peaceful societies, it keeps generating unjust distributions in favour of an elite in possession of wealth and power at the expense of society and nature.[66] In this manner, liberalism poses a threat to democracy.

How does this influence the manner of problem-solving in liberal democracies? In liberal democracies a procedural approach to truth applies that is highly dependent on plurality. Due to legal equality, everybody has the right to make any claim they wish. This requires a rational mode of communication in which the claim can be evaluated. Applied to political decision-making, this mode requires processes where, ideally, everyone possibly affected by the decision can participate and the result is persuasive in a rational manner for everyone affected. This ideal approach, which deeply inspires a deliberative theory of democracy,[67] appears to be problematic while trying to respond effectively to the ecological crisis for two reasons. First, due to its procedural character it tends to neglect material influences of truth although they might be vital

---

[63] The best known two are probably John Rawls and Jürgen Habermas.

[64] See, for example, C. Crouch, *Postdemocrazia* (Laterza, Roma/Bari 2003) published as *Post-Democracy* (Oxford University Press, Oxford 2004); Klaus Bosselmann, *The Principle of Sustainability: Transforming Law and Governance* (Ashgate, Farnham 2008).

[65] See C.B. MacPherson, *The Political Theory of Possessive Individualism* (Clarendon Press, Oxford 1962).

[66] This pattern of argument – with variations, of course – is used by many authors and political groups right now and has gathered new intuitive plausibility from the recent financial crisis. In the realm of political philosophy, the criticism of 'atomistic individualism' led, inter alia, to the theoretical approach of communitarism; see, for example, C. Taylor, 'Atomism', in *Philosophical Papers Volume 2: Philosophy and the Human Sciences* (Cambridge University Press, Cambridge 1985).

[67] See Chapter 2.6.

to society. We will argue below that the ecological crisis constitutes such material truth; and second, those processes tend to be hidden through patterns of rationality claiming to serve social well-being, yet mirror only the shortsighted and selfish interests of some. Insofar as it can be assumed that neo-liberal and pure economic rationality patterns strive to become the rationale of liberal democracies, this calls for developing some ethical approach to the political culture of democracy and the ecological well-being of humankind.

2. Framing earth governance

The destiny of humans cannot be separated from the destiny of earth.
Thomas Berry

Democracy and freedom are more than values to be treasured; they may well be essential to survival.
Noam Chomsky

The idea of earth governance responds to shortcomings of the current system of international environmental law and governance. Its main purpose is to help establish a culture of democracy powerful enough to achieve sustainable societies. This involves governance structures that are capable of serving this purpose. Such structures would feature governance rules able to overcome the democratic and ecological deficit discussed so far.[1]

1. EARTH: OUR HOME

The Earth Charter[2] introduces the term 'earth' as 'our home'. This implies several possible aspects which we can examine briefly: Who is meant by 'our'? Who is it earth gives a 'home' to? Does 'our' only designate humans? Is 'earth' used in a way that grants humanity the (religious) right to exploit nature for its convenience but, maybe, just in a more responsible way? Hence, does 'home' as a notion serve as a metaphor for a humankind having received a place to dwell in which can be altered for convenience purposes, but because it is a home it has to be kept tidy and functional?

Alluding to 'earth' in the sense of 'our home' reminds us of the use earth has in some religious thoughts. Questioning the meaning of 'our', it could be understood in relation to the biblical dominium terrae (Genesis 1: 28) where God grants man dominion over nature ('and have dominion over (. . .)'). Indeed, religious thoughts are one of the sources of the Earth

[1] See generally Klaus Bosselmann, Ron Engel and Prue Taylor, *Governance for Sustainability: Issues, Challenges, Successes* (IUCN, Gland 2008).

[2] The Earth Charter at http://www.earthcharterinaction.org/content/pages/Read-the-Charter.html.

Charter. But it is not exclusively related to Judaism or Christianity, rather it aims to meet the different religious beliefs of all humans.[3] If there is some Judaic-Christian notion included that meets the approach of the Earth Charter, it is rather the 'responsibility for the caretaking of creation' in the sense of reverence for every living being. As Albert Schweitzer's[4] ethical approach tells us, the Earth Charter gives 'our home' an existential quality through reminding us that earth is 'alive with a unique community of life'. Although the Earth Charter somehow differs between the well-being of humans and the 'community of life', it obviously does so only on rhetorical grounds, because it instantly claims the resilience of those two in favour of a 'healthy biosphere'. Ensuring that the 'community of life' and humankind live together in the same biosphere, on which both are existentially relying for their well-being, actually integrates humanity into the 'community of living'. The 'our' in the Earth Charter therefore has a two-layered meaning: it puts humankind in the role of the addressee but only to remind it of being part of a comprehensive community of life relying on a commonly shared healthy biosphere.

This 'our' is combined with 'home', insofar as 'home' is apparently intended to embrace a different meaning than it has in daily use. In day-to-day language, 'home' mostly describes the place where you regularly stay when you want to be on your own, having your privacy, and where you keep your personal items. Legally, it names the place official documents can be sent to, which is important for your status as a citizen, tax-payer, and so on. This daily usage includes the notion of home as a changeable place, but the Earth Charter gives 'home' a much more basic and comprehensive meaning: home is not only the place that gives you shelter, where you are fed and provided with the required resources for well-being, but home is the key dimension for all of existence – for humans, all living beings, ecosystems and their common well-being in a healthy biosphere. It shapes the individuality of people as much as that of their neighbours and prepares the ground for experience and evaluation. And therefore earth as 'home' is not an exchangeable place. Hence, 'home' in the intention of the Earth Charter is a normative focal point. It explains why we should respect life in all its diversity, it asks us to care for 'our' community of life, and so on. But what is the normative source of this focal point?

---

[3] See Klaus Bosselmann and Ron Engel, 'Introduction', in Klaus Bosselmann and Ron Engel (eds), *The Earth Charter: A Framework for Global Governance* (KIT Publishing, Leiden 2010): 19.

[4] Albert Schweitzer, *Ehrfurcht vor dem Leben in Kultur und Ethik* (Beck, Munich 1923).

The normative source of 'home' is 'earth'. The Earth Charter has two intentions here: one was just analysed as 'home'; the other, which is only indirectly addressed, is earth being our entire origin and inspiration while taking us even beyond our perception and comprehension and, probably, surviving us. Earth is bigger than us and always will be bigger. Earth can and shall be the first logical starting point for any thinking and it will always be the first source of inspiration for further thinking; this entitles earth to be a normative category, the source of all normative thinking.[5]

While the Earth Charter applies 'earth' as a normative category, it does so by giving the notion of 'home' a kind of metaphysical surrounding that is not entirely accessible by means of the natural sciences: earth shapes our home, earth is the ultimate category we all rely on and we are all earth, whether we would like to be or not. 'Earth' is used by the Earth Charter in a similar sense to 'nature' or 'wilderness' in European or US thinking, both somehow alluding to the aesthetic category of the sublime and its moral implications and being the inspirational precursors to Aldo Leopold and his Land Ethic.[6]

Summarizing this, we encounter 'earth' as the normative source and frame for all human thinking and striving. The Earth Charter expresses this by calling it 'our home' in a stronger way than daily use would imply. The 'our' is two-layered by addressing humanity but also including it in an all-encompassing community of life. This community of life dwells in the biosphere while sharing ecosystems and suchlike. 'Home' therefore serves as a normative focal point. The normative source for this focal point is earth.

---

[5] Western thinkers who alluded to this include, for example, John Muir (1869), cited in Roderick Nash, 'Limits of American Liberalism', in Thomas Tanner (ed.), *Aldo Leopold: The Man and His Legacy* (Soil Conservation Society of America, Ankeny, IA 1987): 58: 'When we try to pick out anything by itself, we find that it is bound fast by a thousand invisible cords that cannot be broken to everything in the universe. I fancy I can hear a heart beating in every crystal, in every grain of sand and see a wise plan in the making and shaping and placing of every one of them. All seems to be dancing in time to divine music'; see also Martin Heidegger, *Der Ursprung des Kunstwerk* (Reclam, Stuttgart, first published 1950, revised 1960): 43, referring to earth as the 'wesenhaft Unerschliessbare ("intrinsically unrevealable") that keeps itself closed, but makes all things of earth exhale in alternate consistency'.

[6] Roderick Nash, 'Limits of American Liberalism', in Thomas Tanner (ed.), *Aldo Leopold: The Man and His Legacy* (Soil Conservation Society of America, Ankeny, IA 1987): 53.

2. SAVING LIBERAL DEMOCRACY FROM ECONOMIC LIBERALISM

Democracy, in a plain sense, names a state form in which power remains with the people. In ancient times, further differentiations were introduced and some philosophers suspected democracy was in danger of becoming an 'ochlocracy' ruled by a 'mob'.[7] In modern times, democracy as an idea of political philosophy became popular in contract theory, especially following Locke, Rousseau and Kant. One of their main arguments was the innate freedom of every person. Rousseau, for example, entirely blamed culture for turning humans into misguided and sometimes vicious beings while they were born free and good.

As the philosophical insight of an innate right of freedom of any person was shaping a new discussion around state forms and their legitimacy furthered constitutional democracies, the individual and the freedom to act came into focus. The economic side of this was soon discovered and theoretically explained. As Rousseau put it:

> The first man who, having fenced in a piece of land, said 'This is mine,' and found people naïve enough to believe him, that man was the true founder of civil society. From how many crimes, wars, and murders, from how many horrors and misfortunes might not any one have saved mankind, by pulling up the stakes, or filling up the ditch, and crying to his fellows: Beware of listening to this impostor; you are undone if you once forget that the fruits of the earth belong to us all, and the earth itself to nobody.[8]

Both ways of thinking regarding this innate right were soon called liberalism which was considered to be a new kind of political doctrine focusing on the individual above anything else. From here, the ultimate triumph of individual freedom and the cutting back of the state to the basic functions of maintaining services were only a matter of time.[9]

Thus, liberalism as a political doctrine and democracy as a philosophical construct of modernity have become deeply entangled.[10] Although

---

[7] Especially Aristotle; the term 'ochlocracy' was shaped by Polybius. In current literature on democratic theory, this problem is discussed as 'tyranny of the majority'.

[8] Jean-Jaques Rousseau, *Discours sur l'origine et les fondements de l'inégalité parmi les hommes* (first published 1755).

[9] So-called *Nachtwächterstaat* (night-watchman state); Robert Nozick, *Anarchy, State, and Utopia* (Basic Books, New York 1974), is a good contemporary example of this approach.

[10] Compare also Ron Engel, 'Contesting Democracy', in Ron Engel, Laura Westra and Klaus Bosselmann (eds), *Democracy, Ecological Integrity and*

there have been attempts to disentangle the two terms – one well-known attempt was Carl Schmitt's[11] – most contemporary political philosophers consider them mutually dependent.[12] One important reason for this is the normative individualism that current moral and legal theory rely on: the capacity of the individual for responsible self-government and therefore the ability to give (or understand) and comply with moral and legal laws. But this in itself does not necessitate irresponsible economic, neo-liberal behaviour that does not care about its social and ecological consequences, especially in the long term. It appears therefore that we actually deal with two different, yet related philosophical constructs of liberalism: one that can be called original political liberalism and the other that can be characterized as economic liberalism in the sense of an offspring.[13] Assuming that this offspring – now grown to be a monstrous economic 'neo-liberalism' – is detrimental to the prospect of individual freedom, liberalism as a whole has to be re-visited.

Original political liberalism reflects the humanistic assumption of an innate right to freedom as unquestionable and inalienable. In this sense, the Earth Charter commits itself to universal human rights, implying the idea of moral persons being able to be responsible for self-government as the guarantor of individual freedom. Seen in this way, the need for democratic governance becomes inevitable. Economic liberalism, on the other hand, is not inevitable. It may be consistent with the idea of individual freedom, but this is different from being consistent with democracy. Obviously, both are different concepts and only compatible in so far as economic theory and practice can be subjected to democratic control. In other words, ultimate power rests with people not with economic actors or institutions. Arguably, free market ideology undermines the ability of democratic government to guarantee individual freedom for all.

Historically, one of the main intentions of liberalism was to free people from political regimes that would set them apart and above the very people they relied on and were supposed to serve. Liberalism aimed for

---

International Law (Cambridge Scholars Publishing, Newcastle upon Tyne 2010): 26.

[11] Carl Schmitt, *The Crisis of Parliamentary Democracy* (The MIT Press, Cambridge, MA 1988). Original publication: 1923, 2nd edn 1926.

[12] Like John Rawls (e.g. *The Theory of Justice*, 1971; *Law of the People*, 1999) or Jürgen Habermas (e.g. *Faktizität und Geltung*, 1992; *Die Einbeziehung des Anderen*, 1996).

[13] See Michael Schröter, 'Liberalism and Sustainability: Two Colliding Principles?', in Laura Westra, Klaus Bosselmann and Colin Soskolne (eds), *Globalisation and Ecological Integrity in Science and International Law* (Cambridge Scholars Publishing, Newcastle upon Tyne 2011): 286.

individuals to become masters of their own destiny and not dependent on elites unaccountable to them. Enlightenment philosophers from Smith, Hume and Locke to Voltaire, Montesquieu and Rousseau to Lessing, Wolff and Kant all had personal liberty at their core. Liberalization literally meant freeing personal liberty from control by unjust, arbitrary and often incompetent despots. The assumption was – and is – that liberty, rationality and reasonableness will flourish once despotism is removed.

In modern democracies, despotism no longer exists in the form that classical liberalism encountered it. But it has not disappeared, rather it has only changed form. Despotism as the rule of a group or oligarch with absolute power exists in the form of corporate oligarchs. Since the collapse of communism in the early 1990s, democracies grew all around the world, while economic neo-liberalism and associated free market ideology created new centres of power, mostly in a transnational form, but always under the watch of democratic governments. The power of the people (democracy) is being replaced by the power of corporates (corporatism). Yet again, people are becoming passive recipients of decisions in which they have little say, either as consumers or as citizens. The belief in the power of 'the market' has grown so strongly that we can speak of religious market fundamentalism.

Market fundamentalism captures people within nations and throughout the globe. This changes the nature of threats that classic liberalism was familiar with. While there are continued threats of political suppression in both non-industrialized and industrialized countries, the new threats are economic and social suppression. In a world of increasing gaps between rich and poor, the power elites begin to isolate themselves from the rest for their personal protection and to secure their wealth. Like the old despots, the new despots set themselves apart from and above the people they rely on. Unlike the old despots, however, the new despots are not expected to serve people. So things get worse: powerless governments try to serve people, while powerful markets serve themselves. Democracy is being reduced to a ritual of procedural habits.

At this juncture of history, neo-liberalism is the biggest problem. Paradoxically, neo-liberalism follows the logic of individual liberty and in so doing destroys it altogether. As neo-liberalism is hostile to government intervention, it necessitates just that whenever its own pre-conditions are threatened: banks too big to fail will be bailed out, corporates demand low taxes, low wages and low environmental standards and the market dictates the shape and form of public policies.[14] Individuals, while 'free',

[14] A drastic example is the American Legislative Exchange Council (ALEC). ALEC boasts over 2,000 corporate members from Walmart to Exxon Mobile and

are reduced to formal rights of voting – essentially between the hawks and falcons of market-serving political parties – and 'choices' between products and brands. Political liberty is all but gone; 1 percent rules, 99 percent follow. As social and environmental upheavals increase, centralized government intervention will increase[15] – the exact opposite of what political liberalism set out to prevent. Yet, economic liberalism seems to have no problem with it. Only somewhat cynically can we say what big business is telling us: 'Free markets are for you, government intervention and subsidies are for us.'

The only way for political liberalism to remain relevant is to return to its roots and test them against today's liberal democracy. If political liberty requires control of unjustified power in all its manifestations, then democracy has to be much more ambitious than merely controlling governmental power. Controlling market power requires a fundamental rethink of what belongs to 'them' (markets) and what belongs to 'us' (commons). If we, the people, are still in charge then governments have the task of separating markets from the commons. Such a task is typically liberal in the sense that liberalism aims to separate the individual from the collective. But it is also non-liberal or – *horribile dictu* – socialist in its attempt to control markets. Market control does not necessarily mean intervening in somebody's business or in something you don't know anything about. Market control can also mean defining the functions and legitimacy of the market, both arguably indispensable for a functioning society.

Separating the markets from the commons essentially describes the task ahead:[16] how can governments be empowered and the sovereignty of states be restored to ensure market control? And how can democracy be advanced to ensure protection of the commons? This is the key theme of this book and will be explored in the following chapters.

In the remainder of this introductory chapter, we need to identify some of the features that make democracy worthwhile and, as will be argued, indispensable for pursuing the common good or the good of the commons. Among such features are the acknowledgment of what I call ecological

---

plays a key role in writing legislation and determining public policies 'to advance limited government and free markets'. See http://www.alec.org/about-alec/.

[15] With respect to climate change, this point is powerfully made by Naomi Klein in *This Changes Everything: Capitalism vs the Climate* (Simon & Schuster, New York 2014).

[16] Klaus Bosselmann, Peter Brown and Brendan Mackey, 'Enabling Flourishing Earth: Challenges for the Green Economy, Opportunities for Global Governance' (2012) 21 (1) *Review of European Community and International Environmental Law* 20–38.

realism (Section 3), the importance of attitudes and values (Section 4) and the idea of democracy as a covenant (Section 5) A democratic system with such characteristics can be described as a value-based democracy (Section 6). As we are aiming for earth governance, value-based democracy cannot be confined to nation-states, but should be understood as a universal concern, sometimes referred to as earth democracy.[17]

3. DEMOCRACY AND ECOLOGICAL REALISM

An important step towards a value-based concept of democracy was taken in 1945. In that year, the United Nations was established and with it the idea of democracies as agents for peace and nonviolence.

The commitment of the United Nations to conflict-solving mechanisms that exclude violence and to promoting peaceful societies might be one of the most progressive and culture-changing steps in recent political history. And the commitment to a nonviolent but peaceful culture can be considered as an inherent normative feature of democracy.[18] This means, on one hand, that democracies shall provide mechanisms of internal conflict-solving that render violent conflicts such as armed riots, civil wars, revolutions, etc. as superfluous while, on the other, democratic citizens must engage themselves in building a culture of tolerance, mutual respect and solidarity.

Providing nonviolent mechanisms of conflict-solving is a task that will never be completed, but has to be struggled with on a day-to-day basis. Democratic governance therefore has to set up and maintain institutions serving as a formal framework for this task. Those institutions should be able to facilitate conflict-solving processes without preempting them. And, because they are supposed to provide the arenas of democracy, the people themselves are in charge of establishing, maintaining and improving them.

---

[17] Klaus Bosselmann, 'Earth Democracy: Institutionalizing Ecological Integrity and Sustainability', in Ron Engel, Laura Westra and Klaus Bosselmann (eds), *Democracy, Ecological Integrity and International Law* (Cambridge Scholars Publishing, Newcastle upon Tyne 2010): 319–330.

[18] Ron Engel, 'Contesting Democracy', in Ron Engel, Laura Westra and Klaus Bosselmann (eds), *Democracy, Ecological Integrity and International Law* (Cambridge Scholars Publishing, Newcastle upon Tyne 2010). For Engel, commitment to peace and nonviolence is one criterion to distinguish 'thick' from 'thin' forms of democracy. Correspondingly, Jürgen Habermas argues for weak naturalism coercing us into non-violent conflict-solving, developing with socio-evolutionary processes; see Jürgen Habermas, *Wahrheit und Rechtfertigung* (Suhrkamp, Frankfurt 1999).

Institutions of peaceful conflict resolution need to operate at all levels of governance, that is, global, regional, national and local.[19] The Earth Charter describes these as needing to be transparent, accountable and participative while ensuring access to justice for everybody.[20] However, the Earth Charter also asks us to include the community of life and ecological integrity as part of peaceful decision-making. We will not have peace among human communities if the war with nature continues and vice versa: peaceful interaction with nature is predicated on the ability to interact peacefully among ourselves.

Democratic citizens must, first of all, develop an attitude of tolerance as mentioned. In its basic connotation tolerance describes a passive attitude and not a form of active political engagement. It rather asks us to leave 'the other' alone in respect of that other's dignity or, in the case of natural systems, their integrity. But passive tolerance is not enough. In a democracy, tolerance requires active intervention against violence, arbitrariness and intolerance. Again, such negative attitudes can be harmful not just to society, but also to the natural environment.

Mutual respect and solidarity are requirements of a peaceful society. Seeing the viewpoint of 'the other' helps in understanding each other, but also means learning from each other. Mutual learning processes are essential for democratic societies striving for just and fair relations. As citizens develop such attitudes and values, they create the basics of functioning democracies.

The idea of citizenship, however, cannot be confined to nations. Citizens who identify solely with the nation that they are a citizen of, undermine the very conditions under which human relationships flourish. In many ways, our global age functions differently from the Westphalian age of nation-states and one example is citizenship. While citizens may legally be citizens of a nation, practically they are not confined to a nation or, in the case of the European Union, to a region. Effectively, we can all be global citizens and arguably we should be.

While these attitudes and perceptions are all relevant to the idea of democracy as a global concern, they only disrobe the procedural side of democracy. The procedural side of democracy shapes the process of decision-making, but does not tell us anything about shared values or possible outcomes. Democracies are traditionally based on pluralistic

[19] See, for example, Klaus Bosselmann, 'Towards Multilevel Governance for Sustainability: Trends and Challenges', in *Contested Futures: Sustainability, Governance and International Human Rights* (2010) Europe–New Zealand Research Series Paper 1, 11, 26.

[20] Bosselmann, Engel and Taylor (note 1).

approaches to truth. Slightly exaggerated, pluralism shows itself as the source of truth in democracies. That is why procedures to some degree can be considered a technique to make the best possible use of this democratic resource. It also explains why procedure and content are not the same, although it can be argued that good procedures deliver good qualitative outcomes.

But what about values, in particular those relevant to earth governance? As we have discussed above, 'earth' in the sense of the Earth Charter is a normative category with a substantial input. It asks us to consider earth as 'our home' where we are part of a community of life, relying on a shared healthy biosphere and the integrity of earth itself. We must respect this community and take care of it, as well as the biosphere and earth's integrity. Thus, we are asked for quite dramatic changes in our way of thinking and living. How realistic is this? Is 'earth' as a normative category really strong enough to justify such claims of responsibility for the wider community of life?

To answer the question of how realistic such an approach is, we have to be conscious of the fact that its first and most hindering obstacle is the doctrine of sovereign states. This doctrine matches the mindset of a world of plenty rather than of one earth. International law is shaped around this doctrine as, for example, stipulated in Art. 2.2, para. 1 of the UN Charter: 'The Organization is based on the principle of the sovereign equality of all its Members', the members, of course, being sovereign states. In its full meaning the doctrine of sovereign states prevents any consensus on a pre-defined global public good. Rather, it reinforces international negotiations as the key, and often only, method for nurturing a sense of global responsibility. Responsibility conceived in such a way is bound to be weak and potentially in conflict with selfish state interests.

It can be argued that the doctrine of sovereign states was reasonable due to the historical situations (Westphalian settlement and post-WWII) at the time it was introduced, but makes no sense considering today's challenges which are more global than national, with ecological interdependencies being a prime example of the former.[21] Therefore, new and more appropriate approaches should be developed and implemented.[22] Despite some sympathy for this argument in the literature, a 'realistic' view of interna-

---

[21] Walter F. Barber and Robert V. Bartlett, *Global Democracy and Sustainable Jurisprudence: Deliberative Environmental Law* (The MIT Press, Cambridge, MA 2009): 6.

[22] David Held, 'Liberty in the Age of Cosmopolitanism', in Yongjune Park, *Re-evaluation of Values: (A) Journey in Search of Core Values* (Mull Publishing, 2010): 127.

tional relations argues that we have to face the current settlements in the international realm and take it for granted while making further considerations.[23] Although somehow agreeing to this objection, other authors contrast it with another realistic view: the ecological one. This concedes the historical fact of the existence of states and their role at international level, but questions their sovereignty while pointing in an ontological manner to an ecological community that is defined by earth as an ecosystem putting together all living beings in the need of its integrity.[24] This view can be summarized in the expression that earth does not need us for its survival, but we need earth to sustain us, or, as Sara Parkin puts it, in favour of good (sustainable) leadership: 'Get it wrong and we are fossils.'[25]

At the core of ecological realism is a conviction of the urgent need for a global ethical framework to respond to the threats of the ecological crisis in a democratic manner. A possible framework is supposed to be the Earth Charter which therefore can be characterized as visionary, but precisely because of its visionary character it can instantly be dismissed as being too utopian. Critics of this kind would presumably describe themselves as realists. So, who is more realistic – those who insist on ecological realism or those who insist on international relations realism? What is more real – ecology or states? Apparently, two different paradigms or concepts of 'truth' are caught in a clash here.

Current liberal democracies are reliant on procedural approaches, as mentioned above.[26] While those approaches pay high attention to the formal structures of society and the way the individual can and shall participate in the public processes of decision-making, they neglect the material aspect of truth.[27] Simply put, truth is outside the realm of liberal democracies. For procedural theories of democracy, pluralism provides the means and ends of democratic decision-making. Unfortunately, such pluralism does not help us in coming to grips with the complexities of

---

[23] See, for example, Steven Wheatley, *The Democratic Legitimacy of International Law* (Hart Publishing, Oxford 2010): 30; for a more general approach, compare Barber and Bartlett (note 21): 23, 61.

[24] See Klaus Bosselmann, 'Institutions for Global Governance', in Colin Solskone (ed.), *Sustaining Life on Earth: Environmental Ethics and Human Health through Global Governance* (Lexington Books, Lanham, MD 2007): 9.

[25] Sara Parkin, *Positive Deviant: A 21st Century Revolution* (Earthscan, London 2010): 4.

[26] See, for example, Jürgen Habermas, 'Wahrheitstheorien', in Helmut Fahrenbach (ed.), *Wirklichkeit und Reflexion* (Neske, Pfullingen 1973): 211–265.

[27] Ron Engel, 'The Earth Charter as a new Covenant for Democracy', in Klaus Bosselmann and Ron Engel (eds), *The Earth Charter: A Framework for Global Governance* (KIT Publishing, Leiden 2010): 29.

the ecological crisis. For this to happen, we need to do more than collect scientific data and agree on the most reliable. What about aesthetics, for example, which is the branch of philosophy dealing with the nature of art, beauty and taste? No one would deny the importance of art and beauty in our lives and democracies cater well for them, but are aesthetics confined to the human-built environment? What about the natural environment?

Aesthetically, attitudes can be described as the first step towards encountering the moral ground for our actions. We tend to take responsibility for what we 'like' and don't care very much for what we don't 'like'. How come then that indigenous societies tend to genuinely like their natural environments, while Western cultures are more oblivious in this regard or leave it up to the individual whether or not to like nature? According to Western pluralism, this is how it should be: some people are in awe of nature, others are not, and it is nobody's business to decide who may be right or wrong. The currently dominating consensus is that nature is useful in many respects, but foremost a 'useful' natural resource reflecting utilitarian ethics.

Yet, most environmental experts, whether 'Western' or not, see such anthropocentrism at the core of the ecological crisis. One of the implications of anthropocentrism, backed up by a huge number of research findings, is the insight that Western thought has traditionally produced ways of treating nature that are just the opposite of being sustainable. It could be claimed that this insight carries a degree of moral objective truth, although, it should be said, an objective truth only in a negative sense: enabling us to see that wrong ways of acting in the past do not tell us what kind of ethical stance and behaviour may be right in the future.[28] Hence, negative ecological moral realism states that there are certain kinds of behaviour exploiting nature that can be considered morally wrong in an objective sense because they endanger long-term prospects of survival of humans or of the entire community of life.

Moral ecological realism is not telling us that our current system of law and governance is wrong. It does, however, question its moral persuasiveness. It makes claims that ought to be tested in the court of public opinion. If democracy is purely understood as procedural governance, public opinion would arguably take less interest in moral claims of this nature

---

[28] See Michael Schröter, 'Lebensmittelrechtliche Vorsorge als Rechtsprinzip – nationale, europäische und welthandelsrechtliche Aspekte', *ZERP-Diskussionspapier* 4 (University of Bremen, Bremen 2002): 187; on relationships between ecology and ethics, see Klaus Bosselmann, *When Two Worlds Collide: Society and Ecology* (RSVP, Auckland 1995): 317–338.

than in a democracy that is actively engaged in finding truth, no matter how remote or idealistic.

In any case, the quest for sustainability is in need of people actually experiencing and expressing what kind of changes may be necessary for achieving more balanced relations between humans and nature. Ecological awareness is more than feeling guilty about ourselves – it also reflects deeper insights into the human psyche and intellect or, at the very least, generates some practical ideas about how we could be doing better. And, because of moral ecological realism, citizens may be able to interact at a higher level of solidarity, that is, among people and between humans and their natural surroundings.

Effectively, such awareness leads to an expansion of space and time. The local becomes the global (and vice versa) and the present is linked to the future (and vice versa). More particularly, ecological awareness helps in defining earth governance: thinking globally and acting locally is essential to earth governance, but thinking locally and acting globally becomes equally important. We cannot hope for local solutions to solving global problems until we also develop global solutions to local problems. Awareness of interconnections and interrelationships is the key to understanding ecological complexity and in this sense provides accessible knowledge that ought to inform democratic processes.

Earth governance, in sum, contains moral ecological realism. This puts it into competition with, or perhaps in opposition to, liberal democracies. However, both can be reconciled if procedural democracy (based on pluralism) can generate a level of consensus beyond addressing the most immediate issues. Parliamentary debates are, of course, routine around issues such as economic development, energy, social justice, health, education, and so on – most of which have a certain immediacy and singularity to them. A stance based on moral ecological realism would make the connections between (seemingly) singular issues insisting on their systemic character and demanding more ambitious policy measures.

4. MOTIVATIONS AND ATTITUDES

A crucial and probably the most difficult issue of earth governance is the question of motivation towards a culture that enables it. What kind of reason is there to motivate the wider public to overcome egocentric, short-term perspectives in favour of timely and spatially remote humans? And further, how could the concern for future generations include the community of all living beings?

Examining motivational sources requires the distinction between reasons related to egoistic or altruistic behaviour. While the relation to egoistic reasons appears self-evident, some authors question whether altruistic behaviour exists at all.[29] In an ideal world, altruistic behaviour would be performed by entirely neglecting self-interest. Presumably, such a behaviour is not possible because it at least ignores personal values, motivating the agent by the belief to be a better person while doing so. Although this kind of argument is of highly theoretical interest, for our purposes it should be sufficient to call a behaviour altruistic if it is performed related to reasons that do not, under any circumstances, put egoistical preferences above everything else.

One source of possible altruistic behaviour is love. For example, in a life-threatening situation love motivates many parents to sacrifice themselves to save their children. And in the history of nation-states 'love' for the fatherland was misused to motivate people to fight in devastating wars. So far, 'love' has the motivational force to enable people to not behave in line with their first egoistical preference for their own life. But why should people start to 'love' earth and treat it in a manner akin to how they treat 'loved ones'?

Edward Wilson offers the notion 'biophilia' for this purpose.[30] He introduces the term with a theoretical background of evolutionary psychology: the felt attraction to other living beings up to complete ecosystems stops us from destroying them and helps us to survive. It is supposed to be the same psychological process that stops parents killing their children. Indeed, the parallel of the relationship between parents and their children and the attitude we ought to have towards nature is a candidate presented by other authors such as Hans Jonas.[31] The metaphor of 'Mother Earth' nourishing us all also belongs here. Using this metaphor and reflecting evolutionary psychology, humanity lost, at least partially, its innate respect for 'Mother Earth' through the industrial revolution. We might think of ourselves as slowly growing up, as loutish teenagers. But then, all teenagers have to re-learn that their parents are what shaped them and that they will always be with them, whether they like it or not. One obvious difference in this metaphor is that 'Mother Earth' may not be a caring, understanding and all-forgiving parent. From her perspective, it doesn't matter whether there are humans around or not.

---

[29] See, for example, Nigel Barber, *Kindness in a Cruel World: The Evolution of Altruism* (Prometheus Books, New York 2004).

[30] Edward O. Wilson, *Biophilia* (Harvard University Press, Cambridge, MA1984).

[31] Hans Jonas, *The Imperative of Responsibility* (University of Chicago Press, Chicago 1984).

Apart from this hypothetical metaphor,[32] the question of 'biophilia' as a possible source of motivation deserves an answer in terms of its moral quality. As introduced by Wilson, biophilia features more as a function of evolutionary psychology than as a source of an ethical 'ought'. The moral ground on which such a kind of love could be experienced is 'nature' and/or 'wilderness' with their relation to the aesthetic category of the sublime. To grasp this category and why it delivers the moral ground for biophilia, a quote from German poet Friedrich Schiller from 1795 might be useful:

> They (i.e. the objects of nature) *are* what we *have been*, what we are *going to be again*. We have been nature like them and our culture shall lead us on the path of liberty and reason back to nature. Thus they are also representations of our lost childhood which will remain our greatest treasure; and fulfill us with certain nostalgia. At the same time they are representations of our highest perfection in the ideal, that's why they put us in sublime quietness.[33]

The aesthetic stance of the sublime[34] lets us become aware of our freedom inside nature: the difference between humans and nature is not absolute or categorical, but gradual. This aesthetic experience offers the moral insight of a special responsibility for the nature we are essentially part of. And it is an experience that can easily be traced to non-Western cultures; the category of the sublime is just the way Western philosophy (and theology) approach this phenomenon. It does rather appear as a universal ground of humankind, inspiring the different ways of religious and moral thinking. To this end, it appears to have even more universal character than 'human dignity'. Biophilia, therefore, can be considered as the emotional dimension of the sublime, motivating us to listen to its moral claims.

The aesthetic and religious aspects we just touched upon appear to be highly abstract, even if related to more secular notions such as the sublime or biophilia. Yet, the metaphysical aspects of human consciousness are real and inform the way we think and act. When we think of human rights, in particular the concept of human dignity, we strike a similar problem. We seem to have a clear enough idea of what human dignity entails, but may not be aware of the motivations behind it, except for the fact that humanism and the Enlightenment movement of the seventeenth and eighteenth centuries have shaped the idea that today seems so obvious. In a similar vein, we may perceive notions such as biophilia or the concept of ecological integrity as

---

[32] Which, after all, has shaped recent constitutional developments in countries such as Bolivia and Ecuador.

[33] Friedrich Schiller, *Über naive und sentimentalische Dichtung* (Reclam, Ditzinger 1978): 4 (emphasis in original; trans. Michael Schröter).

[34] From the German 'erhaben' or 'ehrfurchtgebietend'.

contemporary expressions of deeper motivations that have always existed and may be cross-cultural as, for example, indicated by reference to Mother Earth. Such expressions of relatedness have their roots in linguistics, of course, but in a sense of reflecting human consciousness as it has evolved through the development of language. Against this long evolution, it would appear arbitrary to assume a moral claim completely based on rational argument. There is, after all, no purely rational argument to support the idea of human dignity.

In law, we usually refer to basic assumptions about human values as expressions of natural law. Arguably, no positive law could function without implicit reference to natural law. Only from a perspective of crude Austinian positivism can legal rules appear to be followed simply because they exist. People obey the law mainly because they believe it is legitimate,[35] but this in turn depends on a range of more subtle factors, including the belief in legitimate authority or resonance with fundamental values. In one way or another, laws are inextricably intertwined with the basic assumptions that society holds precious; they cannot be overruled.

Questions of legitimacy are an essential part of democracy both for its process and its resulting power. They are also issues of trust. Ultimately, we need to ask ourselves to what degree today's political institutions can be trusted to cater not just for immediate needs, but also for long-term environmental security and justice.

Concerns for ecological responsibility are valid at domestic level as much as at international level.[36] In the words of Patricia Mische: 'Ultimately without the development of a global culture of ecological responsibility, it is unlikely that any international law can be fully developed, enforced, or effective . . . An effective system of ecological security requires the development of a powerful cultural force to tell the political forces what to do, and to hold them accountable.'[37]

At this present juncture, political liberalism is closely linked with neo-liberal economics.[38] We may call this a liberal narrative or covenant

---

[35] Tom Tyler, *Why People Obey the Law* (Princeton University Press, Princeton, NJ 2006).

[36] Bosselmann, Engel and Taylor (note 1): 46.

[37] Patricia Mische, 'National Sovereignty and Environmental Law', in Simone Bilderbeck (ed.), *Biodiversity and International Law* (IUCN NL, Amsterdam 1992); see also Dennis Goulet, 'The Ethics of Power and the Power of Ethics', in Dennis Goulet, *The Cruel Choice: A New Concept in the Theory of Development* (University Press of America, Lanham, MD 1985).

[38] See Wolfgang Sachs, *Planet Dialectics: Explorations in Environment and Development* (Zed Books, London 1992).

of modernity, but the question remains whether this is the only covenant under which earth governance would have to operate. There are non-Western covenantal traditions, for example, or global approaches inclusive of all and not just currently dominating cultures.

For the purposes of this chapter, a covenant can be seen as an unconditional commitment to be faithful to others regarding our most fundamental values and behaviours. Understood in this way, a covenant has historically served as the spiritual and moral authority for foundational political agreements such as national constitutions and international treaties.[39] As philosopher and international lawyer Laura Westra has noted, recognition of covenants is 'a powerful heuristic tool for understanding why, of the thousands of charters and agreements, some succeed and others fail. Charters and declarations of moral principles do not of themselves change the world; only the covenants that bear them do'.[40]

5. A NEW COVENANT

The time has come for the creation of a new covenant to govern the international arena which will have the power to transform our current priorities and focus. The values and ethical principles articulated in the Earth Charter are able to provide the basis for such an ecologically founded covenant.[41] This is because the Earth Charter can be seen as the fullest and most comprehensive formulation for a just and sustainable world.[42] It encompasses 'our obligations to ourselves, one another and the greater whole of which we are a part' – the earth, the 'greater community of life'; if not the universe itself.[43] In advocating for the inclusion of the 'greater community of life', the Earth Charter looks beyond the narrow

---

39 Bosselmann, Engel and Taylor (note 1): 49.

40 Laura Westra, 'Future Policy Paths for Ecological Integrity', in Laura Westra, Klaus Bosselmann and Richard Westra (eds), *Reconciling Human Existence with Ecological Integrity: Science, Ethics, Economics and Law* (Earthscan, London 2008).

41 Parveez Hassan, 'Earth Charter: An Ethical Lodestar and Moral Force', in Peter Blaze Corcoran (ed.), *The Earth Charter in Action: Toward a Sustainable Development* (KIT Publishers, Leiden 2005).

42 Ron Engel, 'The Earth Charter as a New Covenant for Democracy', in Peter Miller and Laura Westra (eds), *Just Ecological Integrity: The Ethics of Maintaining Planetary Life* (Rowman & Littlefield, Lanham, MD 2002): 40; Peter Blaze Corcoran (ed.), *The Earth Charter in Action: Toward a Sustainable Development* (Royal Tropical Institute, Amsterdam 2005): 29.

43 Quotations are from the Earth Charter text.

anthropocentrism that characterizes most contemporary conceptions of governance. It argues that the greater community of life should not be respected solely on the basis of future human generations' enjoyment; rather, it is argued that a duty is owed to all sentient beings per se, regardless of their utility to future generations of human beings.[44]

The Earth Charter's plea to include the interests and rights of the community of life in our policies, laws and governmental structures might be dismissed as being unrealistic, and for some as downright laughable. Yet, as Christopher Stone has pointed out, '[t]hroughout legal history, each successive extension of rights to some new entity has been theretofore, a bit unthinkable'.[45] In part, this is because 'until the right-less thing receives its rights, we cannot see it as anything but a thing for the use of "us" – those who are holding rights at the time'.[46] So it was that judges and those in positions of political power were able to easily dismiss arguments for the rights for groups such as women, non-Europeans and children.

Drawing upon the pioneering work of Stone, D'Amato and Chopra have argued that whilst still in a nascent stage of development, international law provides promise for the recognition of rights of non-human forms of life.[47] In particular, these authors, through tracing the development of the international approach to nature, have shown that whales are in the process of being attributed an entitlement to life, which has hitherto only been recognized for the human species. The fact that whales are beginning to be ascribed rights in their own stead, as opposed to recognizing a duty of nations and individuals towards whales, is significant. As D'Amato and Chopra note, '[t]o move from "preservation" to "entitlement" is not just a change of jargon. Rather, it acknowledges the creation of a new subject of international law'.[48] Thus, international law already carries the seeds of possibility for non-anthropocentric conceptions.

Another important aspect of a new ecological covenant and which is articulated in the Earth Charter is the inclusion of future generations.[49] Under current forms of representative democracy, those elected are

---

[44] The Earth Charter. This is not to say that the environment should have the same body of rights as human beings have, rather it is an argument for the proposition that in order to have legally recognizable rights, being part of the human family should not be a prerequisite.

[45] Christopher D. Stone, *Should Trees Have Standing? Law, Morals and the Environment* (Oxford University Press, Oxford 2010): 2.

[46] Ibid.

[47] Anthony D'Amato and Sudir K. Chopra, 'Whales: their Emerging Right to Life' (1991) 85 *AJIL* 21.

[48] Ibid.: 53.

[49] Earth Charter, Preamble and Principle 4.

accountable to their constituencies and do not really feel responsible for those who are not yet born. Of course, the notion that obligations are owed to future generations is not new to international environmental documents; it has been fundamental since the publication of the Brundtland Report.[50] However, to date, the international community is yet to translate these obligations into something where they make a real difference and actually save future generations from a desperately ecologically impoverished world. As Maurice Roche has noted, '[t]he dominant paradigm of social citizenship . . . rests on unspoken and usually barely recognised temporal assumptions. It tends to take for granted that the only issues worth considering are those connected with the social rights and welfare needs of the contemporary set of generations . . . Nothing reveals the outdated character of the dominant paradigm more than this'.[51]

A new ecological covenant should also be informed by the theory of cosmopolitanism. The lacuna of power at international level, in conjunction with the diminishing operation of democracy at state level, has prompted a number of scholars to argue for a new way of conceiving of democracy that allows citizens to exercise political citizenship across borders. Such theorists have asked the question: 'Why must the principles and rules of democracy stop at the borders of a political community?'[52] A leading theorist of cosmopolitanism, Daniele Archibugi succinctly expressed the cosmopolitan project when he wrote that cosmopolitanism is 'the attempt to reconcile the phenomenon of globalization with the success of democracy. It sets out from an acknowledgement of the fact that state-based democracy, the only form we know today, risks being hollowed out by the processes of globalization'.[53]

While traditionally democracy has been rooted in territorially bound nationalism, cosmopolitans argue that despite great diversity there are commonly shared values and interests upon which an expanded 'demos' can be built, which both includes and transcends the nation-states.[54] This expanded conception of 'demos' requires that citizens play a more active

[50] *Development and International Co-operation: Environment*, A/42/427 (1987) Annex ('*Our Common Future*').

[51] Maurice Roche, *Rethinking Citizenship: Welfare, Ideology and Change in Modern Society* (Polity Press, Cambridge 1992): 242.

[52] Danille Archibugi, 'Demos and Cosmopolis' (2002) 13 *New Left Review* 28.

[53] Ibid.: 24.

[54] See Mirian Vilela and Peter Blaze Corcoran, 'History and Provenance of the Earth Charter: Building Consensus on Shared Values', in Peter Blaze Corcoran (ed.), *The Earth Charter in Action: Toward a Sustainable Development* (Royal Tropical Institute, Amsterdam 2005): 178.

role at a dual level – within the state they belong to and the world in which they live.[55] From a cosmopolitan viewpoint, the individual 'is the ultimate unit of concern and all human persons are of equal concern for everyone, not just those linked by the bonds of citizenship, or other contingent relations of nationality, culture etc.'.[56]

Although the notion of cosmopolitanism may seem utopian to some, various factors combined make cosmopolitanism more relevant, and more plausible, than at any other juncture in history. The advent of the International Criminal Court, the rise of human rights, and concerns around economic and environmental crises have all shown that humanity does have common values, common interests and, most importantly, a common future. Of these commonalities, it can be pointed out that the strongest shared value and interest that we have is in our shared environment, the destruction of which is jeopardizing the continued existence of all of humanity. As Archibugi has aptly noted, '[t]o be a cosmopolitan now is no longer simply to feel oneself a citizen *of* the world but also, and above all, a citizen *for* the world'.[57]

The notion of citizenship is pivotal with respect to earth governance and deserves a closer look. While there are various different ways in which citizenship can be understood, in the context of this chapter citizenship can be defined as membership determined by factors such as place of birth, parentage or naturalization, of a political community (generally a nation-state).[58] An important function of citizenship is to define people's rights and duties within their community.[59] While traditionally our understanding of citizenship has been predicated upon the territory of the nation-state, there is much to suggest that the territoriality associated with

---

[55] Ibid.: 31.

[56] Thomas Pogge, 'Cosmopolitanism and Sovereignty' (1992) 103 *Ethics* 48–49.

[57] Archibugi (note 52): 31; emphasis added.

[58] Ibid.: 197. Note, however, the observation made by Deane Curtin that in many colonized countries the concept of citizenship arrived in the early nineteenth century as the language of colonization. The language of citizenship may read very differently for those in the 'third' world. Deane Curtin, 'Ecological Citizenship', in Engin Fahri Isin and Bryan S. Turner (eds), *Handbook of Citizenship Studies* (SAGE, London 2002): 292.

[59] The importance of this function of citizenship is illustrated by the fact that most national constitutions acknowledge the fundamental status conveyed by citizenship and thus contain provisions preventing its denial. This importance is also reflected in the international sphere in Article 15 of the Universal Declaration of Human Rights which recognizes that a right to nationality is a fundamental human right. Klaus Bosselmann, *The Principle of Sustainability: Transforming Law and Governance* (Ashgate, Farnham 2008): 197.

citizenship, and the function of citizenship as demarcating people's rights and duties within communities, are being challenged by the processes of globalization.[60] This is so for a number of reasons.

First, in a globalized world there has been a proliferation of identities so that citizens can no longer rely on their nationality as a sole identity reference point. Through economic globalization and new forms of transport and communication, we have all (to greater or lesser extents) become part of a global culture. The effect of this is that '[t]he foreign becomes the familiar, and the familiar becomes the foreign. As a result, national identity is being replaced by a multinational identity more akin to a global citizen'.[61] A second reason is that there has been an observable shift in the loyalty which citizens feel towards their country of nationality. Thus, '[j]ust as with identity, loyalty has become either weak or split, often detached from nation, state, and territory and more conditional than it used to be, in the sense that it can be challenged more easily. Loyalty nowadays frequently expresses critical commitment rather than blind obedience'.[62] A third effect of globalization, which has challenged traditional conceptions of citizenship is new citizenship laws and the rise of supra- and transnational organizations such as the European Union, World Bank, the World Trade Organization and the United Nations. In particular, the European Union is a striking example of a trend towards a pooling of sovereignty which has challenged how citizenship has previously been viewed.

Contemporaneous with the erosion of traditional understandings of citizenship have been calls for a new conception of citizenship: ecological citizenship.[63] As noted in the above, many environmental problems are international problems – global warming, ozone depletion, acid rain – which are all constitutively international in the sense that they do not, cannot and will never respect national boundaries in their effects.[64] These global ecological problems cannot be solved by states or citizens acting on their own, prompting a number of scholars to argue that a different formulation of citizenship needs to be found. Andrew Dobson, for example, suggests that '[a]t the centre of this intellectual project is the firm conviction that conventional conceptions of justice and citizenship do not

---

[60] Ibid.

[61] Ibid.: 198.

[62] Ibid.: 199.

[63] N. Dower, 'The Earth Charter and Global Citizenship: A Way Forward', in Peter Blaze Corcoran (ed.), *The Earth Charter in Action: Toward a Sustainable Development* (Royal Tropical Institute, Amsterdam 2005): 178.

[64] Quentin Skinner, *States and Citizens: History, Theory, and Prospects* (Cambridge University Press, Cambridge 2003): 211.

provide the human species with an adequate set of tools for resolving the difficulties created by ecological damage today'.[65]

Ecological citizenship can be seen as a radical, re-conceptualized citizenship by taking it outside the realm of activity most normally associated with contemporary citizenship: the nation-state.[66] As Peter Christoff explains, 'because of the territorial boundedness, ecological citizens . . . increasingly work "beyond" and "around" as well as "in and against" the state'.[67] This does not mean that the ecological citizen is global as opposed to national or local. Indeed, it is important that the ecological citizen remains rooted in the local as well as having an appreciation of the global sphere.[68] The crux of ecological citizenship is its adherence to a fiduciary conception of citizenship requiring wide-reaching procedural and participatory rights. Here the Earth Charter is able to provide some invaluable orientation as to what these rights may be. In particular, Principle 13 of the Earth Charter argues that democratic institutions need to be strengthened at all levels, in order to provide transparency and accountability in governance, inclusive participation in decision-making and access to justice.[69]

However, while rights to the environment are central to ecological citizenship, just as important are the limitations placed upon those rights which ecological citizens owe to the environment. As Bart van Steenenberg has argued, '[t]here is one important difference between the environmental

---

65 Andrew Dobson, *Citizenship and the Environment* (Oxford University Press, 2003): 86; see also Andrew Dobson, 'Ecological Citizenship: A Defence' (2006) 15 (3) *Environmental Politics* 447.

66 Ibid.: see also Ralf Dahrendorf, 'The Changing Quality of Citizenship', in Bart van Steenbergen (ed.), *The Condition of Citizenship* (SAGE, London 1994): 13.

67 Peter Christoff, 'Ecological Citizens and Democracy', in Mark J. Smith (ed.), *Thinking Through the Environment* (Routledge, London 1999): 402.

68 Bosselmann (note 17).

69 The Earth Charter. This principle is expounded upon in the following subsections: (a) Uphold the right of everyone to receive clear and timely information on environmental matters and all development plans and activities which are likely to affect them or in which they have an interest. (b) Support local, regional and global civil society, and promote the meaningful participation of all interested individuals and organizations in decision making. (c) Protect the rights to freedom of opinion, expression, peaceful assembly, association, and dissent. (d) Institute effective and efficient access to administrative and independent judicial procedures, including remedies and redress for environmental harm and the threat of such harm. (e) Eliminate corruption in all public and private institutions. (f) Strengthen local communities, enabling them to care for their environments, and assign environmental responsibilities to the levels of government where they can be carried out most effectively.

movement and other emancipation movements. The difference has to do with the notion of responsibility . . . citizenship not only concerns rights and entitlements, but also duties, obligations, and responsibilities'.[70] This raises the question of what these rights and duties are and to whom they are owed. Again, it is argued that the Earth Charter is able to provide us with guidance. In particular, the Earth Charter argues for recognition of the diversity, interdependence, value and dignity of all life.[71] This recognition means that there is a duty to prevent environmental harm, which necessitates taking a precautionary approach to the environment.[72] These and other principles of the Earth Charter put self-restrictions on citizenship rights. In order to exercise our fiduciary responsibility, the right to the use of natural resources, for example, is restricted by respect for the community of life and the duty to prevent harm. Having described the individual components of global ecological governance, we can now describe the collective components of ecological governance, that is, global civil society.[73]

While globalization has curtailed nation-states' capacity to regulate key areas, it has also opened up new spaces to be filled by other actors. Civil society has capitalized upon this political opening, with numerous NGOs[74] emerging as powerful political actors in their own right with sway over the international agenda. In the area of international environmental law, civil society has played a particularly strong role. Indeed, it can be pointed out that this branch of international law would not even exist were it not for the worldwide environmental movement putting global environmental degradation on the agenda of state conferences – the United Nations Environment Programme (UNEP), for example, is largely shaped through the input of environmental groups.[75]

The rise of civil society within the international arena marks an

---

70 Bart van Steenbergen, 'Towards a Global Ecological Citizen', in Bart van Steenbergen (ed.), *The Condition of Citizenship* (SAGE, London 1994): 146.

71 The Earth Charter, Principle 1 (a), (b); Principle 2.

72 The Earth Charter, Principle 2 (a); Principle 6 (a), (b).

73 Bosselmann (note 16): 205.

74 Apart from NGOs, civil society consists of various other groups such as trade unions, business associations, religious bodies, academic institutions, student organizations, ethnic lobbies, community groups, and so forth. This is similarly defined in N. Dower and J. Williams (eds), *Global Citizenship: A Critical Reader* (Edinburgh University Press, Edinburgh 2002): xxi.

75 Alicia Barcena, 'Global Environmental Citizenship' (1997) UNEP 25, Our Planet 8, shows how UNEP's Global Environmental Citizenship Programme has developed strategic alliances with parliamentarians, consumers, local authorities, educators, religious groups, media and other key civil society groups.

important development which raises the possibility for citizens to be actively engaged politically beyond the nation-state. It allows for a multiplicity of voices to be heard, which would otherwise be excluded if states only were represented at international level. As April Carter has noted, 'global civil society builds on the autonomy of civil society bodies within their own nation states and links them within a trans-national realm independent of all nation states'.[76] Furthermore, NGOs and other civil societies can also fulfil an important civil function by holding governments and intergovernmental institutions accountable to the public.[77] The democratic possibilities raised by global civil society have been articulated in the preamble to the Earth Charter when it was noted that '[t]he emergence of a global civil society is creating new opportunities to build a democratic and humane world'.[78] Furthermore, under the Earth Charter, global civil society working in partnership with government and business is seen as essential in moving forward.[79]

However, despite the positive influence global civil society can have on global governance, it lacks democratic legitimacy and accountability in its classical sense. Ultimately, while its policies might impact on citizens' lives, citizens in turn do not have any democratic means to control civil society. The question is thus posed: 'Who – if anyone – do NGOs represent, or are they just unaccountable special interest groups that wear a more friendly disguise?'[80] Moreover, the extreme asymmetry of global networks from the North compared to the South raises the criticism that it is predominantly voices from the North (who often claim the ability to speak for the global South) that are actually represented in global civil society. For example, only 251 of the 1,550 NGOs associated with the UN Department of Public Information come from the South and the ratio of NGOs in consultative status with ECOSOC is even lower.[81] As Scholte has noted, 'hierarchies of social power operate in civil society no

---

[76] April Carter, *The Political Theory of Global Citizenship* (Routledge, London 2001): 80.

[77] Anne Bischel, 'NGOs as Agents of Public Accountability and Democratization in Intergovernmental Forums', in William M. Lafferty and James Meadowcroft (eds), *Democracy and the Environment: Problems and Prospects* (Edward Elgar Publishing, Cheltenham, UK/Northampton, MA 1996).

[78] The Earth Charter, Preamble.

[79] The Earth Charter, 'The Way Forward'.

[80] Michael Edwards, 'Global Civil Society and Community Exchanges: a Different Form of Movement' (2001) 13 *Environment and Urbanization* 145.

[81] Ibid.: see also M. Kaldor, H. Anheir and M. Glasius, *Global Civil Society 2003/4* (SAGE, London 2003).

less than in other political spaces. Civil society is itself a site of struggles to be heard'.[82]

Yet, the lack of accountability and the bias of the North is not an argument for the reduction of the role that global civil society plays in the international arena. Whilst global civil society operates in a less than perfect fashion, its voice adds an essential layer of checks and balances to the international system and helps to ensure that voices beyond the state are heard. The challenge moving forward therefore is to structure global citizen voices in ways that combat, rather than accentuate, existing social, economic and political inequalities.[83] Addressing these problems will require a different way of building international alliances, with more emphasis on horizontal relationships among equals; greater accountability; stronger links between local, national and global action; and a more democratic way of deciding on strategy and messages.[84] It is here that the rise of a truly cosmopolitan notion of citizenship is important as it has the potential to transform global civil society so as to make it representative of the world's citizens. As Attfield points out, legitimizing and monitoring institutions of global governance could be the main effect of global citizenship.[85]

6. TRANSNATIONAL, VALUE-BASED DEMOCRACY

Transnational, value-based democracy is not a form of democracy in which citizens' involvement in politics is restricted to a vote once every three or four years, but rather a democracy which recognizes that active citizen involvement is desirable and even necessary. As Chandra Bhushan has noted, 'If we want to tackle climate change, we will need more democracy not less. Not only within countries, but also between countries'.[86] This is true of course not only for responding to climate change, but for all our ecological problems as well as our economic and political issues. While it

---

82 Jan Aaart Scholte, 'Civil Society and Democracy in Global Governance' (January 2011) CSGR Working Paper 65/01, 21.

83 Edwards (note 80).

84 Ibid.

85 Robin Attfield, 'Global Citizenship and the Global Environment', in N. Dower and J. Williams (eds), *Global Citizenship: A Critical Reader* (Edinburgh University Press, Edinburgh 2002): 197.

86 See https://www.opendemocracy.net/article/international-democracy-day-work-to-do.

is difficult to prescribe exactly the contours of what such a reconstructed political system might look like, some concluding remarks around citizenship, deliberative democracy[87] and the Earth Charter may help to appreciate the changing character of governance designed to protect earth and its global commons.

What is needed is not an abandonment but rather a radical reconstruction of democracy, in order to place decisions back in the hands of the public, thereby opening up the space for different ecological approaches. The question is how do we make democracy and its attendant institutions more participatory so that they are more sensitive to environmental considerations? Deliberative democracy is able to provide some guidance of a way in which democracy can be revitalized. Deliberative democracy, broadly defined, 'refers to the idea that legitimate lawmaking issues from the public deliberation of citizens'.[88] It is a process which 'calls upon citizens to look for the best justifications of the laws, principles and policies that govern their lives and to seek these justifications through processes of public deliberation'.[89] There are three features that can be said to characterize deliberative democracy.

First, this approach to democracy places a premium on the process of decision-making as opposed to outcomes. Importantly, the expectation is that through the process of deliberation itself preferences will be transformed. As Bernard Manin has noted, it is 'necessary to alter radically the perspective common to both liberal theories and democratic thought: the source of legitimacy is not the predetermined will of individuals, but rather the process of its formation, that is deliberation itself'.[90] Consequently, 'the public realm needs to be transformed from a set of mechanisms for aggregating preferences to one for examining them and pursuing those which are in fact-, other- and future-regarding'.[91]

Second, central to deliberative democracy is the notion of unconstrained dialogue. As Jay Bernstein comments on Habermas' theory of discourse ethics, 'the idea of a grounded consensus involves the idea of a

---

87 On the nexus between these two concepts, see Jürgen Habermas, 'Citizenship and National Identity', in Bart van Steenbergen (ed.), *The Condition of Citizenship* (SAGE, London 1994): 20, 32.

88 Graham Smith, *Deliberative Democracy and the Environment* (Routledge, London 2003): 53.

89 Ibid.: 81.

90 Bernard Manin, 'On Legitimacy and Political Deliberation' (1987) 15 *Political Theory* 351–352.

91 David Held, *Models of Democracy*, 3rd edn (Stanford University Press, Stanford, CA 2006): 271.

speech free from coercion and constraint, where only the force of better argument is operative.[92] It requires citizens to take other perspectives seriously; to afford them an equal right to moral authority; to cultivate a disposition towards openness such that they reflect on their own values and preferences in light of conflicting perspectives'.[93] This implies that every participant is equal in the discourse and that every utterance has the same claim of validity. It is important to note that this does not mean that there will necessarily be a complete consensus on issues: in a world of value pluralism, continuing disagreement is a fact of life that cannot be theorized away.[94] Rather, what is aimed at is mutual understanding, which does not mean that people will always agree, 'but rather that they are motivated to resolve conflicts by argument rather than other means'.[95]

Third, deliberative democracy must be inclusive. This means that all people who are in a position to be possibly affected by a decision must be able to participate in the making of that decision.[96] As Habermas has noted, 'deficits [in democratic legitimacy] will always result when the circle of all those involved in democratic decision making does not extend to cover the circle of all those affected by those decisions'.[97]

This facet of deliberative democracy is important and becomes critical in the context of earth governance. How to ensure inclusiveness when the most affected such as the poor and marginalized, future generations and indeed the entire community of life are not represented? In so far as they cannot speak for themselves, they need a voice that can be heard. Such a voice is one of stewardship and trusteeship. Deliberative democracy requires unconstrained and inclusive participation, however in an ecological context participants must give voice to what otherwise remains voiceless. Only a stance of stewardship and trusteeship can ensure that.

Again, the Earth Charter provides for values and attitudes that facilitate such trusteeship. The Earth Charter's Preamble states: '(t)he emergence of

---

92 Jay M. Bernstein, *Recovering Ethical Life: Jürgen Habermas and the Future of Critical Theory* (Routledge, London 1995): 51.

93 Amy Gutmann and Dennis Thompson, *Democracy and Disagreement* (Belknap Press, Cambridge, MA 1990): 79–82.

94 John Rawls, *A Theory of Justice*, 2nd edn (Harvard University Press, Cambridge, MA 1999).

95 Smith (note 88): 59.

96 Those affected include 'anyone whose interests are touched by the foreseeable consequences of a general practice regulated by norms at issue'; Jürgen Habermas, *Between Facts and Norms: Contributions to a Discourse Theory of Law and Democracy* (The MIT Press, Cambridge, MA 1998): 107.

97 Jürgen Habermas, 'Towards a Cosmopolitan Europe' (2003) 14 *Journal of Democracy* 86, 90.

a global civil society is creating new opportunities to build a democratic and humane world', especially with respect to 'universal responsibility' requiring us to 'identify ourselves with the whole Earth community as well as our local communities' in order to discharge of our 'responsibility for the present and future well-being of the human family and the larger living world'.[98] These are reflections of trusteeship for future generations and the community of life. The operating principles and norms of the Earth Charter all underpin this concept of trusteeship. Essentially, the Earth Charter is a covenant of responsibility for the earth,[99] requiring a deep sense of acting on behalf of those who cannot act for themselves. It provides us, therefore, with the contours of earth governance.

Earth governance aims for transnational, global democracy with new institutions that represent people, not states. These institutions are not in competition with states, but complementary to them, in order to complete unfinished business: taking care of the global commons.

---

98 The Earth Charter, Preamble.

99 'It is imperative that we, the peoples of Earth, declare our responsibility to one another, to the greater community of life, and to future generations' (Preamble).

3. Commons

Technology can unite and it can divide. It can elevate and it can degrade. It can create a new civilization of abundance, it may destroy all civilization and life on this globe. . . At stake is the survival of man himself.
Arvid Pardo, 1972[1]

1. INTRODUCTION

Nowadays when we hear the word *wealth* we automatically think of money. How can we not? Champions of the 'market' have ascribed monetary value to everything, transforming our view of nature and its resources. This has been done with little attention to the costs of human impact on the environment (and on other people!) and the ramifications of nature's commodification. These are merely 'externalities' – the unfortunate byproduct of human 'progress'. 'Over the past generation, neoliberalism has steadily expanded to become the default worldview governing economics, public policy and human aspiration more generally.'[2] Modern life has transformed so that 'our economic relations to each other govern our social relations. Our identities as employees and consumers predominate, and so the marketplace becomes our primary source of social and personal meaning'.[3] This has occurred to the detriment of one key fact: human survival depends on a healthy environment. Our shared environment is the site of ever increasing over-use, pollution, congestion, free riding, and conflict.[4] These phenomena occur in a governance vacuum

---

1 Arvid Pardo, 'New Horizons in Ocean Science and Law', in E. Borgese (ed.), *Pacem in Maribus* (Dodd, Mead & Co., New York 1972): 250.

2 David Bollier, 'The Future of the Commons: Notes from a Retreat Exploring the Potential of the Commons to Fight Enclosures and Build Commons-based Alternatives', Retreat on the Future of the Commons, Crottorf Castle, Germany, June 2009: http://commonstrust.global-negotiations.org/resources/Bollier,%20Crottorf%20retreat.pdf.

3 Ibid.

4 Charlotte Hess, 'Mapping the New Commons', Governing Shared Resources: Connecting Local Experience to Global Challenges, the 12th Biennial Conference of the International Association for the Study of the Commons, University of

because of a global political system dominated by individual states' interest and an entrenched belief in the 'market' which ascribes all human action and consumption with the legitimacy of 'progress'.

Today's omnipresence of the market is the epitome of neoliberalism and the result of capitalist order. This is the socio-economic side of the story. The legal side is the emergence of the 'empire of private property'.[5] Private property is the legal vehicle for building markets. As wealth is generated for successful market players, it is secured through property rights. Wealth created by markets is for the few, while wealth created by the commons is wealth for all. Market forces, therefore, can lead to the enclosure of the commons, in particular the natural environment. The state's prime task is to determine and control the boundaries between market forces and protection of the commons.[6]

Over the last 150 years, the systematic appropriation of the environment was justified by the argument that it would increase productivity – 'efficient allocation'.[7] The argument is fundamentally flawed. For 40 years, scientists have pointed to the environmental damage that this path has wrought. Yet, as Clippinger and Bollier explain, when people and cultures are faced with events and ideas that they cannot predict, explain or control, 'they revert to the repetitive assertion of the simplest and most soothing of their founding ideas'.[8] What can be more simple, in the face of devastating evidence of environmental degradation, than to continue on as usual? Chillingly, this anthropological trend, as the authors call it, is perfectly illustrated by the modern-era panacea: sustainable development. It says, we acknowledge the harm, but we will maintain our belief in growth. This we can understand as a 'ghost dance of denial'.[9] It is a

---

Gloucestershire, Cheltenham, England, 14–18 July 2008: http://papers.ssrn.com/sol3/papers.cfm?abstract_id=1356835.

[5] David Bollier, *Think Like a Commoner: A Short Introduction to the Life of the Commons* (New Society Publishers, Gabriola Island, BC, Canada 2014): 97.

[6] Klaus Bosselmann, Peter Brown and Brendan Mackey, 'Enabling Flourishing Earth: Challenges for the Green Economy, Opportunities for Global Governance' (2012) 21 (1) *Review of European Community and International Environmental Law* 20–38.

[7] Silke Helfrich, 'Commons: the Network of Life and Creativity', in Silke Heinrich (ed.), *Genes, Bytes and Emissions: To Whom Does the World Belong?* (Henrich Böll Stiftung, Berlin 2008): http://www.boell.org/web/148-576.html.

[8] John Clippinger and David Bollier, 'A New Renaissance of the Commons: How the New Sciences and Internet are Framing a New Global Identity and Order', in Rishab Aiyer Ghosh (ed.), *CODE: Collaborative Ownership and the Digital Economy* (The MIT Press, Cambridge, MA 2005).

[9] Ibid.

maintenance and repetition of 'ritualistic behaviour that people hope will ward off unpleasant social and economic realities and ecological perils and new global interdependencies that are profoundly threatening to established cultural norms'.[10]

Ideologies borne of the industrial revolution have lost their explanatory power in an age where the very basis of all life is threatened by human choice. It is long past the time to stop the ritualistic burying of our head in the sand, proposing 'market' solutions and finding technological solutions to environmental problems without changing the source of the problem. Current environmental crises speak to a crucial erosion in humans' relationship with each other and with the biosphere.

In response to this picture a new idea is being revived. Commons describes a concept and movement with 'the potential to evolve into a new big story: for a future of social cohesion, supported by ties to our natural, social, and cultural resources'.[11] The commons have always been productive; they are, as Jonathan Rowe puts it, 'the hidden economy, everywhere present but rarely noticed'.[12] Commons management or governance necessitates an approach to this 'production' that embodies sustainability, as opposed to extraction for profit, a neoliberal philosophy which encourages over-use. As Helfrich correctly posits, the capitalist referent – profit – and hence how efficiently we use the commons in a productive sense, contrasts with the central question of the commons: to what end, to whose benefit and in whose interest, and by whom may our shared environment be used.[13] As we shall see, the commons refers to both the material and the immaterial. This volume, which is borne of the grave need for global environmental governance, discusses the natural commons – the environment – as both physical resources and as our knowledge 'commons' for how to manage the relationship between humans and nature.

The point is to recapture the narrative about our shared wealth in the community of life and shed the instrumental approach and market value approach to nature by including more ecological, social, democratic and moral value. In doing so, we move towards a more holistic model of governing our shared wealth. In this way, the commons names the

---

[10] Ibid.

[11] Helfrich (note 7). Also see David Bollier and Silke Helfrich (eds), *The Wealth of the Commons: A World Beyond Market and State* (Levellers Press, Amherst, MA 2012).

[12] Jonathan Rowe, 'The Hidden Commons', *Yes! Magazine* (30 June 2001): http://www.yesmagazine.org/article.asp?ID=443.

[13] Helfrich (note 7).

'species of wealth that classical liberal and neoliberal economics prefers to overlook'.[14]

2. HARDIN'S TRAGEDY OF THE COMMONS

The term 'tragedy of the commons', coined by American biologist Garrett Hardin in 1968 in his seminal article in *Science*,[15] has colloquially become the dominant metaphor for understanding anthropocentrically created environmental harm. Hardin's 'tragedy of the commons' alludes to the degradation of the environment whenever individuals use a scarce resource in common. To illustrate, he used the metaphor of an open pasture for grazing livestock available to all. This he called a commons. According to Hardin, 'rationality' compels people to graze as many livestock as individually possible to increase their individual profits, irrespective of the negative effects of overgrazing and the undermined pasture – 'each man is locked into a system that compels him to increase his herd without limit – in a world that is limited'.[16] Effectively, each herder (all being rational self-maximizers) reaches the same conclusion creating the 'tragedy' – a race to the bottom.

The commoners are portrayed by Hardin in a way similar to the classical economic theory characterization of economic agents: as rational and motivated by self-interest (egoism). The supposed rationality of grazing as many animals as possible arises because of the 'shared' nature of the resource – what you don't take today from the commons may not be there tomorrow. This is essentially the 'logic of mistrust' among people sharing a resource. The costs of overgrazing are externalized (not immediately felt by the individual over-herder) but borne by all who use the resource – the biological carrying capacity of which is undermined. Yet, obviously, when all herders follow the same logic, manifest as opportunism and over-capitalization, the commons is undermined and the outcome is suboptimal for *everyone*. Rational self-interest gives rise to an irrational outcome. In describing this, Hardin said, '[r]uin is the destination toward which all men rush, each pursuing his own best interests in a society that believes in freedom of the commons'.[17]

---

[14] David Bollier, 'The Commons: A Neglected Sector of Wealth Creation', in Silke Heinrich (ed.), *Genes, Bytes and Emissions: To Whom Does the World Belong?* (Henrich Böll Stiftung, Berlin 2008): http://www.boell.org/web/148-576.html.

[15] Garrett Hardin, 'The Tragedy of the Commons' (1968) 162 *Science* 1243.

[16] Ibid.: 1244.

[17] Ibid.

In fact, Hardin's tragedy was a metaphor for overpopulation – which he saw as the most pressing environmental problem.[18] In particular, he was concerned with the right to determine the size of the family or the 'freedom to breed', highlighting the contention between absolute human rights and ecological limits. Yet his observation was not entirely original. Aristotle wrote in *Politics* that people give the least amount of care to those things that jointly belong to the greatest number of individuals. Similarly, Thomas Aquinas, Hobbes and the Scottish philosopher David Hume also made this point. Hardin cites William Forster Lloyd who outlined a theory on the careless use of common property. H. Scott Gordon theorized overfishing in the same way, arriving at the famous conclusion: 'everybody's property is nobody's property.'[19] Hardin also echoes his contemporary Mancur Olson who challenged the assumption that individuals will cooperate (in collective action) to achieve common or group benefits without some form of coercion or other device to ensure common interest.[20]

The 'tragedy' is analogous to the game 'prisoner's dilemma'.[21] As in the pasture, players are more likely to defect if they choose independently of each other, because the risk to one player if he or she cooperates, while the other defects, is catastrophic. In a way the analogy between the tragedy and the prisoner's dilemma is flawed. The prisoner's dilemma is a non-cooperative game – all players possess complete information but they cannot communicate.[22] In a scenario where 'users' cannot communicate, Ostrom follows Hardin's thinking, also arguing that users will overharvest: 'the prediction that users will over-harvest a common-pool resource is supported in experiments where participants do not know the

---

[18] Ibid.: 1245.

[19] H. Scott Gordon, 'The Economic Theory of a Common-Property Resource: The Fishery' (1954) 62 *J. Pol. Econ.* 124.

[20] Mancur Olson, *The Logic of Collective Action: Public Goods and the Theory of Groups* (Harvard University Press, Cambridge, MA 1965).

[21] An example of a prisoner's dilemma game is when two people are held by police in separate rooms. The police offer each the same deal: if one prisoner snitches on the other, he/she will be released while the other prisoner will receive one year in jail; if the prisoner does not cooperate (remains), he/she will receive one month in jail. If both prisoners accept the deal and 'rat' on the other, they both get a three-month sentence. If both prisoners stay silent, they both get one month jail time each. The dilemma is thus: whether to defect or to remain silent (cooperating with the other prisoner).

[22] Elinor Ostrom, *Governing the Commons: The Evolution of Institutions for Collective Action* (Cambridge University Press, Cambridge 1990). She also notes that even where communication is modelled into the game, verbal agreements are non-binding unless expressly deemed to be so.

other individuals who are involved, and when they cannot communicate with each other'.[23] However, when we think back to Hardin's metaphor of the pasture, it becomes apparent that in the open-pasture scenario people *could* communicate.

Critics of Hardin often point out that his example of a pasture is flawed because over-use was generally prevented within these systems through a sophisticated structure of norms practiced by the respective communities. Siefkes describes how large parts of European agriculture were organized around a system of open fields during the Middle Ages and each village had several large unfenced fields that were farmed by the families of the village.[24] Thus, the use by Hardin of the open pasture is a flawed choice in analogy because medieval open pasture areas were unlikely to be 'free access', ungoverned or used by people who did not communicate.

If indeed modern Western society stood in the tradition of Europe's 'other side', that is, the pre-industrial governance of the commons, Hardin would be wrong. We would only have to revive what has always been good practice. Unfortunately, the history of the commons has been 'eclipsed'[25] and forgotten to the point that the commons just describes an empty space without governance or rules. This was certainly Hardin's perception and thus was correct as a description of capitalist society.

Hardin was criticizing free markets, which the actions of individuals acting according to rational self-interest bring about, through the operation of the *invisible hand*, prosperity and greater social good for all. Hardin argued that it simply and clearly doesn't work that way with common resources. Commonly propounded solutions to the tragedy, by Hardin and others, are private property rights (privatization), coercion by a leviathan manifest as state or militarized control or natural resource systems. Hardin assumed that once a resource is privatized, it is in the owner's self-interest to sustainably maintain it and ensure ongoing productive capacity. Political economy means that neither solution is as unitary as it appears – public vs private is not a sterile dichotomy.[26] Ironically, what began as a criticism of classical economic theory became an argument for the privatization of public space and resources, and ultimately for the

[23] Elinor Ostrom, 'Governing a Commons from a Citizen's Perspective', in Silke Heinrich (ed.), *Genes, Bytes and Emissions: To Whom Does the World Belong?* (Henrich Böll Stiftung, Berlin 2008).

[24] Christian Siefkes, 'The Commons of the Future: Building Blocks for a Commons-based Society', in Silke Heinrich (ed.), *Genes, Bytes and Emissions: To Whom Does the World Belong?* (Henrich Böll Stiftung, Berlin 2008).

[25] Bollier (note 5): 79.

[26] Ostrom, *The Evolution of Institutions for Collective Action* (note 22): 14.

implementation of the logic of market economy on new spheres of life, most environmental resources included.[27]

Note, however, that although Hardin proffered private property as an option to avert the tragedy, he did note that 'air and water' (which form part of the 'global commons' – see Chapter 4) 'cannot readily be fenced'.[28] Hence, for those parts of the commons that are not amenable to privatization, Hardin argued that the tragedy 'must be prevented by different means, by coercive laws or taxing devices that make it cheaper for the polluter to treat his pollutants than to discharge them untreated'.[29]

3. DEFINITIONS

At this point you might be asking, 'well what actually *is* the commons?' The answer is not so straightforward, evidenced by considerable confusion, even among scholars and commons advocates. Hence, it is constructive to note some important definitional divergence. Defining the commons is a normative issue and for this reason highly contentious.

If we take Hardin's metaphor, he defines the commons as an open-access area with no rules governing human activity in respect of that area and its resources. Contrastingly, many 'commons scholars' use the term commons to refer to an area which has 'community-defined rules stipulating how a commons could be used, protecting it from overuse, privatization and other forms of damage'.[30] According to Siefkes, 'contrary to the myth spread by Garrett Hardin . . . commons were not "anything goes" areas which anybody could use and abuse at will'.[31] What is effectively being argued is whether 'commons' is a noun (the commons) or a verb (to common). In fact, it is both, summarized thus: '[t]he concept of the commons sheds light on the two sides of this relationship, reveals its two faces. On the one hand, it highlights the nature and function of the resources under discussion. On the other hand, it raises questions about the state of the communities associated with those resources and the conditions required for their success'.[32] John McMurtry[33]

---

[27] Ibid.
[28] Hardin (note 15): 1245.
[29] Ibid.
[30] Siefkes (note 24); Bollier, *The Future of the Commons* (note 2).
[31] Ibid.
[32] Helfrich (note 7).
[33] J. McMurtry, 'The Life-Ground, the Civil Commons and the Corporate Male Gang' (2001) 22 *Canadian Journal of Development Studies* 819.

and Josee Johnston[34] call these the 'natural commons' and the 'civil commons', arguing that the former refers to the biosphere and the 'goods' therein which can be used by humans, and the latter refers to social organization regarding the natural commons, such as access and protection.

3.1 The Verb

To common, commoning or 'civil commons' refers to a social system. Bollier contends that open-access regimes in which the commoners do not truly govern themselves or establish their own rules and sanctions are failed commons.[35] In this way, he limits the word 'commons' to a governed commons. Such a definition is not practicable in light of the fact that 'commons' are also defined as nouns. Commons social systems that limit who has access to a resource and are managed by a select group are better characterized as 'common property regimes'. This is because they behave as property vis-à-vis the entire world except for members of the group who together hold them in common.[36] In other words, they are commons for those in the group but not for those outside the group. But, because the idea of commons is antithetical to the notion of property, to avoid confusion let us adopt Elinor Ostrom's term 'common pool resources management regimes'. Commoning does include several normative principles although these are not always achieved, principally being: fair access, equitably shared benefit, responsibility for preserving the resource for future generations, and democratic, participatory and transparent decision-making.[37]

3.2 The Noun

Commons are areas and resources over which no single person has exclusive control (for example, over use or disposition) but which are 'owned' by all. The fact that the commons are shared assets that belong to us all is the 'salient characteristic which defines [commons] in contradistinction to property'.[38] This definition of commons refers to 'common pool

[34] J. Johnston, 'Who Cares about the Commons?' (2003) 14 (4) *Capitalism, Nature, Socialism* 1.

[35] Bollier, *The Future of the Commons* (note 2).

[36] Yochai Benkler, 'The Political Economy of Commons' (June 2003) 4 (3) *Upgrade IV* 6–7: http://www.cepis.org/upgrade/files/full-2003-III.pdf.

[37] Silke Helfrich and Jörg Haas, 'The Commons: A New Narrative for Our Time', in Silke Heinrich (ed.), *Genes, Bytes and Emissions: To Whom Does the World Belong?* (Henrich Böll Stiftung, Berlin 2008).

[38] Benkler (note 36): 6.

resources'. These commons or 'common pool resources . . . whether material or immaterial – are the basis of all productive, reproductive, and creative processes'.[39] Examples of common pool resources are fish, minerals from the seabed, pasture, water and the common sink (the use of resources for their waste disposal capacity).[40] Commons areas or the fixed spatial dimensions of commons resources are also called 'resource domains'.[41] Resource domains can be imagined as both spatial and physical (collections of substances).[42] The resources within these areas – the common pool resources – can also be called resource units.[43] For example, the pasture is the resource domain, the grass that will be eaten the resource units, a forest is a resource domain and the trees are the resource units.

Another synonymous general term is 'common goods'. These are characterized as essential for human life; unable to be traded; unable to be owned.[44] These include, for example, fresh water, healthy soil and clean air, but also the oceans, the atmosphere and biodiversity. (The 'global commons' is discussed in Chapter 4.) Common goods may be social, cultural and intellectual 'commons', which are all replenishable resources. Or they may be solar, natural and genetic commons, which may be either replenishable or depletable. A third type of commons is material, which consists mainly of depletable resources.[45] All of these commons exist in different geographical spheres – they may be local, regional or global, or all of these.

Note that commons are not the same as common property resources because they are antithetical to the fundament of the concept of property – exclusion. Nor are they 'public goods'. Public goods are non-exclusionary, non-rivalrous resources which the state provides, although often these services are contracted out to private providers as proxy for

---

[39] Helfrich (note 7).

[40] John Vogler, *The Global Commons: Environmental and Technological Governance*, 2nd edn (Wiley, New York 2000). Ostrom also further refines this to 'resource systems' such as grazing areas and lakes, and 'resource units' such as the water withdrawn, the tonnes of grass eaten by livestock, the fish caught on the high seas, the waste absorbed by the lake or atmosphere – Ostrom, *The Evolution of Institutions for Collective Action* (note 22).

[41] Ostrom, *The Evolution of Institutions for Collective Action* (note 22): 30.

[42] Marvin S. Soroos, 'The Evolution of Global Commons', in Ho-Won Jeong (ed.), *Global Environmental Policies: Institutions and Procedures* (Palgrave, London 2001): 42.

[43] Ostrom, *The Evolution of Institutions for Collective Action* (note 22): 30.

[44] Klaus Bosselmann, Peter Brown and Brendan Mackey (note 6).

[45] Global Commons Trust, 'The Commons': http://globalcommonstrust.org/?page_id=11.

the state. Public goods are mostly services that *use* and *distribute* common pool resources.[46] Examples include lighthouses, city parks, healthcare, water provision, sewage systems, public electrification and broadcast programming.[47]

Hess and Ostrom (2007) broadly define the commons as 'a general term that refers to a resource shared by a group of people'.[48] What the social system (verb) definition omits is that 'to share' might not include an organized system of management – 'commoning' might not yet be established. This can be seen in Chapter 4, where the lack of governance of the global commons does not annul the fact that it is a commons. Most important to remember is that *all* definitions of commons have a sense of sharing and joint ownership.[49] 'Commons . . . describes goods and resources [social, cultural or natural] that share a special relationship with a group of people, a community. The group perceives them as being "theirs".'[50] This refers to common ownership – not ownership in the sense of 'property' but ownership as in 'possession'.

'Taking from the commons means taking something as possession (something that will be used) not as property (something that can be sold and commercialized at will).'[51] Common ownership refers to a bundle of rights – a mutually constitutive relationship of access/use (beneficiary) and protection/maintenance (responsibility). Moreover, we own the commons not in our individual capacity but as a group or community. In the broadest sense, common ownership describes the interdependency in the community of life – all living organisms. Ownership conceptualized as a bundle of rights and responsibilities reflects intergenerational equity (the commons as common heritage) and the intrinsic value of nature. Yet, as Vogler points out, be aware that not all people have equal access to the commons or enjoy equitably the benefits thereof even if it belongs to all humankind.[52]

In sum, commons can refer to anything from resources to the areas where these are found, or the collective social systems governing these.[53]

---

[46] Helfrich and Haas (note 37): 5.

[47] On the Commons, 'About the Commons': http://onthecommons.org/about-commons.

[48] Charlotte Hess and Elinor Ostrom (eds), *Understanding Knowledge as a Commons: From Theory to Practice* (The MIT Press, Cambridge, MA 2007).

[49] Hess (note 4): 6.

[50] Helfrich and Haas (note 37): 5.

[51] Siefkes (note 24).

[52] Vogler (note 40): 13.

[53] See Bollier and Helfrich (note 11): xii.

Commons may be governed (commoning) 'under rules that may range from "anything goes" to quite crisply articulated formal rules that are effectively enforced'.[54] Tragedy is linked with the efficacy of governance of the commons.

With this in mind, 'tragedies' can occur in three senses:

- Over-use because of *violation* or *breach* of existing rules;
- Over-use because the rules of access and use are *insufficiently defined* – in other words, doubt begets the temptation or incentives for over-use;
- Over-use because there are no rules or standards of behaviour (open access) and so nothing preventing over-use.

The first two are governed commons (common pool resources with regimes), albeit potentially ineffectually governed, while the latter is an ungoverned commons – an open-access area – which is what Hardin describes but imprudently illustrates through a pasture in a community – something more likely to be a common property regime. Understanding the different locations of 'tragedies', while a fussy exercise, is absolutely *crucial* because in each scenario the problem of over-use, or the incentive to overuse, must be viewed in a more nuanced manner.[55] One cannot be faulted for wondering why, for something as supposedly inherent as the commons, there is such definitional ambiguity. A useful explanation is that the concept of the commons is:[56]

> not part of our modern frame of reference or worldview . . . society is grappling now to understand their meaning. Although we often perceive them, we have lost the specific language for acknowledging and defining our traditional commons. And even for emerging commons like the internet, we are still developing new concepts and vocabulary.

And yet we undertake this complex and contentious task because refining and naming the commons and the kinds of tragedies that can and do occur is a vital precursor to defending and advocating for them.

---

[54] Benkler (note 36): 6.

[55] Achim Lerch, 'The Tragedy of the "Tragedy of the Commons"', in Silke Heinrich (ed.), *Genes, Bytes and Emissions: To Whom Does the World Belong?* (Henrich Böll Stiftung, Berlin 2008).

[56] Global Commons Trust (note 45).

4. FROM COMMONS TO PRIVATE PROPERTY

Originally, the commons were one of the categories of property in ancient Roman law, which distinguished between the exclusive *res privatae* (for example, a private house or a bicycle) and a number of non-exclusive categories of property, among which were the state-created *res publicae* (for example, roads, bridges), the natural *res communes* (the air, the sea and beaches), *res universitatis* – property belonging to a group, and *res nullis* – an unclaimed thing or no-man's land which could become the property of any person or persons, most often invoked in the 'new world' to conquer uncolonized lands.

Things classified as *res communes* were available for the use of all but could not, by their commons nature, become the property of any person or persons.[57] This category reveals most closely what has been discussed as the commons, but do not be fooled by the 'deceptive neatness of these categories, [for] they are of limited usefulness in labelling common pool resources because they lack dimensions that incorporate the flow of resources from the resource domain, the nature of the resource itself and the resource domain in which it is found'.[58] Likewise, when we talk about the commons systems, we conceptualize a regime distinct from property.

Property describes rights, powers and duties between people in relation to something which can be owned. How these rules are constituted determines the type of property something is. Private property is the idea that a 'thing' can be owned by an individual, and that the individual determines how the object shall be used (the right to appropriate) and by whom (the right of exclusion).[59] Private property is most often traced back to the Western liberal theory of John Locke, in particular to the chapter 'Of Property' in the second of his *Two Treatises of Government* appearing in 1689. Locke said that men own their bodies and persons, therefore they own their labors and when this is mixed with something in the state of nature (an unowned resource) it becomes his property.[60] But even Locke assumed that the earth and its resources originally belonged to *all people in common*. However, Locke noted the high transaction costs

---

[57] Prue Taylor, *An Ecological Approach to International Law: Responding to the Challenges of Climate Change* (Routledge, London 1998): 270.

[58] Susan Buck, *The Global Commons: An Introduction* (Island Press, Washington, DC 1998): 4.

[59] William N.R. Lucy and Catherine Mitchell, 'Replacing Private Property: The Case for Stewardship' (1996) 55 (3) *CLJ* 566, 567.

[60] John Locke, *Two Treatises on Government* (Cambridge University Press, Cambridge 1988).

of having to ask everyone else if one could take something as one's own. To address this he emphasized natural limitations on what each man could take. The first was that in each case of appropriation, enough must remain for others. Second, each individual may appropriate only as much as he himself consumes. However, such limits do not work in a monetarized system.

Whereas commons used to be the norm, the advent of individualism over community has made the law of property the norm – private property and public property. Commons as distinct from the patrimony of the state is an altogether foreign concept to our generation. In a sense, the commons asserts a heresy: that there are limits to the claims that private property may make upon the community and upon the earth.[61]

What was offered as a solution to one tragedy (privatization) has created another – the tragedy of markets or the tragedy of enclosure. What has occurred is an encroachment on the commons – our shared wealth – and the gradual demise of the commons system and the dissolution of commons thinking in society.[62] This phenomenon is called 'enclosure' of the commons. Enclosure refers to privatization, commercialization, legal restrictions and scarcity through overconsumption. According to Ostrom, these laws privatized grazing and agricultural lands formerly considered as commons of rural communities, thereby impoverishing the peasants and disintegrating their communities. Nowadays enclosures occur through corporate consolidation, cutting-edge technologies, stricter intellectual property laws and corporate–state partnerships.[63] According to the prominent commons scholar Christian Siefkes, 'the commons did not collapse, they were "stolen", as common sentiment at that time expressed it'.[64] Likewise, Bollier calls the enclosure of the commons into private property 'one of the great injustices of our time'.[65]

Part of the reason why commons were so taken for granted is because they were often beyond the threat of being enclosed. Consider how impossible it might seem to enclose the deep seabed or the atmosphere or the moon. In 1972 the Stockholm Declaration stated that through the 'rapid acceleration of science and technology, man has acquired the power to transform his environment in countless ways and on an unprecedented

---

61 Bollier, 'The Future of the Commons' (note 2).

62 Bollier, *The Commons: A Neglected Sector of Wealth Creation* (note 14).

63 Pat Mooney, Executive Director of the ETC Group, quoted in Bollier, *The Future of the Commons* (note 2).

64 Siefkes (note 24).

65 Bollier, *The Commons: A Neglected Sector of Wealth Creation* (note 14).

scale'.[66] As the epitaph captures, and in the 40 years since, the advent of technology has created the ability for private entities with enough capital to fund such projects to explore previously impossible common pool resources. The commons is no longer a site of commoning and what is taken is 'not in order to be used, but to be consumed; not to be increased in the interest of the common welfare, but to be privately appropriated'.[67] Indeed, many goods that were considered inexhaustible have begun to be threatened and to be subtractable, that is, depletable. The enclosure of the commons poses such problems that these 'private' rights are the locations of a new tragedy – the tragedy of the 'anti-commons'. In these instances, the common good is subordinate to private entities' patented and technologically enforced private access to algorithms, information and knowledge, all encouraged through favourable legal frameworks.

Enclosure does not only occur with material things. Consider the 'enclosure' of common knowledge, perhaps best historically exemplified by enclosures of women's bodies and knowledge of procreation, and now best exemplified by the area of intellectual property.[68] The incursion on indigenous peoples by colonizers is perhaps another apt example of 'enclosure' to the extent that culture, tradition and stores of ecological knowledge have, in turn, been denied, appropriated and commodified. 'This is the real tragedy of the commons: traditional management systems that were effective for thousands of years became obsolete in a few decades, replaced by systems' relentless exploitation of rural people and rural countries.'[69] Furthermore, concerns are frequently cited about the proliferation of patents on biomedical knowledge that impedes production and research on cures for disease and illness.[70] This is similarly the case with ethnobotanical knowledge.

Vandana Shiva refers to enclosure in the area of biology and agriculture as 'biopiracy' and as a new form of 'imperialism', which claims ownership not over territory, but over the inner reaches of genetics, products of nature and traditional culture.[71] Indeed, there are increasing monopolies

---

[66] *Declaration of the United Nations Conference on the Human Environment*, A/Conf/48/14/Revi (16 June 1972) (Stockholm Declaration).

[67] Helfrich (note 7).

[68] Peter Linebaugh in Bollier, *The Future of the Commons* (note 2).

[69] D.W. Bromley, *Environment and Economy: Property Rights and Public Policy* (Basil Blackwell, Oxford 1991): 104; US National Research Council, Board on Science and Technology for International Development, *Conserving Biodiversity: A Research Agenda for Development Agencies* (National Academy Press, Washington, DC 1992).

[70] On the Commons (note 47).

[71] Vandana Shiva, *Biopiracy: The Plunder of Nature and Knowledge* (South End Press, Cambridge, MA 1996).

of money and power in, for example, the seed industry where three companies control half the market. Lately, we are seeing enclosures of 'bytes, atoms, nano-matter and geology' or what is otherwise expressed as the acronym 'BANG'.[72] Likewise, there is a strong impetus for companies to get exclusive rights to biodiversity: 'the revolution in biotechnology is associated with patents on life forms and living processes'.[73] Enclosure is also made more likely because 'the building blocks of knowledge and life that fall prey to this process are permanently shrinking'[74] – the loss of diversity, social, cultural and biological. Likewise, the enclosure of the knowledge commons ensures that the information and knowledge on which economic success is based is controlled and made scarce; and scarcity creates demand and thus a higher price.

Technology has increased our understanding of the commons and hence our ability to exploit it. In turn, this has effected what we see as 'ours' and our concurrent recognition of responsibility to protect it. Instead, the onus of stewardship has been replaced by the pathology of neoliberalism and its mental categories for resources and nature. Enclosure has simultaneously eroded forms of governance for the commons which include non-capitalist social arrangements and institutions and sustainable ethics.

Vogler cites an example which shows how even commons rhetoric has been 'enclosed'.[75] He says, 'the limits of the commons and even awareness of their existence have been defined by the current state of exploration and technology'.[76] Further, 'most of the commons under consideration . . . could not meaningfully be understood as such before the twentieth century. This is because it was either impossible to reach and exploit them (Antarctica, the deep seabed and space), or they were simply beyond the prevailing state of scientific understanding (the radio frequency spectrum and atmospheric commons)'.[77] It used to be that a state's territorial jurisdiction extended three miles from the coastline – the extreme range of a cannon shot. Gradually, this range has extended alongside technological development. For example, when offshore oil exploration and large-scale commercial fishing became feasible, states pressed for Exclusive Economic Zones, and now continental shelves.[78] Will the next step be property rights

---

72 Pat Mooney, Executive Director of the ETC Group, quoted in Bollier, *The Future of the Commons* (note 2).
73 Helfrich (note 7).
74 Ibid.
75 Vogler (note 40).
76 Ibid.: 6.
77 Ibid.
78 Ibid.

in the global commons? The commons, it seems, is being treated as *res nullis* rather than *res communes*.

Technological advancement has allowed for the previously unappropriated and unowned commons to be explored and exploited, giving rise to resource exhaustion, unequal distribution of wealth and negative impacts on vital ecosystems, and in doing so undermining the common interests of humankind in a healthy environment. Thus, we see the 'profound relationship between the new technologies and the new patrimonies, for every day new possibilities appear for fencing in or abusing a good that we only begin to value once it begins to be threatened'.[79] Technology allows for the discovery and capture of new common pool resources in an economic sense. Such enclosures invariably proceed in the private interest. 'Yesterday it was the earth's largely visible natural resources. Today, it is the earth's visible and invisible natural and cultural resources.'[80] Capital and states and the normalization of property over commons have managed to capture the commons' rhetoric and use it to justify expropriation and enclosure as 'in the common interest'. Crucial then is the need for civil societies to examine what is theirs and recapture the debate, and have a stake in reframing environmental policy so that the state's actions truly are reflective of a common good. We are seeing the momentum of such a movement now.

5. A RENAISSANCE: THE COMMONS MOVEMENT

In a rejection of Fukuyama's portent of the 'end of history', in his book *The Beginning of History*, Massimo de Angelis posits the commons movement as the alternative and rival to the predominance of capitalism.[81] Following our discussion of the commons and the gradual normalization of private property, we know that the commons debate is not a new one, so what we are witnessing is a *revival* of commons thinking – a commons debate that has grown into a social and political movement described by Clippinger and Bollier as a 'renaissance of the commons'.[82]

Essentially, it has arisen out of reflection in a 'fundamental, candid,

---

[79] Antonio Lafuente, *The Four Realms of the Commons* in Silke Heinrich (ed.), *Genes, Bytes and Emissions: To Whom Does the World Belong?* (Henrich Böll Stiftung, Berlin 2008).

[80] Helfrich (note 7).

[81] Massimo De Angelis, *The Beginning of History: Value Struggles and Global Capital* (Pluto, London 2007).

[82] Clippinger and Bollier (note 8).

and collective manner on our quality of life and the quality of life of the future generations'.[83] It posits a new kind of economics that takes account of the full cost of market activity by recognizing the environmental and social externalities of production and consumption. Described thus, 'the commons offers not only an affirmative vision of a more equitable, eco-friendly society: it also serves as a countervailing force to keep excesses of the market and government sectors in check'.[84]

These debates have reignited the idea of 'commoning'[85] – the verb – and advocated in favour of a commons-based society called 'commonism'.[86] Those leading the movement tend to hail from commons experiencing mounting enclosure – ecologists, computer programmers, indigenous peoples and ordinary citizens who are concerned about the negative effects of neoliberalism on the environment and on culture. Bollier argues that the commons is appealing because it offers a new master narrative that can connect and coordinate many disparate, seemingly isolated campaigns.[87] 'People are starting to self-identify themselves as commoners with a stake in the resources that neoliberal markets seek to appropriate.'[88] What is being promoted is 'commons-like thinking: a belief in the common good and working toward shared outcomes based on voluntary participation and reciprocity'.[89] This new paradigm rejects the 'competitive, mechanistic, profit-centric mindset that has ruled Western civilization since the dawn of the Industrial Revolution' and replaces it with 'a more humanistic, environmentally aware and holistic world view.'[90] The movement is not only an attempt to 'reclaim the commons' resources but also to reclaim our ways of managing our social, cultural and environmental resources. In this way, it is a revival of notions of the reciprocal relationship between humans and nature – encompassed by terms such as stewardship, guardianship and trusteeship – 'we are resurrecting some forgotten traditions and cultural practices of commoning'.[91]

According to Yochai Benkler, 'one can say that commons and property exist on a spectrum of institutional arrangements. Where along this

---

[83] Helfrich (note 7).
[84] On the Commons (note 47).
[85] Gerhard Scherhorn, 'Transforming Global Resources into Commons', in Bollier and Helfrich (note 11): 395, 396.
[86] Nick Dyer-Witheford, 'Commonism' (2007) *Turbulence* 1: http://turbulence.org.uk/turbulence-1/commonism.
[87] Bollier, *The Future of the Commons* (note 2).
[88] Ibid.
[89] Hess (note 4).
[90] On the Commons (note 47); Siefkes (note 24).
[91] Bollier, *The Future of the Commons* (note 2).

spectrum a resource management system should be so as to be sustainable and efficient depends on technological characteristics of the resource and on patterns of its usage at any given historical moment'.[92] Evidently, the property regime (both public and private), while not problematic per se, has failed to affect sustainability – property is also giving rise to a tragedy. What we need is consideration of a new paradigm for governing the environment.

Yet the prisoner's dilemma and Hardin's 'tragedy', in echoing pessimistic sentiments expressed for centuries, imply the impossibility of rational human beings cooperating for the common good. In other words, unless people have private and exclusive property rights in something, or unless they are coerced, people will not manage a resource sustainably. In fact, many scholars have challenged and rejected this view on both empirical and philosophical grounds, suggesting that the self-interested vision of human behaviour is not as immutable as many economists assert.[93] Many scholars, notably Elinor Ostrom, have sought to demonstrate human beings' capacity to cooperate by citing empirical examples of locally grounded management schemes and cooperatives, particularly in developing countries, which have lasted through generations.[94] Ostrom calls these common-pool resources management.

Ostrom argues that what the putative solutions to the tragedy have in common is 'a faith in the necessity and efficacy of "the state" to change institutions so as to increase efficiency'.[95] According to Ostrom, both the tragedy and the prisoner's dilemma assume fixed constraints and fixed empirical settings, which do not, in fact, reflect the reality of nuanced human and commons contexts.[96] In Ostrom's alternative solution, herders can make a binding contract to commit themselves to a cooperative strategy that they themselves work out.[97] Herders negotiate prior to using the resource (placing their animals in the pasture). There is also the possibility that herders hire a private agent to take on the role of enforcer.[98] Ostrom describes a self-financed contract scenario, which she herself admits is no panacea and has weaknesses in many settings.[99] Furthermore, while

---

92 Benkler (note 36).

93 See, for example, Marco Casari and Charles R. Plott, 'Decentralized Management of Common Property Resource: Experiments with a Centuries-Old Institution' (2003) 51 *Journal of Economic Behavior and Organization* 217.

94 Ostrom, *The Evolution of Institutions for Collective Action* (note 22).

95 Ibid.: 14.

96 Ibid.: 6.

97 Ibid.: 15.

98 Ibid.: 16.

99 Ibid.: 18.

Ostrom's work is integral to challenging the assumption and inevitability of non-cooperation, her work speaks mainly of small-scale and single resource common-pool resource situations. In a small-scale commons situation, individuals can communicate and communities are built on bonds of trust among members that allow for collective management.[100]

However, when talking about the global commons (see Chapter 4), is it so easy to find evidence of cooperation? Despite the ubiquitous yet ambiguous phenomenon of 'globalization', two chief features of which are global communications systems and migration, the world is still dominated by a system of states and thereby a system of national and sub-national identities. Scholars of international relations differ in their perspectives as to what one is likely to see at this level.[101] Hardin assumes it is natural for humans to act purely out of self-interest in open-access areas such as those of the global commons. But this volume neither seeks to ignore the unfortunate reality that actors on the global stage have so far failed to affect ecologically sustainable governance, nor to dismiss out of hand the possibility that cooperation is possible. The simple point is that a commons is not always a tragedy.[102]

The intent of this volume is to argue for a revival of cooperation in environmental management, present throughout history and all over the world – in the form of centuries of stewardship ethics and tradition. In doing so, it is asserted that narrow self-interest is not a foregone conclusion. Implicitly such ideas challenge the economic rationality and inevitability of individual accumulation so central to neoliberalism. What is offered is not a new, but revitalized approach to conceptualizing the relationship between humans and nature. 'The commons "out-cooperates" the market. It does this by itself eliciting personal commitment and creativity and encouraging collective responsibility and sustainable practices.'[103] The challenge for this volume is to translate this into a system of governance for the global commons.

Like Ostrom, the intent of this volume is to pursue a similarly optimistic path by extending the examples of cooperation and stewardship at local levels to the global level. As such, this volume explores the ethical principles that govern humans' relationship with each other and with nature. As put by Bollier, 'the commons values human intentionality and intelligence around shared values. It is not altruistic as such; individual

---

100 Ibid.: Bollier, *The Commons: A Neglected Sector of Wealth Creation* (note 14).

101 For example, contrast realists with liberal internationalists.

102 Bollier, *The Commons: A Neglected Sector of Wealth Creation* (note 14).

103 Bollier, *The Future of the Commons* (note 2).

self interest is simply brought into alignment with collective interests and inscribed within the system itself'.[104] Beyond any formal contractual agreements, trusteeship carries an imperative to act responsibly – socially *and* ecologically – arising out of collective interest. What is proffered is a model of trusteeship that is the embodiment of a cooperative strategy on a global scale. Trusteeship is first and foremost an ethical principle. Transcending the tragedy of the commons begins with the potentiality of something other than that which Hardin attributes to human nature. Governance is about the rules of the game. The commons movement seeks to change the rules of the game – rejecting the inevitability of such behaviour as pre-ordained 'human nature' – because we know that our thoughts, beliefs and actions are socially constructed.

We are at the threshold of environmental and civilizational ruin. Defeatism such as that embodied by Hardin's tragedy – however reflective of the state's failure to address environmental degradation – is an attitude ill-afforded when we have no alternative but to seek solutions.

[104] Michel Bauwens, 'Peer to Peer Foundation', quoted in Bollier, *The Future of the Commons* (note 2).

4. The global commons

> The Earth is the single most important commons that we have; it is an immeasurable gift. That gift is of such complexity and beauty that you just don't tinker with it. The task of any generation is to pass that heritage on. The commons in this sense serves as a secularized version of Creation. This is a powerful discourse for asserting limits on technology and markets.
>
> Wolgang Sachs[1]

1. THE GLOBAL COMMONS – WITHOUT STATUS

In our international system of law and governance, the planet is divided into two realms: areas within and areas beyond national jursidictions – called the global commons. States govern their territories and their environments pursuant to their sovereign prerogative and subject to very little limitation under international law, save a rarely actioned but theoretical duty not to pollute another state's sovereign territory. States can choose to exclude 'outsiders' from access to their territory. In contrast, 'global commons' are resource domains to which all states have legal access. Remember from the discussion of definitions in the previous chapter that the commons (the noun) can be described as comprising resource domains (areas) and resource units. This chapter will discuss the various areas of the global commons – the resource domains – and take this to include the resource units they might hold, both discovered and undiscovered. Although we are indeed talking about the global commons as a mutually constitutive system (and at the same time arguing that its governance is fragmented and the global commons as a whole is without status), it is instructive to discuss each area to gain a thorough understanding of what is included, the current state of international law applicable to these environmental domains and resources, and the state of their governance.

[1] Wolfgang Sachs, quoted in David Bollier, 'The Future of the Commons: Notes from a retreat exploring the potential of the commons to fight enclosures and build commons-based alternatives' (Retreat on the Future of the Commons, Crottorf Castle, Germany, June 2009): http://commonstrust.global-negotiations.org/resources/Bollier,%20Crottorf%20retreat.pdf.

There is no overarching global commons regime but rather an array of regimes that govern the specific resource domains such as Antarctica, outer space and the oceans. Within these regimes are sub-regimes for specific resource units in the area, such as the ozone layer (which performs a function and can be seen as a resource), conservation of marine living resources in Antarctic waters, and so on. These regimes operate in different ways and with various (though usually minimal) success, as this chapter will reveal. Many scholars have noted that many of the commons regimes that do exist (such as the law of sea, the Outer Space Treaty and Antarctica) saw states agree to international management of these commons areas because the economic exploitation of these areas was not yet feasible due to a lack of appropriate technology.[2] But, '[a]s technology has progressed . . . so too have claims of sovereignty over these unclaimed regions'.[3] Shackelford notes that in all of these regimes, calls are becoming louder from capital-exporting nations to permit greater private economic activity.[4]

The common characteristic of existing regimes is voluntariness, a feature which has allowed for the continual politicization of the regimes and the overshadowing of environmental goals. In short, state interests continue to challenge the environmental bona fides of many regimes. As will be discussed in the later chapters of this volume, this is due to multiple reasons, chief among them states' loss of the ecological component of their mandate to govern, and the nature of international relations where states mistrust one another because of the possibility, and frequent occurrence, of free riding. Therefore, as Soroos aptly sums it up, 'international regimes typically display the lowest common denominator of agreement among nations that have conflicting interests and expectations'.[5]

It is intuitive that from time immemorial there have been commons. But because 'global' is an overworked adjective we need to consider why we use the term 'global' and what it really means. Typically, the 'global commons' refers to that which is beyond state sovereignty. Described as *areas*, these are: the oceans, fisheries and seabed beyond state jurisdiction; Antarctica; outer space including celestial bodies, the geostationary orbit and electromagnetic spectrum; and the atmosphere. In their

---

[2] Scott J. Shackelford, 'The Tragedy of the Common Heritage of Mankind' (2008) 27 *Stan. Envt L. J.* 101.

[3] Ibid.: 21.

[4] Ibid.

[5] Marvin S. Soroos, 'The Evolution of Global Commons', in Ho-Won Jeong (ed.), *Global Environmental Policies: Institutions and Procedures* (Palgrave, London 2001): 40.

totality, the global commons areas and the resources therein form an open-access free-for-all of the kind described by Hardin. These areas are generally still open-access, because it has been physically impossible or economically unfeasible to enclose them, although most are experiencing enclosure through the opportunities for private enterprise allowed by ever-improving technologies. This reality has led to the assumption, and in the case of the ocean the tradition, of an open-access global commons. This means that historically the lack of governance has not been problematized. However, the last century gave rise to numerous attempts to create regimes for global commons resources and areas. The driving force behind these efforts was as much about political rivalry and competition as about ever-increasing over-use and enclosure, the effects of which are undermining the environment in global and catastrophic ways through the depletion of resource units, contamination, environmental disruptions through depletion, interference and overcrowding.[6]

There have been various ideas and attempts to green the state's decision-making, among them declarations, treaties, invocation of environmental human rights, and so on. As states decide what rules are applicable to them, international environmental law is still an exercise in persuasion rather than concrete limitation. And persuasion or soft law flies in the face of the pathology of neoliberalism. As this chapter shall explore, economic rationales are still overshadowing the ecological imperatives of cooperation for the various global commons areas and resources. What is happening is unfortunately what Hardin described in the pasture. No matter how cooperative and well behaved a state is, it will still be motivated to do that which will provide dividends. As we will see in Chapter 5, this mandate is overarching and comes before any duty to maintain the health and continuing bounty of the environment (and thus the people). Likewise, the presence of defectors or 'free-riders' seriously undermines any incentive for states to take the environmental initiative. Domestically, if a state invests in environmental clean-up or chooses not to pollute (usually the more expensive route), it will reap 100 percent of the benefits of its choice. In the global commons – the area shared with the rest of the world – if a state does the same, the benefits are divided among all nations, some of whom may not be doing their fair share.[7]

You might be asking by now, surely if the global commons has various regimes of governance it is no longer open-access? This is true perhaps in

---

[6] Ibid.: 55–56.

[7] Christopher D. Stone, 'Defending the Global Commons', in Philippe Sands (ed.), *Greening International Law* (Earthscan, London 1993): 36.

theory, however as long as these regimes rely on voluntariness for compliance, enforcement, and so on, they are in reality still open-access. Various approaches to governance have been taken in an attempt to overcome 'tragedy', however, as we shall see, these have been largely ineffective for a number of reasons. Recall the three types of tragedies in Chapter 1. The global commons is subject to all three. There are rules for specific commons areas but these are transgressed by non-committing states (often the case with fishing and certainly the case with whaling). There are ineffectively defined and enforced rules (often the case with regimes where compliance is voluntary) and there are areas of the commons which simply have no applicable international law. 'The present picture can best be summarized as this: if one looks behind the various lofty declarations and examines the prevailing practices – the law in action – one finds that, aside from a few areas provided for by special treaty, much of the commons is only partially or feebly protected.'[8] In effect, much of the global commons is still open-access whether intended to be so or not.

The commons relay a right of usage. For instance, this is most often interpreted as a right to emit carbon dioxide into the atmosphere. But equally conceivable is the right to *continuing* use, only available with a healthy environment. As Taylor explains, the commons include the right to a clean atmosphere, for example the use of clean air for all living things.[9] Thus, the use of commons is read subject to intra- and inter-generation equity. In this chapter and indeed in this entire volume, the commons is not arbitrarily limited to that which is beyond state territory. In effect, what we are saying is that for this 'commons' – the global commons – there are no boundaries such as one would see in the management of a single common-pool resource. This approach is adopted for two reasons. Under the conventional paradigm of sovereign and global commons areas, environmental damage or 'injuries', if we want to adopt legal parlance, occur in three ways: state-to-commons (emissions); commons-to-commons (oil spills; toxic waste in high seas); and commons-to-state.[10]

The majority of waste originates within national territories and is carried upward or out across the commons by currents of water and air.[11] 'The scale of waste that travels the state-to-commons pathway is gargantuan.'[12] The subsequent degradation of the commons similarly

---

[8] Ibid.: 39.

[9] Prue Taylor, *An Ecological Approach to International Law: Responding to the Challenges of Climate Change* (Routledge, London 1998): 260.

[10] See Stone (note 7).

[11] Ibid.: 72.

[12] Ibid.

degrades environments within state territories, for example through acid rain, rising sea levels, changing weather patterns, and terrestrial and ocean biodiversity losses.

Likewise, resources within national territories, for instance rainforests, provide ecological functions which are commons, such as providing oxygen, maintaining biodiversity, and so on. Essentially, the planet consists of a biosphere which cannot be separated. Any discussion of governance for one part of this biosphere must necessarily include the governance of all. Hence, we arrive at an altogether truthful conclusion: the global commons does not observe territorial boundaries. Ironically, however states may accept this scientific truth, its political implications – that governance ought to cover the entire global environment, conferring status beyond state prerogative – seem to be viewed as entirely radical, even unfeasible. The mandate of this volume is to negate such an assertion and proffer a model of global environmental trusteeship that is long overdue.

2. THE COMMON HERITAGE DOCTRINE

We begin with a discussion of the concept of the common heritage of mankind.[13] It is often used synonymously with the discussion of commons, but it is vital that we have a clear understanding of what the concept actually means and of its status in international law. It is unclear when the concept of common heritage of mankind (CHM) emerged – the sentiments behind it are clearly traceable throughout human history.[14] However, in modern recollection it was first used in a marine context at the first plenary meeting of the 1958 Geneva Conference on the Law of the Sea and again in 1967 by the Ambassador of Argentina to the United Nations, Aldo Cocca. However, it was popularly introduced into discourse by the Ambassador of Malta to the United Nations, Arvid Pardo. The Permanent Mission of Malta submitted a proposal to the United Nations to include a supplementary item in the agenda of the 22nd session of the General Assembly. It was in this document that concern was expressed about the probability that the seabed, ocean floor and its resources, 'the Area', would be progressively and competitively subject to national appropriation and use,

---

[13] See generally Prue Taylor and Lucy Stroud, *Common Heritage of Mankind: A Bibliography of Legal Writing* (Fondation de Malte, Valletta, Malta 2013).

[14] Prue Taylor, 'Common Heritage of Mankind Principle', in Klaus Bosselmann, Daniel Fogel and J.B. Ruhl (eds), *The Encyclopedia of Sustainability, Vol. 3: The Law and Politics of Sustainability* (Berkshire Publishing, Great Barrington, MA 2011).

leading to militarization and to the economic detriment of developing countries.[15] Speaking in the United Nations on 1 November 1967, Pardo proposed a solution which would see the seabed and ocean floor designated the 'common heritage of mankind' and beyond national jurisdiction. The common heritage of mankind principle implied that the resource domain must be used for peaceful purposes only and that all states have a right to share in the benefits thereof, irrespective of whether they have the technical and economic means of exploitation.

Although the concept lacks a commonly agreed definition, there are some underlying features: common heritage areas cannot be appropriated; the area(s) will be used for peaceful purposes; use and access to CHM areas are to fall under a common management system; benefits derived from the CHM shall be equitably shared and technology shall be exchanged and transferred; and the area(s) will be reserved for future generations.[16] Pardo accurately predicted the two lines of logic that have come to characterize the debate over the meaning of the CHM principle. He said that the manner in which the common heritage principle will be used will depend on differing perceptions – the wants, needs, interests and values favoured by world constituencies. Unsurprisingly, given the heterogeneity of world politics, different policies were advanced by developed and developing states.[17]

Thus, some important questions arise about what the concept really means. One allows for the complete freedom of exploration, meaning that technologically advanced countries would benefit most from common resources. The other extreme views exploration on a communal basis. Although this would fulfill the spirit of the CHM principle, it would not generate the amount of commercial activity necessary for substantial economic development due to a complete absence of property rights.[18]

Heritage denotes value transmitted temporally (historically). Given that a healthy environment is necessary for all life, the entire biosphere is arguably the common heritage of mankind. A key question, however, is why

---

[15] Division for Ocean Affairs and the Law of the Sea, Office of Legal Affairs, United Nations, *The Law of the Sea: Concept of the Common Heritage of Mankind: Legislative History of Article 133 to 150 and 311(6) of the United Nations Convention on the Law of the Sea* (United Nations Publications, Herndon, VA 1996): 8.

[16] Daniel Bodansky, Jutta Brunee and Ellen Hey, *The Oxford Handbook of International Environmental Law* (Oxford University Press, Oxford 2007): 562.

[17] Lotta Viikari, *From Manganese Nodules to Lunar Regolith: A Comparative Legal Study of the Utilization of Natural Resources in the Deep Sea Bed and Outer Space* (University of Lapland Publications, Lapland 2002): 58.

[18] Shackelford (note 2): 17.

we value the CHM, and, by extension, why we protect it. Is this merely to maintain humans' ability to use these resources (an anthropocentric approach) or is it because nature has an inherent value unto itself (an ecocentric approach)? Likewise, who is 'mankind'? Obviously the gendered nature of the word is a testament to its historical origins and belies the reality that it includes both men and women, but more complexly we are forced to consider, who are the holders of rights? In the context of a discussion on trusteeship for the global commons, this question necessarily becomes, who is the beneficiary of the trust? Is the state the symbol of mankind? Why not, because states are supposed to be the representatives of people within nations? Or are the beneficiaries every individual citizen, current and future, because states have lost their legitimacy as ecologically astute players?

By now, it is probably apparent that no clear definition of a common heritage of mankind exists, nor does a final decision about its legal implications in international environmental law. Moreover, there is no general acceptance of its legal status, nor even of its existence. Apart from two notable uses of the term – in the Moon Treaty and the Law of the Sea Convention – the term 'common heritage of mankind' has not been included in subsequent international legal documents. Moreover, the Moon Treaty is ratified by only a handful of states, none of which are the major space-faring nations – hardly the token of universal acceptance then. Yet the term still warrants discussion because it is often invoked to describe human obligation of intra- and inter-generational equity in relation to commons areas.[19]

Intergenerational equity requires fairness between past, present and future generations.[20] However, despite this synonymous use, the term has been used as a mechanism for developing countries to challenge the proportion of profits flowing to developed countries from the use of commons resources. Pardo was speaking in a specific social and political context. It was a time of de-colonization, self-determination and independence. Non-appropriation implies that ownership of the common heritage is vested in the whole of humanity and this cannot be altered.[21] Shared benefits

---

[19] Stephen Sec, 'Humanitarian Limits to Sovereignty: Common Concern and Common Heritage Approaches to Natural Resources and the Environment' (2010) 12 *Int. C. L. Rev*. 366.

[20] Edith Brown Weiss, *In Fairness to Future Generations: International Law, Common Patrimony, and Intergenerational Equity* (United Nations/Transnational Publishers, New York 1989).

[21] Jimena Murillo, 'Common Concern of Humankind and its Implications in International Environmental Law' (2008) *MqJICEL* 133, 135.

imply that the benefits of activities (revenue and scientific) which use the commons are distributed among all states, irrespective of geographical location and technological capacity.[22]

International management describes the way that common heritage of mankind objectives can be realized.[23] Examples include the International Authority set up under Article 156 of the Law of the Sea Convention, tasked with distributing the benefits received from exploitation in the 'Area' (the seabed and ocean floor beyond the limits of national jurisdiction). This characteristic closely resembles the trusteeship idea, realized through a neutral international body to act as trustee. Use of the CHM for exclusively peaceful purposes reflects the common anxiety over military confrontation that you will recognize in the discussion of Antarctica and Outer Space later in this chapter. This message found particular resonance with developing countries who adopted it as the tool to challenge developed country dominance. Using the term is fraught with difficulty, because definition is elusive and interpretations differ according to who (read: developed or developing countries) is interpreting the term.

Developing states use the CHM term to create a property regime over common resources, with the objective of ensuring access and entitlement to those resources – distinct from territorial sovereignty but no more environmentally advantageous.[24] Although developed states might use the term to legitimate extraction and exploitation, they treat the term with suspicion because its interpretation focuses on the equitable sharing of benefits. Hence, despite sounding great, the term is less about ecological health and passing on a healthy environment for future generations and more about developing countries' concern over the distribution of profits from exploitation of commons resources.

Hence, as a legal tool to argue for better commons governance, its utility should not be over-stated. CHM is used to argue for a system of common property rights, not a system of common and sustainable use. The term is anthropocentric – 'common heritage of *mankind*' – and recognizes only the interests of current and future generations of humanity, not the necessity of these areas for the continuance of the biosphere as a whole. And in actuality it cannot seriously embody a norm of inter-generational equity because it ignores the fact that ecological sustainability is vital for this.

---

[22] Alexandre Kiss and Dinah Shelton, *International Environmental Law*, 2nd edn (Transnational Publishers, New York 2000): 249.

[23] Murillo (note 21): 136.

[24] Taylor (note 9): 269.

It maintains the arbitrary separation of ecological areas and resources as currently displayed in international law, thereby perpetuating 'the division of the biosphere by false boundaries which ignore the interdependence and interaction of ecosystems'.[25] Perhaps also crucially, CHM does not imply any penalty for breach and so provides little disincentive to be unsustainable. If we want to promote the term as one mandating environmental protection, 'it must be demonstrated that this restrictive interpretation is based on aspects of CHM which are not fundamental or indispensable, but which are products of CHM's historical development in particular contexts'.[26] In effect, to shirk this restrictive interpretation requires a new term, of the kind discussed in the final section of this chapter.

3. COMMON CONCERN

In response to the continual stymieing of use of the CHM term in treaty texts, an alternative term, the common concern of humankind, emerged in the 1980s. The notion of the common concern of mankind was essentially borne from the texts of the United Nations Framework Convention on Climate Change, and the Convention on Biological Diversity, both adopted at the 1992 United Nations Conference on Environment and Development in Rio de Janiero. States wished to avoid the implications of the common heritage principle, which, for developed countries, was read as the probability of interference in sovereign matters by an international commons body, and carried the undesirable obligation of shared benefit.[27]

This language is also found in the 2001 International Treaty on Plant Genetic Resources for Food and Agriculture (ITPGR[28]), adopted by the Assembly of the United Nations Food and Agriculture Organization. The ITPGR retreated from the 'common heritage' language of its forerunner (the 1983 International Undertaking on Plant Genetic Resources, IUPGR) in favour of a less controversial 'common concern' formula.[29] Peter Sand describes this treaty as having succeeded in 'striking a balance

---

[25] Ibid.: 292.

[26] Ibid.: 258.

[27] Murillo (note 21): 138.

[28] International Treaty on Plant Genetic Resources for Food and Agriculture, 2400 UNTS 303 (adopted 3 November 2001, entered into force 29 June 2004).

[29] Peter Sand, 'The Rise of Public Trusteeship in International Environmental Law' (2013) Global Working Paper Series 03/2013, 19: http://globaltrust.tau.ac.il/publications.

between sovereign rights, intellectual property rights and farmers' collective rights'.[30]

Whereas CHM carried some loose ideas about what governance ought to ensue, common concern merely states that something is concerning to all, but carries no implication of what ought to occur in response. Consequently, the definitional and legal debate about 'common concern' is largely academic. According to Jimena Murillo, common concern includes the undertaking that states all take appropriate measures to protect the environment according to their own capacities (analogous to 'common but differentiated responsibility').[31] Likewise, Bodansky, Bronee and Hey state that while common heritage is about equitable sharing of benefits, common concern is about equitable sharing of the burden of cooperation and problem-solving.[32] Boyle suggests it means something is a legitimate matter of international attention and institutions, but it does not challenge sovereign prerogative.[33]

Murillo states that common concern arose as a solution to the disagreements between states, to choose the best system to protect and conserve the environment without generating a high level of interference with their own sovereignty or holding states to the benefit-sharing system.[34] It is curious, then, that she goes on to argue that this duty extends to the protection of the ecosystems located within the jurisdiction of a state, and as such is further reaching than CHM which applies only to areas beyond national jurisdiction.[35] This she calls the spatial element of common concern. The temporal element, she argues, is an aspect of inter-generational equity – that is, the obligation to act now in order to preserve the environment for future generations.[36] A final, social aspect carries the implication of an expanded membership of international participation beyond the state to include all sectors of society. The concept claims a standing for dynamic participants within international environmental law and in front of international courts.[37] Furthermore, and significantly, Murillo argues that notes from the secretariat of the United Nations Environment Programme

---

30 Ibid.

31 Ibid.: 139.

32 Daniel Bodansky, Jutta Bronee and Ellen Hey, *The Oxford Handbook of International Environmental Law* (Oxford University Press, Oxford 2007): 566.

33 Alan Boyle, 'International Law and the Protection of the Atmosphere', in Robin Churchill and David Freestone (eds), *International Law and Global Climate Change* (Graham & Trotman, London 1991).

34 Murillo (note 21): 142.

35 Ibid.: 139

36 Ibid.: 140

37 Ibid.

(UNEP) indicate that common concern is analogous to 'common interest' which posits that common interests enjoy superiority over state interests.[38] Thus, Murillo concludes that 'the secretariat accepted giving the common concept a higher status than the others such as common heritage, shared resources and the like. This would lead to the overriding characteristic of the obligations arising from it'.[39]

The term, so interpreted, reflects a more far-reaching and environmental focus than CHM. It bears noting that, however enticing for international environmental scholars this theoretical legal interpretation may be, the likelihood that states intended to bind themselves to a more rigorous principle is unlikely. Conspicuously, Murillo does not discuss whether states agree with this interpretation of the common concern term. It is highly peculiar that states would agree to a term which ostensibly does not recognize state jurisdiction for common concerns, at a time when they agreed on two conventions (United Nations Framework Convention on Climate Change and United Nations Convention on Biological Diversity) which firmly establish the environmental prerogatives of states within their own territories and in relation to their contribution to environmental problems.

This is not to say that what Murillo suggests is flawed. Indeed, it is exactly what we ought to be striving for. Such obligations to safeguard the earth's ecological balance are erga omnes (as shall be discussed in the following chapters), but whether the term common concern, as used in international treaties, embodies this sentiment is highly contentious. As long as states hold to a different interpretation, one more diluted than even the CHM principle, they will continue to evade their responsibility. We need a new and richer term to embody the types of rights and obligations raised by Murillo. The last section of this chapter discusses the concept of the common heritage of *life*. Conceptually, it offers a departure from both common heritage with its anthropocentric foci and common concern with its definitional ambiguity and likely impotency.

4. THE AREAS OF THE GLOBAL COMMONS

From the preceding discussion we can see that the concept of the commons on international and global levels is more analytical than legal.[40] Currently, there is no one term to encompass what the global commons is

---

38 Ibid.
39 Ibid.
40 Soroos (note 5): 58.

and what status it has in international law. Neither common heritage of mankind nor common concern is satisfactory. Thus, what follows is a segregated examination of the legal regimes for the various global commons areas. Current governance of the global commons areas has formed through slow and highly politicized processes which have produced lowest common denominator outcomes and a fragmented system of domain regimes and even more fragmented sub-regimes.

Before we look at each area of the global commons, it is prudent to note several important observations about the regimes. First, they tend toward three approaches: outright bans (such as that on commercial whaling); limiting the extent to which the commons is used (such as fisheries quotas or emission limits); or the granting or allocation of rights to parts of the commons (such as frequencies in the electromagnetic spectrum).[41] Second, regimes that have established outright bans on activities involving the global commons (Antarctic minerals, atmospheric test ban, ozone depletion) have had more success than those that have merely sought to limit activities (fisheries). This, Soroos explains, is because rules of use require the resolution of additional issues of fairness and the creation of more complicated provisions for enforcement.[42] Third, regimes that govern spatial domains (oceans, seabed, Antarctica, outer space) have evolved further than those that are comprised of physical substances which pass through areas under the jurisdiction of states (atmosphere).[43]

4.1 The Oceans

Oceans cover two-thirds of earth's surface. They account for 97 percent of the planet's living space.[44] They play a crucial role in regulation of the global climate. They are the world's highways because despite the advent of air travel, shipping is still an integral part of the global economy. Despite the oceans being fundamental to our world, the effects of human activity are astonishing. The oceans are a major dumping site for human waste: pollution, sewage, agricultural runoff, munitions – often unfired – and untold quantities of nuclear waste. It has been estimated that approximately 70 percent of the world's fish stocks are depleted, over-exploited or recovering, and yet over-fishing is one of the most pressing ocean issues.

---

41 Ibid.: 56–58.
42 Ibid.: 60.
43 Ibid.
44 Ellen J. Prager and Sylvia A. Earle, *The Oceans* (McGraw-Hill, New York 2000): ix.

Whale species are on the brink of extinction despite years of 'resource management'.

We begin with an overview of the ocean regime because it is the oldest and most complex of all global commons regimes.[45] Ancient Romans acknowledged that the seas were *communes omnium naturali jure* [common to all humankind].[46] Freedom of the seas is an enduring principle. The first recorded statement on the law of the sea was found in the Digest of Roman Emperor Justinian I (483–565). It declared the seas beyond the high water mark and the fish available to all and beyond any state jurisdiction.[47] However, from the fifteenth century debates began about the legal status of the oceans. The recurring motif of this volume – technological advancement – saw a growth in capability and power of mercantile states. Their colonial aspirations led to assertions of sovereignty over oceans and coastal waters and led, for a time, to the dividing up of the world's oceans into two territories. The Treaty of Tordesillas in the fifteenth century drew a line between the poles which assigned Portugal rights to the east of the line and Spain everything to the west.

In 1604–1605, Hugo Grotius wrote *On the Law of Spoils* [*De jure praedae*] at the request of the Dutch. It included a chapter called 'Freedom of the Seas' [*mare liberum*]. Grotius argued that the sea, like the air, cannot be appropriated.[48] This is because no one can leave evidence of their occupation, and because the oceans are unpopulated by humans. In response, the British commissioned John Selden to write a rebuttal, published in 1635, called *Mare clausum* – the right and dominion of the sea. Because Grotius believed that control (and thus enforcement) of an area was central to the legitimacy of the claim, he did not object to territorial or coastal waters. As was said in Chapter 1, 'control' was determined by technological ability. Thus, in the seventeenth century, territorial (controlled) waters were the distance of a cannon shot. Although Grotius's work is the most renowned, these two conflicting perspectives continue to define humans' view of ocean space, and the extent of states' territorial seas has continued to be debated in the centuries following. The universally accepted rule, however, remains that beyond national jurisdiction (whatever this is at the time) the high seas are open to all.[49] However, this enduring principle of

---

[45] Susan Buck, *The Global Commons: An Introduction* (Island Press, Washington, DC 1998): 75.

[46] Ibid.: 76.

[47] Ibid.

[48] Ibid.: 79.

[49] For a more detailed account of the historical development of international maritime law, see Buck (note 45).

freedom of the seas is based on an empirical error – Grotius may well have thought that the oceans were inexhaustible, and he certainly could not have predicted the explosion of population and industry that has given rise to an exceptional ability to degrade the ocean commons.

In 1950 the International Law Commission established a committee to codify existing customary international law for the oceans. At this time, most states accepted the three-mile limit on territorial waters. But many states, notably the United States, wanted to extend these limits for reasons including commercial interests, nationalism, prevention of oil spills, customs and national security. The three United Nations Conferences on the Law on the Sea (UNCLOS) in 1958, 1960 and 1982, codified existing international law of the sea and created new rules in a treaty regime that entered into force in 1994.

At UNCLOS I in 1958 four conventions were passed: the Convention on the High Seas; the Convention on the Continental Shelf; the Convention on the Territorial Sea and the Contiguous Zone; and the Convention on Fishing and Conservation of the Living Resources of the High Seas. Much of this law was a codification of pre-existing customary law of the sea. UNCLOS I is notable for the parties' failure to reach consensus on the width of the territorial sea. In the end, the conference actually escalated the clash over territorial waters. The 1960 UNCLOS II was again a failure after the Arab states and communist bloc stymied a compromise proposal on territorial seas and fishing zones.

Parallel to this, in the 1970s, and following the United Nations Conference on the Human Environment in Stockholm, several treaties were passed creating an oceans sub-regime for pollution. Buck explains the apparent support for pollution control as a cognizance among users of marine living resources that the ability of the resource domain to continue to provide living resources depends in part on lowered levels of pollution.[50] This recognition gave rise to the 1972 Convention on the Prevention of Marine Pollution by Dumping of Wastes and Other Matter (London Convention), and the Convention for the Prevention of Marine Pollution by Dumping from Ships and Aircraft (Oslo Convention); and in 1973 to the International Convention for the Prevention of Pollution from Ships (MARPOL). Since the treaties were adopted, pollution controls have been intermittently strengthened.

In 1990, the parties to the London Convention decided to ban all ocean dumping of industrial waste by 1995. In 1996 the London Convention shifted from regulated dumping to one of absolute prohibition and

---

[50] Ibid.: 101.

introduced an important codification of the precautionary approach and the polluter pays principle. The 1996 Protocol to the London Convention now operates according to a 'reverse list', meaning that all dumping is prohibited except if it is listed in Annex 1 as permissible. Despite these promising movements, the 1992 Earth Summit outcome document, Agenda 21, estimated that land-based sources contribute 70 percent of marine pollutants while maritime transport and dumping each account for 10 percent. This calls into question the overall efficacy of the marine pollution regime, because most pollution originates within state jurisdiction and not through dumping by ships. Both MARPOL and the London Convention rely on states to enforce the regulations and the fulfilment of these obligations is far from comprehensive.[51] Thus, the effectiveness of the maritime pollution regime and any successes from the decline in oil pollution from ships and the dumping of industrial waste is contrasted with the still serious matter of effectively regulating land-based pollution.

In the years following, new 'ocean' issues were emerging such as nuclear and military installations which demanded that new laws of the sea be developed.[52] So, after nine years of negotiations and 22 years after the last conference, UNCLOS III took place in 1982 with the aim of designing a new and overarching international regime for the oceans. It also provided developing countries with the opportunity to further propagate the concept of common heritage of mankind. The result was the Law of the Sea Convention, a 'constitution' for the seas embodied in a treaty of 320 articles and nine annexes. Although a treaty and thus applying only to ratifying states, many of the provisions of the Convention have now gained the status of customary international law by virtue of consensus among parties over certain provisions, and state practice. The Convention separates the seas and oceans into seven zones: internal waters, territorial seas, contiguous zones, exclusive economic zones ('EEZ'), continental shelves, the high seas, and the deep seabed area.

One of the most significant accomplishments of UNCLOS III was the clarification of territorial limits. These are the 12-mile limit for the territorial sea, the contiguous zone extending to 24 nautical miles, the continental shelf to its natural margin or 200 nautical miles, whichever is farther, and an EEZ not to exceed 200 nautical miles. Because the EEZ is subject to the control of the littoral (coastal) states, these waters are no longer an

---

51 John Vogler, *The Global Commons: Environmental and Technological Governance*, 2nd edn (Wiley, New York 2000): 61.

52 Buck (note 45): 87.

open-access regime.[53] The 200-mile EEZs cover 35 percent of the world's sea area but 90 percent of living resources, meaning that most key fishing grounds are within the economic control of particular states.[54] It remains that the high seas and the Area are beyond national jurisdiction and are thus labelled a commons area. The Convention also establishes regimes to govern these respective areas. Additionally, many scholars accept the argument that UNCLOS III has incorporated the London Convention and MARPOL into the Law of the Sea, and that nations are under an international obligation to protect the ocean environment.[55]

4.1.1 Freedom of the seas

The freedom of the seas was a longstanding rule of customary international law prior to it being codified in Part VII of the Law of the Sea Convention. Article 87(1) codifies the principle to include, among other things: freedom of navigation, freedom of flight, freedom to lay submarine cables and pipelines, freedom to construct artificial islands, freedom of fishing, and freedom of scientific research. These freedoms are subject to two provisos – first, to preserve and protect the environment, and second, to exercise these freedoms 'with due regard for the interests of other States'.

4.1.2 Fisheries

Historically, living resources have never been a major concern in the development of the law of the sea. Conservation of marine living resources did not follow an ecological approach, exemplified by its arbitrary separation from fisheries governance. Although, under the Law of the Sea Convention states are required to take necessary measures to preserve and protect the environment (Article 193), the Convention gives the rights of conservation and management in the EEZ to the coastal states, which has clearly not been sufficient to achieve effective conservation.[56] On the high seas, Article 117 places obligations and duties on states to ensure that their nationals do not over-exploit living resources, and Article 118 requires states to cooperate in the management and conservation of living resources. Article 119 requires that states only harvest living resources of the high seas in a sustainable manner, that they agree to total allowable catch figures and that they take into account the effects of harvesting of a particular living resource on associated or dependent species.

---

53 Ibid.: 94.
54 Vogler (note 51): 48.
55 Buck (note 45): 97.
56 Ibid.: 94.

Despite these provisions, adopted at UNCLOS III in 1982, reports of widespread depleting fish stocks prompted the United Nations to call a conference on global fisheries management in July 1993. Fisheries governance sees the frequent tensions between coastal fishing nations such as Argentina, Canada, Chile, Iceland, New Zealand and Peru and the distant-water nations such as China, Japan, Poland, Russia, Spain and the United States.[57] The coastal nations have rights to protect migratory stocks that move between the high seas and their EEZs under Article 74 of the Law of the Sea Convention. They also support binding regulations for high seas fisheries, effectively ending the open-access nature of the high seas.[58] Ultimately, the sustainable management of fisheries still eludes us – demonstrating all three tragedies of a common pool resource – transgression of existing rules, inadequate rules and non-existent rules of governance – made worse by the fact that monitoring compliance in the 'use' of these particular resources is exceptionally difficult.

4.1.3 The deep seabed

Under the Continental Shelf Convention 1958, states acquired the exclusive right to authorize mining under the adjacent sea out to the limit of the continental shelf. These provisions were basically retained in the Convention on the Law of the Sea.[59] The seabed beyond continental shelves was not a salient concern until the 1960s.[60] This changed with the discovery of an important deep seabed resource outside national jurisdiction: manganese nodules. These dark metal balls vary in size from 0.5 to 15 cm in diameter and contain an exceptionally high metallic content which includes iron, zinc, copper, silver and gold. It is estimated that 1.5 trillion tons of manganese, nickel, copper and cobalt in the form of nodules lie on the seabed, mainly in the Pacific Ocean, and the 26 elements found in them are either currently in high demand or soon will be.[61] Like so many other concerns about governance (or lack thereof) of the commons, the concern arose because of the development of technologies that made deep seabed mining of nodules an imminent possibility.

The seabed was the original focus of Arvid Pardo, and when it came to designing the regime for the deep seabed many countries were in favour of classifying the deep seabed and the mineral nodules found there as the common heritage of mankind, as had been done in December 1970

---

57 Ibid.: 95.
58 Ibid.
59 Ibid.: Part VI.
60 Soroos (note 5): 53.
61 Viikari (note 15): 26.

when the UN General Assembly issued a Declaration of Principles stating that the seabed is the common heritage of mankind and must be exploited for the benefits of mankind as a whole, and taking into particular consideration the interests and needs of the developing countries. Developing countries that lacked mining technology and countries that lacked coastlines or ports supported the regime because it would ensure their representation and stake in the profits. According to Buck, developed countries also saw the economic advantages of a common heritage regime, because the potential revenue was a way to reduce developing country dependence on Western funding.[62] Likewise, in the context of increasing concern over military installations, the Superpowers saw UN supervision of the regime as a source of stability should the CHM concept fail and a resource scramble ensue.[63]

Thus, Article 136 of the Law of the Sea Convention states that the seabed and subsoil thereof, called 'the Area' and its resources, are the common heritage of mankind. The resources of the Area are defined in Article 133 as 'all solid, liquid or gaseous mineral resources *in situ* in the Area at or beneath the seabed, including polymetallic nodules'.[64] Article 140 says that activities in the Area shall be: 'carried out for the benefit of mankind as a whole, irrespective of the geographical location of States, whether coastal or land-locked, and taking into particular consideration the interests and needs of developing states.' Because the seabed, the ocean floor and the sub-soil thereof are the common heritage of mankind, all rights of the resources vested in humanity as a whole are represented by the International Seabed Authority. All minerals recovered from the Area are subject to the regulations and procedures of this authority.[65] Another international body, called the Enterprise, was also established by the Convention to control and engage in mining activities, alone or in conjunction with states or private enterprise. Articles 140(2) and 144 state that the norms of equitable sharing of financial benefits and technology transfer between those mining the seabed and the Authority, the Enterprise and developing countries. From an environmental perspective, the regime is far from ideal. Although the ISA monitors mining activities carried out in the Area to ensure that they do not cause damage to the natural resources of the Area and requires that environmental impact assessments be carried out for proposed activities, there is a high

[62] Buck (note 45): 87.

[63] Ibid.

[64] United Nations Convention on the Law of the Sea, 1836 UNTS 42 (adopted 10 December 1982, entered into force 16 November 1994), Art. 133.

[65] Ibid.: Part XI.

standard of proof for harm. The ISA will only prohibit mining activities if there is evidence of *serious harm*.

As such, the seabed is subject to more restrictive rules than the separate regime for the high seas. Some commentators have noted that because resolution of the seabed issue was difficult and the final arrangement highly controversial, the ocean regime was diluted as *quid pro quo* for agreement over the seabed.[66] This 'portmanteau style'[67] Convention, which included the controversial Part XI and favours developing countries, meant that a number of developed countries did not sign it. Some other countries have failed to ratify it. The US, the UK and West Germany were among those that refused the regime, ostensibly for reasons of commercial viability, but in fact many political scientists attribute the policy shift to the abandonment of concepts of interdependence (and hence concepts such as 'common heritage of mankind') and the dogma of free market capitalism that was integral to the Reagan and Thatcher governments.[68]

In the 1990s, consecutive UN Secretary Generals attempted to redesign the regime and bring the developed states on board before the Law of the Sea Treaty came into force.[69] As Buck explains, in the time between the creation of the regime and its expected entry into force, the world of practical politics, market principles, decentralization and deregulation made the regime, and the common heritage of mankind principle, increasingly obsolete.[70] Further negotiations ensued and in 1994 the Agreement Relating to the Implementation of Part XI of the United Nations Convention on the Law of the Sea, known as the 'Boat Paper Agreement', altered the implementation and interpretation of Part XI. Significantly, the commencement of the Enterprise was delayed, states who conducted deep sea activities had a greater voice in the Authority, and technology transfer was abolished. Suffice it to say the advantage now lies with developed, technologically advanced and mining states.[71] Likewise, although the CHM principle has been retained, the regime is now rather different from what was originally intended and held up as the pioneering regime for the common heritage of mankind. The Agreement restricted the scope of CHM to a few rocks sitting on the bottom of the deep seabed. For Pardo, its limited application to 'ugly little rocks' and the transformation

66 Buck (note 45): 88; Vogler (note 51): 47.
67 Vogler (note 51): 46.
68 Ibid.: 64.
69 Ibid.: 90.
70 Ibid.: 91.
71 See Buck (note 45): 89–91 for more detail.

of CHM into a market-based concept was a debasement of the CHM phrase he had championed for nearly three decades.

In the end, it took 12 years for the necessary 60 ratifications to bring the Convention into force in 1994. The US has yet to sign or ratify it. However, in the pursuit of an agreeable solution, the regime's emphasis is on resource development not conservation; and the best interests of humankind are arguably shunted for capital interests.

4.1.4 Whaling

The long history of commercial whaling, or more accurately the exploitation of the 79 species of cetaceans, 'displays the cycles of boom and bust characteristic of unregulated fisheries'.[72] And it is often cited as the quintessential example of a tragedy of a common pool resource. Whaling reached such extents that in the 1980s the small minke whale was the last species at relatively sustainable numbers. After the two world wars, a real push for a management regime emerged from the industry and from whaling nations themselves, cognizant of their rapidly depleted income source. In 1946 the 15 whaling nations signed the International Convention for the Regulation of Whaling (ICRW) and subsequently established the International Whaling Commission (IWC).

In its preamble, the Convention recognizes the 'interest of the world in safeguarding for future generations the great natural resources represented by the whale stocks' and states that it is in the 'common interest' to achieve the optimum level of whale stocks as rapidly as possible. However, it is important to note that the ICRW was originally conceived as a whale harvesting arrangement (hence the word 'resources') which allocated shares to member states, not a conservationist body. The IWC regulated overall catch but did not discriminate between species and it did nothing to protect overfished species. Over the years this ill-conceived approach to resource management proved totally ineffective at preventing further stocks depletion, paralleled with the creation of new and more lethal hunting technologies such as explosive tip harpoons and stern slipway factory ships.

Conservationist countries, such as New Zealand (a 'reformed' whaling nation), have been integral in trying to evolve the function of the IWC from management to prohibition of commercial whaling, something which has met with considerable resistance over the years and required no little diplomatic effort. Gradually, the IWC has increased its conservationist emphasis, and after several failures to gain the required three quarters

---

72 Vogler (note 51): 49.

majority in favour of a global moratorium on commercial whaling, in 1982 the vote passed to wind down commercial whaling catch limits to zero by 1986. Three whaling nations, Iceland, Norway and Japan, remained resolutely opposed to the prohibitionist stance and continue to whale, either in blatant contravention of the moratorium or ostensibly under the Article VIII scientific permit of the ICRW. Whaling is the site of an emotional clash of animal rights advocates and sustainable hunting advocates which reveals 'a heady mix of domestic politics and ethnocentrism'.[73]

The Convention on the Illegal Trade of Endangered Species (CITES) includes whales in its Appendix I, thereby they are subject to an absolute trade ban. Despite this, trade in whale meat is frequently exposed. Many countries have expressed frustration with the IWC while acknowledging the unlikelihood of another regime being established. In 1994, Principle 17 of the Agenda 21 document[74] recognized the IWC as the sole whale management agency. Though not exactly the revolution in terms of whaling conservation that many sought, it does invalidate any other organization from establishing whale catch quotas. In 1994, an international agreement for a whale sanctuary in the southern ocean was agreed, protecting the area around Antarctica where many whales migrate, though Japan still hunts minke and fin whales in the sanctuary.[75] Similar moves to establish sanctuaries in other parts of the world, such as the South Pacific (the habitat, either permanently or during migration, of most living whales), have failed to gain the numbers to pass in the IWC.

While many countries continue to support prohibition on commercial whaling, whether for its easy green credentials or because of the unique affiliation many humans feel towards these mammals, the actions of a few 'defectors' ensure the continuance of a tragedy. The lengthy period it takes whales to grow to maturity and the ecological affronts they face from other sources of environmental degradation mean that numerous whale species remain on the brink of extinction.

4.1.5 A new tragedy: deep sea biodiversity

Historically, the sheer size of the oceans and the obstacles to exploration have hindered our knowledge about, and exploitation of, the deep sea. However, technological development in the form of remote submersibles,

---

73 Ibid.: 51.

74 The non-binding programme which sets out actions for governments, business and organizations for sustainable development.

75 'Whale Sancturies' (Worldwide Wildlife Fund Australia): http://www.wwf.org.au/our_work/saving_the_natural_world/wildlife_and_habitats/australian_priority_species/whales/what_is_wwf_doing_to_protect_whales/whale_sanctuaries.

and submersibles capable of transporting humans into great depths and at intense pressures, has made the deep sea increasingly accessible.[76] As well as mining mineral nodules from the deep seabed, the exploration of deep sea features such as hydrothermal vents, cold seeps, deep sea trenches, seamounts and the abyssal plains has revealed a diversity of biological resources and made the deep sea attractive to bio-prospectors – those interested in developing commercially marketable products.[77] It has been noted that research institutions are increasingly entering into partnerships with industry in order to fund research activities in the deep sea.[78] What is occurring is a blurring of the boundaries between 'pure marine scientific research' and 'applied scientific research' (bio-prospecting).

This is problematic because while there is a clearly established legal regime for scientific research in the Law of the Sea Convention, it does not directly address commercial activity in areas beyond national jurisdiction – a lacuna in the regime.[79] Thus, in terms of regulating bio-prospecting there are no specific rules regulating access to or use of marine biological resources beyond national jurisdiction. Recall that biological resources do not come under the definition of resources of the deep seabed (that are the CHM) under Article 133. It is also doubtful that the provisions in the Convention relating to living resources are sufficient to ensure sustainable practice. While both scientific research and bio-prospecting potentially lead to benefits if done sustainably and certainly contribute to the knowledge of humankind, they also pose a potentially new threat to the unique ocean ecosystem. Should bio-prospecting increase to a level similar to other commercial harvesting exploits, such as whaling or fishing, the over-exploitation and collapse of these species suggests that current regimes would do little to prevent a similar tragedy in deep sea ecosystems.

---

76 Stephanie Adelle Bonney, 'Bioprospecting, Scientific Research and Deep Sea Resources in Areas Beyond National Jurisdiction: A Critical Legal Analysis' (2006) 10 *NZJ Envtl L.* 41.

77 Ibid.

78 Ibid.: 43.

79 Convention on Biological Diversity, Subsidiary Body on Scientific, Technical and Technological Advice, *Marine Coastal Biodiversity: Review, Further Elaboration and Refinement of the Programme of Work: Study of the Relationship between the Convention on Biological Diversity and the United Nations Convention on the Law of the Sea with Regard to the Conservation and Sustainable Use of Genetic Resources on the Deep Seabed*, UN Doc. UNEP/CBD/SBSTTA/8/INF/3 Rev. 1, 39, 11 (SBSTTA Study).

4.2 Antarctica

Antarctica presents probably the most coherent regime of all the global commons – bound by fairly clear geographical limits and governed by a treaty system that originated with scientific exploration.[80] Seven countries (Argentina, Chile, Australia, New Zealand, France, Norway and the UK) have claims to wedges of their continents that originate at the far boundaries of their national land mass and converge at the South Pole. Some of these claims are overlapping. The seven states have differing approaches to territoriality. New Zealand asserts a territorial claim in the Antarctic based on a 1923 British order-in-council that established the Ross Dependency. It has some record of exploration, but New Zealand has not been a strong advocate of territorial claims in the region; in fact, after World War II, New Zealand suggested internationalization of Antarctica. Argentina continues to be the most active claimant in asserting sovereignty; Argentina also contends that the western mountains of Antarctica are geological extensions of Argentina's own land mass.[81]

Many scholars find that the claims to national sovereignty, and the lack of universality and true multilateralism in the operation of the Treaty regime, and the fact that Antarctica is not an open-access domain make it difficult to include the Antarctic and its governance regime in a discussion of the global commons.[82] Yet, ironically, it is the small and exclusive nature of the regime's decision-making procedures that is attributed to its operational success and efficiency.[83]

Ultimately, the question of Antarctica's inclusion as a global commons is mute so long as claims to national sovereignty remain frozen under the Antarctic Treaty of 1959. The Treaty is a framework treaty originally conceived to prevent military confrontation in the region and to maintain scientific cooperation. During the International Geophysical year of 1957 to 1958, the Soviet's launch of Sputnik was the catalyst for a formal accord among states, because it made real the threat that Soviets might position missiles in their Antarctic bases within range of a number of countries. This made necessary a formal accord among states. It neither confirms nor negates the seven states' claims, but it does rule out new claims. In the words of Susan Buck, 'Article IV is

[80] Buck (note 45): 45.
[81] Ibid.: 52.
[82] Graham Nicholson, 'The Common Heritage of Mankind and Mining: An Analysis of the Law as to the High Seas, Outer Space, the Antarctic and World Heritage' (2002) 6 *NZJ Envtl L.* 177, 191.
[83] Vogler (note 51): 81.

masterful in its vagueness. By refusing to clarify the issue of ownership in Antarctica, it defused a volatile situation. A compromise would have been less successful and might even have led to the ultimate failure of the treaty'.[84] Twelve countries with significant scientific research operations in Antarctica were the 12 original parties to the Treaty (the original seven plus Belgium, Japan, South Africa, the USSR and the USA) and form the Antarctic Treaty Consultative Parties (ATCP). The treaty allows other UN member states to accede to it.[85] However, these states must demonstrate an interest in the Antarctic through involvement in scientific activity in order to be able to participate in meetings as a contracting party. Alternately, non-consultative parties are invited to observe, but not participate in meetings.

During UNCLOS III a Sri Lankan delegate proposed that Antarctica be considered CHM alongside the seabed. This was quickly stifled by the ATCPs.[86] Several subsequent attempts were made by developing countries in the 1980s in the General Assembly, all of which were vigorously opposed by the ATCPs who wanted the regime to remain separate from the UN. A compromise was reached wherein the ATCPs report to the General Assembly on a triennial basis.[87] Since then, calls for the classification of Antarctica as CHM have died down, in part because several developing countries are ATCPs. This is further evidence that CHM is used as an equity concept, not necessarily to ensure that environmental sustainability is on the agenda.

Parallel to calls for Antarctica to be a CHM area are calls for Antarctica to be a 'world park', thereby shifting the emphasis from equity of profits of exploitation to a more conservationist and environmental concern. New Zealand took up the cause in 1975, followed by NGOs, the Antarctic and Southern Ocean Coalition (ACOC) and the IUCN. The rhetoric probably had some effect in shifting the emphasis of several sub-regimes to a more environmental standpoint. Due to the minimal range of flora and fauna on the continent itself and the lack of mining thus far due to technical and logistical difficulties, maritime resources constitute the main commercially exploitable resource of Antarctica.[88] Many distant water fleets have headed southwards due to the enclosure of the sea through the establishment of EEZs. The main commercially exploitable marine

---

84 Buck (note 45): 59.

85 Antarctic Treaty, 402 UNTS 71 (adopted 1 December 1959, entered into force 23 June 1961), Art. 13.

86 Vogler (note 51): 79.

87 Ibid.: 79–80.

88 Ibid.: 75.

resources are cod and krill – a new food source for humans, but essential to the Antarctic food chain.

In 1964 the ATCP adopted the Agreed Measures for Antarctic Flora and Fauna, in 1972 the Convention for the Conservation of Antarctic Fur Seals, and in 1980 the Convention on the Conservation of Antarctic Marine Living Resources. Under the CCAMLR, parties agree to conduct harvesting in such a way as to prevent the decline in stocks and also to maintain the ecological relationships between harvested, dependent and related populations. Antarctica is one of the few places where some conservation and sustainability measures were put in place before damage was done. Despite this proactive and ecocentric approach, the Convention is still a normal type of fisheries regime which is both permissive and rather non-specific, including no catch quotas, nor any provisions to deal with non-parties.[89] The waters surrounding Antarctica also form a part of the Southern Ocean Whale Sanctuary.

Parties tried and failed to organize a regulatory regime for mining in Antarctica; the Convention on the Regulation of Antarctic Mineral Resource Activities (CRAMRA) in the 1980s ultimately failed with the refusal of Australia and France to sign the texts. Instead the 1991 Madrid Protocol on Environment Protection to the Antarctic Treaty was adopted. The Madrid Protocol commenced on 14 January 1998 and established Antarctica as a 'natural reserve', following the world park concept formally proposed by New Zealand in 1975. At the time, it included some of the most stringent environmental protections ever before negotiated in an international document. It includes a ban on mining and drilling for oil in the region for the next 50 years unless a unanimous vote is otherwise reached by the ATCP.

Contrasting with the range and specificity of the rules in the Antarctic regime, enforcement is firmly in the hands of states, with whom the prerogative lies to report non-compliance and deal with their own nationals. But in a system of limited numbers of members, where consensus depends on relationships and comity, members are hesitant to upset their counterparts. There are increasing concerns about the environmental impacts of tourism and this, along with the monitoring of fishing activity around Antarctica, are likely to be key issues in the near-future governance of Antarctica. The Antarctic regime is saved, in part, by the continent itself, because tourism is limited to the warmer months and extraction of mineral and energy resources would be difficult under Antarctic conditions.[90]

[89] Ibid.: 86.
[90] Buck (note 45): 68.

Some suggest that the success of the Antarctic Treaty system may result more from the fact that it has yet to be fully tested under conditions of economic pressure.[91] The apparent conservation emphasis must be 'tempered by a sober awareness that if there was any immediate likelihood of economic exploitation of Antarctic mineral resources the situation would, in all probability, be rather different'.[92]

4.3 Outer Space

As Vogler explains, outer space is very much like the high seas because it too is open-access.[93] But as a 'domain' it is difficult to define because there are no clear boundaries to outer space. While the physical characteristics of earth's atmosphere and outer space certainly differ, there is no sharp physical demarcation between the two regions. However, it is also a very different commons because not everyone has access to outer space. The cost of and access to technology are highly prohibitive and exclusionary, meaning that access to this commons is limited mainly to the 'global' north. Yet the space commons provides the technical infrastructure for modern global communication. This, argues Vogler, has given rise to the emphasis on the common heritage of mankind in respect of outer space.[94]

This section considers outer space, the moon and celestial bodies, and the electromagnetic spectrum as part of the same commons area. Celestial bodies such as the moon and the asteroids have vast amounts of untapped natural resources. Gold has now been discovered on asteroids, Helium-3 on the moon, and magnesium, cobalt and uranium on Mars.[95] A mere one percent of this would supply the entire estimated amount of energy to be consumed by humanity in the twenty-first century.[96] But because mining of celestial bodies is not currently feasible, the current use of the space commons is in relation to a set of satellite orbits. Satellites require

[91] John A. Heap and Martin Holdgate, 'The Antarctic Treaty System as an Environmental Mechanism: An Approach to Environmental Issues', in *Polar Research Board, Antarctic Treaty System: An Assessment* (National Academy Press, Washington, DC 1986).

[92] Vogler (note 51): 92; Shackelford (note 2): 40.

[93] Vogler (note 51): 99.

[94] Ibid.

[95] Shackelford (note 2): 43.

[96] This is made economically more feasible by the moon's low gravity easing the transport of bulk materials, especially vis-à-vis a mass driver. A mass driver, or electromagnetic catapult, is a method of spacecraft propulsion that would use a linear motor to accelerate payloads up to high speeds and launch them from the moon to the earth.

choice 'spots' on three orbits located above the equator, along a line running from pole to pole, and along an inclined orbit.[97] These orbits are geostationary (for telecommunications, surveillance and television broadcasting), low earth orbit (for photoreconnaissance, ocean surveillance, electronic surveillance, communications and cell phones, navigation and meteorology) and molniya orbit (for communications).[98] The control and utilization of satellites depends upon the use of radio frequencies. It is the availability and width of these frequencies that determine the allotment of orbital positions.[99]

Despite a history of peaceful and scientific cooperation with regards to outer space, manifest in the 1957–1958 International Geophysical Year and the international approval of the satellite program, dramatic technological advancement substantially affected the development of the space regime. Geopolitics, in the form of the Cold War and the threat of nuclear confrontation, saw the US and the Soviet Union increase their military spending in the 'space race'. This was catalysed by the Soviet launch of the satellite Sputnik I in 1958. By 1969 the USA had beaten the Soviets in the race to put a man on the moon. Nevertheless, like Antarctica, there has been a persistent emphasis on scientific exploration and cooperation with respect to outer space. The Committee on the Peaceful Uses of Outer Space (COPUOS), which became a permanent body of the General Assembly in 1959, maintains close relations with several private groups and with the Office for Outer Space Affairs Division in the UN Secretariat and the International Telecommunication Union (ITU). At the time, COPUOS was unique because it required consensus for decisions to be passed, something which was increasingly difficult to achieve as the membership of the Committee diversified and included more developing states.

The 1967 Treaty on Principles Governing the Activities of States in the Exploration and Use of Outer Space Including the Moon and Other Celestial Bodies (the Outer Space Treaty), negotiated in the COPUOS, was conceived as a regime to prevent the use of space as a military platform for the positioning of weapons, or any other non-peaceful use.[100] Article IV states unequivocally that placing nuclear weapons or weapons of mass destruction anywhere in outer space is prohibited. However, 'peaceful' does not exclude all military activity; it permits non-aggressive military uses.[101] The Treaty's emphasis remains on freedom of scientific

---

97 Vogler (note 51): 98.
98 Ibid.
99 Ibid.: 97.
100 It was passed shortly after the Cuban Missile Crisis.
101 Buck (note 45): 148.

activities and maintaining scientific cooperation. Although it does not use the common heritage of mankind term, it has similar provision. Article I states that while free for exploration and use, outer space shall be for the benefit of all (irrespective of capability) and shall be the province of all mankind. According to Buck, the sovereignty 'issue was agreed on with an astonishing lack of fanfare, but for those familiar with the history of human exploration, it was little short of miraculous'.[102] Several equatorial states challenged this by claiming their rights to the geostationary orbit, as a part of their 'airspace'. The pursuant Bogotá Declaration has not been recognized by most countries. As with other framework regimes, several specific agreements have arisen, such as for the rescue and return of astronauts and space objects (1969), international liability for damage caused by space objects (1972), and registration of satellites and other orbiting anthropogenic objects (1976). The Outer Space Treaty does not address the ownership of outer space, but is unequivocal in declaring that no state may appropriate any part of outer space, the moon or other celestial bodies.

In contrast, the 1979 Agreement on the Moon and Other Celestial Bodies (the Moon Treaty) explicitly states that the moon and other celestial bodies and their natural resources are the common heritage of mankind. This means that resources cannot be exclusively appropriated for one state, as they are for the benefit of all. If extraction became a reality, an international institution, like that for the seabed, would need to be established. However, despite the fact that the Moon Treaty is frequently cited as evidence of recognition of the common heritage of mankind principle in international law, only a handful of states have ratified the Treaty, none of which are the major space-faring nations. Although not feasible for commercial exploitation at the moment, states are obviously wary of binding themselves to such an obligation, or they simply see the Treaty as obsolete. As with the other putatively benign regimes for commons areas, scholars predict the likelihood that the Moon Treaty will also be revised if the possibility of profitable resource extraction becomes a reality.[103] Thus, at present, the Moon Treaty has limited relevance to current space activity.

Concerns about use of the space commons have had little to do with earth's environment. Where environmental concerns have been voiced, it is in relation to the remains of space vehicles re-entering earth's atmosphere, and possible terrestrial contamination by returned spacecraft and

---

[102] Ibid.: 139.
[103] Ibid.: 152.

astronauts.[104] More recent concerns about 'space clutter' left by human activity have been voiced. At the moment, the impact of this debris tends to focus on the potential damage to spacecraft and satellites, because no other non-anthropocentric detrimental impacts are known of. At present, there is no codified regime to manage space debris and no rules of liability, but users cooperate and collaborate through the Inter-Agency Orbital Debris Coordination Committee.[105] Resources extracted from outer space could have profound effects on earth's environment. Some scholars, such as Lotta Viikari, contend that the space commons could potentially improve earth's environment by locating industrial activity in space.[106] However, the converse is also true; if fossil fuels are extractable from the space commons and able to be transported to earth, their continued supply could prevent the shift to renewable energies that is desperately needed yet which moves at an anaemic pace. Furthermore, as space tourism such as via Richard Branson's Virgin Galactic becomes an increasing occurrence, this too could raise environmental issues in the context of the space commons.

Thus, we can see the space regime as a child of its time. While it is currently open-access, humans *so far* lack the technology to give rise to any serious 'tragedy'. However, should such advances be made, it is quite clear that the regime would likely be somewhat obsolete. For instance, the exploitation of outer space is left unresolved. Although the claiming of sovereignty by states is prohibited, the regime does not provide for what would occur if discovery of new resources and exploitation became feasible.

The central issue in the use of the outer space commons relates to geostationary orbits (GSO). As a 'resource', the orbits are not finite because they are not depletable (they are not 'consumed') but they are exclusionary in that there can be only a limited amount of users at any one time. They can be degraded through interference and overcrowding. The control and utilization of satellites depend upon the use of radio frequencies. It is the availability and width of these frequencies that determine the allotment of orbital positions.[107]

Because the radio spectrum is excludable, a regime was necessary to regulate its use. Issues in the regime revolve around national sovereignty, technology transfer, economic development and political control.[108] The

104 Vogler (note 51): 105.
105 Ibid.: 106–107.
106 Viikari (note 15): 123.
107 Vogler (note 51): 97.
108 Buck (note 45): 138.

International Telecommunications Union is the chief regulator, self-proclaimed to be apolitical and focused on technical solutions for efficiency. The ITU is one of the oldest international organizations, founded in 1865 as the International Telegraph Union to regulate the wire services. The present-day ITU was formed in 1932 at the Madrid Plenipotentiary Conference and assumed its new name in 1934. It became a specialized agency of the United Nations in 1947. In 1971, the World Administrative Radio Conference on Space Telecommunications (WARC-ST) formally brought geostationary orbits under ITU control. Because of the constantly evolving nature of technology and the concurrently evolving uses of this commons, the ITU is governed by a series of Conventions that are periodically reviewed. Unsurprisingly equity issues are central. Rights to the radio spectrum were originally allocated on a first-come-first-served basis. The developing nations were concerned that the more advanced countries would establish a permanent monopoly over the resources. They argued that such a system discriminates against them because they lack the technical and financial ability to participate. The 1973 ITU Convention conveys the idea that orbital positions do not confer permanent property rights or sovereignty, but rather a right of equitable access. The International Telecommunications Union refers to the electromagnetic spectrum as a common heritage resource. Following this, the Radio Regulations were revised and in a dramatic departure from the old 'first in time' protocol, all countries were given equal access to the use of space radio communication service frequencies and to the related geostationary orbits. In 1979, developing countries were allocated frequencies for broadcast satellites (despite the fact that they had no satellites) as well as guaranteed 'parking places' if they ever did acquire satellites. As yet there are no claims to specific frequencies.

Because the ITU coordinates worldwide communications, it seeks to ensure that interference is minimized. This is important to all participants, and therefore most nations accede to the ITU regulations, making it a rather successful commons management regime. While states have control of transmissions within their borders, they submit to an international regime under the ITU for beyond-border communications. States that violate ITU protocols may be excluded from access to technological innovations, and interference with their illegitimate broadcasts is likely. International sanctions against 'pirate' broadcasters are stringent; the Law of the Sea even permits nations to take punitive measures on the high seas against broadcasters targeting their territories.

Satellite communications are now being challenged by the new generation of broadband fibre optic cable.

4.4 Atmosphere

The term 'atmosphere' is rarely used in international law.[109] There is much debate on whether the atmosphere is really a global commons. This confusion relates to the fact that as a commons it is unlike any other. Air, a part of the atmosphere, circulates through national jurisdictions (airspace) and beyond in much the same way as sea water. It gives rise to a similar absurdity as the oceans – that units of air or water can be owned at times and not owned at other times. Some scholars mistakenly view the fact that the atmosphere cannot be deemed beyond state jurisdiction as a reason negating its status as a commons. Their problem is analytical. The commons cannot be simplistically defined as that which is beyond state jurisdiction.

The atmosphere has the characteristics of a common pool resource domain. Earth's atmosphere provides water and oxygen to sustain life on earth, and shields us from the sun and from the vacuum of space.[110] It also includes a sink facility. When pollution occurs and the capacity of the sink is exceeded, the quality of air is undermined and ozone is depleted. This means that the atmosphere is highly subtractable but it is difficult to exclude anyone. The atmosphere is made up of five layers, each with an important function. Temperatures increase in each atmospheric layer. The troposhere is closest to the surface of earth and extends between eight and 20 km upwards. It contains around 80 percent of earth's air mass and is where most weather and air pollution occur.[111] This is deemed air space, the international law for which is the 1944 Chicago Convention on International Civil Aviation. According to the Convention, all states have exclusive sovereignty over the airspace above their land and sea territory. Next, the stratosphere extends to about 50 km above the earth's surface where strong winds blow. The ozone layer is contained in the upper limits of the stratosphere where the temperature increases from the absorption of radiation. The mesosphere extends to 80 km, below which lies 99.99 percent of earth's atmosphere.[112] Above this lies the thermosphere where temperatures can reach 1000 degrees centigrade. Its electrified layers reflect high frequency radio waves, allowing long-distance radio communication on earth.[113] The final layer is the exosphere.

In 1988 Malta, a small island threatened by rising seas from global

---

[109] Soroos (note 5): 49.
[110] Buck (note 45): 111.
[111] Ibid.: 112.
[112] Ibid.
[113] Ibid.

climate change, and the country of Arvid Pardo, proposed in the General Assembly that the global climate be deemed CHM. The suggestion was rejected, but the General Assembly did adopt a resolution designating the global climate a 'common concern of humankind'. Unlike Antarctica, outer space and the oceans, the atmosphere is not subject to an overarching framework regime. Instead, regimes have been developed using the framework approach for component atmospheric issues followed by more specific protocols.

Atmospheric pollution and degradation demands a necessarily international regime, because harms cannot be confined to the areas where they originate. In 1979 the Convention on Long-Range Transboundary Air Pollution (Geneva Convention) was adopted. The Convention has been deemed largely toothless, but includes a number of protocols on specific polluting substances.[114] Prominent atmospheric issues include emissions of sulphur dioxide and nitrous oxides combining with atmospheric water and oxygen to form sulphuric and nitric acids which fall to earth in a deposition like snow, hail, fog, clouds or what is colloquially called 'acid rain'. In 1985 the Protocol on the Reduction of Sulphur Emissions or Their Transboundary Fluxes by at Least 30 Percent (Helsinki Protocol) was adopted, but the US, Poland and the UK – all major sources of transboundary sulfur dioxide pollution – are not parties to this convention. In 1988, a second protocol was added to the Geneva Convention: the Sofia Protocol Concerning the Control of Emissions of Nitrogen Oxides or Their Transboundary Fluxes (Sofia Protocol). It mandated an emissions freeze at 1987 levels but allowed many countries, such as the US, to delay compliance until 1994 to compensate for earlier reductions. The apparent failure of the acid deposition regime is the failure of states to determine their internal policy responses, a characteristic translated into the international arena and manifest in the lack of cooperation among states.[115]

In 1985 reports came of an enormous hole over the Antarctic. Countries nearby, including New Zealand, were particularly alarmed because of the potential for high national skin cancer rates, and because they had an economy 'largely dependent on industries such as agriculture,

---

[114] Convention on Long Range Transboundary Air Pollution, 1302 UNTS 217 (adopted 13 November 1979, entered into force 16 March 1983) (LRTAP) includes protocols on sulphur compounds (1985, 1994), nitrogen oxides (1988) and volatile organic compounds (1991). The Vienna Convention (1985) is followed by the Montreal Protocol (1987) and subsequent revisions in London (1990), Copenhagen (1992) and Vienna (1995).

[115] Buck (note 45): 117.

horticulture, fishing and tourism, which are under threat from increasing ultra-violet radiation'.[116] The Vienna Convention for the Protection of the Ozone Layer was adopted in 1985. Another typical framework convention, it is 'important for two reasons: its ecosystem approach, which implies that the natural environment has intrinsic worth, and its emphasis on preventing future harm rather than merely providing remedies for current problems'.[117] A research report prepared through a landmark collaboration between various scientific bodies, catalysed the 1987 Conference in Montreal from which the Montreal Protocol was adopted by even the largest CFC-producing states. The Protocol called for a 50 percent cut in ozone-depleting substances from 1986 levels by 1999.[118] The Protocol included various incentives for developing countries, such as delayed compliance for 10 years. But the need for even further reductions soon became evident. In May 1989, 81 nations adopted the nonbinding Helsinki Declaration on the Protection of the Ozone Layer which called for further reductions and a shorter phase-out timetable. The Copenhagen meeting of parties to the Montreal Protocol in late 1992 again moved the timetable up, due to continuing decline. Several factors led to the successful development of the regime, among them the close relationship between scientists and policymakers, cognizance of developing country concerns and funds to help assist their phase-outs, effective education of the public and policymakers, and the most significant factor which was that manufacturers were able to find alternatives to CFCs.[119]

Similarly, climate change, also characterized as the global warming of the earth from greenhouse gas emissions, entered international consciousness following the first World Climate Conference in 1979. The issue has risen to prominence in the last two decades in part due to the warnings in the First Assessment Report by the International Panel on Climate Change (IPCC) in 1990, which predicted what will occur with even slight alterations to the earth's temperature.[120] Although a measure of climate change is naturally occurring, there is now scientific consensus that anthropocentric activity is increasing the levels of greenhouse gases

---

[116] Philip Woollaston, quoted in (1987) 37 (3) *New Zealand Foreign Affairs Review* 47.

[117] Buck (note 45): 122–123.

[118] New Zealand ratified the Montreal Protocol on 21 July 1988.

[119] Buck (note 45): 124.

[120] Daniel Bodansky, 'The History of the Global Climate Change Regime', in Urs Luterbacher and Detlef F. Sprinz (eds), *International Relations and Global Climate Change* (The MIT Press, Cambridge, MA 2001): 24.

(GHGs), trapping heat in the troposphere and leading to the warming of the earth's surface *at an accelerated rate* which is damaging the planet.[121]

The 1992 United Nations Conference on the Environment and Development (UNCED) in Rio de Janeiro saw the creation and signing of the United Nations Framework Convention on Climate Change (UNFCCC)[122] by over 185 states. The third meeting of the UNFCCC Conference of Parties (COP 3) saw the adoption of the Kyoto Protocol in December 1997.[123] The Protocol entered into force on 16 February 2005, following ratification by Russia.[124] It set legally-binding GHG emissions reduction targets for Annex 1 countries for a commitment period of 2008 to 2012. Failure to meet these targets would require payment for the excess emissions. Initially, the overall target was a global emissions reduction of 5.2 percent below 1990 levels, but it is now established that subsequent compromises, such as the inclusion of land use, land use change and forestry sinks (LULUCF) have reduced the aggregate target to the realm of 0.5 to 1.5 percent below 1990 levels.[125] Since those foundational years, global emissions have grown by roughly 70 percent.[126] Parties to the UNFCCC were tasked with formulating a post-Kyoto (2012) climate regime to present at the UN Conference on Sustainable Development in Rio de Janeiro in June 2012 (Rio+20).

The depletion of the ozone layer unsurprisingly also gave rise to equity issues prevalent in most environmental negotiations. Many states were not major producers or users of CFCs and yet felt the worst effects. Such issues are similarly a major obstacle for climate change negotiations, as developing states deny their complicity in the creation of the problem

---

[121] See R.K. Pachauri and A. Reisinger (eds), 'Climate Change 2007: Synthesis Report. Contribution of Working Groups I, II and III to the Fourth Assessment Report of the Intergovernmental Panel on Climate Change' (Intergovernmental Panel on Climate Change 2007): http://www.ipcc.ch/publications_and_data/publications_ipcc_fourth_assessment_report_synthesis_report.htm.

[122] United Nations Framework Convention on Climate Change, 1771 UNTS 107 (adopted 9 May 1992, entered into force 21 March 1994).

[123] Kyoto Protocol to the Framework Convention on Climate Change, 2303 UNTS 148 (adopted 11 December 1997, entered into force 16 February 2005) (Kyoto Protocol).

[124] Paul Q. Watchman, 'Introduction', in Paul Q. Watchman (ed.), *Climate Change: A Guide to Carbon Law and Policy* (Globe Business Publishing, London 2008): 12.

[125] Anthony Hobley, 'Creating a Global Carbon Market', in Watchman (note 124): 129.

[126] New Zealand Ministry for the Environment, 'Key facts about climate change' (1 November 2010): http://www.mfe.govt.nz/issues/climate/about/key-facts.html.

(despite ever-increasing contributions) and small island and low-lying states espouse their extreme vulnerability to rising sea levels.

4.5 Biodiversity

The World Heritage Convention, adopted by UNESCO in 1972, endeavors to protect and conserve sites of cultural and natural heritage that are of 'outstanding universal value' and located within state borders. This is justified by the belief that world heritage protection is the duty of the international community as a whole.[127] As such, the Convention is balanced between protecting sites of worldwide interest and not excessively interfering in other state territories.[128] The term 'world heritage' was used in preference to the common heritage of mankind in deference to the sovereign rights of states that wished to retain ultimate control over world heritage sites within their boundaries.[129] Nevertheless, while the World Heritage Convention places upon individual states the primary responsibility for identification, protection, conservation, presentation and transmission to future generations of the cultural and natural heritage within their respective territories, the specific standards and requirements for the management of assets in trust for the benefit of present and future generations establishes a yardstick against which the performance of a state can be measured.[130]

Whether or not they are commons depends on whether one's view of global commons starts from states' territories or not. As was seen in the discussion of the atmospheric commons, to define commons only as that which is not owned by states is to have an excessively restrictive view of what all humans own together. Putting aside the question of whether world heritage sites are commons areas (at the very least the citizens and cultures of the state have a strong argument that they are cultural commons), the world heritage regime offers perhaps one of the closest conceptual models to an argument for global trusteeship of the commons which extends even within state territory to include the whole biosphere.

---

[127] Convention concerning the Protection of the World Cultural and Natural Heritage, 1037 UNTS 151 (adopted 16 November 1972, entered into force 17 December 1975) (World Heritage Convention), Arts 6, 7.

[128] Ultimately though, because the Convention relies on goodwill, the actions of the state are only subject to international publicity and criticism for non-compliance, and the committee is not devoid of international politics.

[129] Nicholson (note 82): 195.

[130] Stephen Sec, 'Humanitarian Limits to Sovereignty: Common Concern and Common Heritage Approaches to Natural Resources and Environment' (2010) 12 ICLR 384.

Biodiversity is generally excluded from discussions of the various global commons areas and resources. For one thing, all terrestrial biodiversity and the majority of the sea's biodiversity are within sovereign territory. The CHM principle was rejected when it came to discussing biodiversity governance. Developing states quickly rescinded their support for the common heritage principle which could have led to undue interference in their social and economic development. Unlike the global commons where developing countries can be excluded because they lack the resources necessary to exploit it, many developing countries have rich biodiversity. In the early twentieth century, the Russian scientist Nicolai I. Vavilov noticed that the most varietal (terrestrial) biological wealth of the world was concentrated in only seven or eight mostly subtropical and mountainous regions.[131] Developing countries feared that labeling all biodiversity the CHM could give rise to a new wave of bio-prospecting imperialism.

As Stone points out, telling states to share their biodiversity (genetic information and so on) has as much feasibility as telling the Saudis to share their oil.[132] The nationalistic sentiments that lead many states to secure the genetic resources within their territories parallels the similar movements of coastal states to secure their jurisdiction of the adjacent sea areas.

The global biodiversity 'regime' could be said to consist of several conventions – the 1973 Convention on International Trade in Endangered Species of Wild Fauna and Flora (CITES); the 1979 Convention on the Conservation of Migratory Species of Wild Animals (Bonn); the 1979 Convention on the Conservation of European Wildlife and Natural Habitats (Bern); and the 1980 Convention on the Conservation of Antarctic Marine Living Resources (CCAMLR). Most significant and all-encompassing is the Convention on Biological Diversity (CBD) which was signed at the 1992 Earth Summit in Rio de Janeiro and came into force on 29 December 1993. The Convention is unique in its recognition of the intrinsic value of biodiversity, quite apart from the benefits and advantages it offers humankind. In keeping with the international legal tradition, it is a framework convention, designed as a set of principles to guide state laws and policies.

Article 3 is essentially a codification of customary international law relating to transboundary environmental damage. It sets out the responsibility

---

[131] Nicolai I. Vavilov, *Origin and Geography of Cultivated Plants* (Cambridge University Press, Cambridge 1992).

[132] Christopher D. Stone, *The Gnat is Older than Man: Global Environment and Human Agenda* (Princeton University Press, Princeton, NJ 1993): 211.

of state parties 'to ensure that activities within their jurisdiction or control do not cause damage to the environment of other States or of areas beyond the limits of national jurisdiction'. The components of biological diversity situated in areas beyond the limits of national jurisdiction are not subject to the CBD. This means that bio-prospecting, as mentioned before, is also not covered by the CBD, although Article 5 does require that state parties cooperate in the conservation and sustainable use of biological diversity in areas beyond national jurisdiction. The Convention confirms states' control over biological resources within their territories. States are expected to exercise their judgment in light of the Convention's objectives stated in Article I: conservation of biodiversity; sustainable use of its components; and fair and equitable sharing of benefits arising out of utilization of genetic resources. Beyond these broad guidelines, biodiversity governance is moot.

Yet biodiversity warrants attention as a commons issue for two reasons. First, the rate of disappearance is alarming and is perhaps *the* most pressing global concern. The IUCN estimates that the current species extinction rate is between 1,000 and 10,000 times higher than it would naturally be, caused by human impacts such as farming, introducing alien species into local ecosystems, pollution and exploitation.[133] Slowly the world is waking up to the reality that losses of our 'natural capital' in biodiversity are more of a threat even than terrorism.[134] For instance, the value of pollinating insects alone for the global economy is estimated to be US$190 billion annually,[135] something which makes the collapse of bee colonies potentially disastrous ecologically and financially.

Second, as we saw with the emergent ocean commons tragedy of bio-prospecting, the development of new technology and new uses for biodiversity is similarly threatening to terrestrial biodiversity. Because the world's biodiversity is part of the global and intricate web of the biosphere, the prerogative of states to do what they will within their sovereign territories is an inadequate system for avoiding further tragedy. Yet just like world heritage, the negotiators at the Rio Summit rejected the label of 'common heritage of mankind' for biodiversity and instead called it 'common concern'. Although some commentators would contend that

---

133 See International Union for Conservation of Nature, 'About Biodiversity': http://www. iucn.org/what/tpas/biodiversity/.

134 United Nations Environmental Programme Finance Initiative, Biodiversity and Ecosystem Service Work Stream, 'Demystifying Materiality: Hardwiring biodiversity and ecosystem services into finance' (CEO Briefing, October 2010): 4. http://www.unepfi.org/fileadmin/documents/CEO_DemystifyingMateriality.pdf.

135 Ibid.: 9.

the latter term imposes on states more environmental obligations, the inertia of states since the adoption of the Convention on Biodiversity in 1992 indicates that it is not interpreted thus. As such, this volume includes biodiversity within the ambit of the global commons because of the vital role it plays in the biosphere. Effectively, the concept of the commons pays no heed to socially constructed ideas of territory which parcel out the management of areas to different groups of people if there is sufficient common interest in those areas and resources.

5. AN ECOLOGICAL ALTERNATIVE: THE COMMON HERITAGE OF LIFE

As this chapter has revealed, definition of the global commons is fraught with conceptual and analytical problems. The repetitious narrative is, and seems likely to continue to be, that as resources become increasingly scarce and technology advances to meet surging demand, longstanding principles of communal ownership in the global commons will either be reinterpreted or rewritten outright.[136] As priorities change and technologies develop, states are taking it upon themselves to negotiate bilateral accords and bypass the UN system altogether. This is precisely what is happening today, with a movement towards bilateral agreements.[137]

The fact that the global commons is comprised of discrete commons areas each with their own governance infrastructure reflects another tragedy – the tragedy of ecological fragmentation. Like other tragedies, this tragedy reflects a failure of the human imagination. So it is noted with some irony that the task set forth in this volume is to argue that the elements of life (earth, water, air and energy) and the life therein ought to be protected. How can these not belong to all living things, in common? Competition has reached such a level that we have to design governance regimes for that which is intuitively shared. Not only that, but we have to make the case for which ethical principles ought to apply to these elements – common heritage, common concern, and so on.

In terms of human attempts at dealing with the global commons, the common heritage of mankind is an inadequate way to characterize why certain areas and resources should be protected. It captures one aspect – social equity – while ignoring the overarching reality of ecological limits. It is chiefly an anthropocentric term, and while equity is important the

136 Shackelford (note 2): 2.
137 Ibid.: 45.

global commons must first and foremost be the foci of ecological concerns. Without a healthy biosphere there will be nothing to share. Crucially also, the term has not gained purchase in international law. What is needed is an alternative term – one which encompasses things that are common concern, leaves behind the gendered assumptions of 'mankind' and the anthropocentrism of what is common, with 'all' to include not only human life, but all living things. Such a concept has been mooted. Taylor suggests transforming the concept of CHM to better reflect a new and necessary environmental ethic – that the earth's biosphere is the common heritage of all life on earth, and humanity is the steward.[138] It is called the common heritage of life.

This concept encapsulates the essential elements of a new environmental ethic: the interconnectivity of the biosphere and the impossibility of division, the inherent value of nature and of *all* species, intergenerational equity, and humanity's special relationship with nature.[139] In this sense, the term encompasses what we mean by a global commons. It might seem a dramatic departure from the way we make sense of the world. Helfrich and Haas help to explain why this is so:[140]

> as technological revolutions converge with dramatic imbalances in the various players' ability to assert their interests . . . controlled private appropriation now reaches into the most intimate and remote spheres of our lives – our genes, relationships, and way of thinking and into the resources that are spatially so very distant from us (outer space, deep sea) – that we barely perceive them as being *ours*.

Likewise, at the global level there lacks the same sense of community that frequently exists at the local level, which has complicated our understanding of 'sharing' and the task of developing management systems.[141] Some scholars have tried to re-interpret CHM to give a meaning analogous to that of the common heritage of life. Effectively, they have sought to infuse CHM with more ecological principles. While their intent is admirable, the term is too politically problematic to be used as the kind of norm needed to guide global environmental governance. Re-interpretation of this term is in a way analytically futile, because its history clearly indicates that it does not represent the kind of ecological norm that many seek, but

138 Taylor (note 9): 298.
139 Ibid.
140 Silke Helfrich and Jörg Haas, 'The Commons: A New Narrative for Our Time', in Silke Heinrich (ed.), *Genes, Bytes and Emissions: To Whom Does the World Belong?* (Henrich Böll Stiftung, Berlin 2008).
141 Soroos (note 5).

is/was instead a principle of chiefly social justice concerns. In the end, CHM has created a common property regime, not a viable system of ecological trusteeship, despite this being contrary to the original intention of Pardo to avoid 'property' because it connotes power. In contrast, the common heritage of life sheds the normative ambiguity of the CHM term and offers a better ethical model for approaching the commons and the whole biosphere.

Traditional international law provides that only nation-states can enforce the law against other states. If the source of the legal obligation is treaty law, then only a state party can enforce against another state party. If the source is customary international law, then the obligation must be owed directly to another state and there must be some direct harm to the sovereign interests of the enforcing state. It should be apparent by now that the global commons poses some problems for these parameters of international law. To get beyond these elements, there is a strong argument for CHL to become a special legal norm, similar to a *jus cogens*. CHL would be an obligation owed to the whole international community – *erga omnes*.

Such a status would be binding on all states, irrespective of their express consent. And it would bind all persons, natural and legal, and not just states, which is important because it recognizes that transnational corporations are key actors and often greater perpetrators of ecological harm than states. They could not hide behind the ruse that only states are bound by international law. Any member of the international community can enforce *erga omnes* obligations. However, 'international community' generally means the international community of *states*. This is of little use when states mutually agree not to enforce the law against one another. Humanity and all life having subject status would potentially enable enforcement on their behalf, meaning that not only are all people the subject of international law but nature would have standing too. It could not be amended or derogated from by other agreements, unlike second-order legal rules. Taken together, these qualities go some way to responding to one of the primary 'democratic deficits' in international law. States (and other entities) would not be free to exploit the ecological commons, with no regard for the collective interests of humanity and other life – legal regimes would necessarily deprioritize purely commercially imagined national interests and prioritize common interests in a healthy biosphere.

The Earth Charter is the clearest statement of this CHL concept. As yet, it has only soft law status in international law, unable to move forward in the realm of international legal recognition because of the lack of state subscription. Nevertheless, as the statement of NGOs and civil society worldwide, the Earth Charter is arguably one of the most legitimate international statements of principle ever to be made. It articulates, as a fundamental principle of binding law, the notion that 'natural systems are a common heritage to be safeguarded for present and future generations'. The Preamble embodies the common heritage of life concept: 'we, the peoples of Earth, declare our responsibility to one another, to the greater community of life, and to future generations.' Moreover, it makes links between ecological governance and *all* aspects of human-to-human interaction – social, political and economic.

Moving forward with the concept of the common heritage of life, and with a better understanding of what is meant by the 'global commons', the next two chapters explore the concepts of trust and trusts. Chapter 5 outlines the history of trusts and trusteeship and reveals why this long-standing arrangement is both legitimate in law and appropriate to govern the common heritage of life – the global commons. Characterizing the common heritage of life as essentially 'everything' is a significant imposition on sovereign rights. And in terms of discussing governance regimes for the commons, this delimitation makes the task much more politically challenging.

As Chapter 6 will discuss, if it is in the common interest to ensure the viability of the biosphere for future generations and to use it peacefully, this is entirely what states are mandated to do through their governance of their territories. Thus, Chapter 6 argues that rather than a threat to sovereignty, the notion of the common heritage of life is a reminder of states' essential trusteeship function within their designated territories. In essence, we do not negate the legitimate existence of states and their territories, rather we call for a revival of the ecological components of what it means to be sovereign and to govern. Trusteeship for the global commons is about moving beyond norms in individual agreements towards a more general norm of environmental trusteeship that must be applied at all levels of governance, from global to local levels. This responsibility of humankind to use the biosphere sustainably is non-negotiable; and the role of trustee is non-derogable.

6. FRESHWATER RESOURCES

Edith Brown-Weiss also advocates recognition of the use and availability of the fresh water resource as a 'common concern of humankind', in the same way that climate change was recognized as a 'common concern of humankind' in the 1992 United Nations Framework Convention on Climate Change, and conservation of biodiversity was recognized as a 'common concern of humankind' in the 1992 Convention on Biological

Diversity. [142] She notes that a handful of international agreements already incorporate similar recognition.[143] The Earth Charter, for example, recognizes a 'responsibility to manage the use of renewable resources such as water . . . in ways that do not exceed rates of regeneration and that protect the health of ecosystems'.[144] Similarly, the Draft International Covenant on Environment and Development, also prepared after the UNCED by the International Union for the Conservation of Nature (IUCN) and the World Conservation Union, recognized a responsibility to maintain and restore the quality of water in order to 'ensure the availability of a sufficient quantity of water to satisfy basic human needs and to maintain aquatic systems'.[145]

Building on these agreements, she finds that recognition of the availability and use of water resources as being a common concern of humankind would 'provide a normative basis for all members of the international community to address the multitude of water-related problems'.[146]

---

142 Edith Brown Weiss, 'The Coming Water Crisis: A Common Concern of Humankind' (2012) 1(1) *Transnational Environmental Law* 153.

143 Ibid.: 165.

144 The Earth Charter Principle 5 (c).

145 IUCN Commission on Environmental Law & World Conservation Union, in cooperation with the International Council of Environmental Law, 'Draft International Covenant on Environment and Development, 2nd edn' (2000), Art. 19: http://data.iucn.org/dbtw-wpd/edocs/EPLP-031-rev.pdf. The Covenant recognizes a broad global interest in the environment and provides that '[t]he global environment is a common concern of humanity' (Art. 3).

146 Edith Brown Weiss (note 142): 166.

5. Trusteeship

> The integrated and interdependent nature of the new challenges and issues contrasts sharply with the nature of the institutions that exist today. These institutions tend to be independent, fragmented, and working to relatively narrow mandates with closed decision processes. Those responsible for managing natural resources and protecting the environment are institutionally separated from those responsible for managing the economy. The real world of inter-locked economic and ecological systems will not change; the policies and institutions concerned must.
>
> Our Common Future, Brundtland Report 1987[1]

> [E]ven if everyone ratifies . . . it won't be enough . . . What that suggests to me is that the traditional way of developing international legal standards in small incremental steps, each of which must be ratified before it comes into effect, is simply not equipped to deal with the fast-moving crises of environmental proportions which we face.
>
> Sir Geoffrey Palmer[2]

1. THE MANDATE

By 2050 the world's population may exceed nine billion while industrial output will quadruple. Energy demand will increase exponentially and, as states exhaust their natural resources and exceed the carrying capacity of their ecosystems, marginal costs will reach a point sufficiently high and the commons will be turned to as a source of resources. The question as to who owns the commons, temporarily satiated by weak and insufficient governance regimes, will be reignited. The above epitaphs are an invocation – a call to action. Within the time frame that environmental degradation was alerted to and entered into international political fora in the 1970s, carbon emissions have increased by over 70 percent and ecosystem change has occurred more rapidly and extensively than at any other time in human history, leading to massive and irreversible

---

[1] World Commission on Environment and Development, 'Our Common Future: Brundtland Report' (Oxford University Press, Oxford 1987).

[2] Deputy Prime Minister Geoffrey Palmer, quoted in (1989) 39 (2) *New Zealand External Relations Review* 9–11.

biodiversity losses.[3] Twenty-five years on from the Brundtland Report's narration of the environmental governance deficit, we are still missing the kind of governance that will halt degradation. This chapter introduces what we believe offers an answer to the call. The legal regime that we put in place will determine the future of the global commons, the planet and human beings.[4]

The current crisis is not one of a simply social or environmental character, it is also a crisis of ideas.[5] The crisis of ideas is not due to a dearth of innovation; on the contrary, this proceeds apace. Rather, this stagnation among decision-makers arises from an unwillingness to entertain ideas which transcend the dogma of neo-liberal thought, despite the reality that neo-liberalism has failed to proffer an appropriate and truly sustainable response to degradation. Ideas and action are constrained by moral parameters. Why, in the face of overwhelming empirical evidence, do actors still maintain the status quo? Why do they proffer a system of sustainable development which levels the environment alongside the economy without confronting the productive and consumptive roots of environmental degradation?

Part of this problem is dichotomous thinking. Indeed, this was even the case in Hardin's article – private property or public property, government versus market and cooperation versus competition. According to David Bollier, this is understandable as people are path dependent, seeing these customary arenas of power as the only 'regimes' available to them.[6] This wilful blindness is akin to a schizophrenic's dogged belief in their unreality. By virtue of a keen intelligence unlike any other in the community of life, humans have an enormous potentiality, most often expressed as 'power'. The manifestations of this potential in environmental discussions are usually to the detriment of the environment. However, this same potentiality means that humans can also act as guardians and stewards, because an awareness of our actions means we can consciously choose to

---

[3] Hannah Stoddart (ed.), *A Pocket Guide to Sustainable Development Governance*, 1st edn (Stakeholder Forum, Commonwealth Secretariat, London 2011): 7.

[4] Environmental governance is the various institutions and structures of authority engaged in the protection of the natural environment.

[5] Silke Helfrich, 'Commons: the Network of Life and Creativity', in Silke Heinrich (ed.), *Genes, Bytes and Emissions: To Whom Does the World Belong?* (Henrich Böll Stiftung, Berlin 2008): http://www.boell.org/web/148-576.html.

[6] David Bollier, 'The Commons: A Neglected Sector of Wealth Creation', in Silke Heinrich (ed.), *Genes, Bytes and Emissions: To Whom Does the World Belong?* (Henrich Böll Stiftung, Berlin 2008): http://bollier.org/sites/default/files/Boll%20Foundation%20book%20chapter.pdf.

protect, respect and not cause harm. The ultimate direction of this potentiality is a choice, and, in contrast to the analogy of a mentally ill person who has no control or choice over their illness, we do have a choice and the ability to comprehend our predicament. The disarray of international environmental negotiations for environmental protection, most notably a system to halt rapid climate change, tends to cloud this one crucial factor. That is not to say that the pragmatics of governing the global environment is not a major challenge, it most certainly is, and the beginnings of a recommendation are humbly put forward in the final chapter of this volume. But what we see internationally is that some countries have made their choice, while others have not and believe they can 'have it all'. Inherent in choice is ethics. This has, in turn, given rise to an absence of truly viable ideas among decision-makers. In the poignant words of Sheila Collins:[7]

> [w]hile modern science has given us a picture of how the earth system works, it provides no meaningful way for us to appropriate its lessons. That must come through our cultural institutions; but modern Western culture, with its rapacious capacity for accumulation has so far drifted from this elemental understanding of the earth system that it is fast cutting us off from even the reality on which such an understanding must be based.

We aren't simply missing the right sort of institution. Even the most cursory knowledge of the goings on at inter-state environmental negotiations is enough to tell us that we are missing the right kind of self-reflection by decision-makers. It seems that beyond any technical and adaptive problem that global environmental issues confront humans with, the broad-reaching consequences of environmental degradation, across generations, provokes 'deep moral problems that we cannot avoid, but with which our standard ethical frameworks are ill-suited to cope'.[8]

However, not everyone shares this same malady. Beyond the inner circles of states and representatives, there is lively debate. Manifest in the civil society fora that parallel virtually every international environmental conference and meeting, ideas are rapidly and freely exchanged. Herein lies a commons – of ideas. The inevitable corollary of commons movement is

---

[7] Sheila D. Collins, 'Interrogating and Reconceptualizing Natural Law to Protect the Integrity of the Earth', in Laura Westra, Klaus Bosselmann and Richard Westra (eds), *Reconciling Human Existence with Ecological Integrity* (Earthscan, London 2008): 457.

[8] William B. Griffith, 'Trusteeship: A Practical Option for Realizing Our Obligations to Future Generations?', in Andrew Light and Avner De-Shalit (eds), *Moral and Political Reasoning in Environmental Practice* (The MIT Press, Cambridge, MA 2003).

that attacks on the commons will therefore continue. This, argues Bollier, 'will entail new attempts to criminalize the behaviour of commoners for resisting enclosure – and this will result in various sorts of litigation, social conflict, repression, imprisonment and war'.[9] In the context of the follow-up from the 'Rio+20' Conference in 2012, we need, more than ever, to go beyond the environmental governance deadlock – not only among states, but among the mobilized ecologically minded civil society, and states.

As this chapter will reveal, ideas do exist. Although there are a variety of possible ways to manage the commons, depending on what phenomenon is being discussed, this volume asserts that trusteeship is the logical form of governance for the global commons. Trusteeship is a system of governance imbued with an ethic fundamental to the human–nature relationship and is vitally necessary if we are going to maintain the basis of all life. In the words of Jack Manno, 'it is not the earth that needs healing but our relationship to it'.[10] The challenge is how to affect this in both a moral and legal way. The best way to ensure that this healing happens and lasts is to 'incorporate into our governing institutions, practices that restore relationships of respect, gratitude and reciprocal care between humans, our nations and the rest of the world'.[11]

Unfortunately, dichotomous thinking has served to obscure the ubiquity of trusteeship as a form of governance, one rooted in human history, yet unconsidered as a viable governance system. Hence this chapter is borne of a necessity to remind ourselves of the history and roots of trusteeship in Western and non-Western tradition. The chapter also seeks to locate trusts and trusteeship in existing legal expression and use. The aim is to offer trusteeship as an idea, already existing and proven effective, to be examined and crafted into a model of governance for sustainability of the global commons. So, although this volume discusses what ought to be done about governance of the global commons, the ultimate issue is an ethical one, and ethics will determine how humans, as moral agents, use their potential.

---

[9] David Bollier, 'The Future of the Commons: Notes from a retreat exploring the potential of the commons to fight enclosures and build commons-based alternatives' (Retreat on the Future of the Commons, Crottorf Castle, Germany, June 2009): http://commonstrust.globalnegotiations.org/resources/Bollier,%20Crottorf%20retreat.pdf.

[10] Jack P. Manno, 'Haudenosaunee Great Law of Peace: A Model for Global Environmental Governance', in Ron Engel, Laura Westra and Klaus Bosselmann (eds), *Democracy, Ecological Integrity and International Law* (Cambridge Scholars Publishing, Newcastle upon Tyne 2010): 158.

[11] Ibid.: 158–159.

2. THE STATUS QUO

In order to propose changes to global commons governance, we need to canvas the existing regimes in Chapter 2. Similarly now we revisit the status quo and consider the fact that despite some 40 years of advanced environmental policy and law, international environmental law has failed to halt the continuing rapid decline of earth's ecological systems.[12] Law and governance is failing the environment. At this point, it is instructive to consider again, as we do throughout the volume, what it is we require from law and governance. Chiefly we need a different paradigm within which to place human interaction with nature. We need to establish a non-monetized metric to evaluate the sustainability, quality of life and well-being of a commons and its community of users and producers – human and non-human.[13] The three overarching requirements from environmental governance are, first and foremost, the need to safeguard the environment from exploitation, second the need to ensure the marginalized have access to resources, and third the need to distribute profits from common pool resources equitably and justly. Simply put, the normative principles that are necessary in global commons governance are responsibility, equity – in the form of fair access and shared benefit – and democracy.[14] To the extent that the law fails to facilitate this, we fail to protect that which is most vital to all life.

Because of humans' role in the biosphere and our intelligence, we occupy the role of stewards. The law needs to reflect a fundamental principle of responsibility, recognizable as a fundamental legal principle like justice or human rights.[15] Responsibility is about long-term benefits – thinking about current and future generations of humans, and about the intrinsic value of nature itself. Guiding our actions as responsible actors is the principle of sustainability,[16] in particular the consideration that 'the principle of sustainability has its roots in ecological insights rather than

---

[12] Prue Taylor, 'The Imperative of Responsibility in a Legal Context: Reconciling Responsibilities with Rights', in Laura Westra, Klaus Bosselmann and Richard Westra (eds), *Reconciling Human Existence with Ecological Integrity* (Earthscan, London 2008).

[13] Global Commons Trust, 'The Commons': http://globalcommonstrust.org/?page_id=11.

[14] Silke Helfrich and Jörg Haas, 'The Commons: A New Narrative for Our Time', in Silke Heinrich (ed.), *Genes, Bytes and Emissions: To Whom Does the World Belong?* (Henrich Böll Stiftung, Berlin 2008): http://us.boell.org/sites/default/files/downloads/CommonsBook_Helfrich_-_Haas-neu.pdf.

[15] Klaus Bosselmann, *The Principle of Sustainability: Transforming Law and Governance* (Ashgate, Farnham 2008).

[16] Ibid.

legal anthropocentrism. And it is not compromised in a way that the concept of sustainable development currently is'.[17]

With this in mind we face a major obstacle in the fact that neither of our existing property regimes – private or public – has a mandate to guarantee long-term protection. Responsibility, it seems, is antithetical to how we conceive of the property rights that define our relationship to the earth. The law is traditionally rights focused, meaning that individual freedoms are articulated as legal rights. While this is not inherently problematic, the lack of corresponding duties has given rise to an imbalance. The vast system of 'property' confers rights to protect individual freedoms from interference, by the state or other individuals. These individual rights are framed as the driving force behind economic growth and indeed the entire fabric of societies.

There are two main problems here. First, only human interests are enunciated and given legal status. Second, our property rights are only limited when they impinge on other people's ability to exercise their rights. Responsibility, in the short and long term, for nature, and the collective interest in a healthy environment are not a part of this property paradigm. Where responsibility enters into the legal equation is in terms of post-facto attribution of liability or guilt (responsibility) for the consequences of acts or omissions.[18] Sheila Collins aptly describes the dilemma of modern law:[19]

> While we can be grateful to Locke for advancing the dignity of the human individual at a time of monarchical authoritarianism and providing the intellectual legitimacy for rebellion against tyranny, his philosophy nevertheless, owes its preoccupations to its author's social location on 'this side of the line'. The intellectual memes that his conception of Natural Law perpetuated have left us bereft of the intellectual, ethical, and political resources we need to prevent the swift dismemberment of Mother Earth.

Thus, as Taylor explains, rights need corresponding responsibilities. Collective benefit should define the scope of individual freedoms, not the other way around.[20] Lucy and Mitchell argue that 'it is not feasible to claim the most extensive rights of exclusion, control and alienation over a resource, and yet be subject to a vast range of duties in relation to that resource for the benefit of other persons', as would be the case if we were to constantly amend private property to restrictions.[21] The two are simply

---

[17] Ibid.: 178.

[18] Taylor (note 12): 210.

[19] Collins (note 7): 448.

[20] Taylor (note 12): 207.

[21] William N.R. Lucy and Catherine Mitchell, 'Replacing Private Property: The Case for Stewardship' (1996) 55 (3) *CLJ* 566, 586.

unable to be weighed equally. Ecological health must come before the discretion to use, otherwise how can environmental goals be achieved? Rather than an assault on personal freedoms, environmental responsibilities are designed to ultimately protect freedoms by ensuring that we all, presently and in the future, can enjoy healthy lives via a healthy planet.

3. TRYING FOR A BETTER SYSTEM

So what should we do? If we think about the way that law develops, it is usually in reaction to (more rarely proactive for) a certain social need for regulation. The law is grounded in experience, a set of factual needs, and is subsequently interpreted, putatively 'in flux', and evolved. With regards to the environment, legislators and legal professions 'have clung to the statutory claims that are most familiar to them',[22] meaning that they have sought to apply the law to the environment, rather than develop the law from the environment. It reflects a fundamental methodological flaw in the way the law deals with the environment. Yet this is the most common approach by governments in both domestic systems and at international level to avoid environmental problems; by expanding the body of environmental regulation, essentially adding more subject matter to the law we apply to the environment in an attempt to correct the imbalance.[23]

However, as many scholars have bemoaned over the decades, this approach is slow, piecemeal, reactive rather than proactive, and proceeds without any fundamental problematization of the ideological tenets of the problem: anthropocentric property rights, the sanctity of economic growth and the ensuing commodification of nature and its resources. These are ideological fundaments, which, as Taylor rightly states, are 'core pillars of the legal system which create incentive for ecological harm'.[24] Domestic environmental regulation may attempt to protect 'collective interest' in some well-governed states but the contest between property rights and collective rights in a healthy environment is an imbalanced one. Moreover, too often the true objects of protection are not even recognized as part of a collective interest.

Nor, as White explains, is the problem going to be solved by science and technology, despite most states feeling the most comfortable with

---

[22] Carla A. Wise, 'Green All the Lawyers', Interview of Mary C. Wood, Utne Magazine (September–October 2008): http://www.utne.com/environment/green-all-the-lawyers.aspx.

[23] Taylor (note 12): 204.

[24] Ibid.

'adaptive' strategies available through technological advancement. Technology may be a crucial part of dealing with damage, but in terms of solving the problem it cannot deal with the root of this crisis – the attitudes held by humans towards the environment. Until this can be addressed, there will be no solution. Technology does however have the potential to improve monitoring.

Another broad solution is that of expanding rights.[25] Two themes have emerged, one emphasizing human rights to a healthy environment, the other emphasizing rights for nature.[26] The former are included in many European countries' constitutions. While both sorts of rights are undoubtedly necessary, the concern with the rights approach is that the former is anthropocentric and distracts from the feeling of duty to value nature *for itself* and the latter forces new rights 'holders' (nature) to compete against other rights holders (humans) in a contest of moral norms. And, devoid of a radical shift in ethics, we already know which rights holders have the acute advantage in a flawed legal arena.[27] 'Overcoming the individual rights focus of the law will not be resolved by simply writing "responsibilities" into the law. The task is more complex than that.'[28] Nevertheless, proponents argue that such rights-based approaches are not a panacea, but a first step in the process of more ambitious jurisprudential evolution which grows out of the establishment of a first basic right.[29]

Why does the law find the task of reconciling legal rights with responsibilities for the protection of nature so difficult? We have already outlined the centrality of private property in law. But on an even more elemental level, it boils down to the fact that in most Anglo–American legal systems morality is separate from law.[30] International law has likewise developed in this positivistic philosophical environment and it is only relatively recently that international law has become interested in concepts of fundamental human rights, and moral considerations. Yet, as we saw from the previous chapter, moral considerations such as the rights of future generations and common heritage are not stalwart parts of international law. Nevertheless,

---

[25] Ibid.: 205.

[26] Christopher Stone, 'Should Trees Have Standing? Towards Legal Rights for Natural Objects' (1972) 45 *CLR* 450.

[27] Prue Taylor, 'From Environmental to Ecological Human Rights: A New Dynamic in International Law' (1998) 10 (2) *Geo. Int'l Env. L. Rev.* 309, 377.

[28] Taylor (note 12): 200.

[29] See Tim Hayward, 'Constitutional Environmental Rights: A Case for Political Analysis', in Andrew Light and Avner De-Shalit (eds), *Moral and Political Reasoning in Environmental Practice* (The MIT Press, Cambridge, MA 2003).

[30] Taylor (note 12): 202–203.

there are many noteworthy attempts by civil society groups to inject environmental responsibility into our conceptions of fundamental legal principles, for example, the International Union for the Conservation of Nature (IUCN) Draft International Covenant on the Environment and Development, and the Earth Charter.

The ongoing task of environmental law is 'to understand our place in nature and to reconcile individual (legal) rights with responsibilities toward the collective . . . *all life* on earth'.[31] Christian Siefkes echoes many other commons scholars by calling for a 'paradigm shift' from private property and market emphasis to jointly organized and jointly managed commons.[32] Rejecting the law's private property dogma clears conceptual space for other methods of regulating our relationship with land but his rejection does not automatically make the case for a particular solution, and indeed there are various options for affecting responsibility through commons organization.[33]

Domestically, suggestions include co-management arrangements where everyone has joint responsibility through their shared management role, contracts (such as social charters) which declare intentions and rules that guide behaviour, and trusts where representatives are appointed to hold responsibility.[34] Likewise, courts may interpret the law to include the rights and legal standing of future generations, perhaps even the rights of nature, although as already stated this raises the question of emphases.

Internationally, there are a number of solutions being mooted, mainly by civil society, though some have gained political traction, especially in the EU. Many relate to amending existing international institutions. The Consultative Group of Ministers on International Environmental Governance Reform have made recommendations for reform to the United Nations Economic and Social Council (ECOSOC) and the Commission on Sustainable Development (CSD). The suggestions include merging the two into a Council on Sustainable Development, allowing for greater convergence between the environmental, social and economic pillars of sustainable development, and greater synergy across the UN system.[35]

Another suggestion is upgrading the United Nations Environment Programme (UNEP) into a specialized agency, with the possible name:

---

[31] Taylor (note 12): 199.

[32] Christian Siefkes, 'The Commons of the Future: Building Blocks for a Commons-based Society', in Silke Heinrich (ed.), *Genes, Bytes and Emissions: To Whom Does the World Belong?* (Henrich Böll Stiftung, Berlin 2008).

[33] Lucy and Mitchell (note 21): 579.

[34] Global Commons Trust (note 13).

[35] Stoddart (note 3): 36.

United Nations Environment Organization (UNEO).[36] The proposal has strong support from France, and has been endorsed by the EU Council and UN Secretary General as well as developing countries such as Algeria, Ecuador, Cambodia, Vanuatu, Seychelles, Gabon and Burundi, and various civil society actors.[37] Often called 'the French Proposal', the UNEO would operate similarly to the World Health Organization (WHO) and World Trade Organization (WTO) as the umbrella environmental organization with 'on the ground' functions but without the authority to adjudicate on international environmental disputes.[38] It would be the premier environmental agenda-setting body, as well as the environmental watchdog. Central to this idea is a funding mechanism of assessed contributions rather than voluntary contributions.[39]

The Consultative Group of Ministers for International Environmental Governance have presented the idea of a World Environmental Organization which is similar to the UNEO, although it uses a different name and has some divergence in terms of mandates and functions of the organization.[40] The proposal similarly holds support from European states and developing states. Other suggestions include the creation of an International Environmental Court, with jurisdiction to address issues such as access to justice and scientific understanding.[41] This option is an incentivizing and enforcement mechanism for existing Multilateral Environmental Agreements (MEAs) and governance regimes, and also allows for clarification of treaty obligations, dispute resolution and advisory opinions.

Ultimately, global commons governance would operate through states' MEAs and the Court. Unlike the ICJ, the IEC would grant standing not just to states, but to non-state entities such as corporations, civil society groups and individuals.[42] This option is favoured by many as an adjunct to other institutions such as a UNEO or a World Environment Organization (WEO). Currently, it is being advocated by an international network of

---

[36] Ibid.: 42.

[37] Stoddart (note 3): 42; see also Bharat Desai, *International Environmental Governance: Towards UNEPO* (Brill Nijhoff, Leiden 2014), on proposing such an organization under the name of the United Nations Environment Protection Organization (UNEPO), linking it closely with UNEP. Desai considers the establishment of UNEPO as a useful step towards creating a mandate for a 'new trust' to revive the UN Trusteeship Council (ibid.: xv).

[38] Stoddart (note 3): 42.

[39] Ibid.: 43.

[40] Ibid.: 45.

[41] Ibid.: 53.

[42] Ibid.: 54.

lawyers and advocates.[43] Similarly, proposals for a Global Environmental Parliament make parallels with the International Labour Organization (ILO), advocating in favour of a body with the tripartite structure of an executive bureau, global subject committees and a global court for the environment, and with membership drawn from state nominations.[44] This proposal departs from other options currently being mooted because it concentrates on accountability between the upper echelons of global decision-making and civil society.

Enhancing the UN Security Council to include an environmental mandate is another suggestion that takes account of the growing 'security' dimension of environmental degradation.[45] Such an extension would necessitate amendment to the UN Charter, and unsurprisingly reception to the idea has been unenthusiastic; the idea hindered by the undemocratic nature of the Council. Other solutions include 'clustering' MEAs for less fragmentation, enhancing inter-agency coordination and reforming the WTO and International Financial Institutions (IFIs). While these are interesting ideas, and certainly viewed by states as quite radical, they nevertheless fail to confront the ethical dimensions of the environmental crisis. They are readjustments of the status quo rather than new solutions.

Another much-mooted idea is that of a global environmental ombudsman or commissioner for future generations that would act as an ombudsperson, conveying citizen concerns, ensuring policy coherence, advising on and recommending solutions, and auditing implementation, road blocks and conflicts of interest.[46] This may include bringing judicial review of decisions by the executive but may also include an advisory, educative and mediatory role. The idea of ombudspeople, or at international level

---

43 See ICE Coalition, 'Creating the International Court for the Environment': http://www.icecoalition.com.

44 Stoddart (note 3): 57.

45 Ibid.: 59–60.

46 Maja Göpel, *Guarding Our Future: How to Include Future Generations in Policy Making* (World Future Council, Hamburg 2010): 3; Edith Brown Weiss, *In Fairness to Future Generations: International Law, Common Patrimony and Intergenerational Equity* (United Nations/Transnational Publishers, New York 1989): 124–126; Glen Plant, 'Institutional and Legal Responses to Global Warming', in Robin Churchill and David Freestone (eds), *International Law and Global Climate Change* (Graham & Trotman/Nijhoff, London 1991): 176; Christopher D. Stone, 'Defending the Global Commons', in Philippe Sands (ed.), *Greening International Law* (Earthscan, London 1993); Christopher D. Stone, *The Gnat is Older Than Man: Global Environment and the Human Agenda* (Princeton University Press, Princeton, NJ 1993): 83–88; Nico Schrijver, 'International Organization for Environmental Security' (1989) 20 (2) *Bulletin of Peace Proposals* 115, 120–121.

a possible High Commissioner for Future Generations, is part of a civil society push for global environmental governance to take 'the long view'.[47] The Experts Group on Environmental Law of the Brundtland Commission recommended the appointment of an international ombudsperson in the form of a UN High Commissioner for Environmental Protection and Sustainable Development with a role in both monitoring compliance and policy recommendation.[48] The Maltese also suggested that the role of a guardian of future generations should be included in the 1992 Rio Declaration, an idea ultimately rejected by drafters in favour of a mention in Agenda 21 of 'other institutional initiatives' of the kind discussed here.

There are examples of ombudspeople in many democratic states. They are usually a watchdog on executive, working in conjunction with administrative and public law to maintain accountability and transparency in political governance. New Zealand has had a Parliamentary Commissioner for the Environment since 1986, who effectively acts as an independent environmental ombudsperson. The Commissioner has been a source of serious and genuine analysis of domestic environmental policy and law. In a similar move, Israel's parliament established a Commission for Future Generations in 2001 to provide a voice for sustainable thinkers alongside the usual considerations of money and power.[49] Hungary also has a Parliamentary Commissioner for Future Generations who has an investigative and policy advisory role to ensure the protection of the fundamental right to a healthy environment.[50]

The ombudsperson idea is a prelude to the idea of trusteeship and is encouragingly gathering support within civil society. However, with all these recommendations for an ombudsperson, a commissioner or even a UN guardian, comes the reality that one person will have limited ability to influence the scope of international obligations. The Commission on Sustainable Development that arose from the 1992 Earth Summit has no powers of negotiation or intervention, but maintains a mainly monitoring function despite not being able to review the implementation and effectiveness of MEAs.

---

[47] See Halina Ward, 'Committing to the Future We Want: A High Commissioner for Future Generations at Rio+20', Discussion Paper (Foundation for Democracy and Sustainable Development, World Future Council, March 2012); see also Future Justice at http://www.futurejustice.org.

[48] Experts Group on Environmental Law, 'Proposals for Strengthening the Legal and Institutional Framework', in R.D. Munro and J.G. Lammers (eds), *Environmental Protection and Sustainable Development: Legal Principles and Recommendations* (Graham & Trotman/Nijhoff, London/Boston 1987): 15.

[49] Maja Göpel (note 46): 7.

[50] Ibid.: 8.

4. THE IDEA OF TRUSTEESHIP

Responsibility is 'an affirmative call to guard and protect'.[51] In recalling German philosopher Hans Jonas, Prue Taylor argues that when responsibility is imagined as a positive duty of power, people become committed because something is 'entrusted'. The example that most self-evidently springs to mind is the parent–child relationship.[52] Thus, to affect responsibility this volume proffers the idea of trusteeship because it presents an applicable legal solution and an ethical approach.

Similarly, Lucy and Mitchell argue that the notion of stewardship ought to replace the notion of private property in our thinking and everyday philosophical and legal language.[53] Their goal is not so much to examine stewardship as a notion central to our environmental salvation, but to posit stewardship as the alternative to private property which adequately addresses what the latter lacks.

In domestic law, it would look like people such as landowners with property rights subject to others' rights and environmental regulations, transformed into stewards. Internationally, both states and non-state actors such as large multinationals would likewise become stewards, a role which would define their relationship with nature. Mary Wood, a leading authority on the public trust doctrine, argues that the trust frame allows for the reconciliation of private property and public resources in environmental governance: 'to confront any environmental crisis today, including global warming, we have to be clear on how public resources and private property rights fit together in the scheme of things'.[54] Wood argues that the very act of securing our 'public' property through the trust also anchors our entire system of private property rights.[55] Her logic is flawless: 'all private property depends on Nature's infrastructure. When that infrastructure collapses, it causes natural disasters that make property boundaries irrelevant.'[56] The difference in the human–nature relationship is that it goes from coercion to environmental protection to personal initiative. This is the kind of valuing – the ethical infusion beyond mere rules and enforcement – that must be present in the legal system. Trusteeship for

---

51 Taylor (note 12): 211.

52 Hans Jonas, *The Imperative of Responsibility: In Search of an Ethics for the Technological Age* (University of Chicago Press, Chicago 1984).

53 Lucy and Mitchell (note 21): 566.

54 Mary Wood, 'Nature's Trust: A Legal, Political and Moral Frame for Global Warming' (2007) 34 *Environmental Affairs* 601.

55 Ibid.: 602.

56 Ibid.

the global commons is the intellectual, visible and tangible manifestation of responsibility for the community of life. It provides not only a legal and institutional solution, but a paradigm shift that takes with it the question of environmental ethics.

4.1 Origins

The remainder of this chapter looks at the concept of trusteeship, before, in the final chapters, proposing what trusteeship for the global commons might actually involve and look like. Trusteeship is analogous to stewardship or guardianship, though we use the word 'trusteeship' to describe the arrangement because it is relatable to the legally recognized institution of the trust which we intend to draw on as a source of inspiration.

Most of the world's great cultures, spiritual and religious traditions reflect an ancient wisdom that the land and the people are one. The interdependence of humans and nature provides the impetus for a non-derogable relationship of guardianship and it 'requires humanity to care for and respect nature, beyond the fulfilment of human interests and needs'.[57] The concept of present generations' responsibility, and thus trusteeship for future generations, was famously discussed by the Vice-President of the International Court of Justice, Christopher Weeramantry, in his separate opinion for the *Case Concerning the Gabčikovo-Nagmaros Project*. Judge Weeramantry stated that sustainable development is not merely a principle of international law but one of the most ancient ideas in human heritage.[58] In his view, concepts of trusteeship and sustainable development are, and always have been, a part of international law; much like universal ideals such as human rights. His review took in the ancient irrigation schemes of Sri Lanka, Tanzania, Iran and China, the teachings of Buddhism, the *Tao Te Ching* from China, and African and native American teachings on intergenerational considerations, in each case highlighting the importance of development within the constraints of environmental sustainability.

Religion is an important area to consider when looking into the origins of stewardship, guardianship and trusteeship. This is because how we think about ecology is inextricably linked to how we see ourselves in relation to things around us; that is, our beliefs about nature and destiny.[59]

---

[57] Taylor (note 12): 199.

[58] *Case Concerning the Gabçíkovo-Nagymaros Project (Hungary v Slovakia) (Separate Opinion of Vice President Christopher Weeramantry)* [1997] ICJ Rep 7, 108; 37 ILM 162 (1998).

[59] Lynn Townsend White Jr, 'The Historical Roots of Our Ecological Crisis' (1967) 155 (3767) *Science* 1203.

From time immemorial, it has been the domain of religion to shape our ideas and beliefs. Scholars differ in their opinions about the role of religion in encouraging environmental stewardship. Most critics argue that all major religions are anthropocentric. For example, within Christianity there is a strong association with the dualism of man and nature – that is, man's god-given right to exploit and have dominion over the earth.[60] Genesis 1:28 states: 'be fruitful and multiply' and 'have dominion over the fish of the sea', often quoted in both Judaism and Christianity as justification for the exploitation of nature for man's needs. However, others also point to Genesis 2:15, where God takes the newly created man 'and placed him in the garden of Eden, to cultivate it and to guard it'.[61] Likewise, they highlight the teachings of Saint Francis of Assisi.

In Judaism, God is the owner of all things; man simply has possession rights in varying stages of complexity. The longer-term solution to environmental problems depends upon our ability to re-educate ourselves and our children towards humility – towards *anavah* – and moderation.[62]

Trusts called *waqf* were developed in the Muslim world as early as the seventh century. In Islam, there is an understanding of nature found in the Qu'ran's lack of a clear demarcation between the natural and supernatural, between man and nature. In Islam, God is nature and the environmental crisis stems from a refusal to see the environment as the embodiment of God, surrounding and nourishing life.[63]

In Hinduism, there is a need for harmony with all forms of life, as their destinies are inextricably linked.[64]

In the oneness of Buddhist teaching and the pursuit of awakening, greed and concerns for the self are to be set aside in favour of an appreciation of humanity's place in the environment, the world and all living things.[65]

More recently, the ethical and religious attitude of valuing nature for its own sake and seeing it as divine or spiritually vital has been called

---

60 John G. Walton, 'The Concept of Trusteeship in International Environmental Law' (unpublished LLM thesis, University of Auckland): 5.

61 Ibid.: 15.

62 Rabbi Saul Berman, 'Jewish Environmental Values: The Dynamic Tension between Nature and Human Needs' (Jewish Virtual Library, 1992): http://www.jewishvirtuallibrary.org/jsource/Environment/berman.html, quoted in Walton (note 60): 15.

63 Seyyed Hossein Nasr, 'Islam and the Environmental Crisis', in Steven C. Rockerfeller and John Elder (eds), *Spirit and Nature: Why the Environment is a Religious Issue* (Beacon Press, Boston 1992).

64 Walton (note 60): 14.

65 Ibid.: 15.

'deep ecology'.[66] The crucial point is that although opinion and interpretation differ, there is an identifiable religious recognition of the concept of trusteeship. Barnhill and Gottlieb point out, however, that most religions were blind to the environmental crisis until it was pointed out to them (usually by scientists), although most religions now see nature, or see nature *again*, as deserving of care, stewardship and respect.[67] The reason why stewardship and hence trusteeship arise time and time again in religion is that common to all religions is a deity that is the true owner of the earth, for whom humans act as trustees, and who are also beneficiaries alongside future generations.

Interestingly, indigenous peoples are often associated with stewardship philosophies. For the New Zealand Maori, welfare comes from ethical relations with nature. They say: *Te toto o te tangata, he kai; te orange o te tangata, he whenua* – the blood of humans comes from food, our welfare comes from land. The central concept of *kaitiakitanga* or guardianship arose after the Maori hunted some native New Zealand species to extinction. It is estimated that within the first 100 years of colonization by early Maori, moa, the flightless goose, adzebill, swan and pelican were hunted to the point of extinction. Sea mammals were similarly decimated.[68]

Population pressures and the growth of agriculture also resulted in the descendants of those early settlers abandoning their semi-nomadic lifestyles and adapting their island lore to a new indigenous culture [*Te Ao Maori*]. This approach to respecting all living things and preserving their life forces [*mauri*] brought with it rules governing exploitation necessary to balance human need with preservation, and protection of that life force. Andrea Tunks describes the role of *kaitiaki*, or guardians, as central in maintaining the *utu* [balance or value] and hence mauri of all life.[69] Kaitiaki are both trustee and beneficiary, and they maintain a socially recognized discretion to place ecologically exhausted resources or areas under a *rahui* or ban.

From indigenous and religious narratives is revealed a working model of a healthy human–nature relationship and we see this echo throughout other social and religious mores. Thus, to proffer trusteeship as a means of global commons governance is not a new idea but a revival of an ancient

---

[66] David Landis Barnhill and Roger Gottlieb, 'Introduction', in David Landis Barnhill and Roger S. Gottlieb (eds), *Deep Ecology and World Religions: New Essays on Sacred Ground* (State University of New York Press, Albany, NY 2001): 1.

[67] Ibid.: 3.

[68] Walton (note 60): 11.

[69] Andrea Tunks, 'Tangata Whenua Ethics and Climate Change' (1997) 1 *NZ J Envtl L*. 67.

wisdom. It takes us back to the root of a balance between humanity and nature. Indeed, the citation of indigenous knowledge as a solid basis for environmental governance is at best thought of as a romantic and far-fetched approach quite apart from the environmental credentials of modern-day indigenous populations, or what remain of them.

Such attitudes hark back to racist colonial days when only Europeans were thought to be industrious and rational in contrast to the hunter-gatherer lifestyles of indigenous peoples, thus justifying their large-scale appropriation of uncultivated land for the purpose of rational use and industry guided by a complete lack of ecological knowledge and ethics.[70] What has occurred since is 'a massive epistemicide'[71] of traditional knowledge and language. While one would like to believe that we have moved beyond such narrow-mindedness, the lack of credence for alternative, often indigenous, ways of expressing knowledge and wisdom still reveals these attitudes, especially in the arena of states where such high politics couldn't possibly consider such things as local knowledge and indigenous methodologies with their spiritual trappings.

Commons trusts have existed on a small scale for centuries, it is just that indigenous and peasant peoples offer the most recent examples of this ancient knowledge.[72] Many feudal cultures had common spaces for grazing, foraging, hunting, planting or gathering wood, which were often located on the margins of civilization. In response to the heavily concentrated power and wealth of such societies, commons trusts were attempts to create equity for the people who relied on these commons for their work and sustenance. The Magna Carta of 1215, the armistice in a civil war between the commoners and King John, contained calls against the exploitation of the forests as ordained by the king who wanted to 'degrade the forests to a source of lumber, convert the lumber into money, and invest it in those who promised him their loyalty'.[73] The Magna Carta spoke of common rights of the forest (Chapters 47 and 48) and the common right of the piscary or fishing rights (Chapter 33).[74] Unfortunately, these parts of the Magna Carta have been excluded in its modern version.[75]

---

[70] Collins (note 7): 452.

[71] Boaventura de Sousa Santos, 'Beyond Abyssal Thinking: From Global Lines to Ecologies of Knowledge' (Eurozine, 18 February 2007): http://www.eurozine.com/articles/2007-06-29-santos-en.html.

[72] Vandana Shiva, *Monocultures of the Mind: Perspectives on Biodiversity and Biotechnology* (Zed Books, London 1993): 12.

[73] Helfrich (note 5).

[74] Ibid.

[75] Bollier (note 9).

Technological development has changed people's relationship with nature, from subsistence farmer connected to the rhythms of his environment to a landholder molding his environment to enhance productivity. In 1967, Lynn Townsend White, Jr, a professor in medieval history, documented how the harnessing of wind and water power and the development of the ploughshare allowed artisans to develop efficient methods of farming on a greater scale, forever altering the human–nature relationship from 'part of' to 'exploiter', ushering in an age of the dualism of man and nature.[76] In his view, Christianity moved to legitimate this dualist relationship, thereby separating two moral spheres – religion and ecologism – and portending the central thesis of later legal positivists on the separation of law and morality.[77] Skolimowski argues that our 'cosmology' is now based on mechanistic and empirical science, instead of on humanistic notions and morality toward nature.[78]

According to Sheila Collins, Western culture has appropriated 'knowledge'. Thus, what has been passed down for many centuries now as 'universal knowledge' is very parochial. Collins, like others, believes that '[o]ur ability to reserve earth's integrity is now deeply compromised by our reliance on this one form'.[79] Evernden argues that since the post-Enlightenment period, Western society's humans have been akin to aliens because they have a self-identity distinct from the world around them, which has in turn given rise to the instrumentalist approach to nature.[80] The teachings of St Francis of Assisi are eclipsed by a pervasive religion of consumerism. Although the narrative of environmental attitudes is by no means an exclusively Western one, the spiritual, moral and social context of the attitudes which underlie that most pervasive Western export – economic liberalism – *are* central to understanding the goings-on of international relations in environmental matters. Consequently, 'a process of deep civilizational self-reflection is called for'.[81] This drives the consideration of ethics that must accompany any genuine consideration of anthropocentric environmental degradation and this is why a discussion of indigenous culture and tradition is pertinent to a discussion of environmental ethics.

---

76 Townsend White (note 59).

77 Ibid.

78 Henryk Skolimowski, *Eco-Philosophy* (Boyars, London 1981).

79 Collins (note 7): 445.

80 N. Everdeen, *The Natural Alien: Humankind and the Environment*, 2nd edn (University of Toronto Press, Toronto 1993).

81 Collins (note 7): 445.

CASE STUDY

The Great Law of Peace is the founding constitution of the Confederacy of the Six Nations of the Haudenosaunee [*people of the longhouse*] or Iroquois. It represents a working model of governance which has internalized the concept of trusteeship for the environment.

The Great Law of Peace began when a prophet convinced five rival nations to quite literally bury their weapons beneath the tree of peace on the shore of Onondaga Lake.[82] From thereon, anyone could follow the four roots of the tree back to its trunk and find shelter there, provided they were willing to live by the Great Law of Peace.[83] While the Great Law of Peace grew, not out of an environmental crisis and need for governance, but from blood feuds among different peoples, it is nevertheless an example of overarching cooperation, including for collective environmental responsibility. As Manno states, the Law 'specifically included and reinforced an ethic of responsible resource management, a perspective of respect and gratitude toward the natural world, a requirement to consider the impacts of decisions on future generations . . . and clear assignment of stewardship responsibilities.'[84] Apparently, what impressed even eighteenth-century liberal philosophers, and why the Law remains a model for governance in 2012, is that the Law 'was able to balance individual liberty, national sovereignty and international cooperation.'[85] The Great Law demonstrates what is necessary for a sustainable society: strong covenantal identity wherein sacrifices are made for the common good, including the survival and well-being of all members, self-limitations on individual and collective behaviour are issued, and responsibilities reach across generations.[86] Some fundamental principles of the Haudenosaunee are useful to consider in the conceptual development of global commons governance.[87] First, 'righteousness' refers to the individual aligning their mind to the welfare of the clan, nation and natural law. Diversity and uniqueness flourish within a setting of unity, consensus and checks and balances which are fundamental to the operation of the confederacy. Not only are decision-makers drawn from all representations but women have ritualistically selected chiefs and acted as a 'check' analogous to the judiciary on the leadership council, women's role a vehicle through which people can appeal for justice. As Manno explains, a cognizance of the spiritual natural world and human gratitude toward it underlie all proceedings in the form of ritualistic start and finish addresses.[88] According to the Haudenosaunee, humans were endowed with intelligence so that they might recognize and appreciate their dependence on non-human things. Crucially to our discussion of the commons, the Haudenosaunee

82 Manno (note 10): 161.
83 Ibid.
84 Ibid.
85 Ibid.: 162.
86 Ibid.
87 Ibid.: 164.
88 Ibid.: 165.

also have principles for commons management. Settled areas or 'clearings' were the exclusive management concern of individual nations, but unsettled areas such as woods were open to all Haudenosaunee, although the nation within whose territory the area fell was responsible for its management.[89] Scholars of governance systems and in particular indigenous governance systems have continually emphasized that the success of governance depends on the internalization of these social norms.[90] As the Mohawk scholar Taiaiake Alfred explains, the native concept of governance is based on the primacy of conscience of individuals and persuasion by leaders.[91] The Great Law illustrates how an arrangement can provide for social justice in the sense of shared resources, but also the assurance of sound environmental management and observation of ecosystem limits through collective responsibility that utilizes local leadership and knowledge of natural systems.

While it is important to remember that indigenous peoples are diverse and heterogeneous, the critical element among all indigenous people is an ethic of stewardship arising from a direct relationship with nature and its resources – both practically and within cosmology. To the extent that this balance has been upset in modern times, through the almost universal assault on indigenous peoples the world over, they are the canary in the coalmine – the portent of ecological imbalance and crisis. Importantly, indigenous peoples seem to personify an environmentalism wherein humans and nature can co-exist harmoniously.

Because simply excluding humans from parts of nature does nothing to address the relationship, this principle of harmony and balance is a useful one – representing a truly adequate equilibrium quite distinct from the mythical balance advanced by 'sustainable development'.[92] Ironically, as already stated earlier, in international environmental governance those regimes which have instituted outright bans on certain harmful activity seem to have done better than regulatory regimes. Nevertheless, the challenge of sustainability is finding the human–nature equilibrium. The fact that cultures have in the past been able to manage their commons sustainably for centuries indicates that such balance is possible, but this stems from some eco-philosophical fundaments in spirituality and social organization. To echo Helfrich and Haas, the point is not to speak of a romantic idea of society, but rather to show that indeed there are examples

---

89 Ibid.

90 Ibid.: 163.

91 Taiaiake Alfred, quoted in ibid.: 163.

92 For a discussion of weak versus strong sustainable development, see Bosselmann (note 15).

of governance and relationships between humans and nature that demonstrate we need not reduce the individual to a mere consumer, contractual partner or seller of his labour.[93] An equally compelling role that may be tens of thousands of years old is that of the steward. The purpose of this chapter is to demonstrate how modern law can begin to relax its formalism, and open itself up to an 'important and fertile source of nourishment' found in the traditional wisdom of humanity.[94]

4.2 Academic Literature

Environmental trusteeship is not a new idea in academia either. And in the context of the Rio+20 Conference and the ensuing debates over what governance of the global environment should look like, it is an apt time to rekindle the idea and posit it as a viable and promising option for decision-makers to consider. Arguably, the person responsible for advocating stewardship ethics was Aldo Leopold, a wildlife game manager distressed at what humans were doing to the environment, and who in 1948 published *A Sand County Almanac* which introduced the idea of 'land ethic': 'A thing is right when it tends to preserve the integrity, stability, and beauty of the biotic community. It is wrong when it tends otherwise.'[95] Leopold devoted his career to the meanings and implications of environmental stewardship, arguing that private land owners are responsible as stewards for their property for the common good of humans and nature.[96]

Contemporaries such as Peter Sand and Christopher Stone have drawn on stewardship ethics and advocated in favour of an internationally legal institutional solution of trusteeship for the environment. In Stone's opinion, ecological damage done in the commons by states or private interests is tantamount to theft – meaning that greenhouse gas emissions are a seizure of common property.[97] He posits that a trust fund for the global commons ought to capitalize on revenues from all commons-connected activities by taxing all activity in the sea from beyond the traditional three or 12 miles from the coastline, and that these revenues should be spent on

---

93 Helfrich and Haas (note 14): 12.

94 C.G. Weeramantry, 'Foreword', in M.C. Segger and A. Khalfan (eds), *Sustainable Development and Law: Principles, Practices, and Prospects* (Oxford University Press, Oxford 2004).

95 Aldo Leopold, *The Essential Aldo Leopold* (Curt Meine and Richard Knight (eds), University of Wisconsin Press, Madison, WI 1999): 311–313.

96 Susan Flader, 'Aldo Leopold and Environmental Citizenship' (1999) 87 *Transactions of the Wisconsin Academy of Science, Arts and Letters* 23.

97 Stone (note 46).

projects for the commons, not given back to states to decide how to spend it on development.[98] This mirrors the 'Norwegian model' where natural resource profits go into a national trust fund to support public goods.

Likewise, other scholars have explored various tenets of the idea. Peter Barnes proposed a 'sky trust' – a system of administering rights to the atmosphere not unlike a cap and trade system, only the proceeds from carbon credits are put into a trust fund for people, not held by states.[99] In the same vein, Mary C. Wood proposes a 'nature's trust'.[100] Walton locates global traditions and world religions playing a crucial role in providing context for the notion of environmental trusteeship, and in his view there are clearly created *erga omnes* obligations of current generations as trustees of the environment for future generations.[101] V.P. Nanda and William Ris advocated a public trust doctrine approach whereby the state is trustee for the public, of both territorial and commons areas, a notion which will be explored thoroughly in the following chapter.[102] Similarly, the Legal Experts of the Word Commission on Environment and Development (the 'Brundtland Commission') also advocated the environmental trusteeship role of the state. Redgwell suggests a revamping of the UN Trusteeship Council into a 'collective trusteeship' with an oversight function; ensuring that states and international environmental treaty institutions fulfil their agreed-on obligations for the benefit of present and future generations.[103]

The treatment is cross-disciplinary. Stewardship economics has arisen, infusing considerations of private property and market-based environmental solutions.[104] Similarly in social psychology, the economics of trust as an organizing principle demonstrates how trust is a fundamental human social principle and hence an implicit solution for the management

---

[98] Ibid.

[99] Peter Barnes, *Capitalism 2.0.: Who Owns the Sky? Our Common Assets and the Future of Capitalism* (Island Press, Washington, DC 2001).

[100] Mary C. Wood, *Nature's Trust: Environmental Law for a New Ecological Age* (Cambridge University Press, Cambridge 2013).

[101] Walton (note 60).

[102] V.P. Nanda and W. Jr Ris, 'The Public Trust Doctrine: A Viable Approach to International Environmental Protection' (1976) 5 *Ecology LQ* 291.

[103] See Catherine Redgwell, 'Reforming the UN Trusteeship Council', in W. Bradnee Chambers and Jessica F. Green (eds), *Reforming International Environmental Governance: From Institutional Limits to Innovative Reforms* (United Nations University Press, Tokyo 2005).

[104] Michael D. Young and Bonnie J. McCay, 'Building Equity, Stewardship, and Resilience into Market Based Property Rights Systems', in Susan Hanna and Mohan Munasinghe (eds), *Property Rights and the Environment: Social and Ecological Issues* (Beijer International Institute of Ecological Economics/The World Bank, Washington, DC 1995).

of socially governed problems.[105] Edith Brown Weiss, the leading scholar on intergenerational equity, has advocated in favour of a planetary trust which holds the whole of earth's natural and cultural heritage for present and future generations, although in her scheme the administration of it would be decentralized.[106] Likewise, Mary Wood views the intergenerational promise of trusteeship as a particularly empowering notion for young people.[107] Perhaps this will herald the sea-change of ethics and the re-entrenchment of stewardship among a new generation capable of rejecting an exclusively neo-liberal path dependency. This is an important point, picked up also by Stone who points out that the establishment of guardians is no panacea to this scale of commons degradation, nor other environmental degradation. Rather, the strength of this concept will be in the changes that it precipitates, because once the damage is done the effects can rarely be contained.

However, as Peter Sand rightly points out, 'the topic, it seems, has ceased to be academic'.[108] This is unsurprising given its deep social roots and the uncomplicated premise of the idea of trusteeship, stewardship and guardianship. Several civil society groups who concern themselves with the commons advocate in favour of a Global Commons Trust to promote the creation of trusteeships within broader society, thereby realizing everyone's rights to our commons and its shared benefit for all.[109] The Global Commons Trust is calling for the creation of an inclusive, high-level international panel to discuss global commons problems and recommend solutions.[110]

4.3 What is a Trust?

How does the idea of guardianship, stewardship or trusteeship enable environmental responsibility to be given effect in contrast with the status quo? Lucy and Mitchell explain: '[t]he hallmark of stewardship is land holding subject to responsibilities of careful use, rather than the extensive

---

105 See D.G. Gambetta, 'Can We Trust Trust?', in D.G. Gambetta (ed.), *Trust* (Basil Blackwell, New York 1988).

106 Edith Brown Weiss, 'The Planetary Trust: Conservation and Intergenerational Equity' (1984) 11 *Ecology LQ* 495.

107 Wood (note 54): 600.

108 Peter H. Sand, 'Sovereignty Bounded: Public Trusteeship for Common Pool Resources' (2004) 4 (1) *Global Environmental Politics* 47, 51.

109 Global Commons Trust, 'The Commons': http://globalcommonstrust.org/?page_id=11.

110 Ibid.

rights to exclude, control and alienate that are characteristic of private property.'[111] This definition is analogous to the trust relationship – a legal manifestation of responsibility for the benefit of others. It is ubiquitous in human interaction, and its institutionalization has varying degrees of formalism. Trust relationships are everywhere – non-legal and legal. The most obvious and perhaps central case of a trust relationship is the parent–child relationship. Furthermore, 'all of us, both individually and collectively, act as guardians and hence as trustees to the corpus of knowledge passed down through the generations'.[112]

The essence of a trust is that a trustee has full legal responsibility and usually a large degree of discretion to affect the best interests of the beneficiary or beneficiaries, subject to a fiduciary duty to them, and a duty to act in good faith. Although we have located versions of trusteeship in indigenous social organization, in Western *legal* history traces of the trust model were recognized in legal techniques employed as far back as Ancient Greece and Islamic law.[113] The Islamic law *waqf* was introduced to England by Franciscan friars returning from the Crusades in the thirteenth century.[114] Similarly, Roman law recognized numerous modes by which property was transferred by one person to another with the promise of further transfer to a third entity.[115] Such a person, the property holder in trust, was called the *fiducia* appointed by a 'pact' – *pactum fiduciae*. On the basis of this agreement, the trustee promised the settlor that he would use the property for the fulfilment of a purpose and that he would later return it to him. In case the terms of the *pactum fiduciae* were not adhered to by the trustee, the settlor possessed a claim against him, the action *fiducia directa*.[116] In many civil law countries, only recently embracing the notion of the common law 'trust', the Roman *fiducia* is more akin to the continental civil law concept of fiduciary duty. German jurist Regelsberger adapted the Roman concept of *fiducia* to a role wherein the trustee had secure rights to administer the settlor's trust property.[117] This role was called 'treuhand' which influenced other continental legal systems but each evolved distinctly.[118] In *fiducia*

---

111 Lucy and Mitchell (note 21): 584.

112 Ilias Bantekas, *Trust Funds under International Law: Trustee Obligations of the United Nations and International Development Banks* (TMC Asser Press, The Hague 2009): 2.

113 Ibid.: 14.

114 Evan J. Criddle and Evan Fox-Decent, 'A Fiduciary Theory of Jus Cogens' (2009) 34 *Yale J. Int'l L.* 331, 378–379.

115 Bantekas (note 112): 14.

116 Ibid.

117 Ibid.: 15.

118 Ibid.

relationships, the settlor has substantial ownership of the trust assets and the trustee has formal ownership.[119] In this arrangement, the settlor's rights are more limited than equitable ownership under common law, although all trusts stipulate that assets can be reimbursed to the settlor at the expiry of the trust or through agreement.[120]

It is the Roman *fideicommissum* that is professed by common lawyers to be the forerunner to the common law notion of trusts. 'In its original form it was employed in the field of inheritance in which the testator requested his successor to transfer part or all of the estate to a third person, the beneficiary.'[121] The *fideicommissum* progressed in the Middle Ages to form the immediate predecessor of the common law trust.[122] The concept of the trust is similarly found in non-Western legal history – the Hindu *benimi* and the Islamic concept of *waqf*.[123]

In modern-day legal jurisdictions, the trust arose in medieval England in response to a number of feudal exactions – restrictions and taxes placed on owners of freehold land.[124] Medieval conveyancers devised the concept of 'use' which resembles the trust in that the landowner (called the *feoffer*) or modern-day beneficiary would convey their common law estate in land to another person (called the *feoffee to uses*) – the modern-day trustee.[125] As the most significant generator of wealth, this system of 'use' for land was a substantial hindrance to the collection of royal revenues from previous taxes. In early English law, if the trustee were to abuse his confidence there was no remedy at law. Hence, the institution of the appeal to the Chancellor of England, the King's chief legal officer and cleric, became a means to affect 'justice' and 'conscience' through a distinct enforcement power which later became the court of equity. At the heart of equity is its concern with responding to injustice and preventing unconscionable conduct in particular contexts.[126] As such, it is more flexible than the common law.[127]

The common law and the Chancery with equitable jurisdiction existed alongside each other until the late nineteenth century when they were

---

119 Ibid.: 15.
120 Ibid.: 34.
121 Ibid.: 14.
122 Ibid.: 15.
123 Ibid.: 15–16.
124 Andrew S. Butler (ed.), *Equity and Trusts in New Zealand*, 2nd edn (Thompson Reuters, Wellington 2009): 45.
125 Ibid.: 46.
126 Ibid.: 41.
127 Sarah Wilson, *Todd & Wilson's Textbook on Trusts*, 9th edn (Oxford University Press, Oxford 2009): 9.

fused. Trusts which emerged out of this evolution are often referred to as the 'Anglo–American' trust. However, this terminology is most confusing, for it puts in the same basket the laws of each state of the US, England, Australia, Canada, New Zealand, the laws of offshore jurisdictions, and many others. Nowadays law and equity are merged within 'Anglo–American' judicial systems and courts are granted legal and equitable powers, but still they remain different 'hats'. This historical evolution makes trust law what it is today. The courts also now have the power to declare constructive trusts, or trusts which are 'implied' but do not necessarily conform to the requisites of express or private trusts.

The legal concept of the trust in the common law is predicated on a relationship between the settlor (donor) and the trustee with regard to the administration by the latter of property or assets for the benefit of other persons, the beneficiaries or in respect of a particular charitable purpose.[128] Note that the settlor, trustee and beneficiary are not necessarily different people.[129] But once the trust is created, the settlor's interests in respect of the property cease – only the beneficiaries can enforce a trust.[130] When the trustee is appointed, the trust instrument, as well as the common law, the law of equity, or statute, regulate the rights and duties of the trustee and set the standards against which management of the trust property is assessed.[131] The power trustees have through their trusteeship is subject to the requirement that it be used for the benefit of others, not for their own benefit.[132]

The trust device is unique in law because it gives rise to *two* types of 'ownership' of property simultaneously in existence.[133] These two types of ownership are called legal title and equitable title. This means that in English Law there are two distinctive jurisdictions.[134] Most property is identifiable to an owner who holds all the rights and interests relating to that property. Thus, legal title to property confers rights against the world and a right to deal freely with one's property.[135] When property is held in

---

[128] A. Underhill and D.J. Hayton, *Underhill & Hayton: The Law Relating to Trusts and Trustees*, 15th edn (Butterworths, London 1995): 3.

[129] Wilson (note 127): 6.

[130] Ibid.: 7.

[131] Bantekas (note 112): 172; Jian Liu, 'Trust Funds as Mechanisms for Sustainable Development', in Michael Bothe and Peter H. Sand (eds), *Environmental Policy: From Regulation to Economic Instruments* (Martinus Nijhoff, The Hague 2002).

[132] Butler (note 124): 54.

[133] Wilson (note 127): 1.

[134] Ibid.

[135] Ibid.: 2.

trust by a trustee, they hold legal title and have obligations with respect to the management of the trust and property.[136] The persons entitled to enjoy or benefit from the property hold equitable title over the property and are called beneficiaries or *cestui que trust*.[137] Thus, although the trustee holds legal title it is the beneficiary who has the kind of title and rights in respect of the property that the layperson would understand as 'ownership'. This is equitable title.

The trustee's legal title, unlike conferring a freedom to do as one wishes, is held for the benefit and in furtherance of the entitlements of *another* (the beneficiary), not the holder of the legal rights (the trustee). This obligation owed by trustees to beneficiaries is a fiduciary duty. Familiar fiduciary relationships include the following: trustee–beneficiary, agent–principal, director/officer–corporation, lawyer–client, doctor–patient, partner–partnership, joint venturer–joint venture, parent–child and guardian–ward.[138] The fiduciary relationship can be described as arising 'from circumstances in which one party (the fiduciary) holds discretionary power of an administrative nature over the legal or practical interests of another party (the beneficiary), and the beneficiary is peculiarly vulnerable to the fiduciary's power in the sense that she is unable, either as a matter of fact or law, to exercise the entrusted power'.[139]

There are different types of trusts. Trusts can be classified according to different groups, although these often overlap. These are classification by objects, by duties, by legislation, by commercial purpose, by intention, by subject matter, and so on.[140] Classification by objects (beneficiaries) refers to public or charitable trusts for the benefit of the whole community, or trusts which are private and for the benefit of particular individuals.[141] Whereas private trusts are enforced by the beneficiaries, public trusts are enforced by the attorney general acting on behalf of the whole community of beneficiaries. Another trust able to be classified by its 'objects' are purpose trusts – trusts which benefit non-humans or advance a purpose.[142] Examples are trusts for animals or for the maintenance of tombs.[143] According to Butler, '[t]hese trusts are not easily classified as public or private trusts because they are not for the general public good or for the

136 Ibid.: 3.
137 Ibid.
138 Criddle and Fox-Decent (note 114): 349.
139 Ibid.
140 See Butler (note 124): 57.
141 Ibid.: 58.
142 Ibid.
143 Ibid.

benefit of (living) humans'.[144] Thus, because the 'objects' of these trusts are not able to enforce rights against the trustees, these trusts are also known as trusts of imperfect obligation.[145] Classification by statute refers to trusts which are created by statute. Often, these types of trust relate to public lands held in trust by local bodies.[146]

A significant amount of debate in the case law refers to the powers of local bodies as trustees, specifically whether they hold a discretionary right to dispose of the property as they see fit, as in the case of private trustees.[147] A common type of trust classified by commercial purpose is a unit trust. In such a trust, property such as a company is settled on a trustee in trust for a manager. The manager, now the beneficiary, divides up its beneficial interest into many smaller units or 'shares' which are then offered on the market for a price. Purchasers of these shares are 'investors' and acquire a beneficial interest in the property according to their proportion of shares.[148] Classification by intention may refer to three types of trust: express, resulting and constructive trusts. Express trusts created by private individuals through intentional acts (the settlor's intention to create a trust) are declared either by spoken word or in writing.[149] Various versions of express trusts can exist, depending on whether the trust is intended to operate during the settlor's life (inter vivos trust) or after their death (post-mortem or testamentary trust).

Other versions relate to the amount of discretion the trustee has in relation to the property. These are called fixed (if the instructions are clear and fixed) or discretionary trusts (where the trustee has discretion as to how to distribute the property to the beneficiaries). Protective trusts are designed to protect property from an incapable or irresponsible beneficiary, while family trusts are set up by families to shield family property against such things as taxation, creditors, claims by partners or spouses, or for the benefit of minors.[150] Protector trusts refer to situations where the settlor appoints a person (protector, guardian, advisor) to oversee the trustee and ensure they are discharging their obligations appropriately.[151] Resulting trusts arise because it is presumed that the settlor, or 'testator' if it involves a will, would have wanted a trust.[152] Such an example might be where there is additional

144 Ibid.
145 Ibid.: 59.
146 Ibid.
147 Ibid.: 89.
148 Ibid.: 60.
149 Ibid.
150 Ibid.: 62.
151 Ibid.: 63.
152 Ibid.: 60.

property or assets over and above that which has been directed for use. In such a case, the excess is assumed to be held in a resulting trust for that person's estate.[153] Constructive trusts are trusts arising by operation of law.[154] Constructive trusts can arise from various circumstances, suffice it to say that they are imposed by courts irrespective of the intention of the owner, making them, in effect, an 'imposition of trusteeship in unconscionable situations'.[155]

For courts to recognize a trust, there must be three things: certainty of intention; certainty of subject (property/funds); and certainty of object (beneficiaries). The establishment of a trust is similar to that of gifting one's property. In a gift, the legal owner intends to give their property to another, thereby transferring ownership completely to another. It is different from a sale in that the transfer is not for consideration (anything in exchange). However, a trust is slightly different from a gift in that title is not transferred completely, but rather the ownership of property is split into two forms of title – legal and equitable. The recipient beneficiaries can still enjoy the property but in a more constrained way than if they had been gifted the property outright.

Reasons for favouring the creation of a trust over an outright gift are many. For example, through the creation of a trust the settlor has a say in how the property is used by indicating the instructions and conditions in the trust deed.[156] Reasons for this might be a wish to prevent financial irresponsibility, the particular motivations of the settlor – for instance, an interest in education – or perhaps the desire that certain financial assets are maintained for a long period of time. Likewise, trusts are a useful mechanism to ensure the management of property that the beneficiaries are unable to manage themselves, such as for reasons of age, infirmity or lack of knowledge. On the other hand, in a trust situation beneficiaries are still able to enjoy the benefits of the property but are not directly responsible for it.[157] Usually trusts have a limited lifespan.[158] The exceptions are charitable trusts which can exist indefinitely. This rule exists so that wealth cannot be indefinitely controlled from the grave by the creator of the trust.[159]

---

[153] Ibid.: 63.
[154] Ibid.: 60.
[155] Wilson (note 127): 31.
[156] Ibid.: 7.
[157] Ibid.
[158] This is called the perpetuity period and is either 80 years or the lifetime of any named living person plus an additional 21 years after their death; see Butler (note 124): 49.
[159] Ibid.

4.4 The Trustee

A number of 'types of trustee' can be appointed from family friends to professional, advisory and custodian trustees, and public trusts or the Crown.[160] Where there is more than one trustee, generally, all are expected to act unanimously.[161] Several duties attach to trustees. For the purposes of this discussion, these include the duty to: maintain impartiality between beneficiaries; act in the beneficiaries' best interests – interestingly this includes an obligation for the trustee to consider the welfare of beneficiaries not yet born; not profit from trusteeship; invest; not delegate – although there is a recognized need nowadays for expert advice; be active; keep proper accounts and give information as required.[162]

Trustees have several requirements for the way they carry out their function.[163] They must consciously exercise their discretionary power and do so within the scope of their powers and for its proper purpose (for the benefit of the beneficiaries). They must take into account proper consideration, they must be rational and must exercise their discretion with a duty of care and without delegation, conflict of interest or for their own personal benefit. Finally, the trustee's powers must be exercised in good faith. Generally, a trustee's powers are derived from the trust document or from statute.[164] In modern trust law, most of these powers relate to the financial betterment of the trust, for example through the power to sell, lease, mortgage, make repairs and improvements, develop, and so on – this is also characterized as the duty to invest.[165]

4.5 Beneficiaries

Beneficiaries may restrain, by injunction, trustees who are intending to commit a breach of trust. This equitable relief is available so that beneficiaries can compel trustees to fulfil their duties. Beneficiaries who are injured by the breach of trust can seek a suitable remedy such as suing for equitable compensation or damages.[166] Other rights include beneficiaries' right to compel the trust's due administration, to apply for the appointment of a new trustee, to access information, to control the trustee's

---

160 Ibid.: 108.
161 Ibid.: 112.
162 Ibid.: 124–131.
163 Ibid.: 184–186.
164 Ibid.: 137.
165 Ibid.: 137.
166 Ibid.: 146.

discretionary powers and to trace where the property is being transferred by the trustee.[167]

4.6 Reconciling Trust Law with the Principle of Trusteeship

The account usually given of trusts in legal history relays their English medieval origins. This forms a broad basis of trust law, or what we might call the 'common core' of the Anglo–American trust. Thus, the trust is typically thought of as something arising from common law and adapted into some hybrid legal systems. The 'history' of the trust, it would seem, is entirely blind to the antiquity of the idea, demonstrating the epistemological whitewash of Western narrative, yet again. However, some scholars even suggest that the fundaments of the modern legal trust – the common core of the tripartite relationship – are not even unique to common law systems, but instead belong to the civil law, from whence it was imported in England during the formative period of the Chancellor's jurisdiction over trusts.[168] Lupoi posits that evidence exists that testamentary secret and semi-secret trusts were well known in Europe in the sixteenth and seventeenth centuries and that they were called 'confidentia' – exactly the same name originally attributed to trusts and identical to the structure of the trust.

Accordingly, assertions that there exists a large gulf between Anglo–American and European Continental trust law are exaggerated. There were fiduciary institutions in Roman law and have always been such institutions in the civil law systems influenced by Roman law and also in Germanic customary law.[169] However, in Europe, as in English law, these did not give rise to a separate jurisdiction or the separation of legal and equitable title to property. It is true that some civil law countries avoid the use of the term 'trust' even while adopting the substance of trust law. In civil law jurisdictions, the focus is on the fiduciary nature of the trust relationship. The Spanish call this *fiduciario*, the French *fiducie*, the Germans *Treuhänder* and the Dutch *bewind*.[170]

These institutions provide a legal framework for the administration of the assets of another person, earmarked as separate, in the interest of third persons or an abstract purpose. The people who perform these functions do so similarly to the Anglo–American 'trustee'.[171]

---

167 Ibid.: 147.

168 Maurizio Lupoi, 'The Civil Law Trust' (1999) *Vand J. Transnat'l L.* 967.

169 Tony Honoré, 'On Fitting Trusts into Civil Law Jurisdictions', University of Oxford Legal Research Paper Series, Paper No. 27/2008 (September 2008).

170 Japan, which has the fiduciary institution known as Shintaku.

171 Honoré (note 169): 3.

Importantly though, these institutions lack the supervisory jurisdiction of the court or a public authority that can be called upon to ensure that the purpose for which the assets have been set aside is carried out.[172] Civil law scholars regard the transfer from settlor to trustee as a gift, thus these fiduciary roles amount, rather, to special types of contract that give rise to contractual remedies.[173] However, many of the structural features of the common law trust (such as administration by a non-self-interested party) are matched by civil law institutions such as a guardianship, a curatorship or the administration of deceased estates. According to Honoré, the essence of trusteeship is the holding of an office, that is, a personal responsibility. It is irrelevant whether or not it is subject to detailed control by the state via the courts.

This fact of difference in form, but similarity in the essential fiduciary or responsibility character of the trustee role, in both common and civil law jurisdictions is evident in the 1984 Hague Convention on the Law Applicable to Trusts and on Their Recognition. Article 2 of the Convention gives a broad yet 'essential' 'gateway'[174] definition of trust as the legal relationships created by a person, the settlor, when assets have been placed under the control of a trustee for the benefit of a beneficiary or for a specified purpose. The Convention was created to deal with the private international conflict of law for trusts, particularly the recognition of trusts in civil law countries, that were created in common law countries.[175]

The Convention is a bridging document, not intended to solve all problems or meet all possible variations in the trust practice.[176] It provides that trusts, in accordance with the terms of the Convention, are recognized and protected in signatory states. Thus, the Convention imposes no limitation on the settlor's choice of the law applicable to a trust. A number of common law countries have ratified it but only a handful of civil law countries have done so, their being reluctant to recognize the trust because it makes it possible for citizens of a civil law country to set up in a foreign jurisdiction trusts which will then be recognized in their own country.[177] And if trusts are not available in that country's domestic law, the Hague Convention may encourage overseas investment.[178]

---

172 Ibid.: 4.

173 Ibid.

174 This allows legal professionals to identify trust-like devices without trying to fit them into a comprehensive definition; see Honoré (note 169).

175 Ibid.: 7–8.

176 Adair Dyer, 'International Recognition and Adaptation of Trusts: the Influence of the Hague Convention' (1999) 32 (4) *Vand J. Transnat'l L.* 989.

177 Honoré (note 169): 8.

178 Ibid.

The purpose of this brief overview of the law of trusts was to acquaint ourselves with the modern use of the trust mechanism. The nuance in the law of trusts is immense, and was only touched on as guidance for the later discussion as to what trusteeship for the global commons should look like. The central message from the social and legal origins of trusteeship is that it is a philosophical idea that is enduring but which can be expressed in flexible, adaptive and idiosyncratic legal arrangements.

5. TRUSTEESHIP IN INTERNATIONAL LAW

The trust, as a device, has also been used in public international law, yet it is a surprisingly under-studied feature of international law and politics. At this point however, and in light of the preceding discussion on the differences in common and civil law notions, it is pertinent to note that we need to be careful not to assume the wholesale similarity between domestic and international trusts. This is because there are fundamental divergences in the practical objectives of international and domestic law trust relationships.[179] Indeed, according to one expert, 'the trust concept in international law enjoys very few of the legal commonalities with its domestic law counterpart, apart perhaps from its perceived function'.[180]

Evolution of trusteeship in international law began with 'a racist notion of civilizational differences'.[181] It carries the unfortunate spectre of paternalism due to its early links to empire and its use as a tool in the European civilizing mission. It has followed a varied path from origins such as the East India Company in India, the League of Nations mandate system, the UN trusteeship system and the retaliation, starting in the 1960s, of colonized peoples who successfully challenged the legitimacy of trusteeship and fought, and gained, independence, armed with one of the West's very own ideas: equality.[182] The League of Nations mandate system arose following World War I, when the allies did not wish to grant independence to the former territories of defeated powers, ostensibly because they failed the test as 'civilized' societies with the necessities for statehood.[183]

---

179 Bantekas (note 112): 190.

180 Ibid.: 192.

181 Ralph Wilde, 'Trusteeship Council', in Thomas G. Weiss and Sam Daws (eds), *Oxford Handbook on the United Nations* (Oxford University Press, Oxford 2007): 150.

182 See William Bain, *Between Anarchy and Society: Trusteeship and the Obligations of Power* (Oxford University Press, Oxford 2003).

183 Wilde (note 181): 150.

The mandate system became the institutional embodiment of this 'sacred trust', with individual states as administrators or 'trustees'. This precedent was again followed after World War II when victorious states took on the role of administrating authorities, with UN oversight.

The UN trusteeship system was established by Chapter XII of the UN Charter (Articles 75–85), and Chapter XIII addressed the formation of the Trusteeship Council (Articles 86–91), a principle organ of the United Nations. It continued the League of Nations mandate system in that existing mandate territories were deemed trusteeship territories under the Charter, but it also introduced two new categories: territories detached from enemy states due to World War II and territories voluntarily placed under UN jurisdiction by the administering state. As the institutionalized form of colonial administration, the 1960s ushered in an era of self-determination and post-colonialism which repudiated the legitimacy of foreign state administration.

The basic objectives of the trusteeship system and the obligations of the trustee are set out in Article 76: the promotion of political, economic, social and educational advancement of the inhabitants of the trust territories and their progressive development towards self-government or independence.[184] Unlike the League of Nations mandate system which comprised individuals, membership of the trusteeship council was comprised of states: the five permanent Security Council members, states administering trust territories and additional members – enough to ensure an even balance between administering and non-administering states. Observer status was granted to specialized agencies and other UN bodies. The Trusteeship Council's role was to examine reports and petitions from administering authorities and missions to trust territories.

The trusteeship system essentially dissolved in 1994 when Palau, the last of the trust territories to reach self-government, gained independence. The Trusteeship Council suspended operations and annual meetings. The trusteeship provisions have not been removed from the UN Charter, however, and many have called for a reactivation of the Council, albeit with a different function.

In the 1990s trusteeship was resurrected as a legitimate form of international receivership, in the form of UN territorial administration, for post-conflict and failing states. Such places have included East Timor, Cambodia and Kosovo. In such cases, the temporary multilateral administrator acts like a trustee but does not have the same legal rights of ownership, in this case over territory, that trustees usually have. There also still

[184] Charter of the United Nations, Art. 76 (b).

exist dependent territories such as Greenland and the Cayman and British Virgin Islands who do not possess full sovereignty vis-à-vis their mother countries, Denmark and Great Britain, although they have varying degrees of autonomy.[185] Nevertheless, many countries, particularly developing ones, are still highly suspicious of the interference and paternalism inherent in trusteeship.

Despite its somewhat controversial history in international relations, the problems and failure of trusteeship (in global politics) ought not to detract from its utility as a mechanism for global commons governance. The problems that have been experienced do not stem from an inherently flawed concept, but rather from flawed application. Trusteeship has been a thinly veiled tool of racism wherein it was posited that certain peoples lacked the faculties to govern themselves. More recently, the complexities of establishing stable and diverse societies in post-conflict UN trusteeships have led many to question their efficacy. What becomes clear is that however appropriate the idea of trusteeship is in theory, its success or failure depends on how it is applied.

Similarly, at international level, the United Nations and international development banks draw upon the trust arrangement to manage development funds and in order to distribute aid to beneficiary countries by an intergovernmental entity, with less involvement by donating countries and less reliance on the recipient's administration.[186] These large organizations are intuitive choices because they hold the administrative capacity and know-how to run a trust and are also deemed 'internationally trustworthy' and legitimate distributors of aid.[187] The mechanism also provides a viable alternative to unilateral cash injections into infant governments who have little public accountability and fiscal management experience.[188] Trust funds can be simply bank accounts or they can be imbued with distinct legal personality.[189] This will ultimately depend on the preferences of the donors, but it is not unusual for international trust funds to gain the legal form of an international organization.[190]

Intergovernmental trusts, according to Bantekas, are creatures 'of self-regulation through a sui generis process that is peculiar to international law'.[191] As Bantekas points out, the theoretical benefits of using a trust

---

185 Bantekas (note 112): 16.
186 Ibid.: 18.
187 Ibid.: 7.
188 Ibid.
189 Ibid.: 33.
190 Ibid.
191 Ibid.: 12.

in these circumstances are numerous.[192] For one, it pools funds together which is not only pragmatic and efficient but politically advantageous as the contributors can speak with a combined and compelling voice to achieve what they envision for the beneficiaries. The objective distributor or trustee serves to remove any political friction between donor and beneficiary states, and could serve to dilute the political rhetoric, although states always seem to do their best to prevent this. It avoids mismanagement by corrupt or incapable beneficiary administrations by providing a level of expertise, procedure and accountability in funds distribution and management while still empowering local service providers. Finally, the long-term goals of many funds, whether for disease eradication or for environmental protection, 'require significant planning and human resources . . . which no state would be happy or suitable to undertake unilaterally'.[193] Many of these advantages of trust mechanisms hold true in an environmental context also, and shall be re-visited in the final chapters.

Another essential element to be aware of in regard to intergovernmental trusts is that the beneficiaries of international intergovernmental trusts lack enforceable rights over the trust's assets.[194] The corollary is that they also lack enforceable obligations. This, as we now know, is in contrast to the domestic law of trusts wherein the trustee owes fiduciary duties to the beneficiaries and where the beneficiaries have enforceable equitable rights. The international trusts edict was established in the South West Africa Cases[195] where it was found that although a beneficiary might object to the decisions of the trustees, even with strong moral reasoning, this does not affect the legal relationship between donor and trustee unless provided for in the trust instrument. In this sense, international and intergovernmental trusts resemble more purposeful trusts such as charitable trusts where the beneficiaries are often not named and thus no fiduciary duty attaches between trustee and beneficiary.[196] The World Bank, which often acts as 'trustee', has enshrined the rejection of an enforceable fiduciary duty towards a trust's beneficiaries in its standardized Administrative Agreements with donors.[197] This is putatively

---

[192] Ibid.: 18.
[193] Ibid.
[194] Ibid.: 186.
[195] *Ethiopia v South Africa, Liberia v South Africa (South West Africa cases) (Second Phase)* [1996] ICJ Rep 6.
[196] Bantekas (note 112): 169.
[197] Ibid.: 191.

because many trusts do not have named beneficiaries in advance.[198] And, as Bantekas posits, even if the beneficiaries were designated, the indication by states and by the World Bank is a complete rejection of granting any proprietary rights to beneficiaries.[199] The next essential element is that the trustee(s) are not the agents of the donor.[200] State donors do not confer any of their power as states onto the trustee, nor does the trust alter existing legal relationships.[201] There do exist instances where donors exercise control, do not appoint a trustee and nevertheless call the arrangement a trust. Simply because the name is invoked does not a trust make, and these are arguably examples of a 'Trojan horse of agency disguised as a trust'.[202]

6. INTERNATIONAL ENVIRONMENTAL TRUSTEESHIP

As previously mentioned, a number of proposals have been made to revamp the now defunct Trusteeship Council into an environmental body.[203] In 1994 the President of the General Assembly called for its mandate to be broadened to hold in trust the common heritage and common concerns.[204] Likewise, in 1995 the Maltese proposed the Trusteeship Council be entrusted with CHM for environmental issues.[205] These calls have been echoed by the Commission on Global Governance and by former UN Secretary Generals. The trusteeship question even went to a UN Taskforce on Environment and Human Settlements, chaired by the Executive Director of UNEP, but the 1998 Report of the Taskforce to the General Assembly gave no recommendations regarding trusteeship.[206]

---

198 At international level, there are only three kinds of trusts which name a class of beneficiaries – intergenerational trusts, natural resources trusts and compensations trusts.

199 Bantekas (note 112): 191.

200 Ibid.: 29.

201 Ibid.: 30.

202 Ibid.

203 Stoddart (note 3): 37.

204 *Concluding Statement of the General Assembly President* A/45/PV82 (1991) 21, cited in Carolyn L. Willson, 'Changing the Charter: The United Nations Prepares for the Twenty-First Century' (1996) 90 *AJIL* 122.

205 *Review of the Role of the Trusteeship Council*, GA Res 50/55, A/50/142 (1995).

206 Peter H. Sand, 'Sovereignty Bounded: Public Trusteeship for Common Pool Resources' (2004) 4 (1) *Global Environmental Politics* 47.

Likewise, 'in the last two decades a large number of international environmental law treaties have been interpreted as designating the terms of said conventions as international trusts and the contracting parties as trustees. As a result, the duties of the trustees encompass the implementation of these conventions into domestic law'.[207] 'Intergovernmental trust funds set up to deal with matters pertaining to the environment are perhaps the largest recipients of international funding compared to all other trust arrangements [and] . . . number in the hundreds.'[208]

In contrast to domestic trusts, and even many international trust funds for development or human rights purposes, environmental trust funds do not distribute entitlements which can be personally quantifiable to each beneficiary.[209] Rather, the benefit for the beneficiaries is experienced collectively. We all benefit from a healthier and cleaner environment, but calculating the benefit to each person and other living thing of a reduction in greenhouse gases by X amount is an arbitrary exercise. Also, there are many more interdependencies that simply cannot be fathomed when we consider the environment in a cost and benefit way. Scholars differ greatly on their opinion as to whether 'ecological limits' can actually be calculated, and whether these will ever be truly accurate. As we explored in Chapter 1, it is precisely the collective nature of benefits from sustainability that poses the collective action problem politically.

Bantekas finds that, collectively, beneficiaries of environmental trusts have three broadly identified 'rights' which form a special species of beneficiary rights in contradistinction to other intergovernmental trusts.[210] These are the right to be informed, the right to participate in the decision-making process as to how the state will internally implement the environmental convention, and the right to participate as observers in conference of state parties. In these sorts of obligatory and implied international environmental trusts that arise from treaties, individual states are the de facto trustees as they must formulate ways of dealing with the environmental 'assets' to the benefit of their peoples. Naturally, the fact that the trustee relationship arises from an environmental context would imply that discretion should be used in an environmentally sound way, however more often than not states elevate economic concerns and indeed the economic utility of the environment above ecological health. This is not only because of their individual administrative inclinations, but also because at

---

207 Bantekas (note 112): 202.

208 Ibid.: 262.

209 Ibid.: 203.

210 Ibid.

intergovernmental level these combine to form a dominance of neo-liberal thinking which produces environmental trusts that are based on these same neoliberal principles. As shall be further elaborated on in Chapter 6, this is done despite the fundamental necessity of a healthy environment for human life and therefore fully conceived 'benefit'.

As we have seen, there are examples of trusteeship for environmental issues already present at international level, namely in the form of trust funds such as the Global Environmental Facility. There are also examples in litigation where people have sought to invoke guardianship ethics. Stone mentions a case in 1988 whereby titanium and other heavy metals, the by-product of West Germany's paint complex, were attributed to the death of over 15,000 seals in the North and Baltic Seas.[211] Any of those coastal states might have challenged Germany's actions, but so long as the harm was done on the high seas, the nation-states themselves were doubtful plaintiffs. Moreover, because all the littoral states were probably contributing to the pollution as well, their contributions negated any claims of injury by another. In such an example, an environmental guardian would have been ideal, not only for the seals themselves, but for the other aspects of the biosphere undoubtedly affected by the disaster. On the advice of Stone, a group of environmental lawyers in Germany brought suit, acting as guardians for the North Sea seals – the principal plaintiffs – in the case *Seehunde v. Bundesrepublik Deutschland*.[212] Ultimately, the action failed in the administrative law court because seals could not have standing because they were not 'persons'.[213]

Stone notes however, that the publicity generated by the case forced the government to revoke ocean-dumping permits, so, while not a legal victory, it was a public and political game-changer. Furthermore, Stone cites the case as an important lesson for those advocates of the guardian model. Invoking the guardian principle on an ad hoc basis, and in national jurisdictions where there is no express legislative provision for non-human beings to have legal standing, is not a viable strategy. Ultimately, what is necessary is the institutionalization of the concept of guardianship for the global commons into a concept relevant to multiple, national and international fora. From a legal standpoint, the guardian model has the advantage of avoiding multifarious state litigation, providing one

---

211 Stone, *Defending the Global Commons* (note 46).

212 Verwaltungsgericht [Administrative Court] Hamburg 15 August 1988, *Neue Zeitschrift für Verwaltungsrecht* 1988, 1058; see Klaus Bosselmann, *Im Namen der Natur: Der Weg zum ökologischen Rechtsstaat* (Scherz, Berne 1992): 181–188.

213 Stone, *Should Trees Have Standing*? (note 26): 450.

'injured' voice and conceivably streamlining the legal determination of wrong-doing.[214]

What might a trust for the global commons look like? Although a proposal will be fully explored later, we can sketch the fundaments of a global commons here. Generally speaking, we need a legal entity responsible for protecting the global commons that is inherited from past generations, or is presently being created, on behalf of current and future generations. Because it is common – held in trust and 'owned' by all – the commons are insulated from any exclusive claims by private individuals, business, government or other trusts.[215] Beneficiaries consist of humans *and* other life without existing legal personality, making the beneficiaries what we like to call *the community of life*. Current generations would be the donors or settlors, intentionally deciding to cede management of the trust assets (the global commons) to the trustees.

Trustees themselves, as members of the community of life, are similarly also beneficiaries. What might be the guiding principle for the trustee? Naturally, sustainability is key and also the notion of the common heritage of life. Decision-making would need to be guided by the precautionary principle because weighing up interests is difficult and science imperfect. Likewise, intergenerational equity, meaning that the trustee ensures the planet is passed on to future generations in no worse condition than it received it, can provide equitable access to its resources and benefits.[216] Essentially, intergenerational equity involves conservation of options, quality and access.[217]

However, beyond Weiss's definition there is a necessarily ecological element embodied in the common heritage of life, rather than simply the common heritage of mankind. We also have a responsibility to remedy the damage inflicted on the environment – surely this is also part of our intergenerational responsibility? The trustees' emphasis will need to be on the ecological integrity of the biosphere; only with this can we truly affect justice. Thus, a trusteeship system gives 'nature' standing alongside humans,[218] ensuring that environmental governance is not about preventing the worst harm and simply slowing down exploitation (the impetus behind sustainable *development*), but about overall ecological sustainability. As such, it can avoid the mistakes of previous attempts at

---

214 Stone, *Defending the Global Commons* (note 46).
215 Global Commons Trust (note 13).
216 Weiss, *In Fairness to Future Generations* (note 46): 24.
217 Ibid.: Chapter 3.
218 See in detail Klaus Bosselmann, *When Two Worlds Collide: Society and Ecology* (RSVP, Auckland 1995): 253–260.

governance. Naturally, the trustees will also have a key role in ensuring intra-generational equity, managing the equitable transition for the global South to new types of alternative livelihoods and an environmental sustainability paradigm. The trustee is the legal voice of the voiceless – human and non-human. Personnel could be drawn from existing organizations with expertise, such as the World Meteorological Organization, IUCN, World Wildlife Fund for Nature and Greenpeace, and would need to include a representative sample of cultures and geographies.

The purpose of this chapter has been to fully canvas the idea of trusteeship, from one idea among many that call for responsibility and oversight, whether it be through a trust, a commissioner or an ombudsman. We have looked into the history that trusteeship or stewardship has in religion and tradition and also considered where this dissolved as a mainstream ethic. The examination of trusts and trusteeship, as it currently exists in the legal world, both domestically and internationally, will guide how we design a new trust institution. We know from international intergovernmental funds that there is considerable latitude in how such an institution is designed, given the *sui generis* nature of international trusts. Most often thought of as a construct of medieval English law, it is important to remember that behind the legal notion of trusts is the principle or ethic, which seems to get scant regard in international environmental law. This is what needs to be translated into an institution that will have social and legal effect.

This chapter has taken a twofold approach, first critiquing the law as it stands, and then introducing an alternate idea. Pointing out the shortcomings of our legal status quo is necessary because the success of the guardianship regime will 'depend not only upon legitimation and institutionalization of the guardian as legal representative, but upon significant changes in the substantive law which the guardian would be empowered to invoke'.[219] Our current attitudinal and legal approach demands re-consideration due to the absence of responsibility, both social and ecological, and the separation of these ethics from what we consider the formal 'law'. Our legal solutions are largely devoid of ecological justice. International environmental law needs to take cognizance of the reality of the environmental impact of human activity and to recognize the *erga omnes* obligations of current generations as trustees of the environment for future generations.

It is frankly perplexing that in international law we have *erga omnes* obligations, covering acts of aggression, genocide and basic human rights

---

219 Stone, *Defending the Global Commons* (note 46): 43.

including slavery and racial discrimination, yet no hard-law obligation for humanity to protect the environment from degradation for current and future generations.[220] As Susan Buck argues, we are facing a 'Grotian moment', meaning that we have reached a tipping point in international law, to mirror the corollary in nature.[221] International environmental law is, at present, analogous to the state of the common law before the law of equity intervened to ensure that justice was effected.[222] Arguably, the current UN reform process, following the 2012 Rio+20 Conference, offers windows of opportunity for devising legal and governance changes.[223]

---

[220] Walton (note 29): 18.

[221] Susan Buck, *The Global Commons: An Introduction* (Island Press, Washington, DC 1998).

[222] Walton (note 29): 18.

[223] Ibid.: Chapters 7 and 8.

6. State as environmental trustee

> Society is indeed a contract . . . between those who are living, those who are dead, and those who are to be born.
>
> Edmund Burke (1792)

> Unbelievable as it may seem, the future of humanity rests on our generation being able to reframe government's obligation towards Nature.
>
> Mary C. Wood[1]

1. INTRODUCTION

The current governance of the global commons operates through the prism of national sovereignty. States determine the nature and membership of commons governance regimes. As Christopher Stone aptly puts it, we operate in a 'cramped and mundane vista' wherein the earth in all its ecological wholeness has been artificially divided into a system of political territories.[2] This traditional view posits that nation-states are the only recognized subjects of international law, pursuant to which states are the only entities that can create, directly benefit from, acquire obligations under and enforce international law. Common goods that lie *within* national boundaries fall under the jurisdiction of the nation-state and are precluded from international environmental protection unless expressly agreed upon by the state.

We needn't belabour the point that the state-centric international political system has proven a flawed context for global environmental management. Nevertheless, the reality of state centrism is unlikely to disappear in the near future, despite claims of the dissolution of sovereignty via globalization and international law. This volume has argued that the common heritage of life principle, properly understood, creates humanity and all life as the new 'subjects' of international law. To prevent states' subjugation of the common good of humanity for their own sovereign

[1] Mary C. Wood, 'Nature's Trust: A Legal, Political and Moral Frame for Global Warming' (2007) 34 *Envt Aff.* 577.

[2] Christopher D. Stone, 'Defending the Global Commons', in Philippe Sands (ed.), *Greening International Law* (Earthscan, London 1993): 34.

interests, in the previous chapter we explored the idea of trusteeship as an option for global commons governance. As we saw, trusteeship is a deeply rooted mode of human social organization and exists at many levels from the most micro-levels such as family, through to examples of transnational trusteeship. One very important arena where true trusteeship for sustainability is missing is within the modern nation-state.

In this chapter, we pursue the latter idea, exploring the inevitable role that states will have in any governance regime including one like trusteeship. After all, when it comes to global environmental governance, states are still the players at the negotiating table, despite the usual parallel civil society circuits. This book has advanced a definition of the global commons which permeates the traditional sovereign territorial parameters of the 'global' commons and includes domestic environments in what is deemed 'common' to all humankind.

As explained in Chapter 4, the inclusion of non-discrete environmental aspects such as biodiversity, the atmosphere and the oceans, in the notion of the global commons necessitates such an approach. In this sense, we truly are talking about the *global* environment with its fundamentally 'shared' or 'common' nature. To advance this definition is to venture into a traditionally 'no-go' area for international law. However, the basis of our argument for including the environment within state territory in a system of global commons governance is not merely a belief that international law should know no bounds. Rather, what this chapter discusses is each state's role as a trustee unto themselves. We need to address and scrutinize the role states play as our putative 'representatives', because states' 'sovereign interests' are supposed to be the interests of those governed.

Thus, as well as arguing for a global trusteeship, we are inherently also arguing for a more accurately defined role of the state – more 'accurate' referring to the irrefutable reality that maintaining a healthy environment is essential to ensuring ongoing human prosperity, and, as representatives of the governed, states are tasked with this responsibility. The point of this chapter is to open up states' governance mandate to include other types of wealth and value – ecological, social, democratic, moral – values that need to be fully recognized and actively protected by those who purport to govern on behalf of people.[3]

Responsibly exercised state sovereignty will be vital to preventing further environmental degradation by 'freeloaders' who are willing to

---

[3] David Bollier, 'The Commons: A Neglected Sector of Wealth Creation', in Silke Heinrich (ed.), *Genes, Bytes and Emissions: To Whom Does the World Belong?* (Henrich Böll Stiftung, Berlin 2008): http://www.boell.org/web/148-576.html.

undermine the ecological balance as well as the unique cultural and spiritual value of certain natural areas. However, the challenge is, and always has been, getting states to recognize their obligation to act responsibly and recognize the trusteeship role inherent in their mandate to govern. No small amount of political will is necessary. And political will is ultimately derived from popular will, meaning that the true driver for change will be civil society exercising its influence through the ballot box. After all, a debate on who should be responsible for our collective resources is a debate about the state of society.[4] And yet the entire commons debate tends to be ignored in conventional politics.[5] In a way this is attributable to what we, the people, expect of our political institutions. The discussion of civil society and the commons movement seeks to proffer citizenship as the mode through which the state's role is challenged and reframed into one of trusteeship.

2. STATES' FAILURE – REVISITING THE TRAGEDY OF MARKETS

We live in a situation where climate change, biodiversity loss, toxification of food chains, water shortages and unhealthy consumerism are felt on a daily basis, while all public money is being pumped into economic systems that created these problems in the first place. There is a widespread feeling that political leaders and corporate managers, in their money and power games, are too preoccupied to notice the real needs of people and the planet. The situation, as it now stands, depicts, at its very core, a crisis of human consciousness. This has been the contention throughout this volume and has prompted our calls for a rediscovery of ecological ethics and responsibility now only found in the most 'peripheral' of traditions. What we are witnessing is an extremely high-stakes philosophical competition. Economism is an intellectual attitude which affirms the power and the pretended right of economics to determine the whole of society.[6]

---

[4] Silke Helfrich, 'Commons: The Network of Life and Creativity', in Silke Heinrich (ed.), *Genes, Bytes and Emissions: To Whom Does the World Belong?* (Heinrich Böll Stiftung, Berlin 2008): http://us.boell.org/sites/default/files/downloads/Helfrich_Intro.pdf.

[5] Bollier (note 3).

[6] Johannes Heinrichs, 'A Model of Value-based Democracy as Condition of Ecological Sustainability', in Ron Engel, Laura Westra and Klaus Bosselmann (eds), *Democracy, Ecological Integrity and International Law* (Cambridge Scholars Publishing, Newcastle upon Tyne 2010): 41.

Ecologism is an attitude which is founded on the insight that most of our ecological problems are social problems and must be dealt with accordingly, in our social institutions.[7]

Nowadays, the emphasis of governance is economics as a means to overall human prosperity. The measure of national prosperity, and thus the 'success' of government, is almost always the size of gross national product – how 'rich' the economy is. The state structure is therefore in no way 'neutral'. It favours a way of thinking which sees economic prosperity as the basic requirement for human existence. The 'collective purpose of modern democratic societies [is] maximizing the economic means whereby individuals may freely and fairly pursue their private interests'.[8] One of the earliest contributors to the dismal science, Adam Smith, gave us the concept of the *invisible hand* of the free market. Applying Smith's laissez-faire approach, it is the duty of the economy to exploit all available resources. That results in individual wealth, which leads to communal wealth.

However, economic calculations list only that which increases material prosperity; the rest falls by the wayside and the cost to the environment is irrelevant to GNP. Under the free market theory, once a resource is depleted, technology and market demand will find an alternative. In this way, the market actors move from resource to resource, stimulating growth and consumption. Ironically, repairs to the damaged environment are accounted for on the credit side to such a degree that it is an enormous and lucrative industry. However, the difficulty with Smith's greatest value of labour approach to growth and community well-being is that it assumes that the natural resources required to feed such growth are limitless, or that technology will continually adapt the market to deal with scarcity. It is central to this that the environment is able to accept and digest the waste from production and consumption. Smith has no concern for wasted resources and a deteriorating global environment. Thus, in our economic system the full cost of production is not factored into the price of a product, nor the environmental cost of extracting and exploiting the resource, nor the end cost of disposing of by-products of production, use and disposal of the exhausted product. The free market assumes a *rational actor*, making purchasing decisions on an informed and rational basis. In practice, and in a global marketplace, this is rarely the case. At best, the free market *picks the low hanging fruit* and moves on.

---

[7] Ibid.

[8] Ron Engel, 'Contesting Democracy', in Ron Engel, Laura Westra and Klaus Bosselmann (eds), *Democracy, Ecological Integrity and International Law* (Cambridge Scholars Publishing, Newcastle upon Tyne 2010).

Globalization has exacerbated the issue, as the apparent cost of production is moved to states which have comparative advantage, either in the form of little or no labour protection or lax environmental controls. Under the free global market, producers will automatically relocate to states where the cost of production is lower. While the producing state may claim that both their workers and consumers are better off, environmental costs are not factored into the market pricing.[9] The economy has always been a promise for the future: more outputs, more jobs, a better life for all. This promise has only ever been kept for some, of course, and certainly to the detriment of the environment. Thus, the ideological driver of modern government is economic rationality, despite common sense dictating the wider perspective of ecological rationality.

This framework gives rise to industrialized societies' political-economic context wherein shared resources are regarded as under-leveraged market assets. The environment and its resources are raw inputs for generating corporate profits, GNP and a 'better' society. Restrictions on using the environment for market purposes, such as social or environmental regulation, are often criticized as impediments to wealth creation, and therefore morally suspect and generally unpopular policies.[10] The state therefore shares the ecological blindness which characterizes the traditional economy. This affinity is expressed particularly strongly in the concept of liberty that underlies human and fundamental rights.[11] The corollary of this overriding emphasis on the economy is an 'institutional bias' against sustainability within states.[12] This has been translated into the international arena.

Political institutions function in a world in which power is linked to property.[13] For those who benefit from the economic focus of government, the vulnerability of regulatory agencies to 'capture' by the industries they

---

9 It should be noted that, while the GATT allows under Article XX for measures to be introduced on the grounds of public morals, protection of health, conservation of exhaustible natural resources (in conjunction with domestic restrictions) and the like, the environmental cost of production is not valid grounds for imposing protectionist measures.

10 Bollier (note 3).

11 Klaus Bosselmann, *When Two Worlds Collide: Society and Ecology* (RSVP, Auckland 1995): 71.

12 Klaus Bosselmann, 'Earth Democracy: Institutionalising Sustainability and Ecological Integrity', in Ron Engel, Laura Westra and Klaus Bosselmann (eds), *Democracy, Ecological Integrity and International Law* (Cambridge Scholars Publishing, Newcastle upon Tyne 2010): 93.

13 Peter Barnes, *Capitalism 3.0: A Guide to Reclaiming the Commons* (Berret-Koehler, San Francisco 2006): 34.

were intended to regulate, called 'regulatory capture',[14] has not gone unnoticed. In a capitalist democracy, the state is a dispenser of many valuable prizes. Whoever amasses the most political power wins the most valuable prizes. Lobbying accounts for an enormous amount of money and influence in domestic politics. In the US, the 'influence industry' in Washington now spends $6 billion a year and employs more than 35,000 lobbyists.[15]

Thus, we can see that 'governance' is about a *quid pro quo*, symbiotic relationship between politicians and corporations.[16] The rewards include property rights, friendly regulators, subsidies, tax breaks and free or cheap use of the commons – which are all ostensibly going to lead to the prosperity of the public. What this ultimately means when issues such as environmental degradation arise, is that governments don't govern, they crisis manage, usually while trying to create as little interruption as possible to the *status quo* economic order. In the words of Peter Barnes, 'we face a disheartening quandary here. Profit-maximizing corporations dominate our economy. Their programming makes them enclose and diminish common wealth. The only obvious counterweight is government, yet government is dominated by these same corporations'.[17] The notion that the state promotes 'the common good' is sadly naive.[18]

To appreciate how we reached this point, we need to understand the ontological and epistemological separation of humans and nature. This is part of the Western *conditio humana* – the ego cult, that is, the separation and exclusion of the social and ecological systems of which humans are part.[19] Although capitalism emerged from the industrial era, during the nineteenth century conservation biology based on the evolutionary and ecological sciences was separated from philosophy, science and the art of democratic citizenship and politics.[20] Aldo Leopold called this separation of human matters and the plant and animal community one of the anomalies of modern-day ecology and predicted that the fusion of these two lines of thought would perhaps be one of the most outstanding advances of the century.[21] Alas, what we have is an enduring competition

---

14 Ibid.: 35.
15 Ibid.: 36.
16 Ibid.: 37.
17 Ibid.: 45.
18 Ibid.
19 Bosselmann, *When Two Worlds Collide* (note 11): 71.
20 Engel (note 8): 35.
21 See Curt Meine, *Aldo Leopold: His Life and Work* (University of Wisconsin Press, Madison, WI 1988).

between two ideologies. In one reality, governments continue their modest environmental agenda of energy efficiency and climate measures, while in another reality, they do everything to undermine even the most modest policies of environmental protection. Herein lies the problem, and the reason that states fail, time and time again, to reach agreement as to what must be done to save the environment.

State's very purpose, its reason for existence and the driving force of all policy directly or indirectly, is based on an empirical mistake. Faced with the environment 'problem', states have developed the superficial panacea of 'sustainable development'. In reality, this is 'weak' sustainability, a lowest common denominator idea which balances social, economic and environmental concerns while maintaining the belief that you can have your cake and eat it too – just eat with greater care. Denial is a strong characteristic of the human psyche. Even this weak version has only just started to inform the political economy, giving rise to many attempts at green-wash – the appearance of sustainability without any significant departure from the status quo.

What this shows is a poverty of imagination, a crisis of ideas and a glaring lack of critical analysis into what really defines the scope of a government's mandate to govern. And this is the point – the failure of international environmental law is not simply a failure of cooperation, a display of distrust and competition, it stems from a lack of critical self-reflection. Essentially, states are unable to look beyond the sanctimonious monopoly of economics in 'governance', despite the fact that governance of society is far, far more complex than mere material accumulation. If institutions of governance believe there is no alternative to economic growth, even in the face of ecological and human disaster, then we must doubt their ability to govern responsibly. It is not that states are incapable of governing at all. Recently, we have seen just how willing states have been to help the economy in times of crisis. The response of governments to the current environmental crisis reveals not just helplessness, short-sightedness and denial, but genuine signs of schizophrenia. Caught up in their economic fixations, governments are literally losing a sense of reality.

As the first chapter has discussed, we need to remind ourselves that if our democratic institutions are 'captured' by neoliberal economics and systematically biased against sustainability then many of the characteristics of democracy simply cannot be realized. The unholy alliance between politics and private interests raises serious questions about the ability of the public to influence policy, despite their interests being those that are represented. Furthermore, as Barnes points out, '[n]ot even seated at democracy's table – not organized, not propertied, and not enfranchised – are future generations, ecosystems, and nonhuman species'.[22]

3. STATE SOVEREIGNTY AND INTERNATIONAL ENVIRONMENTAL GOVERNANCE

Sovereignty was first codified with the 1648 Treaty of Westphalia that ended the Thirty Years War, and became vested in the absolute monarch whose authority rested on divine mandate and history, but not the will of the people. The Westphalian Peace followed more than a century of conflict revolving around the Protestant Reformation, which in turn had much earlier roots. In exchange for the protection of freedom of religious confession and freedom of conscience at national level (albeit limited to Catholicism, Lutheranism and Calvinism), states had to agree not to interfere in each other's internal affairs by claiming authority over those of a particular confession. Thus was established the inviolable territorial limits of state sovereignty.[23] The 128 clauses of Westphalia that gave birth to this concept include, among much else, the principle of the sovereign states' monopoly on coercive force as well as the principles of non-intervention in internal affairs, consent as the basis of obligation to comply with international laws, and diplomatic immunity.[24]

Likewise, this emphasis on sovereign rights can be traced back to Grotius's theory of *natural law* in international relations between independent sovereign states, under which there are principles of conduct which are binding on all peoples, regardless of local custom. To Grotius, the sovereign rights of independent states to protect their own property were absolute, and should be respected by all states, regardless of size or power. Coming at a time of considerable conflict in Europe, with the end of the Thirty Years War, the Eighty Years War, the demise of the influence of the Holy Roman Empire (the Peace of Westphalia), Grotius's theory of *natural law*, and the supremacy of state sovereignty, was critically important. As the decades multiplied into centuries, sovereignty transitioned from an absolute right of monarchs to the supreme authority of states, eventually becoming established as 'Westphalian sovereignty', that has

---

[22] Barnes (note 13): 38.

[23] Scott J. Shackelford, 'The Tragedy of the Commons Heritage of Mankind' (2008) 27 *Stan. Envtl L. J.* 5.

[24] Ibid.

to a large part, defined international relations.[25] This original interpretation of sovereignty endured in international law, as seen in Article 15(8) of the Covenant of the League of Nations.[26] This provision stated that the League Council should refrain from dealing with disputes that arose out of a matter solely within the domestic jurisdiction of a party state.[27] This arrangement, which allowed for freedom of political development, ultimately resulted in the global ideological competition of the nineteenth and twentieth centuries.

It was not until after World War II that popular sovereignty became firmly rooted in the international legal system through the United Nations Charter.[28] It was during this same era that the first calls for limitations on sovereignty in the interests of humanitarian concerns were raised. Coupled with the social and environmental impacts of technological advancement, the success of the nation-state began to pose threats that were inconceivable in 1648. The meaning of sovereignty changed. International law now includes, not only the law between states, but law between the individual and the state – international human rights law.

International law, with its decentralized nature, emphasis on state sovereignty and adherence to Austinian legal positivism – the law is what states say it is – ensures that states negotiate and decide when to accept responsibility. International environmental law suffers from this 'inherited congenital defect' shared with public international law – the regulation, only, of legal relationships between states.[29] Let us recap the law. Presently, a state's environmental duties depend on which 'environment' is concerned. For the environment that the state 'owns', they can exploit, use or preserve it at their prerogative. There is no general principle or rule not to degrade one's own environment. For the environment that other states own, there is a principle of international law based on good neighbourliness not to cause damage. For the global commons, there is an abstract duty to cooperate and not to do harm, but no 'plaintiff' to enforce this. There is no example wherein pollution of the commons by a state has been litigated – how could there be when the commons (which is

---

[25] John H. Jackson, 'Sovereignty-Modern: A New Approach to an Outdated Concept' (2003) 97 *AJIL* 785.

[26] Covenant of the League of Nations, Art. 15(8).

[27] Shackelford (note 23): 6–7.

[28] Charter of the United Nations, Art. 1(1). This was largely a response to new power structures in the international system, namely as a result of the Allied victory in WWII, favouring a consensus on popular will as the basis for legitimate governance in much of the Western world.

[29] Bosselmann, *When Two Worlds Collide* (note 11): 79.

not a state and therefore has no legal personality in international law) has no representative or advocate?

That states have the sovereign right to exploit their own resources and form their own environmental policy is the foundational norm of international environmental law. It is enshrined in Principle 21 of the Stockholm Declaration, which also cites the Charter of the United Nations (and in particular Article 2, which establishes the principle of sovereign equality and the exclusive jurisdiction of states in their domestic affairs) and the principles of international law as authority for this proposition. This right is only limited by a responsibility to ensure that the activities within a state's jurisdiction or control do not cause environmental damage for other states or 'areas beyond the limits of national jurisdiction', that is, the global commons. Even with the scope for inter-state liability for pollution, there has been very little invocation of the principle. Pioneering decisions were made by international arbitration tribunals, of which the best known cases are Trail Smelter (1941), Corfu-Channel (1949) and Lac-Lanoux (1957). In these decisions, unintentional exports of harmful substances were, if they were substantial, judged to be violations against the principle of mutual consideration. The offenders were then liable for the damage caused. The Trail Smelter arbitration establishes that a wrongful act and injury must be 'established by clear and convincing evidence'. As Stone explains, to support a lawsuit, or even to deliver a tenable diplomatic protest, the complaining nation generally has to prove some physical 'intrusion' (or threat of intrusion) into its territory.[30] This imposes a high standard of proof. Without this 'infringement', 'many local factors that have in the aggregate, considerable implications for neighbouring states and the biosphere, such as population control, forest maintenance, agricultural techniques, public health administration, cultural attitudes (what constitutes a comfortable life?), are, as a practical matter, beyond the reach of international law'.[31]

This, together with the diplomatic implications of litigating against a political neighbour, means that it is unsurprising this course of action is not more frequently pursued. So, for all the noble concepts of the 'fundamental right to an environment of a quality that permits a life of dignity and well-being' in Principle 1, 16 and the safeguarding of the natural resources of the earth 'for the benefit of present and future generations' in Principle 2, they fall rather flat in the harsh reality of state entitlement to exploitation in Principle 21.

---

[30] Christopher D. Stone, *The Gnat is Older than Man: Global Environment and Human Agenda* (Princeton University Press, Princeton, NJ 1993): 38.

[31] Ibid.

Thus, we can see that state sovereignty is a major impediment to binding international environmental regulation because it prevents intrusion into domestic affairs. But, are we seeing an erosion of sovereignty in global politics? Many see international human rights law as an indication that sovereignty is more porous, and domestic jurisdiction is no longer entirely insulated from interference or from international law which is not voluntarily adopted.[32] Since 2005, the notion of 'responsibility to protect' has been invoked to justify military intervention in a sovereign state on humanitarian grounds, such as genocide, to prevent an imminent catastrophe. This theory considers sovereignty to be contingent upon the good functioning of the state in the discharge of duties of protection towards its subjects, and voidable in the event of a drastic failure of governance.[33]

Certain world leaders have also joined with liberal theorists to bring attention to the inevitable decline of national sovereignty in international relations. Boutros Boutros-Ghali stated: 'The time of absolute and exclusive sovereignty . . . has passed; its theory was never matched by reality.'[34] As Kofi Annan noted, 'Our post-war institutions were built for an *international* world, but we now live in a *global* world'.[35] Further, political theorists such as Susan Strange contend that the waning authority of domestic policymakers over their states' affairs has led to 'territoriality [being] swept away by a pace of change more rapid than human society has ever experienced before'.[36] Furthermore, the World Trade Organization (WTO) and the World Health Organization (WHO) are potent examples of supranational organizations which demand (and receive) a partial immobilization of state sovereignty. However, those examples speak of the voluntary suspension of sovereignty – for causes (trade and pandemics) that states obviously feel override the need for non-interference. Human rights standards, on the other hand, although voluntarily adopted by many states, are norms the recognition of which is hardly an overnight affair. Even now,

---

32 Shackelford (note 23): 7–8.

33 Stephen Stec, 'Humanitarian Limits to Sovereignty: Common Concern and Common Heritage Approaches to Natural Resources and Environment' (2010) 12 *Int. C. L. Rev.* 361, 384–385.

34 United Nations Secretary General, 'An Agenda for Peace, Preventive Diplomacy, Peacemaking and Peace-Keeping', Report of the Secretary General Pursuant to the Statement adopted by the Summit Meeting of the Security Council on 31 January 1992. A/47/277 – S/24111 (delivered to the Security Council, 17 June 1992): http://www.unrol.org/files/A_47_277.pdf.

35 Jackson (note 25): 784.

36 S. Strange, 'The Declining Authority of States', in D. Held and A. McGrew (eds), *The Global Transformations Reader: An Introduction to the Globalization Debate*, 2nd edn (Polity Press, Cambridge 2003).

their enforcement has not been awe-inspiring, leading to the conclusion that, while significant, they are hardly a silver bullet for state sovereignty.

However, economic interdependence, 'globalization' and information flows do continue to alter the *shape* of sovereignty. Furthermore, scholars view international environmental law as manifest evidence that states are willing to concede sovereignty in order to collectively address the environmental 'problem'.[37] Peter Sand calls this the environmental revolution smashing the icon of territorial sovereignty.[38] If this is the case, what gains have we made with decreased sovereignty in terms of sustainability and global environmental governance? Emissions continue to increase worldwide, as do biodiversity losses, all the while states fail to reach consensus in international negotiations, even over the weakest of environmental protections.

Attempts to breach the impermeability of sovereignty via international environmental law have so far failed: there is no clear indication of how 'common concern' affects sovereignty, and in many ways international environmental law has been a vehicle for affirming states' territorial sovereignty, UNCLOS and the Convention of Biodiversity being examples of this. Unfortunately, it seems altogether too soon and too naive to think that international environmental law is the phoenix that many hope it is. A major problem is the lack of enforcement of international law, and lack of compliance even where states subscribe to the rules. 'Practical political considerations continue to emphasize the supremacy of state-to-state interactions and Westphalian sovereignty favoured by realists.'[39] Furthermore, beyond the practical need for resources for human development (something which is viewed relatively and in competition), we forget that identity plays a major part in the way that states behave – what they will and will not do.

As Stephen Stec explains, 'control and exploitation of natural resources . . . also comprise the physical and emotional power base of nation states'.[40] It is perhaps unsurprising that states are naturally inclined to resist the communalization of such valuable assets, which not only means sharing – something entirely contrary to neoliberal principles – but

---

[37] Peter H. Sand, 'Sovereignty Bounded: Public Trusteeship for Common Pool Resources' (2004) 4 *Global Environmental Politics* 47.

[38] Ibid.

[39] J. Thomson, 'State Sovereignty in International Relations: Bridging the Gap between Theory and Empirical Research' (1995) 39 *Int. Stud. Q.* 213. Realists conceive of sovereignty as the state's ability to make authoritative decisions. If interdependence is growing, it is merely a reflection of state preferences.

[40] Stec (note 33): 377.

it also represents a fundamental attack on faith in the nation-state as the main actor in solving global problems.[41]

Yet, is it possible that sovereignty is being eroded without states' concessions? *Jus cogens* are mandatory, non-derogable international norms. Their existence is a lacuna in state sovereignty, surely? Perhaps so, but there has yet to be an environmental rule alongside others such as genocide and slavery.[42] If we consider what drives the various kinds of *jus cogens* – that which is so inherently immoral – surely destruction of the environment, the basis of all life and hence human existence, should be among them. In the opinion of Stone, certain acts can be denominated as 'ecocidal' acts and should be likened to genocide in the international community.[43] However, the reason *jus cogens* tend to be based on human rights, as Stone points out, is because human rights are far more evocative than eco-laws: 'cutting down trees does not arouse the same outrage as cutting down people . . . the tree cutters are at least offering economic development in return for their damage'.[44]

It becomes clear that international environmental law is based on respect for other states' sovereignty which is akin to the Western regime of property rights, but far removed from ecological integrity. And yet it is in this arena that we search for the global solution to this truly grave predicament. Sovereignty is an enduring feature of the global system. This constitutes the basic dilemma of traditional international environmental law. It must get by with a set of tools which has been developed for a totally different scenario. Because neighbours were capable of waging war, states kept a suspicious eye on each other and the conflict model of international law fulfilled its purpose. And it will keep this purpose in economic matters.[45] The sole exception to the system of Westphalian sovereignty has been the international commons. But even all the areas of the commons are not deemed exclusively the common heritage of mankind. And although states do not 'own' parts of the commons, the governance regimes that are in place are the products of states. In this way, 'enclosure' of the commons occurs through both the market and the state, and often the two are indistinguishable. Enclosure is an illustration of how

---

[41] Ibid.

[42] Evan J. Criddle and Evan Fox-Decent, 'A Fiduciary Theory of Jus Cogens' (2009) 34 *Yale J. Int'l* 331.

[43] See Stone (note 30) and more recently Polly Higgins, *Eradicating Ecocide: Laws and Governance to Stop the Destruction of the Planet* (Shepheard-Walwyn, London 2010).

[44] Stone (note 30): 38.

[45] Bosselmann, *When Two Worlds Collide* (note 11): 82.

'sovereignty over the commons has to some extent tracked sovereignty over continental territories, transitioning from communal to national'.[46] Thus, through the reality of sovereignty, it is extremely unlikely that any real initiative will come from states negotiating effective treaties of universal application to protect the global environment.

This reality of neoliberal governance has unsurprisingly also affected how environmental law and regulation is conceived *within* states. Primarily, environmental law is characterized by a 'discretionary frame'.[47] As Mary Wood explains, what this means is that governments have positioned themselves as holding discretionary powers to permit resource exploitation.[48] Domestic environmental commons may be 'government-owned' but this isn't to say it is managed on behalf of future generations, nonhuman species or ordinary citizens.[49]

On the contrary, 'as a general rule, politics – not trusteeship and fiduciary duty – determines what uses are permitted and what prices are charged'.[50] This discretionary frame disguises, behind a 'thick veil of complexity', the unceasing fact that private property rights dictate the direction of discretion, and that the supposed representatives of the environmental interests of the governed actually serve private interests at their expense.[51] To the extent that governments are environmental trustees at present, their primary duty, as they perceive it, is not to preserve the land itself but the income streams it generates.[52] At the same time, techno jargon 'neutralizes' environmental damage, not alerting the public to the problems they should be concerned about and ensuring the requisite level of public ignorance and apathy to maintain this symbiotic relationship.[53] To the extent that the judiciary is supposed to be a check on the executive, they too often deem administrative agencies' discretion beyond their jurisdiction for 'review'.

---

46 Shackelford (note 23): 5.
47 Wood (note 1).
48 Ibid.: 592.
49 Barnes (note 13): 43.
50 Ibid.
51 Wood (note 1): 592.
52 Barnes (note 13): 44.
53 Wood (note 1): 599.

4. SOVEREIGNTY AND TRUSTEESHIP

Fundamentally, the legitimacy of the state rests on its function to act for, and on behalf of, its citizens. This requires the consent of the governed.[54] Governmental duties can therefore be understood as fiduciary obligations towards citizens.[55] Such fiduciary obligations are recognized typically in public law,[56] exist in common law and civil law (although in varying forms and degrees)[57] and are also known in international law.[58] The fiduciary function of the state can also be described as a trusteeship function.[59]

In the following sections, we will explore how state sovereignty can be reconciled with trusteeship. *Prime facie* both seem to have different purposes, yet, as we will see, they are part of the same basic function of the state, that is, to serve the citizens it depends on and is accountable to.

The environmental crisis and the state of the global commons give rise to the need to revisit the relationship between sovereignty and trusteeship.[60] Trusteeship must be pursued at both the international level and the domestic 'internal' level. As Benvenisti notes, the private, self-contained concept of sovereignty is less compelling than it was in the past because of the 'glaring misfit between the scope of the sovereign's authority and the sphere of the affected stakeholders'.[61] This 'glaring misfit' engenders inefficient, undemocratic and unjust outcomes for under- or unrepresented

---

[54] John Locke: '(G)overnment is not legitimate unless it is carried on with the consent of the governed' in Richard Ashcraft (ed.), *John Locke: Critical Assessments* (Routledge, London 1991): 524.

[55] Evan Fox-Decent, *Sovereignty's Promise: The State as a Fiduciary* (Oxford University Press, 2012); T. Frankel, 'Fiduciary Law' (1983) 71 *Calif. Law Rev.* 795.

[56] Including constitutional law, administrative law, tax law, criminal law and environmental law.

[57] For example, the USA, Canada, Australia and New Zealand recognize them with respect to indigenous peoples, ratepayers and (with the exception of New Zealand) in the form of public trusts, whereas continental European countries more fundamentally rely on public law to assume fiduciary relationships between individuals and governments.

[58] Michael C. Blumm and Rachel D. Guthrie, 'Internationalizing the Public Trust Doctrine' (2012) 45 *UC Davis L. Rev.* 741; Henry H. Perritt, 'Structures and Standards for Political Trusteeships' (2004) 8 *UCLA J. Int'l L. & Foreign Aff.* 391; Edith Brown Weiss, 'The Planetary Trust: Conservation and Intergenerational Equity' (1984) 11 *Ecology LQ* 495.

[59] Paul Finn, 'The Forgotten "Trust": The People and the State', in Malcolm Cope (ed.), *Equity: Issues and Trends* (The Federation Press, Leichhardt, NSW 1995): 131–151.

[60] Stec (note 33): 378–380.

[61] Eyal Benvenisti, 'Sovereigns as Trustees of Humanity: On the Accountability of States to Foreign Stakeholders' (2013) 107 (2) *AJIL* 295, 301.

affected stakeholders.[62] Non-citizens, future generations and the natural environment fall into such a category of 'affected stakeholders'.

Trusteeship for sustainability needs to be a ubiquitous principle in all levels of governance down to even the family unit, in the same way that other fundamental ethical principles such as fairness are implicit in our social lives. There are two challenges to advancing the idea of trusteeship and both boil down to sovereignty. On the one hand, to propose a system of international trusteeship is to directly challenge the principle of non-interference in states' domestic affairs. To propose that states become trustees themselves, in addition to an international system of trusteeship, is, again, an intrusion into states' sovereign right to determine their approach to the environment. However, without the latter we will not achieve the former. Regardless of what one thinks about the legitimacy of sovereignty and the entire makeup of international relations, the reality is that states call the shots. Devoid of a radical reorganization of global politics, we need to work within the state-centric context.

Trusteeship is an idea which softens the blow of what would otherwise be seen as an unprecedented intrusion into sovereign state affairs. Consider, what would an international trustee be? Trustees are not states; a trust council might not even be an intergovernmental institution if it were comprised of individuals rather than drawn exclusively from 'states'. Arguably, this represents a less threatening intrusion into sovereignty. After all, this is a type of interventionism that was not envisaged in the UN Charter and which is desirable, necessary and legitimate.[63] As Catherine Redgwell explains, 'trust arrangements do not challenge sovereignty directly, for one of the advantages of trusteeship arrangements is the absence of sovereignty in the exercise of trusteeship functions – there is no transfer of sovereignty to the trust authority'.[64]

But what if trust arrangements were perceived of as a significant intrusion into sovereignty? As we will see later, proposals of trusteeship arrangements at the level of the United Nations have been, more often than not, greeted with hostility. States seem too atttached to the principle of non-interference to appreciate cooperation of this kind. Yet, the

---

[62] Ibid.

[63] Ilias Bantekas, *Trust Funds under International Law: Trustee Obligations of the United Nations and International Development Banks* (TMC Asser Press, The Hague 2009): 19.

[64] Catherine Redgwell, 'Reforming the UN Trusteeship Council', in W. Bradnee Chambers and Jessica F. Green (eds), *Reforming International Environmental Governance: From Institutional Limits to Innovative Reforms* (United Nations University Press, Tokyo 2005): 179.

very origins of the concept of state sovereignty are closely linked with humanitarian concerns. The Peace of Westphalia, as the foundation of state sovereignty, was a key instrument in upholding humanitarian precepts relating to freedom of conscience and religion.[65] To the extent that it resolved a crisis of freedom of conscience and equality before the law and many pre-existing institutions had lost their legitimacy and ultimately collapsed, sovereignty has been and can be justified. But it should also be remembered that humanitarian concerns were at the root of the crisis that the new order resolved. Where new crises emerge, can the principle of non-interference really be justified?

Likewise, with regards to the state itself as environmental trustee for those over whom it governs, it could hardly be refuted that a democratically elected government does not owe its peoples a duty to govern their natural wealth and resources in the interest of their natural development and of the well-being of the people of the state concerned.[66] The first step, then, is convincing civil society that these rights and responsibilities lie with them, despite the state acting as their representative. The second step is convincing them what these rights and responsibilities entail. This is no small task.

Although there is a dedicated green movement, and ever more 'lite' green sentiment, convincing people to alter their engrained, even unconscious neoliberal proclivities in favour of an ethic of stewardship and trusteeship is a very trying task, especially with the economic wind blowing in their faces. But whoever's interests are involved, they must pass through individual countries like a camel through the eye of a needle, and without a mobilized civil society – a *demos* – that is willing to hold governments to account, and demand that they represent their ecological interests internationally, states will continue to behave in the way they always have – reacting to the global environmental crisis according to the conflict model of international law that they are used to.

5. THE MANDATE TO GOVERN

How did we get to this point? Especially if, as we contend, environmental trusteeship has ancient roots and has formed an important part of human social organization throughout history, this question needs to be asked. In

---

65 Stec (note 33): 378–380.

66 See e.g. Declaration on Permanent Sovereignty over Natural Resources, GA Res 1803 (XVII) (1962) [1].

the previous chapter, we discussed how trusteeship carries with it a fiduciary duty. We also saw how states justified colonial rule as a form of trusteeship for peoples who were uncivilized and incapable of self-governance. However, beyond this historical use, the fiduciary relationship still characterizes the relationship between government and the governed. This means that states' sovereignty is premised on trusteeship.

The Peace of Westphalia, besides establishing a sphere of confessional freedom, confirmed the notion of the social contract and empowered the non-ruling classes.[67] Thomas Hobbes, the father of political realism, for all the advocacy for the absolutism of the sovereign, nevertheless argued that political power gained legitimacy through being representative and established at the behest of people. Jean-Jacques Rousseau wrote *Du contrat social ou Principes du droit politique* [*Of The Social Contract, Or Principles of Political Right*] in 1762. Like Hobbes, Rousseau drew on the social contract – the idea that in order to remove ourselves from a 'state of nature' and anarchy, people form a social contract with one another to limit some freedoms in exchange for commonly held duties. The obligation owed among people is manifest in the government who acts, not by divine right, but through the will of the people. The state–people fiduciary relationship originated alongside the republican idea of popular sovereignty.

Criddle and Fox-Decent explain the concept:[68]

> popular sovereignty denotes that the state's sovereign powers belong to the people, and so those powers are held in trust by their rulers on condition that they be used for the people's benefit. Popular sovereignty thus implies that the state and its institutions are fiduciaries of the people, for their justification rests exclusively on the authority they enjoy to govern and serve the people.

'Popular will' was inaugurated as the only legitimate basis for political authority in the English Civil War, in the American Revolution, and then again confirmed in the French Revolution.[69] It is echoed in constitutional documents such as the 1776 Pennsylvania Declaration of Rights: '[A]ll power being . . . derived from the people; therefore all officers of government, whether legislative or executive, are their trustees and servants, and at all times accountable to them.'[70] Locke famously asserted that legislative power is 'only a fiduciary power to act for certain ends' and that

---

[67] Stec (note 33): 378–380.

[68] Criddle and Fox-Decent (note 42): 350.

[69] W. Michael Reisman, 'Sovereignty and Human Rights in Contemporary International Law' (1990) 84 *AJIL* 867, 886.

[70] Criddle and Fox-Decent (note 42): 50; Pennsylvania Constitution of 1776, Art. IV.

'there remains still in the people a supreme power to remove or alter the legislative, when they find the legislative act contrary to the trust reposed in them'. [71]

Likewise, Immanuel Kant drew the moral basis of fiduciary obligations from the duty-bound relationship between parents and children.[72] Kant claimed that children have an innate and legal right to their parents' care. In a similar sense, he believed that state legitimacy was the result of a contract that is necessarily created between people to form a Rousseauian 'general will'. Through this process, Kant claimed, we jointly authorize the state to announce and enforce law.

That state sovereignty is fundamentally a trust relationship cannot be dismissed as a Western ideal. As we saw in the previous chapter, trusts and the implicit fiduciary relationship are traced back to Middle Eastern origins, Roman and Germanic law as well as being inherent in religious teachings. The idea is perhaps even more prevalent in non-Western societies than in present-day Western ones because the former emphasize collective identities (for example, family, clan, nation, religion) over individual freedom and dignity, imbuing implied fiduciary obligations into the structure of public and private legal institutions.[73]

Nowadays, this idea is manifest in the benchmark of our political system – democracy. It is enshrined in Article 21(3) of the Universal Declaration of Human Rights which states that 'the will of the people shall be the basis of the authority of government'.[74] But as Ron Engel points out, 'democracy' can have differing interpretations. There is the 'thin' interpretation which includes procedural democracy, liberal democracy, representative democracy or, simply put, 'the democratic process'.[75] He explains:[76]

> In this view, the democratic ideal is a way of bringing free and equal but competitive individuals and groups (or 'interests') into cooperative and stable relationships by such devices as constitutionally protected civil and political rights, limited government, basic fairness in the distribution of social goods, and opportunities for citizen participation in the formation of public policy through membership in the voluntary associations of civil society and voting in electoral politics.

---

[71] John Locke, *Second Treatise of Government* (Wiley-Blackwell, Oxford 2014): 149, 243 [originally published 1689].

[72] Criddle and Fox-Decent (note 42): 352.

[73] Ibid.: 378–379.

[74] Universal Declaration of Human Rights, GA Res 217 A(III) (adopted 10 December 1948) (UDHR).

[75] Engel (note 8): 28.

[76] Ibid.

Engel contends that the problem with this approach is that 'its principle and narrative, while essential components of the democratic inheritance, are not a complete account of the moral and spiritual requirements of human self-governance'.[77] The role of government is to act as conscientious trustee of citizen resources.[78] We see that in our market-based societies governments fail in both the interpretation and application of what this means – this is a systematic failure of neoliberalism.[79] It has captured how we think about our political arrangements. The state has become, if not the 'engine of market enclosure',[80] then most certainly the conductor.

So, although we may have democracy (and many places do not) in its technical form, we have lost sight of what duty the state owes those it governs. At its most simplistic, the state's legitimacy to govern is based on its ability to serve the common interest. Aristotle saw the purpose of the state as for the 'common good'. John Locke also hinted at such a purpose. But further questions are raised, such as: who defines common interest and what does it include? According to Locke's definition, the 'common good' was what arose from there being surplus produce which could be sold in the marketplace. As Collins explains, Locke's 'definition of the common good is a quantifiable one, not a moral one. From this concept of quantity would flow the modern measure of the common good – the gross domestic product – a poor measure of any society's real quality of life'.[81] But because 'common interests' are socially conceived, they are not static and can be contested – we can argue that new functions and responsibilities ought to become a part of the state's mandate to govern.

Putting aside for a moment the question of what the common good is, let us consider what the relationship between government and the governed ought to be. We have seen that government perceives its role largely as a facilitator of economic growth, seen as analogous with 'prosperity', and thus the protector of private property;[82] that is, the belief that allowing individuals to pursue their own interests will result in the best possible social organization. Few governments could argue that they do not owe a

---

[77] Ibid.: 31.

[78] Bollier (note 3); P. Barnes, J. Rowe and D. Bollier, *The State of the Commons 2003/04: A Report to Owners* (Tomales Bay Institute, Point Reyes Station, CA 2004).

[79] Bollier (note 3).

[80] Ibid.

[81] Sheila D. Collins, 'Interrogating and Reconceptualizing Natural Law to Protect the Integrity of the Earth', in Laura Westra, Klaus Bosselmann and Richard Westra (eds), *Reconciling Human Existence with Ecological Integrity* (Earthscan, London 2008): 455.

[82] Ibid.

fiduciary duty to their constituents. Indeed, now more than ever, governments are scrambling to reduce deficits in order to fulfil their obligation to the public not to overspend. The problem is that states have neglected the ecological aspects of their fiduciary duty – and we, as the voting public, have let them.

Benvenisti conceives of three other normative bases according to which we should ascribe a trusteeship function to states' mandate to govern. The first two grounds lend themselves most easily to the development of rights and obligations under a conception of state trusteeship limited to intra-generational concerns. A normative approach which grounds itself in global resource distribution may be more conducive to the realization of state trusteeship according to principles of inter-generational equity.[83]

First, sovereignty should be viewed as a vehicle for the exercise of personal and collective self-determination.[84] Collective self-determination embodies the freedom of a group to pursue its interests, further its political status and 'freely dispose of [its] natural wealth and resources'.[85] An outdated conception of sovereignty which equates the voting constituency with the affected stakeholders can undermine communities' ability to exercise their right to self-determination. Urbinati and Warren note that this 'geography-based constituency definition' introduces an arbitrary criterion of inclusion/exclusion right at the outset of the discussion on sovereignty.[86] A key challenge in the practical implementation of this principle is thus a clear definition of the 'affected stakeholders'. The Aarhus Convention provides an interesting empirical reference point: it defines the 'public concerned' for the purposes of notification of environmental decision-making[87] as 'the public affected or likely to be affected by, or having an interest in, the environmental decision-making'.

Second, Benvenisti refers to a conception of sovereign states as agents of humanity as a whole.[88] He bases this conception largely on the equal

---

[83] As initially expounded by Edith Brown Weiss, see Edith Brown Weiss, 'The Planetary Trust: Conservation and Intergenerational Equity' (1984) 11 *Ecology LQ* 495.

[84] Benvenisti (note 61): 301.

[85] International Covenant on Civil and Political Rights, 999 UNTS 171 (adopted 16 December 1966, entered into force 23 March 1976), Art. 1 (ICCPR).

[86] Nadia Irbinati and Mark E. Warren, 'The Concept of Representation in Contemporary Democratic Theory' (2008) *Annual Review of Political Science* 387, 397, cited in Benvenisti (note 61): 304.

[87] Convention on Access to Information, Public Participation in Decision-Making and Access to Justice in Environmental Matters, 2161 UNTS 447 (adopted 25 June 1998, entered into force 30 October 2001), Art. 6.2 (Aarhus Convention).

[88] Benvenisti (note 61): 305.

moral worth of all human beings[89] and the corresponding foundation of international law in human rights.[90] He argues that it is humanity at large that assigns to certain groups of citizens the power to form national governments.[91] Accordingly, states can and should be viewed as agents of a global system that allocates competences and responsibilities for the promotion of the rights of all human beings and their interest in the sustainable utilization of global resources.[92] As such, the corollary of states' authority to manage public affairs within their domestic jurisdictions is an obligation to take account of external interests and balance internal against external interests.[93]

Similarly, we could say that the privilege of territorial sovereignty – when given to a group of people – can be legitimized (and respected by other groups and individuals) only when used to promote universal interests of humanity as a whole and not those of the sovereign's citizenry or its (majority or any hegemonic) subgroup. This argument is based on the observation that boundaries of states no longer coincide with boundaries of nationalities or, more generally, with boundaries of groups whose members commonly share a distinct interest or conception of the good.[94]

Benvenisti also refers to a conception of sovereignty as the power to exclude portions of global resources.[95] He notes that both ownership and sovereignty are claims for intervention in the state of nature by carving out valuable space for exclusive use.[96] Such a perception of states as power-wielding property owners provides a solid normative foundation for the imposition of a positive obligation on states to take other-regarding considerations into account when managing the resources assigned to them.[97] Property law theory can thus provide us with a framework within which

---

[89] Ibid., referring to John Stewart Mill, *Considerations on Representative Government* (Prometheus Books, New York, first published 1861).

[90] Joseph Raz, 'Human Rights in the Emerging World Order' (2010) 1 *TLT* 31, 42, cited in Benvenisti (note 61): 306.

[91] Benevisti (note 61): 306.

[92] Ibid.: 308, paraphrasing Huber in Island of Palmas (*Netherlands v United States*) (1928) 2 RIAA 829, 869.

[93] Ibid., paraphrasing Huber in British Claims in the Spanish Zone of Morocco (*Spain v United Kingdom*) (1925) 2 RIAA 615, 641.

[94] Chaim Gans, *The Limits of Nationalism* (Cambridge University Press, Cambridge 2003), cited in Shai Perry, 'Research proposal, May 2013', p. 2.

[95] Benvenisti (61): 308.

[96] Ibid.

[97] Ibid.: 309, 310. Also when making rival claims on transboundary and public resources.

we can translate these moral grounds into legal obligations.[98] Thus, we can and should conceptualize ownership of global resources as originating from a collective regulatory decision at the global level, rather than as an entitlement which inheres in sovereign states.[99]

Although we might all agree that a government has fiduciary duties, there is seemingly little to establish a precedent of state *environmental* trusteeship.[100] However, what many people do not know is that the Magna Carta of 1215, the armistice in civil war between the commoners and King John, 'contained largely unappreciated calls against the exploitation of the forests as ordained by the king at that time'. In a scenario potently familiar to many current governments, 'the king wanted to degrade the forests to a source of lumber, convert the lumber into money, and invest it in those who promised him their loyalty'.[101] The accompanying 'Forest Charter' constitutes landmark statements of commoners' rights. It included a statement of common rights of the forest (Chapters 47 and 48) and of the common right of the piscary or fishing rights (Chapter 33).[102] Yet in the 1870s, the champions of Anglo–American capital recast the Magna Carta to justify their imperial ambitions and racist politics. Certain portions of the Magna Carta have been celebrated and enshrined, while other portions – especially those dealing with commoners' rights to the fruits of the commons – have been portrayed as feudal relics and local particularities.[103] Furthermore, if environmental trusteeship was a seemingly fluent part of ways of life around the world, why did this aspect of social organization not get translated into state governance? And if it was lost, how do we find it again?

---

[98] Klaus Bosselmann, 'Property Rights and Sustainability: Can They Be Reconciled?', in David Grinlinton and Prue Taylor (eds), *Property Rights and Sustainability: The Evolution of Property Rights to Meet Ecological Challenges* (Martinus Nijhoff, The Hague 2011): 23–42.

[99] Benvenisiti (note 61): 309.

[100] See generally Klaus Bosselmann, *The Principle of Sustainability: Transforming Law and Governance* (Ashgate, Farnham 2008): 145–74.

[101] Helfrich (note 4): 1.

[102] Ibid.

[103] David Bollier, 'The Future of the Commons: Notes from a retreat exploring the potential of the commons to fight enclosures and build commons-based alternatives' (Retreat on the Future of the Commons, Crottorf Castle, Germany, 25–27 June 2009): http://commonstrust.global-negotiations.org/resources/Bollier,%20 Crottorf%20retreat.pdf.

6. STATES AS TRUSTEES

It is time for our political institutions to shed their exclusively economically imagined mandate and adopt an ethic of care for the commons. This includes recognizing that they are responsible for maintaining the health of the environment, and this can only be achieved through sustainability. The prosperity that governments are designated to affect is a much larger concept than material well-being, and involves maintaining the common ecological basis of the economy. Only the state is in a position to make and enforce rules based on fundamental principles, and only the state has the power to govern.[104] The way to achieve this, and the alternative to Engel's 'thin' democracy, is a 'thick' interpretation which includes what can be termed 'the democratic way of life'.[105] Thick democracy includes 'respect for others and respect for self, non-violence and mutual persuasion, critical reason and empirical inquiry, trust and hospitality for the stranger, and compassion for the suffering of others; as well as the distinctive political goods associated with the rule of law based on equal justice, reason and consent; universal political, civil, economic, social and cultural rights', and so on.[106] It is 'a narrative that consequently finds in the struggle to assure the conditions for a life of free and equal dignity for all persons living in community with one another and the Earth as the ultimate end and meaning of human history'.[107]

That states can reconceptualize their mandate to govern is not a pipe dream. We can point to empirical examples of specific treaty obligations, state practice and domestic legislation, in which states have adopted 'other-regarding obligations': requirements to take into account the effects of policies on both non-citizens and the environment.[108]

Such requirements with respect to non-citizens can be seen in WTO law. For example, the exception under GATT Article XX(j) that members may deviate from their GATT obligations in adopting and enforcing measures 'essential to the acquisition or distribution of products in general or local short supply' is qualified by a requirement to observe 'the principle that all contracting parties are entitled to an equitable share of the international supply of such products'.

Similarly, the Agreement on Agriculture requires that states instituting 'any new export prohibition or restriction on foodstuffs [. . .] shall give due

---

104 Bosselmann (note 100): 145.
105 Engel (note 8): 29.
106 Ibid.
107 Ibid.
108 Benvenisti (61): 316.

consideration to the effects of such prohibition or restriction on importing Members' food security' (Article 12).

Other procedural obligations flowing from a trusteeship conception of states are explored in the following two chapters.

We can also point to examples in which states have adopted other-regarding obligations with respect to the natural environment. Ostrom has pointed to numerous local examples where cooperation is based on an acknowledgement of sustainable management of the environment.[109]

Likewise, the Great Law of Peace is an example where political leaders are trustees and recognize the vital ecological component of that role, going beyond the mere economic development of peoples. Only with this aspect of governments' mandate firmly entrenched can we redeem the concept of national sovereignty for our modern-day context. Globally, about 100 countries have constitutional environmental protections of some kind, and half of them incorporate environmental rights in some form.[110]

Within Europe, the constitutions of 14 EU member states as well as all Eastern European states contain express environmental provisions.[111] In some other constitutions, more expansive environmental rights have been proclaimed, for example Brazil, Costa Rica and Paraguay's constitutions refer to the preservation of 'ecological balance', while Ecuador and Bolivia's constitutions mention specific rights relating to Mother Earth. In the US, some state constitutions refer to the preservation of natural, scenic, historic and aesthetic values of the environment.

What remains is for all these states to pragmatically realize their role as environmental trustee. Like a constitutional obligation, this needs to be a non-derogable function of government, to the extent that deviating from trusteeship would trigger the courts' jurisdiction to invoke trusteeship to halt contrary policy. The German constitution, for example, contains a specific state obligation to protect the environment for future generations.[112]

As Benvenisti notes, states' failure to comply with the majority of existing 'other-regarding' obligations under international law does not trigger direct legal consequences imposed by third parties through effective enforcement mechanisms.[113] He suggests furthermore that such

---

[109] Elinor Ostrom, *Governing the Commons: The Evolution of Institutions for Collective Action* (Cambridge University Press, Cambridge 1990).

[110] Bosselmann (note 100): 126.

[111] Ibid.: 125.

[112] Art. 20a: 'Mindful also of its responsibility toward future generations, the State shall protect the natural bases of life (. . .).'

[113] Benvenisti (note 61): 316.

an 'imperfect' recognition of these obligations may in fact be desirable. He lists three reasons for this: first, an external, sanction-imposing regime may be comparatively less competent than states in striking the right balance between domestic and foreign interests; second, such a regime may compromise equality and reciprocity by unduly burdening certain sovereigns but not others; and third, such a regime could displace and stifle democratic processes.[114]

Such a system is closely related to the public trust doctrine, an example of trusteeship in action. The public trust has 'intimations of guardianship, responsibility, and community'.[115] As a doctrine of environmental protection, it evolved primarily though US courts and jurisprudence. It arose from the Roman law notion of *res communes* and embodies the principle that certain common resources or areas such as fisheries, air, running water and wild animals belong to all and are held in trust by the state for the benefit of the general public. Under the doctrine of *res communes*, the king could not grant exclusive rights of access to a common resource. So, things that are under a public trust cannot be given away or sold. The US Supreme Court decision in *Illinois Central Railroad v. Illinois*[116] was the landmark case wherein the Court invoked the public trust doctrine to prevent the government from alienating the public right to lands under navigable waters. The public trust originally held that certain resources such as lands beneath navigable waters or tidal areas are either inherently the property of the public at large or are at least subject to a kind of inherent easement for certain public purposes.[117]

In the 1970s, Joseph Sax 'unhooked [the doctrine] from its traditional moorings on or around water bodies and applied it to dry land as well',[118] through his highly influential article 'The Public Trust Doctrine in Natural Resources Law'.[119] According to Sax's analysis, the public trust doctrine required the collection of adequate information, public participation in decisions, informed and accountable choices, and close scrutiny of private giveaways of environmental resources.[120] Also in

---

114 Ibid.: 317.

115 Carol M. Rose, 'Joseph Sax and the Idea of the Public Trust' (1998) 25 *Ecology LQ* 351.

116 (1892) 146 US 387, 452; 135 Sc. Ct. 110, 118.

117 See Patrick Deveney, 'Title, Jus Publicum, and the Public Trust: An Historical Analysis' (1976) 1 *Sea Grant L. & Pol'y J.* 13, 14.

118 Carol (note 115): 352.

119 Joseph Sax, 'The Public Trust Doctrine in Natural Resources Law' (1970) 471 *Mich. L. Rev.* 509–546.

120 Ibid.: 557–565.

the 1970s, Nanda and Ris advocated a public trust doctrine approach whereby the state is trustee for the public, of both territorial and commons areas.[121]

The doctrine has since been incorporated into numerous states' court cases, constitutional language and environmental statutes.[122] Blumm and Guthrie find that the evolution of the US's public trust doctrine has in fact been outpaced by courts and legislatures in other states.[123] They point to legislation and jurisprudence in India, Pakistan, the Philippines, Uganda, Kenya, Nigeria, South Africa, Brazil, Ecuador and Canada, which have proved to be a more accurate reflection of Joseph Sax's original vision than that in the US, for two key reasons.[124]

First, the doctrine in these ten states incorporates the principles of precaution, sustainable development and intergenerational equity. This linkage is often due to courts' interpretation of the doctrine as a part of constitutional and statutory declarations of the public's right to a healthy environment or the right to life, which remain largely unrecognized in the US.[125] Furthermore, the doctrine now applies to many more natural resources, both aquatic and terrestrial, than Joseph Sax suggested it should in 1970.[126] Blumm and Guthrie conclude that the rapid embracing of the public trust doctrine in these diverse countries evidences an evolution of the doctrine towards becoming a general principle of international law – a development perhaps beyond what Sax envisioned in his pioneering article four decades ago.[127] Figure 6.1 outlines the states in which public trust doctrine and 'public trust doctrine-like' laws and policies have been introduced.

While many , mostly common law, countries have introduced public

---

[121] V.P. Nanda and W. Ris Jr, 'The Public Trust Doctrine: A Viable Approach to International Environmental Protection' (1976) 5 *Ecology LQ* 291.

[122] Mary Turnipseed, 'Operationalizing Ubiquitous Stewardship Mandates in Ocean Law and Policy with the Public Trust Doctrine or Using the Public Trust Doctrine to Achieve Ocean Stewardship' (2013): 3: https://law.uoregon.edu/assets/facultydocs/mwood/turnipseed.doc.

[123] Michael C. Blumm and Rachel D. Guthrie, 'Internationalizing the Public Trust Doctrine: Natural Law and Constitutional and Statutory Approaches to Fulfilling the Saxion Vision' (2012) 45 *UC Davis L. Rev.* 741, 748.

[124] Ibid.: 1. The study analyses and compares the origins and scope, bases, purpose, public standing and remedies under the doctrine in each respective country.

[125] Ibid.: 70.

[126] Ibid.

[127] Ibid.: 9.

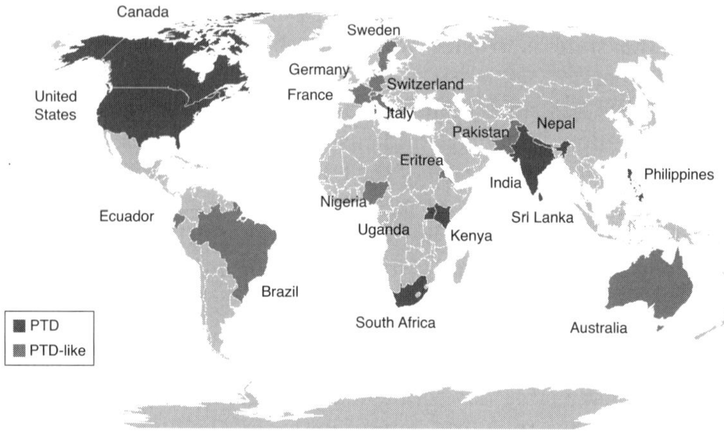

Note: Reprinted from Sagarin and Turnipseed 2012.

Source: Blumm and Guthrie 2012; Sand 2004; Turnipseed et al. 2010.

Figure 6.1 The PTD and 'PTD-like' 128 laws and policies in state laws

trust-type laws into their respective jurisdictions, the process of the incorporation and [128] expansion of the public trust doctrine into domestic law is a prime example of a 'creeping cross-cultural process of diffusion between legal systems'.[129] Peter Sand adopts Arnold Toynbee's concept of 'memesis' to describe such processes.[130] Toynbee defines 'memesis' as 'the reception and adoption of elements of culture that have been created elsewhere and have reached the recipients by a process of diffusion'.[131]

Like the public trust, there are numerous examples of stakeholder trusts – assets managed by trustees on behalf of a specific group – which convey a notion of commons ownership and equitable benefit. In Alaska, the state government established the Alaska Permanent Fund to serve as a trust fund for revenues derived from the sale of oil on state lands. The

[128] 'PTD-like' laws refer to those protecting public access to common natural resources or discussing trusteeship-like governmental responsibilities without using the term 'public trust'. These States include Ecuador, which recently rewrote its constitution to provide a right to exist for nature.

[129] Peter Sand, 'The Rise of Public Trusteeship in International Law' (2013) Global Trust Working Paper Series 04/2013, 21: http://globaltrust.tau.ac.il/national-courts-as-trustees-of-humanity/.

[130] Ibid.

[131] Arnold Joseph Toynbee, *A Study of History: Reconsiderations*, Vol. 12 (Oxford University Press, Oxford 1961): 343, cited in Sand (note 128): 21.

Fund, now worth US$40.1 billion, generated dividends of $1,107 for every citizen in the state in 2006, making it a policy mechanism for equitable sharing of benefits. These sorts of trusts are a good model for a more centralized system of trusteeship at international level – as long as permission to commodify commons resources is done sustainably and in a way that maintains the essential character of the resource as a shared one.

The one problem with the idea of the public trust is that it creates two distinct categories of government duties – that which is under the public trust and common property (which belongs to the people) and that which is state property (which can be controlled and mismanaged by government).[132] Arguably, all of the domestic environment should be part of this public trust, not just small pockets set aside for conservation. So, while the idea is appropriate, it needs wide application. Sustainability needs to be a fundamental principle of governance, such as justice or human rights, not merely a choice to apply to certain things. Pennsylvania's constitution, for example, declares: 'Pennsylvania's public natural resources are the common property of all the people, including generations yet to come. As trustee of these resources, the Commonwealth shall conserve and maintain them for the benefit of all the people.' As Barnes correctly notes of this constitutional dictum, 'serving as trustee of natural resources isn't an *option* for the state, it's an affirmative duty'.[133]

Mary C. Wood has been instrumental in furthering this idea, carving out a bold new legal strategy for government accountability for climate change based on the public trust doctrine.[134] It dictates that it is the government's duty to maintain certain natural resources for the benefit of its citizens. Through Wood's approach, which she terms 'atmospheric trust litigation', lawsuits would establish that the atmosphere is one of those resources, and that by not taking action against climate change, the government is shirking its legal responsibility.[135] Wood also believes that as trustees, governments have an enforceable fiduciary obligation. As she says, the courts will be essential in checking the runaway politicization

---

[132] *On the Commons: A Commons Movement Strategy Centre*: http://www.onthecommons.org.

[133] Barnes (note 13): 34.

[134] Mary C. Wood, *Nature's Trust: Environmental Law for a New Ecological Age* (Cambridge University Press, Cambridge 2013); Michael Blumm and Mary C. Wood, *The Public Trust Doctrine in Environmental and Natural Resources Law* (Carolina Academic Press, Durham, NC 2013).

[135] Carla A. Wise, 'Green All the Lawyers', Unte Magazine (September–October 2008): http://www.utne.com/environment/green-all-the-lawyers.aspx?PageId=1.

(read: the favouring of short-term economic interests and hence political capital) of the other two branches of government.[136] In Woods' opinion, courts 'have been on the sidelines in climate crisis. With atmospheric trust litigation the courts become enforcers'.[137] In such a system, 'the public would have clarity on its own government's responsibility',[138] thus reducing the political fallout for those politicians who advance a green agenda.

There are, however, plenty of examples where states appear to subscribe to a trustee role and nevertheless exploit it. For instance, Section 1 of Nigeria's 1978 Land Use Act is an example of legislation which designates national land and subsoil (including mineral oils) as held in trust by the governor of the state territory 'for the common benefit of all Nigerians'. By designating it as trust property, the Act separates out state title to land and the Nigerian people's beneficial ownership of it.[139] However, at the same time, this removes their ability to enforce their previously enforceable rights under the previous regime, revealing something of a shrewd manipulation of the trust mechanism.[140] Moreover, the fact that 90 percent of marine living resources are within the 200 mile EEZ fishing grounds of particular states and the problem of overfishing persists, it is clear that where states would conceivably adopt a trustee role they have been seriously ineffective.

So, although we see the public trust concept gaining traction in the modern context with calls for guardians and ombudsmen to hold governments to account for their trusteeship role, these 'watchdogs' will be nothing more than lap dogs unless we can get states to acknowledge this role for themselves. As Peter Sand notes, the somewhat inflationary invocation of trusteeship as an ethical equivalent of 'stewardship', 'custodianship' or 'guardianship' is often purely metaphoric and devoid of legal substance.[141]

One of the reasons for such confusion is the absence of a uniform concept of public trust. As mentioned, depending on national legal traditions public trust can have different meanings and connotations. With

---

136 Mary C. Wood, 'Atmospheric Trust Litigation', in W.H. Rogers and M. Robinson-Dorn (eds), *Climate Change Reader* (Carolina Academic Press, Durham, NC 2011).

137 Ibid.

138 Ibid.

139 M. Banire, *The Nigerian Law of Trusts* (Caxton Press, Caldwell, ID 2002): 18.

140 Bantekas (note 63): 198.

141 Peter Sand, 'The Rise of Public Trusteeship in International Environmental Law' (2013) Global Working Paper Series 03/2013, 16: http://globaltrust.tau.ac.il/publications.

respect to natural resources, there are similarities across most common law countries.

For example, the Supreme Court of India declared the public trust doctrine part of the land:

> The State is the trustee of all natural resources which are by nature meant for public use and enjoyment. [The] public at large is the beneficiary of the sea-shore, running waters, airs, forests and ecologically fragile lands. The State as a trustee is under a legal duty to protect the natural resources. These resources meant for public use cannot be converted into private ownership.[142]

In both jurisdictions, natural resources are considered common property of all the people with the state acting as trustee. The same can be said of civil law countries, although not as an expression of the public trust doctrine and not in the same terms. Here, the more elaborate field of public law (including constitutional and administrative law) assumes fiduciary relationships between the state and its people. Trusteeship concepts with respect to the commons are visible throughout a number of continental European countries.[143]

Peter Sand is correct in concluding that, while there is no universal understanding of the public trust doctrine or the concept of environmental trusteeship, we can observe a transnational convergence of environmental rules.[144] In fact, the worldwide coherence of constitutional obligations to protect the environment has reached such a degree that we can speak of 'global environmental constitutionalism'.[145] This new area of legal scholarship and advocacy holds great promise for perceiving states as trustees for the natural commons.

7. RECLAIMING THE COMMONS

How then can the state be understood to act as an environmental trustee? Hardin proffers two alternatives to avoid the tragedy of the commons: privatization and state coercion. But what we know is that 'neither the state nor the market is uniformly successful in enabling individuals to sustain long-term productive use of natural resource systems'.[146] Moreover, Hardin

---

142 Ibid.: 41.

143 Ibid.: 41–44; Bosselmann (note 99): 169–170.

144 Sand (note 141): 45.

145 Klaus Bosselmann, 'Global Environmental Constitutionalism: Mapping the Terrain', *Widener Law Review*, Special Issue: Global Environmental Constitutionalism (forthcoming, May 2015).

146 Ostrom, *Governing the Commons* (note 109): 1.

assumes that private property owners will act sustainably because this is in their long-term economic interest; however, we know from experience that this is not borne out in reality. Profit is too far removed from the natural resource base for long-term considerations to vary accumulation. Hardin also forgets that states, at least democratic ones, operate at the behest of voters. States will not coerce if their constituents do not demand it; to do so would be political suicide. Obviously states see it as their responsibility to act in situations of economic crisis. What prevents them from extending this responsibility to the task of adjusting the economy to ecological realities is their own obsession with growth. Behind all the state interventions we have ever seen was the expectation of growth. To turn this around and promote a sustainable economy, quite simply, seems beyond the imagination and ability of governments.[147] Thus, at present, asking the sovereign state to accept a fundamental fiduciary duty is a bit like asking the fox to look after the chicken. The appetite of states to exploit the global environment is greater than their interest in preserving it.

To negate this we need to link the protection of the commons and natural resources to sovereignty and legitimacy to govern in the same way that the social contract forms the basis of the state. This can only be done through civil society – those who are governed. Mary Wood, in her work on public trusts, calls this the 'reframing'; people taking control of the language – the discourse – that we use to hold governments accountable.[148] As author George Lakoff says, 'reframing is changing the way the public sees the world. It is changing what counts as common sense'.[149]

States are trustees and citizens are the beneficiaries and settlors – they choose the trustee and have equitable benefit. Given the fact that both the environmental debate and the sustainability agenda are closely associated with civil society, the prospect of democratic, sustainable societies and states that are trustees is ultimately determined by the role that civil society is willing and able to play. This is because democracy has the sovereign of the people at its core. Governments are elected by the *demos*, its citizens. It is only by virtue of citizens that governments are able to reaffirm the idea of economic growth, hence missing the point of sustainability. As constituency and counterpart of governments, civil society can

---

[147] Tim Jackson, *Prosperity Without Growth? The Transition towards a Sustainable Economy* (Sustainable Development Commission, London 2009).

[148] Wood (note 1): 577–603.

[149] George Lakoff, *Don't Think of an Elephant! Know Your Values and Frame the Debate* (Chelsea Green Publishing, White River Junction, VT 2005): xv.

either be critical or supportive of economic growth. Likewise, civil society can either be indifferent or proactive with respect to sustainability.

Representative democracies have become sclerotic and throughout OECD member states there is a widespread decline of public trust coupled with political apathy. Politicians cannot challenge vested consumer and producer interests for fear of losing votes, media support, lobbyist and associated funding. This makes democracies incapable of mobilizing citizens to tackle collective action problems on a large scale. If governments have stuck to their rhetoric of economic prosperity, social justice and environmental protection without actually changing things for the better, then they have only responded to the needs of the system, for example the short-term cycles of governmental power. Obviously, the demos wasn't sufficiently interested to demand a change in the system. In this regard, the ball is still firmly in the court of civil society in terms of what public concerns enter the democratic process. Thus, while this volume is about proposing a new global environmental governance regime, the continual emphasis has been on what the world community needs even more – new values and ethics which will act to guide us through this current impasse.

We will need strong leadership and environmental literacy and sustainability knowledge. Citizens can make a real difference, but only if and only insofar as they act as responsible citizens. In essence, this means a rejection of the consumer status that economies and increasingly governments have bestowed upon us in lieu of citizenship. In contemporary society, the system of citizenship is instrumental in the reproduction and expansion of capitalism.[150] Economic relations govern our social relations, and our identities as employees and consumers predominate, making the marketplace our primary source of social and personal meaning.[151] Thus, 'the most formidable process of commons encroachment takes place through the expansion of capitalist forms of social organization [private property over forms of common property], and particularly through the commodification process'.[152]

We are so divorced from the externalities of our transnationally produced goods and so accustomed to the operation of the market in provision of these goods. Global warming has achieved the 'think global' dimension of environmental degradation that was absent previously (though arguably not enough to truly curb consumer habits). Thinking

---

150 José Esteban Castro, 'Commons and Citizenship: The Contradictions of an Unfolding Relationship', in Silke Heinrich (ed.), *Genes, Bytes and Emissions: To Whom Does the World Belong?* (Heinrich Böll Stiftung, Berlin 2008).

151 Bollier, *The Future of the Commons* (note 102).

152 Castro (note 150): 3.

in terms of the commons is another conceptual leap for many people, not only because of the globality of the environment and all its constituent and mutually interdependent parts, but because in the day of capitalism and privatization we simply do not think in terms of shared resources. Economic rationality needs to be reduced to size. It has its origins – and rightful place – in the development of business and market strategies. To this end, it is also part of the public sphere and an important one at that. But economic rationality has little to offer some of society's basics, that is, motivations, values and ethical guidance for policy, law and governance. Yet, economic rationality has become a foundation of ethics.

We know what causes the tragedy of the commons – overharvesting. But why, with the plethora of environmental information and warnings that exist today, is it so challenging to cooperate for better commons management? We have already discussed the unfortunate realities of real-politik and its effect on agreement over what to do. But beyond that there is a conceptual problem in the way that people – civil society – approach the issue. As the late Elinor Ostrom explained, we tend to over-harvest a common-pool resource when we do not know the other individuals who are involved, and when we cannot communicate with each other.[153] Not only is this a problem of space (intra-generational), it is also a problem of time (inter-generational). It seems we fundamentally lack a sense of responsibility towards one another borne from a lack of perception of common fate.

Avoiding, or ending, the tragedy of the commons will depend on the strength of the commons community and the widespread assumption of responsibility within civil society.[154] Ostrom has found that there are plenty of examples of communities with citizens who do know each other and can communicate who have effective systems of commons management. However, the necessarily high degree of communication, reciprocity and cooperation that is necessary for this is rare in heavily individualized societies or in those under enormous socio-economic pressure.[155]

At the global level this is even more challenging. The multifarity of

---

[153] Elinor Ostrom, 'Governing a Commons from a Citizen's Perspective', in Silke Heinrich (ed.), *Genes, Bytes and Emissions: To Whom Does the World Belong?* (Heinrich Böll Stiftung, Berlin 2008).

[154] Christian Siefkes, 'The Commons of the Future: Building Blocks for a Commons-based Society', in Silke Heinrich (ed.), *Genes, Bytes and Emissions: To Whom Does the World Belong?* (Heinrich Böll Stiftung, Berlin 2008).

[155] Silke Helfrich and Jörg Haas, 'The Commons: A New Narrative for Our Time', in Silke Heinrich (ed.), *Genes, Bytes and Emissions: To Whom Does the World Belong?* (Heinrich Böll Stiftung, Berlin 2008).

cultures, language, religion, political systems, and importantly socio-economic disparity, mean that not only do citizens not know each other, they are invariably viewed with suspicion as the 'other'. Granted, globalization and communications technology have affected something of a dissolution of the barriers to intermingling and communication, but at the same time they have created something of a backlash against encroaching cultural imperialism.

How do we overcome these challenges to civil society mobilization? First, we need to start practising rejection of the objectifying assumption that the individual is a strictly utility-maximizing *homo economicus* – 'Economic Man'.[156] People are also guided in their actions by reputation, a sense of solidarity and reciprocity.[157] There are three 'layers' that affect an individual's decision to cooperate in a common-pool situation:[158] their own identity; the group context in which decisions are being made; whether the situation is repeated and it is possible to use reciprocity and gain a reputation for trustworthiness: 'These turn out to be among the important micro-level variables that explain the diversity of decisions to overcome the strong temptations of common-pool resource dilemmas.'[159]

To achieve these changes, covenantal bonds, that is, obligations accepted towards one another, are important. The Governance for Sustainability report (GfS) finds that the existence of covenantal bonds, typically underpinning traditional and indigenous communities, is likely to generate more sustainable processes and decisions.[160] Such a finding parallels the work of Elinor Ostrom and others on the ability for smaller communities to sustainably manage commons because of their closer proximity and social bonds. According to Karl Polanyi, '[m]an's economy, as a rule, is submerged in his social relationships. He does not act so as to safeguard his individual interest in the possession of material goods; he acts so as to safeguard his social standing, his social claims, his social assets . . . In every economic system, the maintenance of social ties is crucial'.[161]

Likewise, as Judge Weeramantry states, the value in people obeying the

---

156 Ibid.

157 Ibid.

158 Juan Camilo Cárdenas and Elinor Ostrom, 'How Norms Help Reduce the Tragedy of the Commons: A Multi-layer Framework for Analyzing Field Experiments', in John N. Droback (ed.), *Norms and the Law* (Cambridge University Press, Cambridge 2006).

159 Ostrom, *Governing a Commons from a Citizen's Perspective* (note 153).

160 Klaus Bosselmann, Ron Engel and Prue Taylor, *Governance for Sustainability: Issues, Challenges, Successes* (IUCN, Gland 2008).

161 Karl Polanyi, *The Great Transformation: The Political and Economic Origin of Our Time* (Beacon Press, Boston 1990): 75.

law is not in the threat of police power and the sanction of the law 'but because they feel bound in conscience to observe it without coercion of any kind'.[162] What we feel bound by in ethics is fundamentally determined by how we see ourselves in relation to the things around us, that is, our beliefs about nature and destiny. Traditional and indigenous societies did not have the same separation between man and nature that persists in modern thought.

Crucial to a civil society mobilization is challenging this philosophical perspective. Economic rationality needs to be replaced with *ecological* rationality, to the tune that economic concerns are enmeshed in a wider conceptual framework which acknowledges that the environment is foundational to everything. Sustainable development is, therefore, only possible within ecological limits. This gives rise to a contemporary conception of the *demos* with the whole community of life in mind. And from this will grow ecological citizenship – a new relationship between humans and the natural world that stresses non-reciprocal obligations and responsibilities. This would operate like a 'new ecological covenant' – a non-anthropocentric conception of the demos which recognizes the rights of future generations and the rights of non-human forms (ecological integrity).

GfS found that effective democratic institutions are more likely to result in good quality decisions. Another important feature is a sense of 'place' and citizenship. People are, in most instances, more motivated within neighbourhoods or communities than in anonymous cities with less defined local governance structures. Essentially, what these findings show is that central to repairing humans' relationship with nature is the state of the relationships they have with other humans. The more socially affiliative the governance institution, the better the sustainable outcomes. So, when we consider the concept of future generations and our – current generation's – responsibility towards them, we are perhaps also missing the requisite sense of responsibility toward our present peers. In the words of one scholar, with the rise of stewardship 'it can be expected that new social forms will emerge that may help to re-equilibrate the system in a higher level of human organization that privileges intra- and inter-generational cooperation and solidarity over the blind dynamics of competition and the survival of the fittest'.[163]

It should be noted, however, that public opinion of judicial decisions

---

[162] C.G. Weeramantry, *Law in Crisis: Bridges of Understanding* (Capemoss, London 1975): 25.

[163] Castro (note 150): 10.

and courts generally may be guided by principles different from those in simple votes or opinion polls. National courts can readily take a long-term view, and their 'touchstone of legitimacy "is" the ability of a judicial pronouncement to sustain itself in dialogue and the power of the judicial action to generate assent over the long haul'. Courts do not have to persuade the public with all their judgements and it is often more relevant that important changes in doctrine will be viewed favourably in the future. This observation is pivotal to a proper institutionalization of trusteeship at a global level. It suggests that the general direction or trend of public sentiment is more important than a present opinion poll for influencing courts' willingness to endorse the trusteeship conception.[164]

But however necessary civil society is in changing the way that it and governments and ultimately the international system approach the global environment, the question remains, *how* do we embolden and mobilize an ecologically minded civil society? Nature is expertly abstracted from citizens' everyday lives, so how do we make people, many of whom have paid scant regard to the pragmatic and philosophical human–nature relationship, feel like they have a stake in nature and therefore an obligation to protect it?

It seems like there is no dearth of information about the environmental crises that afflict earth, and indeed 'green' sentiment is very much in vogue, even among the most ecologically dislocated populations. Yet this hardly amounts to a civil society groundswell, and it certainly has not tipped the balance of the majority of the population's conception of what role the government should have in the greening of society. As we have said, denial is a powerful feature of the human psyche. The psychological tenets of anthropocentric environmental damage are well acknowledged and there is no dearth of literature exploring these issues. Another limitation is the efficacy of environmental NGOs in endearing civil society to their cause. Much of the time, the tactics of environmental NGOs are seen as too radical, too disruptive and essentially too-much-too-soon for a citizenry unaccustomed to such rhetoric. The contrast is simply indigestible for the 'mainstream' and consequently people react oppositionally (how well known is the derogatory term 'tree-huggers'?) rather than affiliatively. Internationally, despite ground-breaking research and ideas among civil society networks, the achievements of non-state actors in normative development in the environmental field and their recognition

---

[164] Paul Merternskoetter, 'National Courts as Trustees of Humanity?' (2013) Global Trust Working Paper Series 04/2013, 35: http://globaltrust.tau.ac.il/national-courts-as-trustees-of-humanity/.

have lagged behind the activity and recognition of human rights NGO networking in the development of norms in other fields of humanitarian concern.[165] Crucially, 'there has been no clear set of cosmopolitan norms in the environmental field to pose a challenge to existing neoliberal norms in the same manner as, for example, human rights protections'.[166]

Essentially, what this means is that there are NGOs who advance a strong sustainability agenda, and there are those who advance a weak sustainable development agenda, and the message to civil society is unclear. Environmental NGOs are more diverse, less organized and less integrated globally than NGOs for other causes and therefore they pose less of a threat.[167] The fact that at almost every environmental conference there is an equally potent civil society forum, and yet states do little to take these ideas on board, is a testament to this obstruction. The simple truth is that humans are disinclined to respond to long-term threats, and this mental weakness is aided by the discretionary frame put forth by governments which allows the maintenance of complacency and the encouragement of consumption, and ultimately drives the economic growth model.[168]

Wood suggests that the way to appeal to the citizenry to hold governments to the trust paradigm is to appeal to their sense of 'ownership', albeit collectively, of the commons.[169] Wood calls this a 'reframing' of environmental law. The *status quo* approach to environmental law – the discretionary frame – has four sides, discretion characterizing each facet.[170] Protection of the environment is an aspiration and carried out through the discretionary frame.[171] As she explains, this approach never captures the commons element of natural resources, but rather 'it allows government to damage the resources until they are all gone'.[172] Similarly, Bollier argues that 'once a resource is considered "government property" its moral and legal connection to the citizenry begins to wane'.[173] In considering shared resources as commons belonging *to the people*, Bollier argues that the commons emphasizes the prior claims of the citizens (commoners) over and above government. This process is called communalization.[174]

---

165 Stec (note 33): 374.
166 Ibid.
167 Ibid.
168 Wood (note 1): 600.
169 Ibid.: 599.
170 Ibid.: 593.
171 Ibid.
172 Ibid.: 594.
173 Bollier, *The Commons: A Neglected Sector of Wealth Creation* (note 3).
174 Stec (note 33): 362.

Through reframing, the 'four sides' of environmental law would be obligation, obligation, obligation, obligation.[175] This is the nature of trusteeship. And it essentially portrays the difference between viewing the environment as our property, to do with as we choose, and viewing the environment as a gift, something that we are tasked with preserving and which, at the same time, will maintain us.

The power to reframe, as Wood correctly conveys, resides in citizenship.[176] The first step is disseminating the idea that the state is an environmental trustee, and not a trustee whose duty is above all revenue generation, but a 'duty to invest' that is perceived through the sustainability of the trust assets, so to speak. A good investment should increase value and pay dividends in the future. Thus, the choices that the state as trustee should make, in relation to the environment, and indeed everything, should necessarily go beyond the short election cycle and take into account future generations. That way, when governments grant rights of exploitation that undermine citizens' ownership of the commons, the analogy becomes one of trustees selling off the beneficiaries' assets, not only with a long-term loss to the beneficiary, but often with seriously detrimental and immediate environmental ramifications for beneficiaries such as contamination and pollution.

Wood argues that people's perceptions change remarkably when they think of their trust being mismanaged.[177] Arguably, this impetus is so strong that it can even overcome the challenges of collective action. After all, arguably the strongest shared value and interest that we have is in our shared environment, the destruction of which is jeopardizing the continued existence of all of humanity. The 'collectivization of particular objects' idea works with the reality that private property is a central referent of modern societies and a strong philosophical frame for how we interact with the world. Once people understand they have a property right in something, they are inclined to protect it.[178] People, she argues, 'understand a freewheeling grandfather spending down all of their rightful inheritance'.[179] It is possible that it will take the present generation of youth to alter the neoliberal path dependency. As Wood says:[180]

The trust frame has particular empowerment for youths, because it recognizes a property right of natural inheritance for the children of the

---

175 Wood (note 1).
176 Ibid.
177 Ibid.: 601.
178 Ibid.: 600.
179 Ibid.: 601.
180 Ibid.: 600.

world. It gives children an entitlement, as beneficiaries with no lesser standing than our own, to natural wealth, even though they are not yet old enough to exercise any voting power over their government. Children get angry when they think of our generation spending down a trust that they are entitled to take in the same abundance we have enjoyed.

By tapping into concepts that are already resonant in the public, perceptions of a government's mandate can begin to change. It superimposes the trust frame on government.

However, the important corollary of this approach is ensuring that people, beneficiaries, similarly acknowledge their agency as guardians and stewards; it is just that for efficiency's sake they delegate this role to an elected government. Although children now may be far more aware of environmental issues, consumption is ever-increasing, especially with new and vulnerable markets. Stewardship ethics do need to imbue people's worldview too though, in order for the mandate to stick. Achieving a trust frame and then not moving beyond the property characteristic that we can do with it what we choose, would be counter-productive. Rather, this realization of common 'ownership' of the commons is a kind of property holding that requires sustainability as *the* fundamental guiding principle.

8. ECOLOGICAL CITIZENS, ECOLOGICAL STATES

This chapter has been about challenging and changing the role of states from 'engines of market enclosure' into ecologically mandated sovereigns – our trustees. As the role of the state has responded to popular sovereignty, we have also looked at the role that civil society necessarily plays in this process. In the end, it is the crisis of human consciousness that underlies all material, economic and environmental manifestations and is the ultimate cause of self-destruction.

However, the potential of human consciousness also allows the opportunity for the opposite of self-destruction, that is, sustainability through responsibility, for nature and future generations, given effect through trusteeship. The purpose of this chapter has not been to attack the nation-state. It is indeed the symbol of the current system. Rather, we have sought to attack how the nation-state perceives its role and function in respect of those governed. It is overwhelmingly and devastatingly misperceived as primarily involving economic growth, with consequences of environmental degradation and a yawning gap between rich and poor. However, this chapter and indeed this volume is about eschewing the stalemate in solution-finding and looking for an option that addresses both the ethical and institutional deficits that maintain environmental crisis worldwide. As sovereign and trustee of the environment, the state would not lose its sovereignty, but foster it in a moral and factual sense, which, far from being utopian, would better reflect the realities of our situation than current conceptualizations of state sovereignty.

We stand now at a 'Grotian moment'.[181] We will either choose to acknowledge the physical and ecological preconditions of human existence – the necessity for a sustainable way of life and the changes this requires – or we will choose to fail. Those making the choices are those we appoint as our political representatives. Until 'we' the citizenry mandate them with something other than economic gatekeeping, they will continue their path dependency and they will ultimately fail us, and in turn humanity at large will fail future generations, if indeed they are around.

What needs to happen in this moment is the setting of new universal ethical and legal standards for human rights and the preservation of ecological integrity in international law.[182] This will not happen unless states make it happen. An internal revolution predates the international one. And even more immediately this means embracing a new kind of individual and collective responsibility among citizens. Trusteeship says that the duty to protect the environment should not have to be negotiated. Sustainability is the goal – this will never change. Like justice and human rights, sustainability should be a foundational norm of humanity that guides the functions of states rather than be guided by them.[183] Territorial sovereignty over natural resources (or 'fruits' of the environment) can only be perceived, therefore, as inherently linked to an obligation to protect the environment. The use of resources is covered by territorial sovereignty only within the parameters of ecological sustainability. This would read as: 'the sovereign right of states to exploit their resources pursuant to the principle of sustainability.'

Global commons governance cannot abide the traditional rule that international law and governance ends where a state's borders begin. This is a legal fiction that ignores ecological reality. States need to exempt transnational aspects of the domestic environment from the concept of territorial sovereignty, making way for global commons governance. Through sustainable governance at state level, territorial sovereignty is conceptually restricted at the global level, leading to a paradigm shift in international environmental law. Instead of state sovereignty setting limits

---

[181] Susan Buck, *The Global Commons: An Introduction* (Island Press, Washington, DC 1998).

[182] Engel (note 8): 36.

[183] Bosselmann, *The Principle of Sustainability* (note 100): 149.

to environmental protection, environmental protection would set the limits to state sovereignty. This is not an unprecedented idea; 'limiting the self-interest of states by taking into account global concerns of humanity has become a fundamental aspect of international law'.[184] But because the theory of cooperation comes up against the reality of competition, it simply will not suffice for a few conscientious states to try and influence the rest. All states need to recognize that it is their imperative to preserve the environment.

Having discussed the impetus for states adopting the role of environmental trustee, how do we ensure that this is translated into a willingness to abide by global commons trusteeship? Sovereign territories are part of the indivisible, interdependent global environment, and it follows that if states are trustees or guardians of their territories they are, together, responsible for the global environment. There needs to be a system of trusteeship for those areas for which it is infeasible and inefficient for single states to act as trustee; these would be the commons areas that are beyond state territory and that belong to all of humanity to preserve and protect. As Ostrom points out, resource users 'tend to be most interested in goods and services generated at a local level and take less notice of those generated by larger scales'.[185]

It is a far more complex task to mobilize global citizenship, especially when there are significant social, cultural and religious differences that tend to 'other' people from one another. Ultimately though, we all share our reliance on the environment and it is the strength of the imperative for guardianship that can overcome other differences. After all, we have seen this as a common thread throughout all cultures and religions. It is not a 'hegemonic' idea; it is a fundament of human existence. Thus, citizenship exists in two senses – as a constituent of a nation-state, and as a global citizen – a part of humanity – and citizens have an equally important role in legitimizing and monitoring institutions of global governance.[186]

The Earth Charter is the clearest example of this undertaking and is testimony to the fact that civil society is willing to embrace this turning point, even if states cannot yet get past inertia. The Earth Charter propounds the comprehensive principle of 'respect and care for the community of life', based on the ontological presupposition that 'all beings are interdependent and every form of life has value regardless of its worth to

---

184 Stec (note 33): 364.

185 Ostrom, *Governing a Commons from a Citizen's Perspective* (note 153).

186 Robin Attfield, 'Global Citizenship and the Global Environment', in N. Dower and J. Williams (eds), *Global Citizenship: A Critical Reader* (Edinburgh University Press, Edinburgh 2002): 197.

human beings'. Moreover, the Earth Charter not only explicitly affirms 'ecological integrity' but sets forth a thick version of democracy through its principles of social and economic justice, non-violence and peace.[187] The Charter puts forward a truly universal ecological understanding of democracy, which can be termed 'earth democracy'. According to Ron Engel, earth democracy is 'a revival of some of the deepest historical and normative roots of the thick interpretation of democracy'.[188]

Thankfully, 'global civil society' or 'transnational publics' are more possible today than ever, due to new information technologies that allow members to gain 'access to global knowledge, the sharing of experiences, the division of mental labor and the local connectedness'.[189] It is through this avenue that 'commoning' has become a formidable phenomenon worldwide. First though, we have to be clear what 'cosmopolitan' norms we need guiding this 'revolution'. It can only ever be sustainability – anything else is empirically false. People need to understand the difference between living within ecological limits and the current 'solutions' that are proffered. As a framework for global governance, the Earth Charter can reliably guide us.[190]

In the next chapter, we move on to putting the idea of trusteeship into action. We discuss what is needed of an institution that can transform, rather than merely reform, international environmental governance.

---

187 Engel (note 8): 36–37.

188 Ibid.: 37.

189 Global Villages Network, http://globalvillages.ning.com.

190 Klaus Bosselmann and Ronald J. Engel (eds), *The Earth Charter: A Framework for Global Governance* (KIT Publishing, Leiden 2010).

7. Trusteeship and the United Nations

More than ever before in human history, we share a common destiny. We can master it only if we face it together. And that is why we have the United Nations.
Kofi Anan

At present, there is no international organisation that is granted the broad jurisdictional authority and governance powers required to compel countries to recognize their collective duty to combat climate change. Law, without credible institutional arrangements to implement and enforce it, remains nothing more than just an abstract idea.
McGoldrick, Feaver and Maver[1]

1. THE TRUSTEESHIP MANDATE OF THE UN

1.1 Why the UN?

The United Nations is an institution with practical experience in international trusteeship. The UN oversaw the operation of the International Trusteeship System, under which (after World War II) states were entrusted with territories of particular ex-colonies. The object was to assist the inhabitants of the territories to gain independence. The World Trade Organization (WTO) and World Health Organization (WHO) can also be analysed in terms of trusteeship. As 'trustees', the overriding objective of their respective regimes is constructed as a putative 'beneficiary'.[2] In addition, the governance structures of the WTO and WHO entail specific trusteeship duties and powers. It emerges from the following analysis that the UN provides a solid conceptual and practical setting for the institutionalization of environmental trusteeship at the global level. Before considering the World Trade Organization, the

---

[1] Will McGoldrick, Donald Feaver and Andrew Maver, 'Fiduciary Duty and Climate Governance: Challenges for International Diplomacy and Law', in Ken Coghill, Charles Sampford and Tim Smith (eds), *Fiduciary Duty and the Atmospheric Trust* (Ashgate, Farnham 2012): 27.

[2] Karen J. Alter, 'Agents or Trustees? International Courts in their Political Context' (2008) 14 *Eur. J. Int'l Rel.* 33, 40.

World Health Organization and the United Nations Trusteeship System in detail, an assessment is offered of the current UN framework in relation to environmental issues.

The UN reform process following Rio+20 is strongly supportive of the establishment of multi-level global governance for sustainability. The strong nexus between intergenerational equity and sustainable development has been repeatedly stressed within the UN.[3] Collective trusteeship is increasingly being linked to emerging concepts of global governance.[4] A large number of interventions within the Sustainable Development Goals (SDG) Committees, in particular, have stressed the importance of this nexus.[5] This provides fertile normative ground for the establishment of a UN body charged with a fiduciary obligation to protect the planet's ecological integrity for current and future generations.

The mandate of the UN is particularly well-suited to an adoption of this function. As Judge Weeramantry recently noted:[6]

> It is the duty of the United Nations to provide leadership and long-term vision in this area by spreading awareness of the problem, the causes of the problem and the steps needed to address it. An outstanding step in this direction would be the appointment of a dedicated representative of future generations who can provide the necessary long-term perspectives, both internationally and to legal systems across the world.

Similarly, Dodds, Strauss and Strong have recently emphasized that: 'The UN provides our best chance to all live together on this planet in a fair and equitable way. The question will be: are we clever enough to realize

---

[3] See, for example, Report of the Secretary-General, *Intergenerational Solidarity and the Needs of Future Generations*, UN Doc A/68/100 (5 August 2013); Jan-Gustav Strandaneas, *A Council for Sustainable Development: A Possible Outcome of the Rio+20 Process* (2012): http://www.uncsd2012.org/content/documents/JGS-SDC-final.pdf; United Nations, *The Future We Want: Zero Draft of the Outcome Document* (2011): 57: http://www.uncsd2012.org/index.php?page=view&type=12&nr=324&menu=20; Global Conference on Implementing Intergenerational Equity, *Conference Synopsis* (Geneva, July 2013): http://future-justice.org/wp-content/uploads/2013/07/Global-Conference-Synopsis.pdf.

[4] United Nations University, *International Sustainable Development Governance: The Question of Reform: Key Issues and Proposals Report* (2001): http://www.uncsd2012.org/content/documents/ISDGFinalReport.pdf.

[5] See, for example, 'Intervention of the Permanent Observer Mission of the Holy See to the United Nations Tenth Session of the Open Working Group on the Sustainable Development Goals, Cluster 1, Poverty Eradication and Promoting Equality' (31 March 2014): http://www.holyseemission.org/statements/statement.aspx?id=455.

[6] World Future Council, 'Judge C.G. Weeramantry calls for the UN to provide leadership' (9 October 2013): http://www.futurejustice.org/.

that in time?'[7] Ultimately, the concept of 'sovereigns as trustees' demands an institutional arrangement such as that offered by the UN. The power of sovereigns has been entrusted; therefore, sovereigns have an obligation to 'mutually explore and develop the most effective . . . supranational institutions that can meet the challenges . . . that result from the system of sovereign states'.[8] Observations such as those noted above display an awareness of thc practical and ethical challenges arising from the collapse of life-sustaining global ecological systems. There is also an awareness of the pressing need to develop an effective institutional response.

1.2 Why a Fiduciary Mandate?

In the previous chapter, the potential for sovereignty to be 'reclaimed' for humanity was discussed. This requires, first, that states recognize that environmental crises are one of the greatest threats to the public interest; second, that as representatives of the general will they are mandated as environmental trustees. Until these requirements are acknowledged by states, the effectiveness of solutions to the global environmental crisis will be limited. This is because the predominance of the state-centric system will remain; that is, the very system which created the conditions for the emergence of the crisis in the first place.

Although a state's abuse of the natural environment may occur within its own sovereign territory, there are obviously many cases where the effects are extra-territorial. This blurs the line between what is 'internal' and what is 'external'. Reflecting this ecological reality, the definition of the global commons used in this volume has not been limited to those traditional 'commons' areas, which are currently beyond the sovereign territory of states. Any attempt to govern the environment must take a holistic approach, safeguarding the entirety of the global natural environment. However, this does not entail an argument against the validity of state sovereignty. Rather, the argument is that the mandate of states to govern for the common interest must include an ecological component. Indeed, attempts made by states to maintain the life-supporting environmental systems of their own 'sovereign' territories will be seriously undermined if states fail to work together to mitigate global environmental problems. Thus, environmental governance becomes an issue of global governance.

---

7 Felix Dodds, Michael Strauss and Maurice F. Strong, *Only One Earth: The Long Road via Rio to Sustainable Development* (Routledge, London 2012): 185.

8 Eyal Benvenisti, 'Sovereigns as Trustees of Humanity: On the Accountability of States to Foreign Stakeholders' (2013) 107 (2) *American Journal of International Law* 295, 333.

Without a fundamental reconceptualization of the nature and gravity of the problem at hand, barriers to ambitious action will persist.[9] A growing number of commentators are now recognizing that a fundamentally new approach to international climate negotiations is required.[10] Francesco Francioni, for example, calls for 'the sovereign State as a trustee of global common goods'.[11] Furthermore, Peter Sand asserts that a transfer of the public trust concept from the national to the global level is 'conceivable, feasible and tolerable'.[12]

It has been proposed by McGoldrick, Feaver and Maver that there are three key ways in which a fiduciary-based approach to climate governance would contribute to the goal of achieving an ambitious global response to climate change.[13] First, it would 'compel governments – based on a legal duty to their citizens – to do everything within their power to reduce greenhouse gas emissions occurring within their jurisdiction'.[14] Second, because the threat of climate change can only be resolved through international efforts, it would 'compel governments to intensify diplomatic efforts aimed at achieving an effective, globally coordinated response'.[15] A third argument is that 'a fiduciary duty can be extended beyond national governments to the realm of international organizations'.[16]

The theoretical benefits of using a trust are numerous. For one, it would pool funds together in a way which is not only pragmatic and efficient, but politically advantageous.[17] As a fiduciary distributor, the trustee serves to

---

9 McGoldrick, Feaver and Maver (note 1): 9.

10 Ibid. The authors refer to Ved P. Nanda and William K. Ris Jr, 'The Public Trust Doctrine: A Viable Approach to International Environmental Protection' (1976) 5 *Ecology LQ* 291; Peter H. Sand, 'Sovereignty Bounded: Public Trusteeship for Common Pool Resources?' (2004) 4 *Global Environmental Politics* 47; Mary C. Wood, 'Advancing the Sovereign Trust of Government to Safeguard the Environment for Present and Future Generations (Part I): Ecological Realism and the Need for a Paradigm Shift' (2009) *Env. Law* 39, 43.

11 Francesco Francioni, 'International Common Goods: An Epilogue', in Frederico Lenzerini and Ana Filipa Vrdoljak (eds), *International Law for Common Goods: Normative Perspectives on Human Rights, Culture and Nature* (Hart Publ., Oxford 2014): 443, 448.

12 Peter H. Sand, 'Sovereignty Bounded: Public Trusteeship for Common Pool Resources?' (2004) 4 *Global Environmental Politics* 47.

13 McGoldrick, Feaver and Maver (note 1): 10.

14 Ibid.

15 Ibid.

16 Ibid.

17 Ilias Bantekas, *Trust Funds under International Law: Trustee Obligations of the United Nations and International Development Banks* (TMC Asser Press, The Hague 2009): 18.

remove any political friction between donor and beneficiary states, which 'could serve to dilute the political rhetoric'.[18] Moreover, entrusting funds to a trusteeship institution would reduce the danger of mismanagement of funds by corrupt or incapable beneficiary administrations. A trusteeship regime would provide a high level of expertise and accountability in distribution and management, while still empowering local service providers.[19] A further point of relevance is the fiduciary duty to manage entrusted funds with a long-term orientation. This is a benefit, because the long-term goals of environmental protection 'require significant planning and human resources . . . which no state would be happy or suitable to undertake unilaterally'.[20]

1.3 Why a Centralized Institution?

Safeguarding the earth's life support systems, such as the atmosphere, might be thought a fairly crucial aspect of global governance. The absence of an institution with the broad jurisdictional authority to compel countries to combat climate change leads to the sentiment that '[l]aw, without credible institutional arrangements to implement and enforce it, remains nothing more than just an abstract idea'.[21] Therefore, the development of a rule of international law concerning the protection of the environment must be accompanied by effective means for ensuring enforcement and compliance.[22] Benvenisti accurately observes that in the absence of such a framework, 'sovereigns are subject only to certain minimal obligations that do not impose substantial burdens on them'.[23] In the face of this problem, it is crucial for states to collectively make a commitment to an institutional configuration which can 'correct, or at least minimize, the systemic democratic failures that inhere in the sovereign-based system'.[24]

A formal institution of environmental trusteeship would give a coherent identity to the mass of disparate obligations to protect the environment which are currently falling upon states. The present 'climate change regime' exists in a conceptual, rules-based sense, but lacks organizational identity.[25] A coherent and appropriately empowered international

---

18 Ibid.
19 Ibid.
20 Ibid.
21 McGoldrick, Feaver and Maver (note 1): 23.
22 Ibid.
23 Benvenisti (note 8): 300.
24 Ibid.: 303.
25 McGoldrick, Feaver and Maver (note 1): 25.

institution of trusteeship would provide a 'credible foundation' from which international obligations of a collective nature, such as a clean and safe atmosphere, can be asserted.[26] Crucially, this will lend legitimacy to enforcement measures applied to states that fail to fulfil their obligations. A climate change regime *might* achieve widespread consent for substantive obligations. However, without a well-designed, coherent institutional framework, the long-term viability of such specialized systems of law is likely to be undermined.[27]

The current proliferation of organizations in the field of international environmental governance amounts to 'too many cooks in the kitchen' and simply cannot deliver the kind of collective action that is necessary for effective environmental governance. The United Nations Environment Programme (UNEP), established in 1972 to coordinate UN environmental programmes, is supposed to be the overall coordinating body. However, in reality it competes with the Global Environmental Facility, the Commission for Sustainable Development, the United Nations Development Programme (UNDP), the World Trade Organization (WTO), other UN specialized agencies, and regional institutions and programmes. Significantly, the UNEP's lack of financial resources means that it is unable to exert the intended leading role that was envisioned at the time of its creation.[28] Likewise, there are over 300 multilateral environmental agreements, each with its own secretariat. These can be financially burdensome for states. For example, a single national communication or report (pursuant to a treaty requirement) can cost a small industrialized state between US$350,000 and $500,000, and around 70,000 hours of consulting time to produce.[29] With such costs and human resource demands, multiplied over numerous multilateral agreements, it is unsurprising that states lack enthusiasm.

The complicated institutional structure of the present regime of environmental governance mirrors its conceptual fragmentation. Not only are there a multitude of players, but their messages and agendas are different. Greater prominence and support is currently enjoyed by 'environmental' development projects, which aim for economic growth under the rubric of a weak form of 'sustainable development' (chiefly at the behest of international financial institutions such as the World Bank and the International

---

[26] Ibid.

[27] Ibid.: 24.

[28] See Adil Najam, Mihaela Papa and Nada Taiyab, *Global Environmental Governance: A Reform Agenda* (International Institute for Sustainable Development, Winnipeg 2006).

[29] Ibid.: 86.

Monetary Fund (IMF). These projects have resources which vastly exceed those of the UNEP.[30] This lack of conceptual coherence does not enhance the regime's status as perceived either by civil society or states. The aims of environmental governance must be unambiguous, able to be clearly understood and presented in a tangible form. An institution of global environmental trusteeship would arguably satisfy these requirements in a superior way. An unambiguous mandate and a motivating ethic would lend legitimacy to its clearly defined powers and duties.

Thinking on environmental issues has progressed to a point where finding a substantive basis for a duty to preserve the global environment is not a major problem. The more difficult questions concern the 'enforcement of this duty in an international context'.[31] The willingness of states to bestow a sufficient degree of trusteeship powers upon a body charged with upholding global ecological integrity remains to be seen. This will determine the enforceability of obligations against states in practice. Ultimately, it may determine whether the aim of safeguarding the earth's life support systems is achieved or not.

1.4 Trusteeship Theory in the Law of International Organizations

International Relations theory has typically characterized the relationship between states and international organizations as one of *agency*, whereby legitimacy is derived from the agent's ability to represent and respond to the principal's interests.[32] This is typically labelled 'principal–agent theory'. Only recently has it been suggested that some international organizations operate to serve the interests of some 'putative beneficiary that differs from the principal'.[33] That 'beneficiary' may be an entirely artificial construction.[34] In these circumstances, legitimacy is derived from adherence to an external reference point, conferring a *triadic* nature on the relationship between states and international organizations. This relationship can be ascribed a *trusteeship* function, and this constellation of relations is typically labelled 'principal–trustee'.[35]

---

[30] Steve Charnovitz, 'A World Environment Organization' (2002) 27 *Colum. J. Envtl L.* 323, 346.

[31] McGoldrick, Feaver and Maver (note 1): 25.

[32] See, for example, Mark Pollack, *The Engines of Integration: Delegation, Agency, and Agency Setting in the European Union* (Oxford University Press, Oxford 2003).

[33] Alter (note 2): 40.

[34] Ibid.

[35] Ibid.: 33.

International organizations can be described as 'trustees' of the values that inhere in the treaties that constituted them, entailing various 'fiduciary' duties. The 'beneficiary' is usually cast in terms of an 'external reference point' or the 'overarching values of the regime'.[36] The normative content of the 'beneficiary' generally represents the principal's previously defined *long-term interests*. The trustee ought to honour this external point of reference, even when facing pressure to adapt to the principal's case-specific preferences. Issues of hierarchy and power must not, therefore, determine the decision-making process of fiduciary international organizations.

Why do states agree to this? A trusteeship approach can be useful when the collective, long-term interests of states differ from their short-term interests. Such an approach can also bolster political legitimacy for unpopular decisions in the short term.[37]

The main identifying characteristics are:

- There is a trustee;
- There is a putative beneficiary which differs from the agent;
- The trustee exercises discretion in the administration of the trust corpus in the beneficiary's interest;
- The exercise of the trustee's discretion is bound by certain fiduciary obligations.

1.5 Analysing Selected International Organizations

The following sections analyse the fiduciary nature of the WTO, the World Health Organisation (WHO) and the United Nations Trusteeship Council (UNTC) as currently existing UN institutions. First, features of each regime which entail an institutional configuration of trusteeship will be highlighted. This serves to illustrate that, empirically, trusteeship is a well-established concept within the UN. Second, the fiduciary obligations which emerge will be outlined. Third, the transferability of such concepts to a new environmental trusteeship organization will be

---

[36] Alec Stone Sweet and Thomas L. Brunell, 'Trustee Courts and the Judicialization of International Regimes: The Politics of Majoritarian Activism in the European Convention on Human Rights, the European Union and the World Trade Organization' (Spring 2013) 1 *Journal of Law and Courts* 60, 62.

[37] See Thomas Gehring and Isabel Plocher, 'Making an Administrative Trustee Agent Accountable: Reason-Based Decision Making within the Kyoto Protocol's Clean Development Mechanism' (2009) 53 *International Studies Quarterly* 669.

Table 7.1 Key characteristics of trusteeship

	Beneficiary	Corpus	Trustee	Key points
WTO *Judicial trustee*	Liberalization of trade	WTO agreements (for example, GATT, TRIPS)	Appellate body	Judicial law-making can get around legislative paralysis. Majoritarian activism gets politically difficult law through
WHO *Executive trustee*	Attainment of highest possible level of health	Governance powers (with respect to public health)	WHO Executive Board	Key example of 'logic of delegation' to a trustee (as opposed to an agent). Has a specific zone of discretion within which trustee powers can be exercised
UNTC *Executive/ administrative trustee*	Inhabitants of ex-colonies	Physical territory of ex-colonies	UNTC	Structure already exists; support to revive. Well-developed accountability mechanisms
WEO *Executive/ administrative trustee*	Present and future generations	Entire biosphere	WEO Trust Council	Support among states and civil society groups

examined. (Details of a proposal for a new environmental trusteeship will be discussed in Chapter 8.)

Table 7.1 shows the key characteristics of the trusteeship components of the WTO, the WHO, the UNTC and an environmental trusteeship institution, such as a World Environment Organization (WEO).

2. WORLD TRADE ORGANIZATION

The World Trade Organization's Dispute Settlement System was established as a result of the Understanding on Rules and Procedures Governing the Settlement of Disputes (Dispute Settlement Understanding, DSU).[38] The Appellate Body (AB) is the highest adjudicative body in this regime. It hears appeals from first-instance Panel hearings.[39] Appellate Body decisions become legally binding when they are adopted by the Dispute Settlement Body (DSB), which is made up of the WTO Members collectively.[40] Adoption by the DSB effectively occurs automatically, because a consensus decision of the General Council (that is, all WTO Members, including the winning party) is required *not* to adopt the AB's report.[41]

Recent advances in trusteeship theory in international law have established the foundations for an analysis of the WTO's Dispute Settlement System, particularly its Appellate Body, in terms of 'trusteeship'.[42] The basic structure of the AB-as-trustee model is as follows: *principals* (WTO Member States) delegate discretion to the *trustee* (the Appellate Body) to enforce and interpret the *corpus*. The corpus consists of the relevant instruments of the WTO regime, such as GATT, GATS, TRIPS and SPS. The trustee administers and implements the trust on behalf of the 'beneficiary' (the WTO objectives of the liberalization and stability of trade).[43] As noted above, Alter argues that the beneficiary may be 'entirely an artificial construction'.[44] However, trusteeship with an abstract principle as the 'beneficiary' does not entail merely abstract outcomes. This is because, of course, behind the 'beneficiary' (the WTO objective of free and stable trade) stand the WTO Members (to whom, in practice, benefits of the trust flow). Given the broad nature of the values with which

---

[38] World Trade Organization, *Understanding on Rules and Procedures Governing the Settlement of Disputes, Marrakesh Agreement Establishing the World Trade Organization*, Annex 2, *The Legal Texts: The Results of the Uruguay Round of Multilateral Trade Negotiations* 354 (1999), 1869 UNTS 401, 33 ILM 1226 (1994).

[39] Ibid., Articles 16.4 and 17.

[40] *Marrakesh Agreement Establishing the World Trade Organization*, Apr. 15, 1994, *The Legal Texts: The Results of the Uruguay Round of Multilateral Trade Negotiations* (1999), 1867 UNTS 154, 33 ILM 1144 (1994), Article IV: 3.

[41] Dispute Settlement Rules (note 38): Article 17.14.

[42] Alter (note 2): 33.

[43] Dispute Settlement Rules (note 38): 3.2.

[44] Alter (note 2): 40.

the AB is entrusted, domestic publics may also be considered a 'larger beneficiary'.[45] The trustee's discretionary authority in the administration of the trust is bound by the *terms of the trust* (the Dispute Settlement Understanding).[46]

2.1 Trusteeship as the Appropriate Model for the WTO Appellate Body

As noted above, concepts of 'agency' and 'trusteeship' have been used to provide models of international institutions. The former can be conceptualized as a 'mere agent' or 'pure agent',[47] whereas the latter may be denoted by the terms 'trustee', 'trustee–agent'[48] or 'super-agent'.[49] 'Trustee institution' is a more appropriate conceptualization for the WTO AB than that of mere 'agent'. This is because the WTO regime's settlement of discretionary powers upon the AB go beyond those of mere agency.

2.2 Settlement of Discretionary Powers

How can we distinguish trustee courts from simple courts-as-agents? Stone Sweet and Brunell propose three factors which indicate hallmarks of a 'trustee' court.[50] These include: (1) extreme difficulty in practice for states to override the court's decisions, (2) compulsory jurisdiction, and (3) the court as the authoritative interpreter of the regime's law.

2.2.1 Difficulty for states to override the court's decisions

Under the 'pure agent' model, principals create agents by conferring authority to make decisions. However, an element of ultimate control remains with the principal, particularly through procedures which allow for the principal to override the agent's decisions. An example of courts-as-agents in this sense can be seen within a system of parliamentary supremacy. Interpretative practices may lead textualist critics to call for judges to be more 'faithful agents'.[51] However, even in the face of extensive judicial law-making, the principal has the last say. Through a majority

---

45 Ibid.: 55.

46 Dispute Settlement Rules (note 38).

47 Alter (note 2): 41.

48 Ibid.: 35.

49 Stone Sweet and Brunell (note 36): 62.

50 Ibid.

51 Antonin Scalia, *A Matter of Interpretation* (Princeton University Press, Princeton, NJ 1997): 93.

vote in parliament, lawmakers can overturn unwanted judicial decisions by amending (or creating) a statute.[52]

However, in the case of the WTO AB, it is virtually impossible for states to reverse rulings. As noted above, a 'negative consensus' is required *not* to adopt an AB report.[53] The fact that the 'principal' in international regimes is a composite, not a unified, entity further weakens the threat of override. Therefore, the AB effectively occupies a position of structural supremacy in relation to states.[54] The existence of the third-party 'beneficiary' means that the principal's position is no longer hierarchically supreme. Unlike 'courts as agents' in a parliamentary supremacy regime, the WTO as a 'trustee court' is more akin to the US Supreme Court and many constitutional courts around the world, which are trustees of their respective constitutions (empowered to enforce the constitutional law against any contrary public act, including acts of the legislature).[55] The AB's supremacy has been borne out in practice as well as in theory, as no ruling has been overturned by the DSB.

Alter observes that should a trustee stray beyond what the power elite or body politic can accept, the option of removing a trustee or eliminating the office altogether remains.[56] However, a far more likely response (to circumvent a trustee whose decisions one does not like) would be for issues to be settled outside the realm of the trustee to avoid their interference.[57] As discussed below, powerful states (such as the US in the *United States–Safeguard Measures* case)[58] have recognized the benefits flowing from a commitment to the overarching objective of 'free trade' and have continued to use the system despite adverse decisions in particular cases.

2.2.2 Compulsory jurisdiction

WTO AB exercises compulsory jurisdiction over questions concerning state non-compliance and states are under a legal obligation to comply with their rulings. Article 19.1 of the DSU provides: 'Where a panel or the AB concludes that a measure is inconsistent with a covered agreement,

---

52 Examples of subsequent statutory amendment or creation can be seen in the aftermath to the New Zealand cases: *Ministry of Health v Atkinson* [2012] 3 NZLR 456 and *Attorney-General v Ngati Apa* [2003] 3 NZLR 643.

53 Dispute Settlement Rules (note 38): Article 17.14.

54 Stone Sweet and Brunell (note 36): 62.

55 Ibid.: 65.

56 Alter (note 2): 44.

57 Ibid.

58 *United States: Safeguard Measures on Imports of Fresh, Chilled or Frozen Lamb Meat from New Zealand and Australia*, AB-2001–1, WT/DS177,178/AB/R (01–2194), adopted by Dispute Settlement Body, 16 May 2001.

it shall recommend that the Member concerned bring the measure into conformity with that agreement'. Despite the mild language, in reality states have no discretion regarding the AB's 'recommendations'. The extent of power entrusted to the AB is reinforced by its ability to invoke strong compliance mechanisms. The member found to be in violation of an agreement either has to provide compensation with the agreement of the complainant, or it may face retaliatory countermeasures. Ultimately, the member must achieve conformity with the agreement.[59]

2.2.3 Law-making function

The focus of GATT and WTO regulation has moved from trade rounds to a judicial process.[60] The AB can be considered a 'trustee' because authority was effectively 'settled' upon it to control the institutional evolution of the regime through 'judicial law-making'.[61] The WTO system requires consensus for its members to make or change rules, such that it is 'virtually immune to change except through litigation'.[62] As a result, 'judicial action routinely becomes a substitute for legislative action'.[63] In addition, states left key provisions of agreements vague, so that the WTO agreements are 'incomplete contracts that, in practice, are completed through adjudicating state disagreements over treaty interpretations'.[64] One example of this is Article XX of the General Agreement on Tariffs and Trade (GATT, 'General Exceptions'). Exceptions include measures such as those 'necessary to protect human, animal or plant life or health'.[65] This is an example of an incomplete norm of crucial significance, because its 'open language' constitutes an 'implicit delegation of authority to judges'.[66] Another point supporting the AB's interpretative authority is

---

[59] Dispute Settlement Rules (note 38): Article 22.

[60] Judith Goldstein and Richard Steinberg, 'Regulatory Shift: The Rise of Judicial Liberalization at the WTO', in Walter Mattli and Ngaire Woods (eds), *The Politics of Global Regulation* (Princeton University Press, Princeton, NJ 2009): 211.

[61] Ibid.: 227.

[62] Stone Sweet and Brunell (note 36): 82.

[63] Judith Goldstein and Richard Steinberg, 'Negotiate or Litigate? Effects of WTO Judicial Delegation on US Trade Politics' (Winter 2008) 71 (1) *Law and Contemporary Problems* 257, 259.

[64] Stone Sweet and Brunell (note 36): 82.

[65] General Agreement on Tariffs and Trade (15 Apr. 1994), *Marrakesh Agreement Establishing the World Trade Organization*, Annex 1A, *The Legal Texts: The Results of the Uruguay Round of Multilateral Trade Negotiations*, 17 (1999), 1867 UNTS 187, 33 ILM 1153 (1994), Art. XX(b).

[66] Stone Sweet and Brunell (note 36): 82.

its ability to use 'autonomous reasoning' (that is, it is not limited to the parties' arguments).[67] Although past cases are not legally 'binding', the AB ensures that panels apply its jurisprudence in a consistent manner.[68] This means that the AB governs through the production of what is, in effect, a precedent-based jurisprudence.[69] This is consistent with the WTO regime objective of 'security and predictability of the multilateral trading system'.[70]

2.3 Fiduciary Duties

2.3.1 Constructing the regime's law

The Appellate Body's 'trustee' role is displayed in its pursuit of the values of the WTO regime (the constructed 'beneficiary'), without undue influence from outside interests. The AB has pursued trade liberalization and stability – the values enshrined in treaty instruments – while clarifying and progressively constructing the regime's law.[71] Related to this enforcement and refinement of the meaning of provisions (with reference to the WTO's fundamental goals) is the AB's lack of deference towards member states. The AB has held that the defendant state failed to meet its obligations under WTO agreements in almost 90 percent of its decisions.[72] These statistics support Gering and Plocher's reference to the Appellate Body as among the most autonomous trustees in international relations.[73]

2.3.2 Ascertaining views of beneficiaries

The AB has a fiduciary obligation of 'deliberative engagement'.[74] It fulfils this duty by examining indicators of wider state consensus, such as multilateral treaties and positions taken by international organizations. The court's treatment of cases concerning Article XX of GATT[75] illustrates

---

[67] Appellate Body Report, *EC–Hormones*, para. 156. WT/DS26/AB/R, WT/DS48/AB/R, adopted 13 February 1998. DSR 1998: 1, 135.

[68] Stone Sweet and Brunell (note 36): 82.

[69] Ibid.: 61.

[70] Dispute Settlement Rules (note 38): Article 3.2.

[71] Stone Sweet and Brunell (note 36): 82.

[72] Ibid.

[73] Gehring and Plocher (note 37): 670.

[74] In Leib, Ponet and Serota's account of fiduciary judging, 'deliberative engagement' is held to be one of the most important fiduciary duties of a trustee court, along with 'loyalty' and 'accountability'; see Ethan J. Leib, David L. Ponet and Michael Serota, 'A Fiduciary Theory of Judging' (2013) 101 *California Law Review* 699.

[75] General Agreement on Tariffs and Trade (note 65).

this approach. Under Article XX, the AB has adopted a 'proportionality analysis' to determine the validity of claims by states regarding necessary exceptions to GATT obligations.[76] In conducting this assessment, less restrictive alternatives 'reasonably available' to the defendant state are considered. In *EC–Asbestos*, the court assessed 'reasonably available' alternatives by considering industry standards and other states' practices.[77] In *US–Shrimp*, the AB examined a number of multilateral treaties, in particular the Convention on Trade in Endangered Species.[78] In reaching decisions after taking account of the views of the majority of WTO Members, the AB fulfils its duty of deliberative engagement and enhances the legitimacy of its decisions.

2.4 Benefits of Judicial Trusteeship in the Context of the WTO Regime

There are a number of benefits that accrue from judicial trusteeship. One benefit of the AB's functioning as an independent trustee is that it can free WTO Members from 'capture by entrenched domestic interests'.[79] Another benefit is improved compliance within the WTO regime.[80] This has led to enhanced open trade. It has been suggested that 'WTO judicial liberalization may be as, or even more, efficient at reaching the stated goal of the WTO to liberalize trade than the traditional trade rounds'.[81]

Analogous benefits, resulting from the discharge of trustee duties, could be enjoyed by a trusteeship regime with the object of environmental protection. However, there is a notable point of difference between the systems. That is, the WTO emphasizes a pragmatic approach to 'settling' as early as possible (for example, through negotiation) and getting back to business-as-usual.[82] This is negotiation done 'in the shadow of the law'.[83] Nevertheless, it is bargaining focused on relations between the individual parties.

Indeed, the majority of disputes in the WTO have not proceeded beyond consultations, either because a satisfactory settlement was found

---

[76] *Korea–Beef*, WT/DS161/AB/R [2001].
[77] *EC–Asbestos*, WT/DS135/AB/R [2001].
[78] *US–Shrimp [I]*, WT/DS58/AB/R [1998].
[79] Goldstein and Steinberg (note 60): 214.
[80] Ibid.: 236.
[81] Ibid.
[82] World Trade Organization, 'Settling Disputes: A Unique Contribution': http://www.wto.org/english/thewto_e/whatis_e/tif_e/disp1_e.htm.
[83] Robert Mnookin and Louis Kornhauser, 'Bargaining in the Shadow of the Law: The Case of Divorce' (1979) 88 *Yale Law Journal* 950.

or because the complainant decided for other reasons not to pursue the matter further.[84] In contrast, with an environmental trusteeship regime, one state's breach of any 'agreement' affects *all* other states due to the global interconnectedness of environmental issues. This is not to say that speedy compliance, in contrast to lengthy litigation, would not be desirable in an environmental trusteeship system. However, an ADR-type 'quick bargain settlement' approach would have to be carefully monitored to ensure settlements achieve results consistent with the values of global ecological integrity.

2.5 Majoritarian Activism as a Strategy of the Trustee Court

'Majoritarian activism' occurs when the court produces law that reflects standard practices or a high degree of state consensus, but that would not have been adopted under unanimity rules.[85] Article 19 of the DSU provides that the panel and the AB 'cannot add to or diminish the rights and obligations provided in the covered agreements'.[86] However, due to 'weak constitutional constraints', the AB has an inherent capacity 'to engage in expansive law-making'.[87] An example of 'majoritarian activism' can be seen in the AB case *United States–Safeguard Measures on Imports of Fresh, Chilled or Frozen Lamb Meat from New Zealand and Australia*.[88] Following the earlier case of *Argentina–Safeguard Measures on Imports of Footwear*,[89] the AB held that Article XIX of GATT 1994 allows 'Emergency Action on Imports of Particular Products' only if unforeseen developments lead to or threaten to lead to 'serious injury to domestic producers'. 'Unforeseen developments' was a requirement the AB discovered on proper construction. The US failed to establish that import damage was unforeseen, meaning industry 'safeguards' were not legitimate. This

---

84 World Trade Organization, 'Stages in a Typical WTO Dispute Settlement Case': http://www.wto.org/english/tratop_e/dispu_e/disp_settlement_cbt_e/c6s2p1_e.htm.

85 Miguel Poiares Maduro, *We, the Court: The European Court of Justice and the European Economic Constitution* (Hart Publ., Oxford 1998), cited by Stone Sweet and Brunell (note 36): 63.

86 The same phrase appears in Article 3.2 of the Dispute Settlement Understanding (note 38), under 'General Provisions'.

87 Richard Steinberg, 'Judicial Lawmaking at the WTO: Discursive, Constitutional, and Political Constraints' (2004) 92 (2) *Am. J. Int'l L.* 247, 249.

88 *United States–Safeguard Measures on Imports of Fresh, Chilled or Frozen Lamb Meat from New Zealand and Australia* (note 58).

89 *Argentina–Safeguard Measures on Imports of Footwear*, WT/DS121/AB/R, Report of the Appellate Body, 14 December 1999.

case shows how the AB has scope to interpret the law in ways that are unwanted by powerful actors, and thus are unlikely to have been agreed to by the collective principal either before or after the ruling.[90]

A 'trustee court' has the authority to say what international law means, to apply the law to concrete cases and thus to indicate what compliance with international law entails.[91] Though there was fierce rhetoric following the *US–Safeguard Measures* decision, the US complied with the decision. Goldman and Steinberg observe that:[92] 'as long as the AB does not deviate too far from underlying interests of Member States, they can rule, countries will comply, and liberalization moves forward – albeit with a Greek chorus of politicians and the public complaining about judicial activism and a loss of sovereignty.'

Normatively, the trustee court's approach of 'majoritarian activism' in relation to its discretionary use of delegated interpretative authority is an attractive approach. The possibility of achieving decisions beyond the reach of states, yet which can be recognized as acceptable, is a key benefit of trusteeship. It is a crucial element which international efforts at environmental protection need to capture in order to be effective.

2.6 Trustee Neutrality?

When interpretative authority is delegated to a 'trustee court', the trustees of the legal agreement and their legal interpretations are presumed to be more independent and disinterested compared to states (evident in self-serving arguments put forward in litigation). However, Alter notes that being a trustee does not mean that international judges are entirely neutral or fully independent actors.[93] In recognition of the contextual influences impacting upon decision-makers' perceptions of international trade rights and obligations, the DSU holds that the seven AB members must be broadly representative of membership of the WTO.[94] In practice, this has meant that either three or four Appellate Body members have always been citizens of a developing country member.[95] This aspect of the trustee role

---

[90] Alter (note 2): 52.

[91] Karen J. Alter, *The New Terrain of International Law: Courts, Politics, Rights* (Princeton University Press, Princeton, NJ 2014): 6–7.

[92] Goldstein and Steinberg (note 63): 280–281.

[93] Alter (note 91): 7.

[94] Dispute Settlement Rules (note 38): Article 17.3.

[95] World Trade Organization, 'WTO Bodies Involved in the Dispute Settlement Process': http://www.wto.org/english/tratop_e/dispu_e/disp_settlement_cbt_e/c3s4p1_e.htm.

of the WTO AB is significant. Given the tensions between developed and developing countries in relation to rights and obligations regarding environmental protection, a similar structure is arguably needed in a trusteeship approach to global ecological integrity.

3. WORLD HEALTH ORGANIZATION

The World Health Organization is the directing and coordinating authority for health within the UN system.[96] It is responsible for providing leadership on global health matters, shaping the health research agenda and setting norms and standards.[97] It also articulates evidence-based policy options, provides technical support to countries and monitors health trends.[98] It is the sole intergovernmental organization with the constitutional capacity to develop global public health policy.[99] The governance structure of the WHO is constituted by two bodies – the World Health Assembly and the Executive Board. The Secretariat is the third organ of the WHO.[100] Headed by the Director-General and numbering approximately 8500 technical and administrative staff, it carries out the WHO's day-to-day work.[101]

3.1 Trusteeship as the Appropriate Model for the WHO

3.1.1 Fiduciary nature of the WHO

The WHO has a 'fiduciary' nature in the sense that there is an overriding objective that constituent member states have agreed to pursue. Threats to global health (such as pandemics) do not have borders, so joining the WHO may be considered to have an aspect of enlightened self-interest. However, in forming and joining the WHO, in addition to benefitting from WHO services, states undertake to act on behalf of the broad objective of 'attainment by all peoples of the highest possible levels

---

[96] The WHO is a specialized UN agency, brought into relation with the UN Social and Economic Council through Articles 57 and 63 of the UN Charter and Article 69 of the WHO Constitution.

[97] *WHO: Working for Health* (World Health Organization, Geneva 2007).

[98] Ibid.

[99] J. Kendall, 'The Third Sector and the Development of European Public Policy: Frameworks for Analysis?', Civil Society Working Paper 19 (London School of Economics, London 2001): http://www.ucc.ie/archive/hdsp/Kendall_Third_sector.pdf.

[100] Constitution of the World Health Organization, 14 UNTS 185, Art. 9.

[101] Ibid., Art. 30.

of health',[102] and not purely in terms of self-interest. This is a 'trust' in the sense of having an overarching 'commission or charge'.[103] As with the WTO regime, 'no property need be involved'.[104] Further hallmarks of fiduciary obligations include 'vulnerability' (of populations to health emergencies) and the discretionary power to affect the interests of beneficiaries. WHO decisions in prioritizing allocation of scarce resources have very real practical effects on the health levels of populations of different world regions. Broadly, therefore, the WHO can be said to have been entrusted with its mandate.

3.1.2 An ethic of stewardship and trusteeship

It is useful to note that the WHO perceives *itself* as a steward or trustee of its mission in a broad sense. The WHO's *World Health Report 2000* emphasizes the importance of an ethic of stewardship in health systems. Stewardship was defined as 'the careful and responsible management of something entrusted to one's care'.[105] People entrust both their bodies and their money to the health system, 'which has a responsibility to protect the former and use the latter wisely and well'.[106] The report explained that effective stewardship requires 'oversight and trusteeship',[107] explicitly recognizing the interrelated nature of these concepts.

The *World Health Report 2000* urged governments to be the 'stewards' of their national resources, maintaining and improving them for the benefit of their populations.[108] Though the state's task as 'overall steward or trustee' of the system involves careful regulation, the concept of stewardship when properly conducted 'has a pervasive influence on all the workings of the system'.[109] The report also emphasized that trusteeship or stewardship applied to its own mission: 'At the international level, stewardship means influencing global research and production to meet health goals. It also means providing an evidence base to guide countries' efforts to improve the performance of their health systems.'[110]

Building upon this general ethic of stewardship and trusteeship, the

---

102 Ibid., Art. 1.

103 L.S. Sealy, 'Fiduciary Relationships' (1962) 20 *Cambridge Law Journal* 69, 76.

104 Ibid.

105 World Health Organization, *World Health Report 2000: Health Systems, Improving Performance* (World Health Organization, Geneva 2000): 45.

106 Ibid.

107 Ibid.: 119.

108 Ibid.: 117.

109 Ibid.: 45.

110 Ibid.: 117.

sections below will consider the degree to which the WHO's institutional structure entails trusteeship in the specific sense of a legal role with defined discretionary powers and fiduciary obligations.

3.1.3 The World Health Assembly in relation to individual states

The World Health Assembly (WHA) is composed of delegates from all member states of the WHO.[111] Each country has one vote.[112] The Assembly can be understood to be a 'principal' (like the General Council of the WTO), while the WHO's Executive Board has a trusteeship role. Before considering the Executive Board, it is useful to outline the powers of the Assembly itself. The Assembly determines the policies of the WHO.[113] It usually does so by issuing 'recommendations' under Article 23 of the Constitution (which, though not legally binding, have weight with member states due to moral pressure). The Constitution makes provision, in Articles 19 and 21, for the Assembly to adopt conventions and to pass legally binding regulations. These powers make the WHA a 'quasi-legislative' body.[114] The WHO Framework Convention on Tobacco Control, significantly, is the first convention to be adopted under Article 19. Like other international law treaties, the consent of states was required to make it binding on them.[115] The Convention has an obligation to report, entailing international accountability.[116] However, there is no legal mechanism to enforce compliance.

The International Health Regulations (IHRs) provide a legal framework to deal with the international spread of diseases.[117] The IHRs are legally binding, unless members choose to opt out of them within the prescribed time limit.[118] Notably, however, the IHRs contain no provision for enforcement or penalties for non-compliance.[119] The WHO relies on

---

[111] WHO Constitution (note 100): Article 11.

[112] Ibid., Art. 59.

[113] Ibid., Art. 18(a).

[114] Elisabetta Minelli, *World Health Organization: The Mandate of a Specialized Agency of the United Nations* [I.2.1.3]: http://www.gfmer.ch/TMCAMWHO_Minelli/Index.htm.

[115] *WHO Framework Convention on Tobacco Control*, 2302 UNTS 166 (adopted 21 May 2003), Art. 21; see also WHO Constitution (note 100), Art. 35.

[116] *WHO Framework Convention on Tobacco Control* (note 115), Art. 62.

[117] *WHO Revision of the International Health Regulations*, WHA Res. 58.3, World Health Assembly, 58th Ass. (23 May 2005). See also WHO Constitution (note 100), Art. 21(a).

[118] WHO Constitution (note 100), Art 22; International Health Regulations (note 117), Art. 59.

[119] See World Health Organization, 'Frequently Asked Questions about the International Health Regulations' (2005): http://www.who.int/csr/ihr/howtheywork/faq/.

'peer pressure' and 'public knowledge' to ensure voluntary compliance by states.[120] In explaining why states comply, reference is also made to the possible *practical* consequences of non-compliance: increased mortality of affected populations, economic and social disruption and the danger of unjustified measures being adopted unilaterally by other states.[121]

This raises the question of the scope of the WHO's legal authority in the case of a severe infectious outbreak within an uncooperative state. The Constitution provides that the WHO shall enjoy in the territory of each member 'such legal capacity as may be necessary for the fulfilment of its objective'.[122] Article 68 goes on to say: 'Such legal capacity . . . shall be defined in a separate agreement'. These individual agreements between the WHO and its members preserve the ultimate autonomy of states, as WHO assistance is 'on request of the [g]overnment'.[123] This is reinforced by Article 2 of the Constitution itself, which stipulates that one of the WHO's functions shall be 'to furnish appropriate technical assistance and, in emergencies, necessary aid *upon the requestor acceptance* of Governments'.[124] Therefore, the WHO cannot, through the WHA *or* the Executive Board's 'emergency powers' (discussed below), legally compel an individual state to comply with the IHRs. Nor could the WHO require, through coercive measures, that the uncooperative state receive emergency assistance. The WHO is limited to 'recommendations'.[125]

Concerning the question of broader legal authority of the international community to respond to a severe infectious outbreak in an uncooperative state, legal power is more likely to rest with the UN Security Council (acting under Chapter VII powers of the UN Charter).[126] The most relevant Security Council resolution in this area is one which stressed that HIV/AIDS may pose a risk to international security.[127] However, actual use of coercive measures in response to such a risk is an area untested in practice. Dopplick observes that in such a case a range of measures could

---

[120] Ibid.

[121] Ibid.

[122] WHO Constitution (note 100), Art. 66.

[123] See, for example, *Agreement Between the Government of Thailand and the World Health Organization for the Provision of Services by the World Health Organization in Thailand* (signed in Bangkok, 12 August 1949) 178 UNTS 348, Article 1(a).

[124] WHO Constitution (note 100), Art. 2(d) (italics added).

[125] International Health Regulations (note 117), Art. 15–19.

[126] Renee Dopplick, 'Emergency Preparedness for a Pandemic under International Law' (PhD thesis, 2008): 8: http://papers.ssrn.com/sol3/papers.cfm?abstract_id=1232762.

[127] S.C. Res. 1308, UN Doc. S/RES/1308 (17 July 2000).

be utilized, from disease surveillance, and travel and trade restrictions under Article 41 of the Charter to increasingly intrusive measures requiring the use of force, such as law enforcement or military action to enforce quarantines or to maintain order, under Article 42.[128]

Such measures against individual states are unavailable in the WHO's legal framework. Indeed, some argue that in the context of health objectives, a 'soft law' approach is preferable to a 'hard law' approach.[129] One reason is that a successful response to containing a pandemic requires system-wide activation of resources and personnel, including capacity at decentralized, local clinics.[130] A top-down, command-and-control model (stressing mandatory requirements) may be of little effectiveness in this regard, in contrast to an approach of exhortation and encouragement of voluntary compliance with recommendations. Furthermore, the concrete reality of health threats (due to the immediate effects of disease) is easily visible to states, making it more likely that they will feel a need to voluntarily comply with WHO recommendations (which are generally perceived as being based on sound technical underpinnings).

An environmental trusteeship and the WHO health regime share significant similarities. Both issues know no borders. Both involve scientific underpinnings, with persons of technical expertise entrusted with decision-making power. However, basic human psychology suggests a key difference between health and environmental issues. The less immediate nature of environmental threats may mean that an environmental trustee's 'recommendations' are less likely to be implemented with urgency by states.

3.1.4 Executive board in relation to the WHA

The Executive Board (the Board) is made up (currently) of 34 persons delegated by members and 'technically qualified in the field of health'.[131] The Board's functions are primarily preparatory (such as in preparation of the agenda for the Assembly) and executive, in that the Board gives effect to the decisions and policies of the Assembly.[132] Besides these preparatory and executive roles, the Board can also have an 'autonomous role' in

---

[128] Dopplick (note 126): 14.

[129] See Kevin A. Klock, 'The Soft Law Alternative to the WHO's Treaty Powers' (2013) 44 *Geo. J. Intn'l L.* 821; see also Belinda Bennett and Terry Carney, 'Law, Ethics and Pandemic Preparedness: the Importance of Cross-jurisdictional and Cross-cultural Perspectives' (2010) 34 (2) *Australian and New Zealand Journal of Public Health* 106.

[130] Dopplick (note 126): 31.

[131] WHO Constitution (note 100), Art. 24.

[132] WHO Constitution (note 100), Art. 28.

dealing with events requiring immediate action, such as an epidemic or a calamity (discussed in detail below).[133]

The WHA and the Board's legal powers in relation to individual member states are restricted. However, the Board can be understood in terms of trusteeship due to the nature of its role in relation to the WHA. This arises from the 'logic of delegation' of power to the Board. Majone proposes that there are two different 'logics of delegation' – namely, delegation to capture efficiency gains and delegation to increase the credibility of the principal and of political decision-making.[134] Credibility will be enhanced when agents are made independent, because 'an Agent bound to follow the directions of the delegating politician could not possibly enhance the credibility of the commitment'.[135] Building on this framework, Alter suggests that the concepts of 'agent' and 'trustee' are two categories which sit at opposite ends of a continuum. She says that:

> Principals choose to delegate to Trustees, as opposed to Agents, when the point of delegation is to harness the authority of the Trustee so as to enhance the legitimacy of political decision-making. Trustees are (1) selected because of their personal reputation or professional norms, (2) given independent authority to make decisions according to their best judgment or professional criteria, and (3) empowered to act on behalf of a beneficiary.

In terms of (1), the persons serving on the Board are required to be 'technically qualified' persons. Regarding (2), the Board has authority to make decisions, which can involve significant 'political responsibility' (as well as issues of a purely technical nature).[136] For example, the Board's decision-making authority includes preparation of the agenda of the Assembly, which can involve the inclusion or omission of 'sensitive' questions.[137] Also, the role of the Board is a determining factor governing the choice of the Director-General. Considering (3), the Board as trustee is meant to act in the interest of the WHO's overarching objective of global health

---

[133] Minelli (note 114), [I.2.2.3]. See WHO Constitution (note 100), Art. 28(i).

[134] Giandomenico Majone, 'Two Logics of Delegation: Agency and Fiduciary Relations in EU Governance' (2001) 2 *European Union Politics* 103, 104. A similar distinction was made by Edmund Burke, who contrasted a 'trustee model of representation' with a 'delegate model of representation'. See Edmund Burke, 'To the Electors of Bristol' (1774) in *The Works of the Right Hon. Edmund Burke*, Vol. I (Holdsworth and Ball, London 1834): 179–180.

[135] Ibid.: 110.

[136] Gian Luca Burci and Claude-Henri Vignes, *World Health Organization* (Kluwer Law International, The Hague 2004): 48.

[137] Ibid.

(the putative 'beneficiary', which provides an orientation away from the self-interest of individual WHO members).

3.1.5 Change in the executive board's logic of delegation

The 'logic' of delegation (from the WHA as principal to the EB) has undergone a change. The WHO Constitution's framers and more recent Assemblies have conceptualized the role of the EB differently, the former as 'trustees', the latter as 'delegate representatives' (that is, as representatives of their countries' interests). The unique nature of the EB member election process sheds light on the nature of members' role as intended by framers of the WHO Constitution. First, the WHA selects member states, with regional proportionality a relevant consideration. Then, member states appoint to the Board a technically qualified 'person'.[138] This process indicates that Board members were to serve not as representatives of their respective governments, but as 'the collective expression of the total membership of WHO and the conscience of its member states'.[139] The *personal* nature of board membership was a 'fundamental principle, untouched for years'.[140] Indeed, an earlier attempt to amend Article 24 by giving members of the Board the status of 'government representatives' was flatly rejected by the Assembly.[141] This emphasis on the role of members of the Board as objective professionals was a mode of delegation which aimed at 'enhanc[ing] the credibility of the commitment'.[142] This conception of the Board's role is well removed from the 'mere agent' end of the agent–trustee continuum.

Sweet Stone and Brunell explain that the notion of trusteeship is a concept which 'denotes a specific institutional configuration'.[143] However, how those entrusted with authority actually use it is 'an empirical, not a conceptual, question'.[144] In the case of the EB, the normative intention of the framers of the WHO Constitution was that Board members would exercise their powers with reference to the global WHO objective

---

[138] Ibid. The language of Article 24 of the WHO Constitution refers specifically to 'persons', in contrast to the language of Article 10, which refers to Assembly 'delegates'.

[139] Commonwealth Department of Community Services and Health, *World Health Organization, A Brief Summary of its Work* (Australian Government Publishing Service, Canberra 1988): 15. See also *WHO Official Records* (OR) No. 1, 72.

[140] Burci and Vignes (note 136): 45.

[141] *Official Records of the World Health Organization*, OR 28, 165.

[142] Majone (note 134): 104.

[143] Stone Sweet and Brunell (note 36): 62.

[144] Ibid.

of health for all. However, a large number of Board members did in fact act as government representatives, so that the principle was no longer being respected.[145] The result was that EB members acting as representatives caused the nature of the role to be legally 'redefined' by the WHA. It was decided in 1998 that members of the Board should, from then on, act 'as government representatives'.[146] In terms of Alter's 'continuum', the change in the role of EB members can be visualized as a significant shift closer to the 'agent' end.

The history of the Board provides empirical evidence of elements of 'trusteeship' in this UN agency. As will be explained below, there remain specific 'zones of discretion' in which the Board has trustee powers. However, it is worth noting at this point that the 'reinterpretation' episode provides a cautionary tale for any proposed environmental Trust Council. Though the ideal of apolitical, loyal service in the interests of the object of the regime may be intended, factors must be considered which make the ideal difficult to apply. In the case of the EB, the five permanent UN Security Council members were 'quasi-permanent' members of the Board, which was not in line with the demand that Board members serve in their personal capacity.[147] The de facto rotation between regions for the position of Chairman of the Board was not really compatible with this idea either.

3.2 The Executive Board's Zone of Discretionary Power

Decision-makers can be highly reputed experts, but if they are able to be 'kept on a tight leash'[148] they will be mere agents, rather than 'trustees'. The EB has broader powers than those of a mere agent, because it has a specific area in which it can exercise autonomous decision-making power. This can be understood in terms of a 'zone of discretion', which is determined by the trustee decision-maker's 'sum of competences . . . minus the sum of control instruments'[149] with which the principal can override an unwanted decision of the trustee. The zone of discretionary power of the EB emerges from the

[145] Burci and Vignes (note 136): 46.

[146] *Status of Members of the Executive Board: Clarification of the Interpretation of Article 24 of the Constitution* Res. WHA51.26, WHA51/1998/REC/1, p. 29. Interestingly, this was achieved not through a constitutional amendment, which would have taken several years, but through a 'clarification' of the meaning of Article 24, which was possible due to a difference between the English and French versions of the section. See Burci and Vignes (note 136): 46.

[147] Burci and Vignes (note 136): 46.

[148] Sweet Stone and Brunell (note 36): 68 (fn 10).

[149] Ibid.: 65. The term was used in that context to analyse a trustee court.

Constitution's provision of emergency powers to the Board under Article 28(i). These powers entail a 'trustee' role, because it is possible that the EB could override a particular kind of decision of the WHA – that is, the 'suspension' of a member under Article 7 of the Constitution.

3.2.1 The case of Portugal's suspension

The case of Portugal in the 1960s is useful for considering the Board's zone of discretionary powers. Article 7 of the WHO Constitution gave the WHA the power to implement sanctions on its members based on late fee payment or other 'exceptional circumstances'. Doing so would result in loss of voting privileges and possibly the suspension of WHO services. This was applied in 1964 to South Africa, in relation to voting privileges at the WHA, owing to the *apartheid* regime.[150] In the 1960s, Portugal's policy on retention of its colonies (and military action against independence movements) was viewed critically by the international community.[151] In 1966, the WHA decided (with the requisite two-thirds majority) to suspend Portugal's right to participate in the Regional Committee for Africa *and* to suspend technical assistance services to Portugal and its overseas territories (including malaria eradication measures).[152] This is the only example of suspension of WHO *services* being enforced under Article 7.[153] In 1967, at the Assembly, the Director-General reported on the implementation of the suspension. In his report, it was noted that he considered the suspension of technical assistance to be 'subject to the exercise of discretion in the event of any emergency where, in his opinion, there is a serious danger to public health, or where it may be necessary to organize health relief for the victims of a calamity'.[154]

The perspectives of different members expressed at the Assembly shed light on this issue. Dr Keita (of Guinea) argued that the purpose of the resolution had been to persuade Portugal to follow a more humane policy in its African territories and that 'there was nothing in the attitude of Portugal to justify any change of attitude'.[155] Therefore, he said, 'it would be a contradiction of the terms of the resolution to give the

---

[150] WHA 17.50, *Official Records of the World Health Organization*, OR 135, 23.

[151] Resolution 2107 (XX) of the United Nations General Assembly appealed to specialized agencies to refrain from granting technical assistance to Portugal.

[152] Res. WHA 19.31, *Official Records of the World Health Organization*, OR 151, 13.

[153] Burci and Vignes (note 136): 31.

[154] *Official Records of the World Health Organization*, OR 161, 515–518 (Twentieth World Health Assembly, Geneva, 8–26 May 1967).

[155] Ibid.: 516.

Director-General free hand'.[156] In contrast, Professor Aujaleu (of France) said he supported the Director-General's 'request' as contained in his report.[157] Interestingly, the Director-General stressed he was not asking for any action by the Assembly; 'he was merely stating what he considered should be his prerogative'.[158] Though there were no specific objections raised to this claim, it was not clarified as to whether the Director-General did indeed have this prerogative power. Pursuant to the Director-General's request, the report was simply noted.

In terms of the WHO Constitution, it is doubtful whether the Director-General has such 'prerogative' power, because this power is held by the EB. In fact, during the discussion, Dr Otolorin (of Nigeria) had suggested that rather than the WHA granting the Director-General authority directly, *if* an emergency situation arose, it should be referred to the Health Assembly or the Executive Board. This was an expression by a member of WHA that the EB had the power in an emergency to override an Article 7 suspension passed by the WHA. Indeed, the Director-General's language echoed Article 28 of the Constitution, which says that the functions of the Executive Board shall be:[159]

> (i) to take emergency measures within the functions and financial resources of the Organization to deal with events requiring immediate action. In particular it may authorize the Director-General to take the necessary steps to combat epidemics, to participate in the organization of health relief to victims of a calamity and to undertake studies and research the urgency of which has been drawn to the attention of the Board by any Member or by the Director-General.

Article 28(a) provides that one of the Board's functions is 'to give effect to the decisions and policies of the Health Assembly'. However, Article 28(i) would likely, in emergency circumstances, prevail over Article 28(a). If so, the Board could authorize the Director-General to take 'necessary steps', even though there had been a WHA decision to suspend services to a country. The significance of the EB's powers is reinforced by provision in the Constitution for a special fund to be used at the discretion of the Board, which may be established to meet emergencies (Article 58). Thus, the Board, entrusted with discretionary power to override WHA decisions regarding suspension, has trusteeship powers in this area.

A similar attitude has been expressed by succeeding Director-Generals when faced with comparable situations, though such powers have not been

---

156 Ibid.
157 Ibid.
158 Ibid.
159 WHO Constitution (note 100): Art. 28(i).

applied in practice.[160] It is worth reiterating an observation made above, that trusteeship denotes a specific institutional configuration (a conceptual question) whereas what happens in practice is a separate, empirical question. The next conceptual question to consider is: what if the Board exercises its discretionary power, but the WHA subsequently does not approve? For example, if WHA states wished to continue the suspension of health services to a racist regime undergoing a health emergency, how easily could the WHA override the Board's proposed emergency action?

There is a notable difference between the WTO and WHO regimes in this regard. In contrast to the WTO General Council's unanimity requirements, in the WHA only a two-thirds majority is required for 'important questions'.[161] This less stringent requirement entails a lesser degree of trusteeship for the Executive Board than the Appellate Body of the WTO. However, Burci and Vignes note that the suspension of services in the case of Portugal raises an important question of principle. That is, whether the suspension of health services to a population is compatible with the spirit of the WHO's Constitution.[162] This was a concern even in the absence of a significant health emergency. In the case of a health emergency, upholding a sanction to withhold WHO services would be even more incompatible with the spirit of the WHO Constitution. Therefore, the EB's measures would be more consistent with the overarching objective of the WHO regime, lending them the weight of legitimacy.

A conceptual discussion of institutional powers contains an element of the speculative. However, the events surrounding Portugal's suspension by the WHO raised issues which are worth considering in relation to a body empowered for the purpose of environmental trusteeship. For example, to what extent could a Global Commons Trust Council override certain decisions of an Assembly of states? How large a 'zone of discretionary power' will states bestow upon such a body? (See Chapter 8).

3.2.2 Fiduciary duty of loyalty to the 'beneficiary'

The political aspect involved in the use of Article 7 in 'exceptional circumstances' has been noted in relation to South Africa and Portugal. One further perspective from the 1967 World Health Assembly is worth noting. The Portuguese delegate stated that he found it:[163] 'impossible to see any connection between certain controversial political decisions and

160 Burci and Vignes (note 136): 32.
161 WHO Constitution (note 100): Art. 60.
162 Burci and Vignes (note 136): 31.
163 *Official Records of the World Health Organization*, OR 161 (note 154): 517.

the struggle to improve world health . . . Any departure from that basic aim was a threat to the humanitarian principles which should inspire all WHO's action.'

Using its Article 28(i) power in times of emergency, the EB would be eschewing political considerations and single-mindedly pursuing its duty of loyalty to the overarching purpose of the WHO regime ('health of all peoples'). Political use of Article 7 was also contemplated by the Assembly against Israel in 1971; however, no practical action was taken.[164] Burci suggests that such a move could have led to the withdrawal of a significant contributor to the WHO, the USA.[165] Given the reality that powerful states can have a significant influence on the practical implementation of sanctions in 'exceptional circumstances', an approach which affirms the (albeit narrow) trusteeship power of the Board is normatively attractive.

4. UNITED NATIONS TRUSTEESHIP SYSTEM

The notion of an international institution exercising a trusteeship function is not new. Indeed, the UN Trusteeship Council was established to oversee the transition of certain territories from colonization to independence. Under the International Trusteeship System (TS), states were entrusted with territories which did not have legal standing as nation states. After World War II, 11 territories were placed under 'trusteeship'. All have now achieved independence (the last being the trust territory of Palau, which gained independence in 1994).

The Trusteeship System is an example of an *executive or administrative trustee*. In this system, an Administering Authority was entrusted with a territory. Administering Authorities were overseen by the UN Trusteeship Council and the General Assembly.[166] The physical territory of ex-colonies constituted the corpus of the trust, while the beneficiaries of the trust were the inhabitants of those territories. The principal objective of the Trusteeship System was to ensure that territories placed under the system ('trust territories') were governed for the benefit of their inhabitants.

---

164 Ibid.

165 Ibid.

166 Andriy Y. Melnyk, 'United Nations Trusteeship System', in R. Wolfrum (ed.), *The Max Planck Encyclopedia of Public International Law* (Oxford University Press, Oxford 2013): 15: http://opil.ouplaw.com/home/ORIL.

4.1 Trusteeship Characteristics

Trusteeship was defined as a legal concept, the framework of which is found in Chapters XII and XIII of the UN Charter. The present section will explore how and why Administering Authorities can be considered 'trustees' and the nature of fiduciary obligations such a position of trust entails. Following this, the relevance of these principles to trusteeship of the global commons will be considered.

4.1.1 Nature of authority over territories held in trust

The notion of trusteeship in international law can be traced to a number of sources.[167] Particularly important are Article 76 of the UN Charter and Article 22(1) of the Covenant of the League of Nations.[168] These provisions emphasized the core principle that the trustee's discretionary powers must be exercised with reference to the best interests of beneficiaries. The relevant sections of the Charter and the Covenant indicated what 'best interests' meant, with a key difference. The League focused on the 'tutelage of . . . peoples',[169] without reference to eventual independence or self-determination. In contrast, the UN trusteeship system aimed above all to steer subject territories toward 'self-government or independence'.[170]

In the *South-West Africa* case, Sir Arnold McNair identified three basic features of trusteeship authority:[171]

> (a) that the control of the trustee, *tuteur* or *curateur* over the property is limited in one way or another; he is not in the position of the normal complete owner who can do what he likes to with his own, because he is precluded from administering the property for his own benefit; (b) that the trustee . . . is under some kind of legal obligation, based on confidence and conscience, to carry out the trust or mission confided to him for the benefit of some other person or for

---

[167] For example, Edmund Burke's speeches in the eighteenth century regarding British policy in India. See the 'Speech on Mr Fox's East-India Bill' in Burke (note 134): 276; see also A.J.R. Groom, 'The Trusteeship Council: A Successful Demise', in A.J.R. Groom and P. Taylor (eds), *The United Nations at the Millennium: The Principal Organs* (A&C Black, London 2000): 143.

[168] Carsten Stahn, *The Law and Practice of International Territorial Administration: Versailles to Iraq and Beyond* (Cambridge University Press, Cambridge 2008): 456.

[169] League of Nations, *Covenant of the League of Nations* 225 Parry 195; 1 Hudson 1; 112 BFSP 13; 13 AJIL Supp. 128 (1919), Art. 22, para. 1.

[170] See Art. 76 of the *Charter of the United Nations* 145 BSP 805 (adopted 26 June 1945, entered into force 24 October 1945).

[171] *International Status of South-West Africa (Advisory Opinion)* [1950] ICJ Rep 128. Separate Opinion of Judge McNair, 149.

> some public purpose; (c) that any attempt by one of these persons to absorb the property entrusted to him into his own patrimony would be illegal and would be prevented by law.

These general principles shed light on the International Trusteeship System because of the institution's analogy with trusteeship in private law (particularly in the vesting of property in trustees).[172] Stahn observes that '[t]he authority exercised by the administering powers under the Trusteeship System was trusteeship authority *per excellence*'.[173] In terms of the above test, all elements were satisfied. Article 76 of the Charter and specific trusteeship agreements (which defined the terms of the trust) gave trustee-states control over the territories, but prevented them from exercising ownership. The element of conscience is reinforced by the vulnerable nature of the beneficiaries. The League of Nations mandate system was established for 'peoples not yet able to stand by themselves'.[174] Similarly, the Trusteeship System was established to protect the weak, in cases where there was 'great might on the one side and unmight on the other'.[175] Finally, violations of obligations under trusteeship agreements and the Charter were subject to accountability under the Trusteeship System. Judicial review was also possible at the International Court of Justice. This was stipulated in individual trusteeship agreements.[176] Therefore, trusteeship became 'a legal principle of administration with clear cut obligations for administering powers'.[177]

4.1.2 Voluntary undertaking of trusteeship duties

In private law express trusts, the trustee must agree to the trusteeship. Similarly, with the Trusteeship System, 'states directly concerned'[178] were to voluntarily enter trusteeship agreements with respect to individual trust territories.[179] All but two states which held territories under the League of Nations 'mandate' system consented to bring their mandates into the Trusteeship System and submitted draft trusteeship agreements to the

---

[172] Ibid.
[173] Stahn (note 168): 114.
[174] Covenant of the League of Nations (note 169): Art. 22(1).
[175] McNair (note 171): 149.
[176] See, for example, Art. 16 of the *Trusteeship Agreement for the Mandated Territory of Western Samoa* (submitted by the Government of New Zealand to the General Assembly, First Session, Second Part, as Revised by the Assembly) (1947) 1 (1) *International Organization* 216, 219.
[177] Stahn (note 168): 114.
[178] UN Charter (note 170), Art. 79.
[179] Ibid., Art. 77(1).

United Nations General Assembly.[180] Trusteeship agreements can be considered treaties between an administering power and the UN, which are intended to be binding.[181] The voluntary nature of trusteeship undertakings reinforced the 'confidence' element inherent in the relationship between the Administering Authority and the beneficiaries.

4.2 Fiduciary Duties

4.2.1 Obligation of loyalty

The obligation of loyalty is perhaps the most crucial duty of trusteeship. The trustee must exercise its powers in the best interests of the beneficiary without a conflict of interests and without making an unauthorized profit. The relevance of these obligations is illustrated by the Australian *Phosphate* case.[182] Australia was the Administering Authority of the island of Nauru. Australia sought to move the native population off a phosphate-rich island, in order to facilitate phosphate mining operations. In December 1965, the General Assembly reaffirmed the 'inalienable right of the people of Nauru to self-government and independence' and resolved that Australia should take immediate steps to restore the island 'for habitation by the Nauruan people as a sovereign nation'.[183] These events eventually led to the creation of a domestic Legislative Council in 1966 and the acquisition of the phosphate industry by the Nauru Local Government Council.[184] Parker observes that the history of colonialism – and, therefore, by logical extension, decolonization – is in many ways entwined with concepts of international trusteeship.[185] However, though in practice tendencies characteristic of colonialism may have persisted, the Trusteeship System was able to hold trustees accountable in performing their fiduciary obligations.

4.2.2 Accountability

The Trusteeship System utilized accountability practices established in the League of Nations mandate system (such as the duty to submit annual

---

180 Melnyk (note 166): 8. The two exceptions were South Africa regarding South-West Africa (Namibia) and the UK with respect to Palestine.

181 Ibid.: 9.

182 A. Anghie, 'The Heart of my Home: Colonialism, Environmental Damage and the Nauru Case' (Spring 1993) 34 *Harv. Intn'l L.J.* 445, 454–455.

183 G.A. Res. 2111 (XX), UN GAOR, 20th Session, 1407th plen. mtg (1965).

184 Anghie (note 182): 452.

185 Tom Parker, *The Ultimate Intervention: Revitalising the UN Trusteeship Council for the 21st Century*, Report Centre for European and Asian Studies (2003): 22.

reports).[186] By the time of the formation of the Trusteeship System, in Groom's words, 'the genie of international accountability could not be put back into the bottle of untrammelled colonial possession'.[187] International supervision of the Trusteeship System was exercised through an annual obligation of the administering power to report to the Trusteeship Council, written and oral petitions by inhabitants of trustee territories and periodic visits to the trust territory.[188] The visits amounted to 'a projection of the Trusteeship Council and its supervisory activities into the Trust Territories'.[189] For example, the 1948 report of the Visiting Mission for Ruanda-Urundi and Tanganyika led to the Trusteeship Council recommending to the Administering Authority of Ruanda-Urundi to review its legislation to remove all traces of racial discrimination.[190]

Overall responsibility for the operation of the TS (except for 'strategic areas') was assigned to the UN General Assembly, such that the General Assembly may be characterized as 'the highest instance of review' within the TS.[191] Furthermore, though UN Charter does not provide for an enforcement mechanism or sanctions in case of non-compliance with obligations under the TS, the Trusteeship Council's status as a 'principal organ' of the United Nations gave its recommendations enhanced weight.[192] Even though these UNTC and General Assembly decisions were not legally binding, they were generally followed in practice.[193]

A related principle emerges under accountability – that the administrative trustee must *bear responsibility* for unlawful acts committed in breach of its fiduciary duty.[194] Following the Australian *Phosphate* case, the Nauruans, in a case for restitution, claimed that Australia had failed to make any provision to rehabilitate the land it had mined or to ensure that the Nauruans received proper compensation for the deposits extracted.[195] Australia agreed to a AUS$107m settlement. This suggests recognition of the strict nature of fiduciary obligations which it was required to fulfil as an administrative trustee.

---

[186] League of Nations Covenant (note 169): Art. 22(7).
[187] Groom (note 167): 145–146.
[188] UN Charter (note 170): Art. 87(a)–(c) and Art. 88.
[189] Parker (note 185): 27.
[190] Ibid.
[191] Melnyk (note 166): 14.
[192] Parker (note 185): 26.
[193] Melnyk (note 166): 19.
[194] Ibid.: 41.
[195] *Certain Phosphate Lands in Nauru [Nauru v Australia]* [Preliminary Objections] 1992 ICJ 240 (26 June).

4.2.3 Applicability of UN Trusteeship Council principles

The historical evolution of the International Trusteeship System shows that the international supervision of ex-colonies was better than leaving it to states themselves. It is useful to consider an earlier occurrence of the 'trusteeship' idea in relation to colonies. At the Berlin West Africa Conference of 1884–5, the idea was promoted that colonial rule over a foreign people must be exercised for the benefit of the local population.[196] While a laudable sentiment, Chowdhuri argues that entrusting native protection to individual states without supervision was a 'grave blunder'.[197] It left the indigenous populations of the colonized territories at the mercy of individual governments and irresponsible trading companies. In contrast, the Trusteeship System was 'one of the most sophisticated occurrences of international territorial administration and good governance'.[198] Trust territories gained independence relatively quickly (within half a century), upon which the Trusteeship System was regarded as having successfully completed its mission.

The Trusteeship System's principles of loyalty and international accountability endure as 'more timeless than their historical origins in the colonial era would suggest'.[199] As such, there is arguably a valid continuing place for trusteeship in international law. One possibility involves transferring the administration and reconstruction of collapsed states to a renewed trusteeship system.[200] While this is an idea not without merit, such proposals have met with opposition, due to parallels between trusteeship and colonialism. One writer has argued that 'trusteeship has always been, and would remain, a form of colonialism'.[201]

Proposals for trusteeship of the global commons do not suffer from being tainted by a lingering colonialism. Such ideas were rejected in the early days of the Trusteeship System. For example, in 1947 there were proposals to include Antarctica and the Polar Regions in the system. However, such proposals were not considered seriously by states, because

---

[196] General Act of the Berlin Conference, Art. VI and IX, *Consol. TS* (26 Feb., 1885) 165: 485.

[197] R. Chowdhuri, *International Mandates and Trusteeship Systems: A Comparative Study* (Nijhoff, The Hague 1955): 21.

[198] Melnyk (note 166): 38.

[199] Parker (note 185): 50.

[200] See Saira Mohamed, 'From Keeping Peace to Building Peace: A Proposal for a Revitalized United Nations Trusteeship Council' (Apr., 2005) 105 (3) *Columbia Law Review* 809; see also Parker (note 185).

[201] Ruth E. Gordon, 'Some Legal Problems with Trusteeship' (1995) 28 *Cornell Int'l L.J.* 301, 346–347.

(as was noted with irony) the Trusteeship System 'applied only to people not to penguins'.[202]

In the twenty-first century, it is time to re-evaluate that position. In the twentieth century, decolonization was one of the big projects. In the twenty-first century, the decolonization project is finished. However, a root concern of earlier adventures of colonization, resource extraction and use,[203] continues as a source of difficulty between states. At post-war conferences of both World Wars I and II, colonies were one of the most contentious issues.[204] International environmental protection talks can be similarly contentious, because both issues relate to the use of natural resources and the 'feeding' of states' resource (and energy) hungry economies.

Just as similar points of contention can be identified between issues of colonization and environmental protection, parallels can be discerned between the functioning of the Trusteeship Council and key features of any future environmental trusteeship body. Administrative trustees of 'trust territories', under the supervision of the Trusteeship Council, acted on behalf of entities that were vulnerable and which lacked legal standing. Likewise, an environmental trusteeship would need to act in favour of public goods and ecological communities which have no legal standing and no representation. There are a number of serious threats to crucial life-supporting ecological systems. As Chowdhuri observed at the Berlin conference, it would be a 'grave blunder' to ignore the benefits of international trusteeship of the global commons. Such a model furnishes superior safeguards and long-term benefits.

---

[202] P.J. Beck, *The International Politics of Antarctica* (Croom Helm, London 1986): 271.

[203] Eric Hobsbawm *The Age of Empire: 1875–1914* (Weidenfeld & Nicholson, London 1987): 73.

[204] See Parker (note 185): 6, 10.

8. Institutionalizing trusteeship for the global commons

> For the real question is whether the brighter future is really always so distant. What if, on the contrary, it has been here for a long time already and only our own blindness and weakness has prevented us from seeing it around us and within us, and kept us from developing it?
>
> Vaçlav Havel

1. THE PERPETUAL STRUGGLE FOR ENVIRONMENTAL TRUSTEESHIP

For over 40 years now, the United Nations has (in one way or other) considered the duty of nations to act as trustees of the global commons. In December 1970, the Secretary-General circulated a background note to the UN Stockholm Conference on the Human Environment. He proposed that the Declaration of the conference should refer to: 'the duty of all nations to carefully husband their natural resources and to *hold in trust* for present and future generations the air, water, lands, and communities of plants and animals on which all life depends.'[1]

The 'trust' language was not retained in the final text of Principle 2 of the Declaration as adopted in 1972.[2]

Following the 1992 Rio Earth Summit, the Commission on Global Governance (CGG) recommended the transformation of the UN Trusteeship Council in its 1995 report, *Our Global Neighbourhood*: 'The Trusteeship Council should be given a new mandate over the global commons in the context of concern for the security of the planet.'[3]

---

[1] UN Doc A/Conf48/PC/WG1/CRP4 (1971): 13, cited in Louis B. Sohn, 'The Stockholm Declaration on the Human Environment' (1973) 14 *Harv. Int'l L. J.* 423, 456 (italics added). See also Peter H. Sand, 'The Concept of Public Trusteeship in the Transboundary Governance of Biodiversity', in Louis J. Kotzé and Thilo Marauhn (eds), *Transboundary Governance of Biodiversity* (Brill, Leiden 2014): 34.

[2] Sohn (note 1): 457. See also Sand (note 1): 36, 49.

[3] Report of the Commission on Global Governance, *Our Global Neighbourhood* (Oxford University Press, Oxford 1995).

During the 1990s, many environmental and legal scholars proposed an environmental trusteeship council.[4] Among states, Malta was (and is) a particularly active supporter, putting the proposal on the agenda of the 45th (1991), 50th (1995) and 55th (1997) sessions of the UN General Assembly.[5]

In 1997, the Secretary-General took up the Maltese initiatives and proposed a 'new concept of trusteeship' to address the issue of global ecological integrity.[6] The Report *Renewing the United Nations: A Programme for Reform* recommended that the Trusteeship Council:

> be reconstituted as the forum through which Member States exercise their collective trusteeship for the integrity of the global environment and common areas such as the oceans, atmosphere and outer space. At the same time, it would serve to link the United Nations and civil society in addressing these areas of global concern, which require the active contribution of public, private and voluntary sectors.[7]

Among the measures recommended by the Secretary-General was the establishment of a high-level UN Task Force in 1998 to review existing structures and arrangements. The work of the Task Force was accompanied by a note from the Secretary-General on a 'new concept of trusteeship', proposing the reconstitution of the Trusteeship Council.[8] This note supported the concept of a 'high level deliberative forum that could take a comprehensive, strategic and long-term view of global trends and policy guidance in those areas to the world community. A new high level council with a well-defined mandate that does not create overlaps or conflicts with existing intergovernmental bodies could serve that purpose'.[9]

---

4 See, for example, C. Tinker, 'Environmental Security in the United Nations' (1992) 59 *Tennessee Law Review* 787, 821; Klaus Bosselmann, *Im Namen der Natur: Der Weg zum Ökologischen Rechtsstaat* (Scherz, Munich 1992): 400–406; Christopher Stone, *The Gnat is Older than Man: Global Environment and Human Agenda* (Princeton University Press, Princeton, NJ 1993): 217; H. Cleveland, 'The Global Commons: A Global Commons Trusteeship Commission is Needed', *The Futurist* (May/June 1993); Klaus Bosselmann, *When Two Worlds Collide: Society and Ecology* (RSVP, Auckland 1995): 277.

5 Kemal Baslar, *The Concept of the Common Heritage of Mankind* (Kluwer International, The Hague 1998): 69.

6 Felix Dodds, Michael Strauss and Maurice F. Strong, *Only One Earth: The Long Road via Rio to Sustainable Development* (Routledge, London 2012): 174.

7 Report of the Secretary-General, *Renewing the United Nations: A Programme for Reform*, UN Doc. A/51/950 (1997): 85.

8 Note by the Secretary-General, *United Nations Reform Measures and Proposals: A New Concept of Trusteeship*, Note, UN Doc. A/52/849 (1998).

9 Ibid.

The Task Force made 24 recommendations, mainly around strengthening the role of the United Nations Environment Programme (UNEP),[10] but fell short of addressing the trusteeship concept. Instead, the Task Force chose to assign this task to an environmental forum, to be held as part of UNEP's annual meetings of the Governance Council, where it eventually died an 'inglorious death by committee'.[11] Other recommendations of the Task Force have not been implemented, meaning that UNEP continues to suffer from underfunding and lack of competence. The only tangible change to date is an upgrade of UNEP's Governance Council to a UN Environment Assembly, which is open to all UN member states and which had its inaugural session in June 2014.[12]

The idea of an Environmental Trusteeship Council (ETC) was also taken to the 2002 World Summit on Sustainable Development in Johannesburg, but was not further discussed there. A Report in preparation for the Summit called for building upon the original trusteeship system and establishing a new ETC.[13]

Unlike the original Trusteeship System, the objectives of which could be satisfied, an ETC will need to function in perpetuity, much like the UN itself. Given the normative character of environmental obligations and the continuing capacity of States (and other entities) to irrevocably alter or harm the human environment, there is no prospect of the ECT achieving a fixed goal of perfect conditions. Moreover, if an intergenerational dimension is to be expressively integrated in the functions of the ETC, unlimited duration is essential. To establish a permanent ETC would require an amendment to the UN Charter.

Membership of the ETC would not be confined to states. It would include representatives of global civil society comprising individual experts, NGOs and UN agencies. Its functions would reach from treaty implementation (streamlining and reporting) to initiating petitions on behalf of present and future generations.[14]

A new mandate for the Trusteeship Council would indeed require an

---

[10] Report of the Secretary-General, *Environment and Human Settlements*, UN Doc. A/53/463 (1998).

[11] Sand (note 1): 50.

[12] UNEP News Centre, 'Historic UN Environment Assembly' (28 June 2014): http://www.unep.org/newscentre/Default.aspx?DocumentID=2791&ArticleID=10931.

[13] Dodds et al., *International Sustainable Development Governance. The Question of Reform: Key Issues and Proposals* (2002) UNU/IAS Final Report prepared for the World Summit on Sustainable Development, 21–22, http://www.uncsd2012.org/content/documents/ISDGFinalReport.pdf.

[14] Ibid.: 22.

amendment of the UN Charter, in particular with respect to composition (Article 86) and functions and powers (Articles 87 and 88). A broadening of its mandate to include representatives from global civil society (acting on behalf of present and future generations) would require amendments to Articles 75 and 76. Such far-reaching changes to the Charter are difficult to imagine. Many states would perceive them as threatening the principle of sovereign equality (Article 1), hence as going to the heart of the United Nations' mandate.

On the other hand, sovereignty and trusteeship are not diametrically opposed to each other. On the contrary (and as discussed throughout this book),[15] the legitimacy of states rests on their ability to meet their trusteeship obligations. At the international level, these obligations translate to 'collective trusteeship', as the UN Secretary-General termed it. To put collective trusteeship into practice requires a joint effort of states, the UN and civil society.

So far, states have shirked their trusteeship obligations, but the issue is not going to go away. The process leading up to the 2012 Rio+20 Summit and developments since demonstrate this quite clearly. Rio+20 attracted numerous proposals for more effective UN governance of sustainable development. Paragraphs (a)–(h) outline a selection:

(a) The Consultative Group of Ministers on International Environmental Governance reform recommended reforms to the United Nations Economic and Social Council (ECOSOC) and the Commission on Sustainable Development (CSD). The suggestions include merging the two into a Council on Sustainable Development, allowing for greater convergence between the environmental, social and economic pillars of sustainable development, and greater synergy across the UN system.[16]
(b) Another suggestion was the upgrading of the UNEP into a specialized agency, with the possible name United Nations Environment Organization (UNEO).[17] The proposal had strong support from France, and has been endorsed by the EU Council and UN Secretary-General; developing countries including Algeria, Ecuador, Cambodia, Vanuatu, Seychelles, Gabon and Burundi and various civil society actors also supported the proposal.[18] Often called 'the

---

[15] In particular, Chapters 5 and 6.

[16] Hannah Stoddart (ed.), *A Pocket Guide to Sustainable Development Governance*, 1st edn (Stakeholder Forum, Commonwealth Secretariat, London 2011): 36.

[17] Ibid.: 42.

[18] Ibid.

French Proposal', the UNEO would operate in a manner similar to the World Health Organization (WHO) as the umbrella environmental organization with 'on the ground' functions but without the authority to adjudicate on international environmental disputes.[19] It would be the premier environmental agenda-setting body, as well as the environmental watchdog. Central to this idea is a funding mechanism of assessed rather than voluntary contributions.[20]

(c) The Consultative Group of Ministers for International Environmental Governance presented the idea of a World Environmental Organization (WEO), which is similar to the UNEO, although it uses a different name and has some divergence in terms of mandates and functions of the organization.[21] The proposal similarly holds support from European states and a number of developing states.

(d) Other suggestions include the creation of an International Environmental Court (IEC), with jurisdiction to address issues such as access to justice and scientific understanding.[22] This option is an incentivizing and enforcement mechanism for existing multinational environmental agreements (MEAs) and governance regimes, and also allows for clarification of treaty obligations, dispute resolution and advisory opinions. Ultimately, global commons governance would operate through states' MEAs and the Court. Unlike the ICJ, the IEC would grant standing not just to states, but to non-state entities such as corporations, civil society groups and individuals.[23] This option is favoured by many as an adjunct to other institutions such as a UNEO or WEO. There is support for such an option among international networks of lawyers and advocates.[24]

(e) Similarly, proposals for a Global Environmental Parliament drew parallels with the International Labour Organization (ILO), advocating in favour of a body with the tripartite structure of an executive bureau, global subject committees and a global court for the environment, with membership drawn from state nominations.[25] This proposal departs from other options that have been mooted, because

---

19 Ibid.

20 Ibid.: 43.

21 Ibid.: 45.

22 Ibid.: 53.

23 Ibid.: 54.

24 See, for example, Stephen Hockman, 'The Case for an International Court for the Environment' (International Court for the Environment Coalition 2010): http://www.icecoalition.com.

25 Stoddart (note 16): 57.

it focuses on accountability between the upper echelons of global decision-making and civil society.

(f) Enhancing the UN Security Council to include an environmental mandate is another suggestion. This suggestion takes account of the growing 'security' dimension of environmental degradation.[26] Such an extension would necessitate amendment to the UN Charter, and, unsurprisingly, reception to the idea has been unenthusiastic; the idea is hindered by the undemocratic nature of the Council.

(g) Other proposals include 'clustering' MEAs for less fragmentation, enhancing inter-agency coordination and reforming the WTO, the IMF and the World Bank.

(h) Finally, the German Advisory Council on Global Change proposed an independent 'Earth Commission' to safeguard the rights and interests of future generations and 'to place on the international agenda, in a manner that catches the world's attention, issues which would otherwise be neglected despite their vital importance'.[27] Its members would be appointed by the UN General Assembly.

At Rio+20, considerable attention was drawn to the Draft Peoples' Sustainability Treaties (2012), designed to follow up on the recommendation of the 1987 'Brundtland Report' to create a charter articulating principles to guide nations in transitioning to sustainable development.[28] Such a charter was initially proposed at the Earth Summit in 1992, but was not adopted.

The 2012 Draft Treaties embrace and recognize the importance of established principles and declarations, such as the Stockholm Declaration, the Rio Declaration, the Johannesburg Declaration, the One Planet Living Principles, the Green Economy Coalition, the Trade Union Council 'Just Transition' principles and alternative models of economics of the New Economics Foundation. Furthermore, it places a strong focus on the Earth Charter; for example, the preamble specifically outlines the recognition of the earth's 'vitality, diversity and beauty as a sacred trust'.[29]

Although not expressed in the wording of the document, the foundations of the Draft Sustainability Treaties facilitate a trusteeship role of states.

---

[26] Ibid.: 59–60.

[27] German Advisory Council on Global Change (WBGU), *New Structures for Global Environmental Policy* (Earthscan, London 2001): 179.

[28] Peoples' Sustainability Treaties, 'Synthesis Report for Rio+20' (2012): http://sustainabilitytreaties.org/.

[29] The Earth Charter Initiative, *The Earth Charter* (2000): http://www.earthcharterinaction.org/.

This is outlined most strongly in the recognition of intergenerational equity and restoration of natural habitats. These are principles which can be directly expanded to implement binding trusteeship roles for states.

To see these trusteeship principles entering discussions at UN level, a high-level political body would need to be established with the purpose of monitoring and promoting international environmental agreements, such as the proposed Draft People's Sustainability Treaty.

For Rio+20, the Earth Charter Initiative released a report calling for a world environment organization with a global trusteeship mandate. The report, entitled *Enabling a Flourishing Earth: Challenges for the Green Economy, Opportunities for Global Governance*, makes the point that the green economy agenda is an attempt to correct market failures and argues that governments must separate markets from the commons.[30] It recommends an organization with a trusteeship function over global public goals and common goods, with an oversight of markets to ensure that they are protective of non-market common goods.[31]

Most subsequent proposals and discussions locate 'trusteeship for the environment' within the rubric of sustainable development, often couched in the language of 'intergenerational equity'. The institutionalization of intergenerational equity represents one of the key elements of environmental trusteeship. The best representation of the interests of the beneficiaries is the trust.

The Rio+20 outcome document *The Future We Want* indicates that strong governance is necessary for achieving sustainable development at all levels,[32] namely, the local, national, regional and global levels.[33] At the international level, state governments considered that the General Assembly should retain its role on issues of concern to the international community[34] and integrate sustainable development as a key part of United Nations activities.[35]

---

[30] Klaus Bosselmann, Peter Brown and Brendan Mackey, *Enabling a Flourishing Earth. Challenges for the Green Economy, Opportunities for Global Governance* (Stakeholder Forum, London 2012).

[31] Ibid.

[32] Laura Horn, 'Rio+20 United Nations Conference on Sustainable Development: Is this the Future We Want?' (2013) 91 (1) *MqJICEL* 18, 29.

[33] Resolution of the United Nations General Assembly, *The Future We Want*, UN Doc. A/RES/66/288, Annex (2012): 76: 'We recognize that effective governance at the local, subnational, national, regional and global levels representing the voices and interests of all is critical for advancing sustainable development.'

[34] Ibid.: 80: 'We reaffirm the role and authority of the General Assembly on global matters of concern to the international community.'

[35] Ibid.: 81.

The earlier draft of *The Future We Want* had suggested that the office of an ombudsman (or a High Commissioner) for future generations should be introduced at international level.[36] Unfortunately, this proposal for the establishment of an ombudsman was not agreed to in the final version of *The Future We Want*.[37] Instead, paragraph 86 of the 2012 outcome document invited the Secretary-General to prepare a report on the issue of 'promoting intergenerational solidarity *for the achievement of* sustainable development'.[38]

It is crucial to note here that paragraph 86 conceptualizes the promotion of intergenerational solidarity as merely instrumental to the achievement of the broader goal of sustainable development. The report thus does not view the protection of future generations against political short-termism as *an end in itself*, in a Kantian sense. Rather, intergenerational solidarity is placed as a subordinate component of the paradigm of balancing economic growth with the protection of such interests. This is far removed from sustainability as an overall objective: the preservation of the global environment for future generations *can* and *must* constitute the ultimate *telos* of any international regime orientated towards sustainability.[39]

Pursuant to paragraph 86 of *The Future We Want*, the Secretary-General produced a report entitled 'Intergenerational solidarity and the needs of future generations' in August 2013.[40] The purpose of the report was to 'consider the need for intergenerational solidarity, taking into account the needs of future generations', and '*to evaluate how this need could be addressed by the UN system*'.[41]

The report is relevant in three key ways. First, it outlines possible models for institutionalizing concern for future generations at the United Nations, suggesting the way forward.[42] Second, it reviews the fundamental ethical

---

[36] United Nations, 'The Future We Want: Zero Draft of the Outcome Document' (2012): 57: http://www.uncsd2012.org/futurewewant.html: 'We agree to further consider the establishment of an Ombudsperson, or High Commissioner for Future Generations, to promote sustainable development.'

[37] Horn (note 32): 33.

[38] *The Future We Want* (note 33): 86.

[39] Rakhyun Kim and Klaus Bosselmann, 'International Environmental Law in the Anthropocene: Towards a Purposive System of Multilateral Environmental Agreements' (2013) 2 *Transnational Environmental Law* 285–309; Klaus Bosselmann, *The Principle of Sustainability: Transforming Law and Governance* (Ashgate, Farnham 2008): 9–41.

[40] Report of the Secretary-General, *Intergenerational Solidarity and the Needs of Future Generations*, UN Doc. A/68/100 (2013).

[41] Ibid.: 2.

[42] Ibid.

underpinnings of intergenerational solidarity and future generations. Paragraph 12 suggests a general acceptance of the ethical framework on which a trusteeship model would be founded and reinforces the UN's observation of a growing link between collective trusteeship and the emerging concepts of global governance. It states: 'it has been argued that the notion that each generation holds the earth as a trustee or steward for its descendants strikes a deep chord with all cultures, religions and nationalities.'[43] Third, the report evaluates how the need for intergenerational solidarity is embedded in the concept of sustainable development and existing treaties, declarations, resolutions and intergovernmental decisions.[44]

Despite the report's location firmly within the rubric of sustainable development, it is still of strong empirical utility. It indicates the nature of the discourse currently present within the UN; it indicates a strong emphasis on public input and the desirability of multi-stakeholder outcomes; and it lists current actual proposals for change. We can build on this platform.

The report affirms four key points which are relevant for our purposes. First, the report affirms the basis of our moral obligations towards future generations as 'simply the equal concern and respect we owe to all humans, regardless of where and when they may have been born'.[45] In doing so, it draws explicitly on Article 1 of the Universal Declaration of Human Rights.[46] The report also recognizes the universal nature of these obligations, beyond the sustainable development agenda:

> The dedication to future generations is visible worldwide and across cultures. It is a universal value shared amongst humanity. This value is foundational to constitutions and international treaties; it is a driving force in the economy; in households it manifests itself even in religious beliefs, traditions and culture. It is also recognized that living members of a community benefit from the sacrifices and investments made by previous generations.[47]

Second, the report notes the close nexus between discourses on intergenerational justice and the agenda on sustainable development. Highlighting the interconnectedness of global challenges, it also notes that 'the sustainable

---

[43] Ibid.: 12.
[44] Ibid.: 32–61.
[45] Ibid.: 13.
[46] *Universal Declaration of Human Rights*, GA Res 217A (III), A/810 (1948), Art. 1: 'All human beings are born free and equal in dignity and rights. They are endowed with reason and conscience and should act towards one another in a spirit of brotherhood.'
[47] Report of the Secretary-General (note 40): 3.

development agenda is deeply intertwined with issues of *intra*-generational equity and justice'.[48]

Third, the report strongly endorses adoption of the precautionary principle as a normative underpinning of any institution protecting the interests of future generations. Avoiding and minimizing harm was taken to entail the practical requirement of '*avoiding irreversible* impacts on the ecosystems that provide the basis for human life – today, as well as in the future'.[49]

Fourth, and most importantly, the report recognizes the imperative to translate this moral obligation into political and legal terms: 'Despite this cultural value, a sense of responsibility towards future generations, in theory and even more so in practice, is a relatively new concept in the legal and political arenas.'[50]

The imperative to implement theory in practice is reinforced by the observation that future generations are 'politically powerless, with the representation of their interests limited to the vicarious concern of present generations'.[51]

The report astutely recognizes the difficulty in identifying the 'interests' of future generations – the interests of the 'beneficiaries' – as the key practical issue in the institutionalization of responses to these concerns. It finds that 'the needs of future generations should be identified and articulated as precisely as possible – current generations should not forego benefits unless it seems reasonable that it would make a difference'.[52]

The report drew heavily on input from academics and civil society. This included such events as an Expert Panel on Intergenerational Solidarity, which took place in May 2013. Furthermore, the discussion paper 'Committing to the Future We Want: A High Commissioner for Future Generations at Rio+20'[53] was referred to in the report as having 'created solid ground for the section of the report dedicated to policy options with regard to institutionalizing concerns for future generations'.[54]

In many ways, complementary to this UN Report (and the UN reform process in general) has been a series of interactive dialogues of the UN

---

48 Ibid.: 15.
49 Ibid.: 25.
50 Ibid.: 4.
51 Ibid.: 5.
52 Ibid.: 17.
53 Halina Ward, 'Committing to the Future We Want: A High Commissioner for Future Generations at Rio+20' (Discussion Paper, Foundation for Democracy and Sustainable Development, 2012).
54 Report of the Secretary General (note 40): 33.

General Assembly, under the title *Harmony with Nature*. On an annual basis, since 2011, the General Assembly has engaged with leading academics and global governance activists, to discuss a general shift from an anthropocentric to an earth-centred perspective on governance. Initiated by Bolivia, and based on a UN General Assembly resolution in 2009,[55] the *Harmony with Nature* dialogues have, so far, produced five reports of the Secretary-General, a database of documents and an extensive bibliography of non-anthropocentric jurisprudential perspectives.[56] Clearly, these perspectives call for governance based on stewardship and trusteeship, as highlighted at the inaugural *Harmony with Nature* dialogue in 2011[57] and again in 2014.[58]

The post-2015 development agenda of the United Nations is a logical platform for trusteeship governance. The new development framework will have a set of Sustainable Development Goals (SDGs), but also requires arrangements for more effective governance. To this end, member states have expressed the importance of 'good governance' in the context of SDGs: 'Democracy, good governance and the rule of law at the national and international levels, as well as an enabling environment, are essential for sustainable development including sustained and inclusive economic growth, social development, environmental protection and the eradication of poverty and hunger.'[59]

The ongoing discussions around SDG-related governance have mainly focused on well-known features such as democracy, transparency, accountability, participation, justice and the rule of law. In terms of methodology, there is a debate on whether there should be a stand-alone SDG on governance – as an enabler as much as an outcome of SDGs – or an incorporation of governance across all development goals.[60] However, better institutional arrangements are equally important. As the SDG process aims to achieve its goals by 2030, now is the time to push for institutions of trusteeship.

---

55 A/Res/64/196.

56 United Nations Harmony with Nature, 'UN Documents on Harmony with Nature', http://www.harmonywithnatureun.org/index.html.

57 With the presentation of the report, *Enabling a Flourishing Earth* (note 30) by Peter Brown, First Interactive Dialogue of the UN General Assembly on Harmony with Nature (2011).

58 Frank Biermann, 'Governance in the Anthropocene: Towards Planetary Stewardship', Fourth Interactive Dialogue of the UN General Assembly on Harmony with Nature (2014).

59 *The Future We Want* (note 33): 10.

60 United Nations Development Programme, *Governance for Sustainable Development* (Discussion Paper, 2014).

This overview of current developments towards a UN environmental trusteeship organization in some form suggests that the future is open. It is neither certain nor unlikely that UN member states will eventually muster the necessary political will. Much depends on the leadership of individual states which have, in the past, supported the idea of a World Environment Organization or a revival of the UN Trusteeship Council. However, the political will is unlikely to be strong enough without the voice of global civil society. Only a loud and clear voice has a chance to be heard by the UN and its member states. It falls therefore mainly upon civil society, including networks of activists, experts and scholars, to push for environmental trusteeship for all levels of governance.

2. INSTITUTIONALIZING TRUSTEESHIP OF THE GLOBAL COMMONS

The main obstacle against effective global governance remains unrestrained state sovereignty. Judging by the actual behaviour of states at international level, notably of the most powerful, the myth of absolute state sovereignty seems to be in the DNA of states and governments. As long as they perceive themselves as having a monopoly on determining the role of international institutions, they will follow *their* needs, not the needs of ecological governance. As governments favour short-term economic objectives over long-term environmental goals, they are not likely to choose the tools which are most effective in achieving these goals. Rather, they will choose tools which will benefit them most politically. It may be helpful, therefore, to perceive states not so much as static legal entities, but as dynamic organizations capable of learning and thereby adopting a trusteeship attitude to the global environment.[61]

On that basis, we can assume that knowledge and experience do matter. To a degree, the 'perpetual struggle' for UN reform is an illustration of this. There is a growing consensus that the intergovernmental system will only change if states themselves are changing. This is particularly true for a stewardship or trusteeship approach to global governance. As long as states, especially the most powerful, compete over natural resources, nothing will change and the tragedy of the commons will take its full course. The reverse needs to happen: as a global commons, natural resources need to be protected and shared by all, not by a few at the expense of the rest. The required change of mindset is less a problem of

---

[61] Bosselmann, *The Principle of Sustainability* (note 39): 180.

state sovereignty per se, and more a problem of outdated thinking about national interests. The challenge is to incorporate global interests into the formulation of national interests.

It is helpful, therefore, to remind ourselves of the rich traditions of environmental stewardship and trusteeship. They have existed in all cultures, across nations and throughout time. For our present time and purposes, the essentials of trusteeship for the global commons can be summarized in the following way.

2.1 Earth-based Governance

First of all, environmental trusteeship does not stand in opposition to the institution of the state; to the contrary, trusteeship provides the institution of the state with the legitimacy that it currently does not have. The global commons defy territorial boundaries, do not belong to states and cannot be exploited by individuals (private or public) at the expense of all. The pursuit of individual interests undermines the interests of all and creates a *jurisdiction gap*: the 'discrepancy between the global boundaries of today's major policy concerns and the essentially national boundaries of policy-making'.[62]

To overcome this discrepancy and close the jurisdiction gap, the global commons need to be recognized as an entity that is currently without jurisdiction, but which urgently needs one. Global commons belong neither to states nor can they be governed without them. Any governance structures, so far, have been sketchy and fragile. What passes for governance of the global commons is a loose bundle of treaties and principles that are unambitious and barely implemented. The existing treaty regimes for the oceans,[63] the atmosphere,[64] biological diversity[65] and Antarctica[66] lack overarching objectives, are full of loopholes and have virtually no effect in preventing continued degradation. There is no functioning governance of the global commons.

Yet, the real problem is not the bad shape that these regimes are

---

62 Inge Kaul, I. Grunberg and M.A. Stern (eds), *Global Public Goods: International Cooperation in the 21st Century* (Oxford University Press, Oxford 1999): 450.

63 United Nations Convention on the Law of the Sea, 1833 UNTS 3 (1982).

64 Following the United Nations Framework Convention on Climate Change, 1771 UNTS 107 (1992).

65 Following the Convention on Biological Diversity, 1760 UNTS 79 (1992).

66 Protocol on Environmental Protection to the Antarctic Treaty, 30 ILM 1455 (1991).

currently in, but their fundamentally flawed design. They are basically beyond repair. As long as states operate on the basis of negotiated consensus, they are locked into settling for the lowest common denominator. The consensus-based system gives each country a veto. More often than not, the US has exercised its veto and has been the least cooperative of all countries. But other countries, too, have been strategic, selfish and basically uninterested in preserving the global commons. Instead, the commons have been left in a dangerous vacuum that continues to be filled with other hard law: state sovereignty (nurturing 'land grab') and property rights (nurturing free use). It is no overstatement to suggest that the present system of governance does not protect the global commons at all, but protects powerful states and corporations at the expense of us all (living today and in the future). This is a regime of global exploitation rather than protection.

To turn this perverse logic around, we must insist that the global commons belong to all humankind, not to states and not to individuals. This automatically requires an understanding of governance that has the common good at its focus, not the competing interests of states or people.

The focus shifts from states to earth. This is the core meaning of earth governance. It may appear revolutionary, but is only so against the backdrop of current power structures. Considering the rich tradition of governance for the commons in all cultures, earth governance is merely its application at a global level. It is nothing more, nothing less.

2.2 Trusteeship Governance

Any form of protection of the global commons must occur in a non-competitive, cooperative and trusting manner. In this sense, trusteeship governance is the most elementary requirement of any state that is a member of the international community. So what does such requirement entail? We can now turn to some basic, practical questions for any governance based on trusteeship:

- What is the inalienable core of a trusteeship function, that is, what cannot go missing in the extrapolation to the international context?
- What is the ultimate aim of trusteeship, that is, what are the 'terms of the trust' in law parlance?
- What is the *corpus* of the trust, that is, what is the object to be protected by international law?
- How can the *beneficiaries* be most effectively represented?
- How can the beneficiaries most effectively *enforce the terms of the trust* against the trustees?

2.2.1 The core of a trusteeship function

It is important to identify the inalienable normative core of a trusteeship function, before proceeding to institutional models. We must ask ourselves: what elements of the trusteeship doctrine cannot be excluded from the institutionalization process? The most appropriate authority in this regard is Joseph Sax, the 'father' of the modern public trust doctrine in the environmental context. He argued that the underlying concept of the public trust doctrine is 'readily adaptable to the whole range of issues that comprise our environmental dilemma'. He suggested, however, that if the doctrine is to be a satisfactory tool, it must meet three requirements:

- It must contain some concept of a legal right in the general public.
- It must be capable of an interpretation consistent with contemporary concerns for environmental quality.
- It must be enforceable against the government.[67]

Similarly, Fox-Decent notes that there are three fundamental conditions from which a fiduciary relationship arises:

- The fiduciary holds 'administrative powers over the beneficiary or certain of her interests'.
- 'The beneficiary is incapable of controlling the fiduciary's exercise of power' ('or of exercising the type of power held by the fiduciary').
- 'The relevant interests of the beneficiary are capable of forming the subject matter of a fiduciary obligation'.[68]

These normative principles have been recognized by organs of the United Nations and also by treaty law. As noted above, Secretary-General U Thant presented to the 1972 Stockholm Conference the concept that nations 'hold in trust' resources for future generations.[69] Along the same lines, UN Secretary-General Kofi Anan described a re-constitutionalized UN Trusteeship Council as 'the forum through which member states

---

[67] V.P. Nanda and W. Ris Jr., 'The Public Trust Doctrine: A Viable Approach to International Environmental Protection' (1976) 5 *Ecology LQ* 291, 306. See also Joseph Sax, *Defending the Environment: A Strategy for Citizen Action* (Alfred A. Knopf, New York 1971): 172.

[68] Evan Fox-Decent, *Sovereignty's Promise: The State as a Fiduciary* (Oxford University Press, Oxford 2012): 93.

[69] UN Doc. A/Conf48/PC/WG1/CRP4 (1971), 13 (note 1).

exercise their collective trusteeship for the integrity of the global environment and common areas such as the oceans, atmosphere and outer space'.[70]

The subject of 'collective trusteeship' can be described as protecting the integrity of common areas – or global commons – that have been legally recognized as a 'common concern of humankind'.[71] These areas include, for example, the atmosphere[72] or biological diversity.[73] As Catherine Redgwell points out, these trusteeship duties should apply to the global commons, whether located *within* or beyond national boundaries.[74]

An even stronger expression of public trusteeship is the concept of the 'common heritage of mankind',[75] as we have seen in Chapter 4. The concept is embedded in the UN Convention on the Law of the Sea, although limited to the deep seabed[76] and only with respect to mineral resources.[77] Nevertheless, the United Nations Convention on the Law of the Seas (UNCLOS) has been described as 'one of the most developed applications of trusteeship or fiduciary relationship in an environmental context'.[78]

Other examples of treaty-embedded trusteeship include the 1946 International Convention for the Regulation of Whaling, which formally recognizes 'the interest of the nations of the world in safeguarding for future generations the great natural resources represented by the whale stocks',[79] and the 1972 World Heritage Convention, with its duty for states

---

70 *Renewing the United Nations* (note 7).

71 Catherine Redgwell, 'Reforming the United Nations Trusteeship Council', in W. Bradnee Chambers and Jessica F. Green (eds), *Reforming International Environmental Governance: From Institutional Limits to Innovative Reforms* (United Nations University Press, Tokyo 2005): 179.

72 Under the 1992 UN Framework Convention on Climate Change (note 64).

73 Under the 1992 Convention on Biological Diversity (note 65).

74 Redgwell (note 71).

75 Prue Taylor, 'The Future of the Common Heritage of Mankind: Intersections with the Public Trust Doctrine', in Laura Westra, Prue Taylor and Agnes Michelot (eds), *Confronting Ecological and Economic Collapse* (Routledge, London 2013): 32–46.

76 United Nations Convention on the Law of the Sea (note 63), Art. 135.

77 Ibid., Art. 133.

78 Patricia Birnie, Alan Boyle and Catherine Redgwell, *International Law and the Environment*, 3rd edn (Oxford University Press, Oxford 2009): 198. See also Mary Turnipseed et al., 'Using the Public Trust Doctrine to Achieve Ocean Stewardship', in Christina Voigt (ed.), *The Rule of Law for Nature* (Cambridge University Press, Cambridge 2013): 365–379.

79 International Convention for the Regulation of Whaling, Preamble, 2 December 1946, 62 Stat. 1716, 161 UNTS 74.

to ensure 'the identification, protection, conservation, presentation and transmission to future generations of the cultural and natural heritage'[80] situated within their territories. Similarly, the UN Framework Convention on Climate Change postulates the duty of states to 'protect the climate system for the benefit of present and future generations of humankind'.[81]

While international law does not recognize environmental trusteeship as a customary or general principle, the concept forms part of its architecture. There are certainly no legal barriers that would prohibit the concept from being applied domestically or internationally.

2.2.2 The aim of environmental trusteeship

Trusteeship's ultimate aim is to preserve the integrity of earth's ecological systems. Global commons, such as the oceans or the atmosphere, each possess an integrity that allows them to maintain their ecological functions.

The concept of ecological integrity is, of course, well known in international environmental law. Some 23 international soft and hard law agreements contain specific reference to it. The first of such agreements was the Convention on the Conservation of Antarctic Marine Living Resources, adopted in 1980, which recognized in its preamble the importance of 'protecting the *integrity* of the ecosystem of the seas surrounding Antarctica'.[82] Another example is the preamble of the 1992 Rio Declaration on Environment and Development, which calls for 'working towards international agreements which respect the interests of all and protect the *integrity* of the global environmental and developmental system'.[83]

Principle 7 of the Rio Declaration then defines the generally recognized duty of states to cooperate: 'States shall cooperate in a spirit of global partnership to conserve, protect and restore the health and *integrity* of the earth's ecosystem.'[84] This is repeated in key documents such as Agenda 21 and the 2002 Johannesburg Declaration. Even the 2012 Rio+20 outcome document, *The Future We Want*, widely perceived as unambitious and weak, calls for 'holistic and integrated approaches to sustainable

---

[80] Convention Concerning the Protection of the World Cultural and Natural Heritage, 27 UST 37, 1037 UNTS 151, (1972), Art. 4.

[81] United Nations Framework Convention on Climate Change (note 64): Art. 3.

[82] Convention on the Conservation of Antarctic Marine Living Resources, 1329 UNTS 48 (1980) (italics added).

[83] Rio Declaration on Environment and Development, UN Doc. A/CONF.151/26 (vol. I); 31 ILM 874 (1992) (italics added).

[84] Ibid. (italics added).

development which will guide humanity to live in harmony with nature and lead efforts to restore the health and *integrity* of the earth's ecosystem'.[85]

Further, the Brundtland Report itself described the 'integrity of the natural system' as the basic condition for 'the survival of life on earth', and in this way described the core idea behind sustainability as a prerequisite for development.[86]

The Earth Charter has the concept of ecological integrity at its very core. It urges 'all individuals, organizations, businesses, governments, and transnational institutions' to '[p]rotect and restore the integrity of Earth's ecological systems, with special concern for biological diversity and the natural processes that sustain life'.[87] Despite its uncertain legal status,[88] the Earth Charter is significant because of its inclusiveness[89] and widely accepted role in complementing the 1992 Rio Declaration.[90]

In the same vein, Article 2 of the International Union for the Conservation of Nature (IUCN) Draft International Covenant on Environment and Development states: 'Nature as a whole and all life forms warrant respect and are to be safeguarded. The integrity of the Earth's ecological systems shall be maintained and where necessary restored.'[91] The Draft Covenant is a product of decades of work of leading scholars and practitioners, and has been regularly revised to reflect new developments in the field of international environmental law.

Applying the usual standards for the recognition of concepts as international law, we can say that the repeated and consistent references to ecological integrity amount to an emerging fundamental goal or *grundnorm*

---

85 *The Future We Want* (note 33): 40 (italics added).

86 Report of the World Commission on Environment and Development, *Our Common Future*, UN Doc. A/42/427, Annex, (1987); Part I.1.3.[23]: 'Nature is bountiful, but it is also fragile and finely balanced. There are thresholds that cannot be crossed without endangering the basic integrity of the system. Today we are close to many of these thresholds; we must be ever mindful of the risk of endangering the survival of life on Earth.' See also Bosselmann, *The Principle of Sustainability* (note 39): 29–34.

87 Earth Charter (note 29), Principle 5.

88 Klaus Bosselmann, 'Earth Charter (2000)', in R. Wolfrum (ed.), *Max Planck Encyclopedia of Public International Law* (Oxford University Press, Oxford 2009).

89 The participatory process during the 1990s included hundreds of civil society organizations aiming for a consensus across cultures, religions and nations.

90 The Charter has been formally endorsed by over 2,000 organizations including UNESCO, IUCN and a number of states and major cities.

91 IUCN Environmental Law Programme, *Draft International Covenant on Environment and Development. Fourth Edition: Updated Text* (IUCN, Gland 2010), Art. 2.

of international environmental law.[92] But, even independently of any legal status under international law, the fundamental importance of preserving the ecological integrity of earth's ecological systems should not be in any doubt.

Relating this fundamental goal to intra- and intergenerational equity describes the key issue for trustees.[93] While sustainability is defined as preserving the integrity of ecological systems, the concept of sustainable development applies sustainability to human development.[94] Hence, ecological integrity sets the limits for social and economic development. Trustees need to ensure, therefore, that our responsibilities for future generations are being met by following the goals of sustainable development as defined here.[95]

2.2.3 The corpus of the trust

The object or corpus of the trust can be defined either in general terms or in more specific terms, depending on the exact role of a trusteeship institution. Generally speaking, the earth and its ecological systems function as a whole and cannot be divided up into discrete elements. On the other hand, governance can be more efficient if focused and localized. Institutions such as, for example, a World Environment Organization or a UN Trusteeship Council could conceivably have responsibility for the entire biosphere, which would leave them with a more general monitoring, coordinating or advisory role. Other institutions such as, for example, an Antarctic authority or a global climate authority would be confined to their respective objectives and hence play a more focused administrative or legislative role.

Peter Sand has identified a whole spectrum of possibilities and proposals:

---

[92] Kim and Bosselmann (note 39): 294, 305 and 308. See further Klaus Bosselmann, 'Grounding the Rule of Law' in Christina Voigt (ed.), *The Rule of Law for Nature* (Cambridge University Press, Cambridge 2013): 75–93, and Klaus Bosselmann 'The Rule of Law Grounded in the Earth: Ecological Integrity as a Grundnorm', in L. Westra and M. Vilela (eds), *The Earth Charter: Ecological Integrity and Social Movements* (Routledge, London 2014): 3–11.

[93] Peter Sand, 'Sovereignty Bounded: Public Trusteeship for Common Pool Resources' (2004) 4 (1) *Global Environmental Politics* 47.

[94] For more on the difference between these two concepts, see Klaus Bosselmann, Ron Engel and Prue Taylor, *Governance for Sustainability: Issues, Challenges and Successes*, IUCN – The World Conservation Union, Environmental Law and Policy Series (2008) Vol. 70, Bonn/Germany; http://cmsdata.iucn.org/downloads/governance_final_fur_web.pdf.

[95] So-called 'strong' sustainable development; see Bosselmann (note 39): 55–57.

trusteeship institutions for the Antarctic, for the Amazon rainforest, for genetic resources, for designated endangered species, for shared water resources, for regional seas, for ocean resources, for the atmosphere as a whole, for the global commons or for all elements of the environment.[96] Each has its advantages and disadvantages and they do not have to be mutually exclusive. In fact, the whole point of earth governance is to identify trusteeship models at the appropriate level – whether domestic, regional or global – and with a corpus appropriate to the situation at hand. The actual terms of trust will have to determine the specifics of the corpus and the beneficiaries.

In section 3, we will discuss trusteeship institutions at international level that appear best suited for the global commons.

2.2.4 Effective representation of beneficiaries

A common denominator of all considerations for beneficiaries is the rights and interests of future generations. They feature in numerous proposals for effective representation.[97]

The 1997 United Nations Educational, Scientific and Cultural Organization (UNESCO) Declaration on the Responsibilities of the Present Generations towards Future Generations is the 'most pronounced political recognition of the need to consciously and comprehensively protect the needs and interests of future generations'.[98] A campaign in

---

[96] Sand (note 1): 51–52. With respect to the global commons, some of the most relevant texts include Simone Borg, 'The Trusteeship Council as a Keeper of the Global Commons for Future Generations, and the Role of Diplomacy in Implementing Effective Environmental Protection', in David Attard (ed.), *Colloquium on the Legal Protection of the Environment Beyond the Limits of National Jurisdiction* (Mediterranean Academy of Diplomatic Studies, Malta 1992); Stone (note 4): 83; Burns Weston and David Bollier, *Green Governance: Ecological Survival, Human Rights and the Law of the Commons* (Cambridge University Press, Cambridge 2013): 238–255; and Mary Wood, *Nature's Trust: Environmental Law for a New Ecological Age* (Cambridge University Press, Cambridge 2014): 129–142.

[97] See, for example, Centre for International Sustainable Development Law (CISDL) and World Future Council (WFC), 'National Policies & International Instruments to Protect the Rights of Future Generations' (Working Paper): http://www.worldfuturecouncil.org/library.html; Maja Göpel, 'Guarding our Future: How to Protect Future Generations' (2011) 1 (6) *Solutions Journal*: http://www.thesolutionsjournal.com/node/821; Simon Caney, 'Climate Change and the Duties of the Advantaged' (2010) 13 *Critical Review of International Social and Political Philosophy* 203; Andrew Dobson (ed.), *Fairness and Futurity: Essays on Environmental Sustainability and Social Justice* (Oxford University Press, Oxford 1999).

[98] Maja Göpel, 'Intergenerational environmental justice: tacking a democratic deficit with Ombusdpersons for future generations': http://www.worldfuturecouncil.org/library.html.

the early 1990s by the Cousteau Society catalysed the adoption of the Declaration. The Society campaigned for a Bill of Rights for Future Generations.[99] Article 1 of the proposed bill said: 'Future generations have a right to an uncontaminated and undamaged Earth and to its enjoyment as the ground of human history, of culture, and of the social bonds that make each generation and individual a member of one human family.'[100]

Over 9 million people in 106 countries signed the petition in support of this Bill of Rights. In 1993, UNESCO became a partner and in 1997 the UNESCO General Conference adopted the Declaration on the Responsibilities of Current Generations towards Future Generations.[101] Importantly, Article 8 of the Declaration refers explicitly to the 'Common Heritage of Humankind',[102] invoking the concept of trusteeship. Crucially, the Declaration provides an authoritative basis for recognition by the UN of future generations as legal subjects:

> States, the United Nations system, other intergovernmental and non-governmental organisations, individuals, public and private bodies should assume their full responsibilities in promoting, in particular through education, training and information, respect for the ideals laid down in this declaration, and encourage by all appropriate means their full recognition and effective application.[103]

Given this authoritative basis, we turn to the question of the 'most appropriate and effective representation of the beneficiaries'.[104] What kind of institutional arrangements would best give effect to the overarching aims of trusteeship? Do we need to empower 'guardians' with rights of standing and legal representation on behalf of civil society? How can effective public participation on a transboundary level be organized? These are some of the key political questions; none will have an indisputable answer that everyone and every political body – states or international organizations – would agree with.

From the perspective of earth governance, however, it is obvious that states cannot have a monopoly on answering these questions. States are part of the problem as much as part of the solution, so they need to pause

---

[99] Ibid.: 3.

[100] Ibid.

[101] United Nations Educational, Scientific and Cultural Organization, 'Declaration on the Responsibilities of Current Generations towards Future Generations', adopted 12 November 1997 (Records of the General Conference, 29th Session, Vol. 1, Paris, 1998): 69–71.

[102] Ibid., Art. 8.

[103] Ibid., Art. 12(1).

[104] Sand (note 1): 56.

and reflect on what essentially legitimizes their decision-making power. As has been argued throughout this book, justification for political power rests ultimately with the people, on whom it depends and to whom it is accountable.

With respect to the beneficiaries, future generations cannot speak for themselves. Similarly, the global commons and the community of *all* life cannot speak for themselves. They rely on guardians or trustees who need to be trustworthy and capable of truly representing the beneficiaries' interests. States may qualify here, but surely not exclusively so, given their rather dismal track record to date. They may have to share the privilege with other institutions or groups which are less likely to put national and sectoral interests over global and common interests.

The representation of future generations may be in good hands by appointing a High Commissioner or Ombudsman for Future Generations. Offices of this nature have been established in a few countries.[105] It has to be said, however, that none of these have had any tangible impact on the development of national policies and laws. And while in principle the case for creating an institution to uphold responsibilities to future generations is strong,[106] the fact that governments do not consider this important enough for their own jurisdictions suggests that a UN-based High Commissioner or Ombudsman will either not be approved or, if so, only in a subordinate advisory role.[107]

It is only through a profound re-conception of the state as a trustee for the global commons (and for future generations) that we may find the kind of powerful representation that we are looking for.[108] In the meantime, this power needs to be found either entirely outside the jurisdiction

---

[105] Such offices include: a Parliamentary Commissioner for Future Generations in Hungary; a Parliamentary Commissioner for the Environment in New Zealand; an Environment and Sustainable Development Commissioner in Canada; and a Parliamentary Commission functioning as an Environmental Ombudsman in Israel. See Heloise Miereanau, 'Representing the "Unrepresentable"?', in Saki Bailey et al., *Protecting Future Generations through Commons* (Council of Europe, Strasbourg 2013): 147, 149.

[106] See, for example, Maja Göpel, *Ombudspersons for Future Generations as Sustainability Implementation Units* (Stakeholder Forum, London 2011): http://www.stakeholderforum.org/sf/.

[107] The initial draft of the Rio+20 outcome document *The Future We Want* (note 36) expressly referred to such an institution, but the final version of para. 86 is less specific ('consider the need for promoting intergenerational solidarity for the achievement of sustainable development taking into account the needs of future generations').

[108] See Chapters 2 and 6.

of nation-states, such as in the form of an independent body with highly respected, ethically motivated and skilled personalities,[109] or a mixed solution must be found that ensures both a democratic mandate and the utmost moral integrity. The *democratic element* could be provided for by the representation of three different political sectors, that is, governments, the United Nations and civil society. Each of these three sectors could nominate its own representatives. The *moral integrity element* could be provided for by establishing criteria that candidates have to meet if they seek nomination. They ought to be knowledgeable of the ethics of trusteeship, experienced with trustee obligations and have a proven track record of independence and integrity.

Whether the current system of international environmental law will ever allow for more democracy, as envisaged here, is an open question. Some are sceptical, for example, about the legitimacy of new institutions to speak on behalf of future generations.[110] Sand suggests, however, that this problem may be 'more academic than real: with regard to environmental issues of "common concern", the interests of future beneficiaries are inevitably shared by at least the younger generation of contemporary civil society'.[111] There is no alternative to developing more democratic structures and giving effect to future interests.

2.2.5 Enforcing the terms of reference

Another contentious issue is the enforcement of trusteeship obligations. If we agree that Sax's first two requirements of environmental trusteeship can be met in the international context,[112] then the third remains a challenge. How would civil society be able to enforce 'the terms of the trust against the trustee'?[113] Beneficiaries will need administrative and judicial remedies.[114] Traditional international law is geared for nation-states and their acceptance (or non-acceptance) of being held legally accountable.

'Democratic accountability' of governments to citizens is considered

---

[109] For example, in the form of an 'Earth Commission' as proposed by the German Advisory Council for Global Change (note 27).

[110] See, for example, Michael Bothe, 'Whose Environment? Concepts of Commonality in International Environmental Law', in Gerd Winter (ed.), *Multilevel Governance of Global Environmental Change: Perspectives from Science, Sociology and the Law* (Cambridge University Press, Cambridge 2006): 539, 555. It is noted that 'some screening of those able to serve as the attorney of future generations would be necessary'.

[111] Sand (note 1): 56–57.

[112] See above – 2.2.1.

[113] Sand (note 1): 53.

[114] Nanda and Ris (note 67): 307.

an essential part of international environmental trusteeship,[115] but sufficient accountability will be difficult to achieve by this means. There are precedents of transnational accountability, but they are traditionally confined to commercial interests, for example in private international law (or conflict of laws). Environmental interests do not fit the rigid divide between (enforceable) private interests and (non-enforceable) public interests.[116] And international environmental law has its focus on states, not citizens. There are two major obstacles that make it difficult for citizens to seek remedies against transboundary environmental harm. One is the no-act-of-the state exemption, which means that a state is not liable towards persons who suffer harm outside its jurisdiction.[117] The other is the due diligence exemption, which means that a state has no transboundary liability for actions of non-governmental activities, as long as the government itself has acted with due care.[118] The emergent field of international environmental administrative law[119] and growing case law makes the general acceptance of transboundary procedural rights of individuals or groups more likely.[120]

For the time being, however, we have to rely on states themselves to commit to transboundary procedural rights as, for example, recognized in the 1998 Aarhus Convention on Access to Information, Public Participation in Decision-Making and Access to Justice in Environmental Matters.[121] Regional in scope, only European countries have so far been signatories, despite the fact that the Aarhus Convention is open to all

---

[115] Catherine Redgwell, *Intergenerational Trusts and Environmental Protection* (Manchester University Press, Manchester 1999): 68.

[116] C.S. McCaffrey, 'Liability for Transfrontier Environmental Harm: The Relationship between Public and Private International Law', in C. van Bar (ed.), *Internationales Umwelthaftungsrecht* (vol. 1, Carle Heymanns, Cologne 1995): 81, 83. See further Julio Barboza, *The Environment, Risk and Liability in International Law* (Brill, Leiden 2011).

[117] Rene Lefeber, *Transboundary Environmental Interference and the Origin of State Liability* (Kluwer Law International, The Hague 1996): 182.

[118] Ibid.

[119] Wolfgang Durner, 'Internationales Umweltverwaltungsrecht', in Christoph Möllers et al. (eds), *Internationales Verwaltungsrecht: Eine Analyse anhand von Referenzgebieten* (Mohr Siebeck, Tuebingen 2007): 121–165. See generally Jörg Menzel, *Internationales Öffentliches Recht* (Mohr Siebeck, Tuebingen 2011).

[120] Sand (note 1): 54; and Peter Sand, 'The Evolution of Transnational Environmental Law: Four Cases in Historical Perspective' (2012) 1 *Transnational Environmental Law* 183, 195.

[121] Convention on Access to Information, Public Participation in Decision-Making and Access to Justice in Environmental Matters (Aarhus, 25 June 1998), 2161 UNTS 447.

countries. In a sense, environmental democracy is currently confined to Europe.

The lacking recognition of enforceable transnational (and intergenerational) rights remains a stumbling block for effective environmental trusteeship. Its feasibility and practicality is, however, not dependent on it. The main challenge for now is to build a 'robust institutional infrastructure that sovereigns could trust to make impartial and competent decisions on allocations among sovereigns or their citizens'.[122]

3. WORLD ENVIRONMENT ORGANIZATION AS A MODEL

Based on the essential features outlined so far, we can now consider what a UN-related environmental trusteeship organization may look like. Using a World Environment Organization as a model here does not mean that a WEO would per se be preferable to other proposals for supranational or intergovernmental institutions.[123] Similar institutional proposals include: a United Nations Environment Programme Organization (UNEPO);[124] a United Nations Environment Organization (UNEO);[125] a Global Environment Organization (GEO) with a global parliament and global court for the environment;[126] and an Environmental Security Council.[127]

---

[122] Eyal Benvenisti, 'Sovereignty as Trustees of Humanity: On the Accountability of States to Foreign Stakeholders' (2013) 107 (2) *American Journal of International Law* 295, 320.

[123] See section 1, above.

[124] Bharat Desai, *International Environmental Governance: Towards UNEPO* (Brill, Leiden 2014).

[125] The 'French proposal' supported by the EU, some African and Latin American countries and many civil society actors. See Frank Biermann, 'Reforming Global Environmental Governance: The Case for a United Nations Environment Organisation' (Stakeholder Forum, London 2011): http://www.stakeholderforum.org; Andreas Rechkammer, *UNEO: Towards an International Environment Organization: Approaches to a Sustainable Reform of Global Environmental Governance* (Nomos, Baden-Baden 2005).

[126] See Narito Harada, 'Campaign for a Global Environment Organisation: A French Perspective', (Yale Center for Environmental Law and Policy, New Haven, CT 2003), http://www.agirpourlenvironnement.org/pdf/harada.pdf.

[127] See Maria Ivanova, *International Environmental Governance Reform: Options and Implications* (Report for the IEG Chatham House Workshop, 16–17 July 2007), 7; Lorraine Elliott, *Expanding the Mandate of the UN Security Council to Account for Environmental Issues* (2002): http://archive.unu.edu/inter-linkages/docs/IEG/Elliot.pdf.

Some of these proposals would be complementary to the establishment of a WEO, while others differ only in name.

Most proposals are either silent about trusteeship ambitions or give it very little attention; this includes proposals towards a WEO.[128] In contrast,

---

[128] Here is a selection (in alphabetical order): Frank Biermann, 'The Case for a World Environment Organization' (2000) 42 *Environment* 23–31; Frank Biermann, 'The Emerging Debate on the Need for a World Environment Organization: A Commentary' (2001) 1 *Global Environmental Politics* 45; Frank Biermann, *Reforming Global Environmental Governance: The Case for a United Nations Environment Organisation (UNEO)* (Stakeholder Forum 5, London, Feb. 2011) [discussing the history of debate surrounding the creation of a WEO, three models of a WEO, and the case for a UN Environment Organization]; Frank Biermann, 'World Environment Organization', in J.-F. Morin et al. (eds), *The Essential Guide to Global Environmental Governance* (Routledge, London 2014): 236; Frank Biermann, *Earth System Governance: World Politics in the Anthropocene* (The MIT Press, Cambridge, MA 2014); Stephen Charnovitz, 'Toward a World Environment Organization: Reflections upon a Vital Debate', in R.B. Mitchell (ed.), *International Environmental Politics* (SAGE, London 2008): 173–193; Daniel Esty, 'The Case for a Global Environmental Organization', in Peter B. Kenen (ed.), *Managing the World Economy* (Peterson Institute for International Economics, Washington, DC 1994): 287; Daniel Esty, 'Toward a Global Environmental Organization', in C.F. Bergsten et al., *Toward Shared Responsibility and Global Leadership: A Report to the Leaders of the G-8 Member Countries* (Recommendations for the G-8 Genoa Summit from the G-8 Preparatory Conference, 2001): 30, 31; Daniel Esty and Maria Ivanova, 'Revitalizing Global Environmental Governance: A Function-Driven Approach', in *Global Environmental Governance: Options and Opportunities* (Yale School of Forestry & Environmental Studies, New Haven, CT 2002); Thomas Gehring and Sebastian Oberthür, 'Was bringt eine Weltum weltorganisation? Kooperationstheoretische Anmerkungen zur institutionellen Neuordnung der internationalen Umweltpolitik' [World Environment Organization: What on Earth For? Cooperation Theory and the Debate on the Institutional Reorganization of International Environmental Politics] (June 2000) 7 (1) *Zeitschrift fur Internationale Beziehungen* 185–211; Thomas Gehring and Sebastian Oberthür, 'Reforming International Environmental Governance: An Institutionalist Critique of the Proposal for a World Environment Organisation' (2004) 4 (4) *International Environmental Agreements: Politics, Law and Economics* 359–381; Nils Goeteyn, 'Legal Challenges in the Creation of a World Environment Organization', in Robert Percival et al. (eds), *Global Environmental Law at a Crossroads* (Edward Elgar Publishing, Cheltenham, UK/Northampton, MA 2014): 295–312; C. Ford Runge, 'A Global Environment Organization (GEO) and the World Trading System' (2001) 35 *Journal of World Trade* 399; Nico Schrijver, 'Pros and Cons of Establishing a UN World Environment Organisation', in (2012) *Report of the 75th Conference/the International Law Association* 912–914; Udo Simonis, 'Global Environmental Governance: Speeding up the Debate on a World Environment Organization' (Wissenschaftszentrum Berlin für Sozialforschung, Papers FS II 02-404, 2002); John Whalley and Ben Zissimos, 'What Could a World Environmental Organization Do?' (2001) 1 *Global Environmental Politics* 29–34.

discussions around a new UN Trusteeship Council have mostly involved environmental trusteeship functions.[129] The following suggestions would, for the most part, be relevant to the establishment of a UN Trusteeship Council for the Global Commons or a WEO.

Essentially, what is needed is an institution capable of transforming, rather than merely reforming, international environmental governance. For many years, there has been discussion over the possibility of a World Environment Organization (WEO). Renato Ruggiero, then executive director of the World Trade Organization (WTO), drew much attention when he advanced the idea of a world environment organization as a counterweight to the WTO.[130] Before that, in 1997, the German government had proposed – supported by Brazil, Singapore, South Africa and New Zealand – the establishment of a 'global umbrella organization for environmental issues'.[131] Ever since then, proponents have focused on particular aspects such as the mandate or legitimacy of a WEO.

3.1 Mandate

There are two ways in which a WEO could be created. The first is by way of a treaty, thereby bringing it under normal UN structures. Alternatively, it could be created by way of a General Assembly Resolution, which would endow it with independent institutional status. An accompanying aspect of a United Nations General Assembly Resolution should be a recognition of the fiduciary nature of state sovereignty.

It is suggested that a WEO should be mandated with power that is not dependent upon the assent of states, but that instead would function independently of the UN. Endowing a WEO with an independent function and power would reflect the importance of ecological integrity as a matter of global concern, a concern fundamental to all other global concerns (such as social justice and economic prosperity). It could, therefore, be seen as a step towards a meaningful understanding of 'sustainable development'. Furthermore, such an institution would not be hindered by states acting in self-interest or deadlock politics, giving it needed flexibility which would be impossible if it were subject to the power struggles of states. Like the EU, which sometimes acts in conflict with state interests in the greater

---

[129] A suggestion raised in the report, *Our Global Neighbourhood* (note 3).

[130] Renato Ruggiero, 'A Global System for the Next Fifty Years', Address to the Royal Institute of International Affairs, 30 October 1998, http://www.wto.org/english/news_e/sprr_e/sprr_e.htm.

[131] Frank Biermann, 'The Case for a World Environment Organization' (2000) 42 (9) *Environment* 22, 24.

interests of the EU as a whole, a WEO would similarly act not in the interests of states, but in the greater interests of the environment.

The mandate and functions currently performed by UNEP will no doubt need to be an important part of a WEO. Reliable scientific information, monitoring and reviewing of environmental policies are crucial in creating a successful international response to the ecological crisis. However, in order to address the more systemic issues which have crippled previous international environmental institutions, the mandate for a WEO must go beyond this in a number of ways.

First, in order to avoid Hardin's 'tragedy of the commons',[132] a WEO should be mandated with a trusteeship function over the 'global commons' or 'global environment', so as to stop individuals or states exploiting these common areas to the point of destruction.[133] A wide view of what this entails should be adopted by a WEO, thereby including the atmosphere, outer space, the high seas and Antarctica.

The trusteeship function of a WEO would not be new, as we have seen in Chapter 7. An obvious parallel can be drawn between the functioning of the – currently defunct – UN Trusteeship Council and the trusteeship role that a future WEO would need to play in order to be effective.[134] The Trusteeship Council acted on behalf of entities that were not legally recognized; similarly, a WEO would need to act in favour of the global commons, which has no legal standing and no representation.

Second, a WEO should be mandated with the power to resolve disputes. A major issue which has hampered the advancement of an international response to ecological issues is the lack of accountability for states in breach of their legal obligations. Traditionally, it has been up to states to call upon the International Court of Justice (ICJ) when another state has acted outside the bounds of its legal obligations. However, problematically, *both* states have to agree upon the court's jurisdiction. In the past, states have been able to avoid the legal ramifications of decisions by political manoeuvring within the UN system.[135] Furthermore, in the case of the

---

132 G. Hardin, 'The Tragedy of the Commons' (1968) 162 *Science* 1243.

133 Christopher D. Stone, 'Defending the Global Commons', in Philippe Sands (ed.), *Greening International Law* (Earthscan, London 1993): 34.

134 See, for example, M. Imber, *Environment, Security and UN Reform* (Macmillan, London 1994): 106, referring to comments made by the UNCED Secretary-General Maurice Strong; G. Palmer, 'New Ways to Make International Environmental Law' (1992) 86 (2) *American Journal of International Law* 259, 279; *Renewing the United Nations: a Programme for Reform* (note 7).

135 For example, the events surrounding the case: *Military and Paramilitary Activities in and against Nicaragua (Nicaragua v United States of America)* [1986] ICJ 14 (27 June 1986).

global commons, there is also the issue of the lack of a plaintiff clearly qualified to demonstrate both standing and injury.[136]

On this basis, it is suggested that a two-tier mechanism could be installed, similar to that of the WTO, which would allow states to unilaterally be able to take another to court.[137] Further, the possibility is raised for other recognized entities to be able to take a case on behalf of the environment. Such 'guardians' could either be drawn from existing international agencies that have the appropriate focus, such as the United Nations Environment Programme and the World Meteorological Organization (WMO), or from the many non-governmental organizations (NGOs, such as Greenpeace and the World Wide Fund for Nature). Another possibility is the establishment of a system of guardians, who would be legal representatives for the natural environment.[138]

The idea of a guardianship role for the benefit of natural entities is similar to the concept of legal guardians (sometimes 'conservators') in familiar legal systems.[139] Presented with possible invasions of the interests of certain persons who are unable to speak for themselves (such as unrepresented infants, the insane and the senile), courts are empowered to appoint a legal guardian to speak for them. So, too, can guardians be designated to be the legal voice for the otherwise voiceless environment.[140] This does not mean that the guardians would be given plenary powers to halt any activity of which they disapproved. Rather, the role of the guardian would be built into the institutional process, to ensure that environmental values were being identified and accounted for.[141] The judgements of an environmental dispute resolution panel would be most effective if they were legally binding. However, at the very least, the panel could issue an advisory opinion, which states would ignore at the cost of the international community's moral opprobrium.

---

[136] See Christopher D. Stone, *Should Trees Have Standing? And Other Essays on Law, Morals and the Environment* (Oceana Publications, Dobbs Ferry, NY 1996).

[137] Numerous scholars have argued for the need for an international environmental court. See, for example, Alfred Rest, 'The Indispensability of an International Environmental Court' (1998) 7 *RECEIL* 63; Alfred Rest, 'Need for an International Court for the Environment?' (1994) 24 *Environmental Law and Policy* 173; Amedeo Postiglione, 'An International Court for the Environment?' (1993) 23 *Environmental Law and Policy* 73. Compare with Ellen Hey, *Reflections on an International Environment Court* (Martinus Nijhoff, The Hague 2000).

[138] Christopher D. Stone, 'Defending the Global Commons', in Philippe Sands (ed.), *Greening International Law* (Earthscan, London 1993): 43.

[139] Ibid.: 40.

[140] Ibid.

[141] Ibid.

3.2 Legitimacy

If a powerful environmental institution were to be created, it would be imperative that it be seen as an institution of legitimate standing. The question is thus raised as to how such legitimacy may be attained. The creation of a WEO along the lines proposed here would have the requisite legitimacy for two reasons.

First, a WEO would be legitimate if it was widely democratic, representative and participatory. As noted in Chapter 1, globalization has reduced the ability of states to exercise power over their territories, while simultaneously the international arena operates undemocratically with powerful states manipulating outcomes according to their own state interests. Given widespread adherence to the value of democracy as the yardstick of 'legitimate political authority', this democratic deficiency begs to be addressed.[142] Furthermore, it can be argued that democracy is particularly important in relation to the environment,[143] because it is an issue which will affect everyone and often, particularly those with the least power. Given that ecological issues are caused by hundreds of millions of individual actions, part of the challenge lies in convincing individuals that they need to take responsibility for their own actions and alter their current ways of life. In order to achieve this, it is imperative that international institutions become more participatory. Accordingly, the conception of the *demos* is much wider, under this view, than that which we have under existing institutional frameworks. On this basis, it may be that such a WEO could function as a model for transforming the international arena to be more democratically inclusive.

It is suggested that the administration of a WEO body should be bipartisan and representative of the actual global population by having representatives from all regions of the world. These representatives should be politically independent and of high eminence and moral integrity so as to be seen to be both legitimate and an authoritative voice for environmental issues. The question is then raised as to how the composition of these eminently qualified people would be reached. One solution is that it could be similar to the International Court of Justice, with its eminently qualified lawyers from a wide range of the world's jurisdictions.

Another option, which holds further democratic appeal, is to select individuals from a pool of best qualified individuals representing a wide

---

142 John Dunn (ed.), *Democracy: the Unfinished Journey* (Oxford University Press, Oxford 1993): 239.

143 See Chapter 2.

spectrum of civil society, including indigenous peoples, peoples without a state, NGOs and persons with environmental, ethical and scientific expertise. The actual nomination could occur either through the UN General Assembly, the newly established UN Environment Assembly[144] or a yet to be established UN Parliamentary Assembly.[145]

Second, the creation of a WEO would gain legitimacy by virtue of the urgent need to protect the environment. As noted in Chapter 1, the scale of the ecological crisis which we face is staggering in its enormity. The urgency of addressing this crisis, before it becomes too late, demands that collective and decisive action be taken. On this basis, the creation of a WEO is legitimized by the common concern that humanity has in its own survival. Legitimacy also arises from the moral imperative to cease the destruction of the earth for the community of all life.[146] The creation of a WEO, therefore, is not only legitimate but incalculably necessary.

Critics would argue that such an institution would be impossible to create. Indeed, the obstacles are many. It is by no means suggested that it would be politically easy. Almost certainly, proposals for a WEO will be vehemently opposed by numerous states, probably including the world's most powerful states, the USA and China. Yet, it is important that the success of a future WEO is not seen to hinge on the backing of superpowers. Rather, as the example of the International Criminal Court serves to illustrate, when a norm of society emerges, even the fact that it is vehemently opposed by the world's most powerful cannot stop it from being an institution of instrumental value to the global community.

Furthermore, while critics may dismiss the creation of such a democratically mandated WEO as utopian, given the reality of the state-centred international arena, here it is argued that the existence of other realities make such a move not only plausible but inestimably necessary.

First, it must be pointed out that while the current political paradigm is undoubtedly a reality, the dynamics of ecological destruction and the processes of globalization are also very real. They threaten our continued security and in fact our entire existence, hence they demand that the reality of the political paradigm be transformed. Only then will we be able to address the threats with which humanity is collectively confronted. In this

---

[144] United Nations Environment Assembly, 'First United Nations Environment Assembly' (23–27 June 2014): http://www.unep.org/unea/en/.

[145] See Campaign for a United Nations Parliamentary Assembly, 'Developing International Democracy': http://en.unpacampaign.org/documents/index.php.

[146] Earth Charter (note 29), Principle I, 'Respect and Care for the Community of Life'.

sense, what is viewed as being 'realistic' must itself be reclaimed in favour of the global environment.

Second, it can be pointed out that in other areas, where there has been a strong common interest, states have managed to reach agreements which have effectively transferred national powers to international institutions. For example, because economic development according to neo-liberal policies is such an important concern to states, wide-reaching agreements have been, and continue to be, reached under the auspices of the WTO. A further example of the international community collectively working together to address a common concern is when, under the organization of the WHO, states managed to successfully coordinate mass vaccinations for small pox, leading to the successful eradication of the disease. What greater common concern could there be than ensuring the physical conditions of life and ecological integrity?

3.3 Funding

The creation of such an institution and its continuing success would be heavily dependent upon securing sufficient, predictable and coherent funding. The experience with UNEP has highlighted a massive shortcoming in the current environmental regime. As one commentator has pointed out, the budget of UNEP is currently less than the price of a Boeing 747 and a number of environmental NGOs have budgets which significantly outstrip it.[147] Furthermore, when international institutions are reliant upon the benefaction of states, they are in jeopardy of having their values and mandate corrupted by political necessity. States are well aware that institutions are only able to function if they have sufficient funding. A number of states have used this as a point of leverage in manipulating UN organizations into rescinding policies they disagree with and creating those they desire. Indeed, for states whose contributions are substantial, the withholding or contributing of funds has often been a political tactic which has been engaged on numerous occasions. For example, in the past, the US has cut funding to show its disagreement with the newly created Human Rights Council, which was lambasted as a 'vehicle for anti-Israel resolutions'.[148]

---

[147] Stefania Prestigiacomo and John Njoroge Michuki, 'Why We Need a World Environment Organization', *The Guardian* (28 October 2009).

[148] John Bolton, 'Prepared Statement of the Honourable John Bolton, Former United States Permanent Representative to the United Nations', in Future of the United Nations under Ban Ki Moon: Hearing Before the Committee on Foreign Affairs in the House of Representatives (One Hundred Tenth Congress, First

The question, therefore, is how to secure funding which is not reliant upon the machinations of states. This is an issue which deserves to be explored at greater length than is possible here, but one possible solution is provided by Christopher Stone. He proposes the creation of a 'Global Commons Trust Fund'.[149] Rather than being dependent upon voluntary contributions, this arrangement would impose levies based on legal obligations, thereby ensuring a relatively dependable flow of money each year.[150] While under present practices, common areas can generally be used and abused free of charge and with relative impunity, the creation of a Global Commons Trust Fund would impose levies on use of the commons areas themselves. The funds could then be used to service and repair the damage caused by use of the global commons. Such a market-based financial mechanism would be able to secure funding from those who are responsible for the creation of the issues in the first place. In Stone's words, 'What could be more reasonable? Or, given the afflictions of our planet, more crucial?'[151]

3.4 Governance

Based on our discussions of the WTO, the WHO and the UNTC[152] and the essentials of trusteeship governance,[153] we can summarize some preferable governance arrangements for a WEO.

First, we propose an executive or administrative arm similar to the UNTC and the WHO. We name this arm the Trust Council. The Trust Council would comprise representatives from member states, NGOs and epistemic communities – representing the *trustees*. These trustees administer the *corpus* of the trust (the biosphere) on behalf of the *beneficiary* (current and future generations). The Council's discretionary authority in the administration of the trust is bound by certain *fiduciary obligations* (respect for ecological integrity) contained within the *terms of the trust* (the aims as defined in the body's constitutional documents). The Trust Council would also play a key role in the *implementation* of WEO policy.

Second, we propose a legislative arm based on the World Health

Session, 13 February 2007, Serial No. 110–7): 28. For a summary on the issue, see also Luisa Blanchfield, *The United Nations Human Rights Council: Issues for Congress* (United States Congressional Research Service, RL33608, 30 April 2013).

149 Stone (note 133): 34.

150 Ibid.

151 Ibid.: 40.

152 See Chapter 7.

153 This chapter, under 2.2.

Assembly of the WHO, but strengthened in terms of decision-making power and trusteeship functions. The World Environment Assembly (WEA) could be organized along various groupings of global commons issues (commons areas groups). For example, an Antarctica Group would comprise trustees chosen from states, civil society groups and special experts. Similarly, members in an Oceans Group, an Atmosphere Group, an Outer Space Group and a Biodiversity Group would be trustees from states, civil society groups and special experts. The various commons area groups would gather information, initiate policies and develop rules or treaties in their respective areas for adoption by the WEA.

Third, we propose a judicial arm based on the powers of the Dispute Settlement Bodies (DSB) of the WTO. To this end, the concept and scope of the proposed International Court for the Environment (ICE) could be drawn upon. An adjudicatory body with a special focus on environment-related disputes (for example, the special environmental chamber in the International Court of Justice, an international environmental court or, at least, a set of arbitration rules specifically designed for environment-related disputes) has been proposed for several decades, but yielded limited results.[154] Instead, and aside from a small number of cases brought before the International Court of Justice, environment-related disputes have 'borrowed fora'[155] normally devoted to other fields, such as human rights courts and commissions, the WTO DSB or investment tribunals.

Viñuales sees the key to establishing a genuine environment court in the need for 'prevention' and 'balance'.[156] Undoubtedly, the need for prevention is determined by a general awareness of global ecological degradation, but courts need to adjudicate on the basis of precise law. The idea of prevention is only vaguely reflected in an array of principles such as no harm, precaution, cooperation, prior informed consent and environmental impact assessment. While all relevant, these principles do not adequately express the fundamental concern for the integrity of ecological systems. There is as yet no overarching rule, *grundnorm* or *raison d'etre* that an environment court could rely upon.[157]

Unlike human beings, with clearly defined human rights, the environment

---

[154] Jorge E. Viñuales, 'Managing Abidance by Standards for the Protection of the Environment', in Antonio Cassesse (ed.), *Realizing Utopia: The Future of International Law* (Oxford University Press, Oxford 2012): 326, 330–332.

[155] Ibid.: 331.

[156] Ibid.: 326.

[157] Douglas Fisher, *Legal Reasoning in Environmental Law: A Study of Structure, Form and Language* (Edward Elgar Publishing, Cheltenham, UK/ Northampton, MA 2013): 433.

has no rights or legal bottom-lines. To rectify this gross imbalance, there are a number of options, including rights of nature, ecological limitations to property rights[158] or Mother Earth-type international conventions or national constitutions.[159] It is possible, however, to build on existing international environmental law and derive from it the emerging *grundnorm* of integrity of the earth's ecological systems. [160] This could be acknowledged by the judicial arm of a WEO or, alternatively, promoted by its legislative arm.

4. CONCLUSION

Establishing a WEO as sketched here does not face insurmountable obstacles. These can be overcome, given sufficient political will. What is important is to realize its potential. Indeed, there is potential in various proposals for international institutions based on environmental trusteeship. Like a WEO, a World Climate Authority, for example, would dramatically improve prospects for effective climate protection, if based on trusteeship. Understood as a global commons, the atmosphere could be governed through trusteeship measures to complement, direct and speed up states' negotiations towards legally binding targets.

Through the lens of the global commons, the concept and role of state sovereignty appears in a different light. As has been argued throughout this book, rethinking sovereignty is not only legally possible, but also – and crucially so – indispensable. In a world of profound interdependencies there are no winners, only losers, if we do not get this right. Every state is bound to accept limits to its own jurisdiction and to act as a trustee to humanity under international standards,[161] but it cannot and must not do this alone. Exercising trusteeship for the global commons is the responsibility of states, the United Nations and civil society alike.

---

158 Bosselmann (note 39): 111–143.

159 Klaus Bosselmann, 'Global Environmental Constitutionalism: Mapping the Terrain', *Widener Law Review*, Special Issue on Global Environmental Constitutionalism (forthcoming, May 2015).

160 Kim and Bosselmann (note 40); Rakhyun Kim and Klaus Bosselmann, 'Operationalizing Sustainable Development: Ecological Integrity as a *Grundnorm* in International Law', *Review of European Community and International Environmental Law* (forthcoming, 2015).

161 Francesco Francioni, 'International Common Goods: An Epilogue', in Frederico Lenzerini and Ana Filipa Vrdoljak (eds), *International Law for Common Goods: Normative Perspectives on Human Rights, Vulture and Nature* (Hart Publ., Oxford 2014): 443, 448.

9. Conclusion: there is another way

> Never measure the height of a mountain until you have reached the top. Then you will see how low it was.
>
> Dag Hammarskjold

Shifting from states to earth as the centre of environmental governance is not really one of choice, but one of necessity. As long as innovative ideas are exclusively derived from what states are willing to support, no genuine progress will be made. This has been the problem of the United Nations from day one when it began to address the global environmental crisis at the 1972 Stockholm Conference. There has never been enough support for *effective* institutional reform. States allowed for a United Nations Environment Programme (UNEP), but no World Environment Organization; negotiations, but no trusteeship; political declarations, but no binding law; and talk, but no action. The global environmental crisis has been fitted into existing practices and institutional arrangements, rather than the other way round: if existing arrangements are insufficient to meet ecological challenges, they need to be changed.

The problem is not disinterest. There is no shortage of proposals for giving UNEP more power or establishing new environmental organizations. The problem is the lack of conceptual foundation. Any new organization, whether a World Environment Organization or United Nations Trusteeship Council or World Climate Authority, would need additional properties and instruments that existing legal regimes do not have. Proponents of institutional reform have largely failed to address the fundamental question of how and why new organizations can make a difference. Only more effective forms of collective decision-making and enforcement could achieve that, including, for example, rules that are enforceable against states.

Unsurprisingly, calls of this kind have attracted little support. Few states are prepared to accept enforcement of supranational rules against their will. Yet, the erosion of national sovereignty has been taking place for decades. Examples include the governance systems of the European Union or of international trade. In both instances, supranational rules override domestic law and can be enforced in courts. Moreover, state sovereignty has been fundamentally undermined by global corporate power:

states compete with each other in making their territory as economically attractive as possible, even if this means a lowering of social and environmental standards. Ironically, states have insisted on their national sovereignty with respect to the global commons, only to surrender it to market fundamentalism. This contradiction reveals not just a misconception of ecological challenges, but a most serious erosion of sovereign power. States no longer control the markets, rather markets control the states.

The irony of wanting to improve the living conditions of citizens by sacrificing national sovereignty to global markets has been described as the 'sovereignty paradox':[1] states hold on to outmoded ideas even in a situation where only global cooperation can aid prospects for sovereignty and prosperity. They remain shackled to their territories, unable to realize that global economic forces threaten the very integrity of the social and ecological systems that they are trying to protect.

The way out of the sovereignty paradox is differentiation: more sovereignty where possible, less sovereignty where necessary. In a globalized world, this means protecting citizens and the environment from global economic forces ('more sovereignty') and protecting the global commons and regulating global financial and economic markets through international cooperation ('less sovereignty'). The perspective of differentiated sovereignty, also referred to as 'responsible' or 'smart' sovereignty,[2] inevitably calls for reforming and strengthening global institutions. Nothing could be more urgent than matching political institutions to the global challenges that we face.

The drivers for responsible and smart sovereignty are not states per se, of course, but real people, that is, citizens, activists, advocates and decision-makers in a bottom-up approach called democracy. But how is it possible to practise national democracy when most critical decisions are made at the global level? Currently, the global level is the playing field of forces that operate beyond the radar screen of democratic control. To change that, some form of global democracy is needed.

Global democracy is not a mere accumulation of states functioning through democratically elected governments. If this were so, hopes for global democracy would indeed be very slim. After all, the erosion of national sovereignty was caused by global institutions accountable to no one but themselves, that is, the Word Trade Organization, the

---

1 Dominik Zaum, *The Sovereignty Paradox* (OUP, Oxford 2007): 226–231; Inge Kaul, 'Meeting Global Challenges: Assessing Governance Readiness', in Hertie School of Governance (ed.), *Governance Report 2013* (OUP, Oxford 2013): 33–34.

2 Inge Kaul (note 1): 34–58.

International Monetary Fund, the World Bank, big banks and multinational corporations. It is impossible to restore lost sovereignty and accountability if democratic action remains confined to the national level.

There is another way. Democratic action must involve all levels, that is, the local, the national, the regional and the international. This is also the only way to reclaim the global commons that we are so rapidly losing. The concern for the commons is a unifying feature of humanity. If we see ourselves as stewards of the earth and states as trustees of the common good, then this is a crucial step towards earth governance, perhaps to be called earth democracy.[3]

Trusteeship for the global commons is the noblest form of democracy and the best hope for the *demos* to take charge of its own destiny.

[3] Klaus Bosselmann, 'Earth Democracy: Institutionalizing Ecological Integrity and Sustainability', in Ron Engel, LauraWestra and Klaus Bosselmann (eds), *Democracy, Ecological Integrity and International Law* (Cambridge Scholars Publ., Newcastle upon Tyne 2010): 319–330.

Bibliography

Alter, Karen J., 'Agents or Trustees? International Courts in their Political Context' (2008) 14 *Eur. J. Int'l Rel.* 33.

Alter, Karen J., *The New Terrain of International Law: Courts, Politics, Rights* (Princeton University Press, Princeton, NJ 2014).

Anghie, A., 'The Heart of My Home: Colonialism, Environmental Damage and the Nauru Case' (Spring, 1993) 34 *Harv. Intn'l L. J.* 445.

Antarctic Treaty 402 UNTS 71 (signed 1 December 1959, entered into force 23 June 1961).

Archibugi, Danielle, 'Demos and Cosmopolis' (2002) *New Left Review* 13.

Argentina: Safeguard Measures on Imports of Footwear, WT/DS121/AB/R (Report of the WTO Appellate Body, 14 December 1999).

Arndt, Birger, *Das Vorsorgeprinzip im EU-Recht* (Mohr Siebeck, Tuebingen 2009).

Ashcraft, Richard (ed.), *John Locke: Critical Assessments* (Routledge, London 1991).

Attfield, Robin, 'Global Citizenship and the Global Environment', in N. Dower and J. Williams (eds), *Global Citizenship: A Critical Reader* (Edinburgh University Press, Edinburgh 2002).

Bain, William, *Between Anarchy and Society: Trusteeship and the Obligations of Power* (Oxford University Press, Oxford 2003).

Banire, M., *The Nigerian Law of Trusts* (Caxton Press, Caldwell, ID 2002).

Bantekas, Ilias, *Trust Funds under International Law: Trustee Obligations of the United Nations and International Development Banks* (TMC Asser Press, The Hague 2009).

Barber, Nigel, *Kindness in a Cruel World: The Evolution of Altruism* (Prometheus Books, New York 2004).

Barber, Walter F. and Robert V. Bartlett, *Global Democracy and Sustainable Jurisprudence: Deliberative Environmental Law* (The MIT Press, Cambridge, MA/London 2009).

Barcena, Alicia, 'Global Environmental Citizenship' (1997) UNEP 25: http://www.ourplanet.com/imgversn/85/barcena.html.

Barnes, Peter, *Capitalism 2.0: Who Owns the Sky? Our Common Assets and the Future of Capitalism* (Island Press, Washington, DC 2001).

Barnes, Peter, *Capitalism 3.0: A Guide to Reclaiming the Commons* (Berret-Koehler, San Francisco 2006).
Barnes, P., J. Rowe and D. Bollier, *The State of the Commons 2003/04: A Report to Owners* (Tomales Bay Institute, Point Reyes Station, CA 2004).
Barnhill, David Landis and Roger S. Gottlieb, 'Introduction', in David Landis Barnhill and Roger S. Gottlieb (eds), *Deep Ecology and World Religions: New Essays on Sacred Ground* (State University of New York Press, Albany, NY 2001).
Benkler, Yochai, 'The Political Economy of Commons' (June 2003) IV (3) *Upgrade* 6–9.
Benvenisti, Eyal, 'Sovereigns as Trustees of Humanity: On the Accountability of States to Foreign Stakeholders' (2013) 107 (2) *American Journal of International Law* 295.
Berman, Rabbi Saul, *Jewish Environmental Values: The Dynamic Tension Between Nature and Human Needs* (Jewish Virtual Library, 1992).
Bernstein, Jay M., *Recovering Ethical Life: Jürgen Habermas and the Future of Critical Theory* (Routledge, London 1995).
Biermann, Frank, 'The Case for a World Environment Organization' (2000) 42 (9) *Environment* 22.
Birnie, Patricia, Alan Boyle and Catherine Redgwell, *International Law and the Environment*, 3rd edn (Oxford University Press, Oxford 2009).
Bischel, Anne, 'NGOs as Agents of Public Accountability and Democratization in Intergovernmental Forums', in William M. Lafferty and James Meadowcroft (eds), *Democracy and the Environment: Problems and Prospects* (Edward Elgar Publishing, Cheltenham, UK/ Northampton, MA 1996).
Blumm, Michael and Rachel D. Guthrie, 'Internationalizing the Public Trust Doctrine' (2012) 45 *University of California Davis Law Review* 741.
Blumm, Michael and Mary C. Wood, *The Public Trust Doctrine in Environmental and Natural Resources Law* (Carolina Academic Press, Durham, NC 2013).
Bodansky, Daniel, 'The History of the Global Climate Change Regime', in Urs Luterbacher and Detlef Sprinz (eds), *International Relations and Global Climate Change* (The MIT Press, Cambridge, MA 2001).
Bodansky, Daniel, Jutta Bronee and Ellen Hey, *The Oxford Handbook of International Environmental Law* (Oxford University Press, Oxford 2007).
Bollier, David, *The Commons: A Neglected Sector of Wealth Creation* (Henrich Böll Stiftung, Berlin 2008).
Bollier, David, 'The Future of the Commons: Notes from a retreat exploring the potential of the commons to fight enclosures and build commons-based alternatives', Crottorf Castle, Germany, 25–27 June 2009.

Bollier, David, *Think Like a Commoner: A Short Introduction to the Life of the Commons* (New Society Publishers, Gabriola Island, BC, Canada 2014).

Bollier, David and Silke Helfrich (eds), *The Wealth of the Commons: A World Beyond Market and State* (Levellers Press, Amherst, MA 2012).

Bollier, David and Burns H. Weston, *Green Governance: Ecological Survival, Human Rights and the Commons* (Cambridge University Press, Cambridge 2013).

Bonney, Stephanie Adelle, 'Bioprospecting, Scientific Research and Deep Sea Resources in Areas Beyond National Jurisdiction: A Critical Legal Analysis' (2006) 10 *New Zealand Journal of Environmental Law* 41.

Bosselmann, Klaus, *Im Namen der Natur: Der Weg zum ökologischen Rechtsstaat* (Scherz, Berne 1992).

Bosselmann, Klaus, *When Two Worlds Collide: Society and Ecology* (RSVP, Auckland 1995).

Bosselmann, Klaus, 'Institutions for Global Governance', in Colin Solskone (ed.), *Sustaining Life on Earth: Environmental Ethics and Human Health through Global Governance* (Lexington Books, Lanham, MD 2007).

Bosselmann, Klaus, *The Principle of Sustainability: Transforming Law and Governance* (Ashgate, Farnham 2008).

Bosselmann, Klaus, 'Earth Democracy: Institutionalising Sustainability and Ecological Integrity', in J. Ronald Engel, Laura Westra and Klaus Bosselmann (eds), *Democracy, Ecological Integrity and International Law* (Cambridge Scholars Publishing, Newcastle Upon Tyne 2010).

Bosselmann, Klaus, 'Towards Multilevel Governance for Sustainability: Trends and Challenges', in *Contested Futures: Sustainability, Governance and International Human Rights* (Europe – New Zealand Research Series Paper, 2010): 1–72.

Bosselmann, Klaus, 'Property Rights and Sustainability: Can they be Reconciled?', in David Grinlinton and Prue Taylor (eds), *Property Rights and Sustainability: The Evolution of Property Rights to Meet Ecological Challenges* (Martinus Nijhoff, The Hague 2011).

Bosselmann, Klaus, 'Values for Governing Ourselves: the Earth Charter' (2011) 4 *Indigo* 112.

Bosselmann, Klaus, 'Grounding the Rule of Law', in Christina Voigt (ed.), *The Rule of Law for Nature* (Cambridge University Press, Cambridge 2013).

Bosselmann, Klaus, 'The Rule of Law Grounded in the Earth: Ecological Integrity as a Grundnorm', in L. Westra and M. Vilela (eds), *The Earth Charter, Ecological Integrity and Social Movements* (Routledge, New York 2014).

Bosselmann, Klaus, 'Global Environmental Constitutionalism: Mapping the Terrain' (2015) 21 *Widener Law Review, Special Issue Global Environmental Constitutionalism*.

Bosselmann, Klaus and Ronald J. Engel (eds), *The Earth Charter: A Framework for Global Governance* (KIT Publishing, Leiden 2010).

Bosselmann, Klaus, Peter Brown and Brendan Mackey, 'Enabling a Flourishing Earth: Challenges for the Green Economy, Opportunities for Global Governance' (2012) 21 (1) *Review of European Community and International Environmental Law* 20–38.

Bosselmann, Klaus, J. Ronald Engel and Prue Taylor, *Governance for Sustainability: Issues, Challenges, Successes* (IUCN, Gland 2008).

Bothe, Michael, 'Whose Environment? Concepts of Commonality in International Environmental Law', in Gerd Winter (ed.), *Multilevel Governance of Global Environmental Change: Perspectives from Science, Sociology and the Law* (Cambridge University Press, Cambridge 2006).

Boyd, David, *The Environmental Rights Revolution* (UBC, Vancouver 2012).

Boyes, Roger, 'World Agenda: Riots in Iceland, Latvia and Bulgaria are a Sign of Things to Come', *Times Online* (21 January 2009).

Boyle, A., 'International Law and the Protection of the Atmosphere', in Robin Churchill and David Freestone (eds), *International Law and Global Climate Change* (Graham & Trotman, London 1991).

Bromley, D.W., *Environment and Economy: Property Rights and Public Policy* (Basil Blackwell, Oxford 1991).

Bromley, D.W. (ed.), *Making the Commons Work: Theory, Practice, and Policy* (ICS Press, San Francisco, CA 1992).

Brown, Peter, *Restoring the Public Trust* (Beacon Press, Boston 1994).

Brown, Peter, *Right Relationship: Building a Whole Earth Economy* (Berrett-Koehler, San Francisco 2009).

Buck, Susan, *The Global Commons: An Introduction* (Island Press, Washington, DC 1998).

Burci, Gian Luca and Claude-Henri Vignes, *World Health Organization* (Kluwer Law International, The Hague 2004).

Burdon, Peter, *Exploring Wild Law: The Philosophy of Earth Jurisprudence* (Wakefield Press, Adelaide, SA, Australia 2012).

Burdon, Peter, *Earth Jurisprudence: Private Property and the Environment* (Routledge, London 2015).

Butler, Andrew S. (ed.), *Equity and Trusts in New Zealand*, 2nd edn (Thompson Reuters, Wellington 2009).

Cárdenas, Juan Camilo and Elinor Ostrom, 'How Norms Help Reduce the Tragedy of the Commons: A Multi-layer Framework for Analyzing Field Experiments', in John N. Droback (ed.), *Norms and the Law* (Cambridge University Press, New York 2006).

Carter, April, *The Political Theory of Global Citizenship* (Routledge, London 2001).
Casari, Marco and Charles R. Plott, 'Decentralized Management of Common Property Resources: Experiments with a Centuries-Old Institution' (2003) 51 *Journal of Economic Behavior and Organization* 217–247.
Case Concerning the Gabçíkovo-Nagymaros Project (Hungary/Slovakia 1997 ICJ; 37 ILM 162 (1998), Separate Opinion of Vice President Christopher Weeramantry.
Castro, José Esteban, *Commons and Citizenship: The Contradictions of an Unfolding Relationship* (Heinrich Böll Stiftung, Berlin 2009).
Certain Phosphate Lands in Nauru [Nauru v Australia] [Preliminary Objections] 1992 ICJ 240 (June 26).
Charnovitz, Steve, 'A World Environment Organization' (2002) 27 *Colum J. Envtl L.* 323.
Chowdhuri, R., *International Mandates and Trusteeship Systems: A Comparative Study* (Nijhoff, The Hague 1955).
Clippinger, John and David Bollier, 'A New Renaissance of the Commons: How the New Sciences and Internet are Framing a New Global Identity and Order', in Rishab Aiyer Ghosh (ed.), *CODE: Collaborative Ownership and the Digital Economy* (The MIT Press, Cambridge, MA 2005).
Collins, Sheila D., 'Interrogating and Reconceptualizing Natural Law to Protect the Integrity of the Earth', in Laura Westra, Klaus Bosselmann and Richard Westra (eds), *Reconciling Human Existence with Ecological Integrity* (Earthscan, London 2008).
Commission on Global Governance, *Our Global Neighbourhood* (Oxford University Press, Oxford 1995).
Commonwealth Secretariat, 'Reform of International Environmental Governance: An Agenda for the Commonwealth', paper prepared for the Commonwealth Heads of Government Meeting on Reform of International Institutions, London, 9–10 June 2008 (May 2008).
Concluding Statement of the General Assembly President A/45/PV82 (1991) 21, cited in Carolyn L. Willson, 'Changing the Charter: The United Nations Prepares for the Twenty-First Century' (1996) 90 *AJIL* 122.
Constitution of the World Health Organization, 14 UNTS 185.
Convention Concerning the Protection of the World Cultural and Natural Heritage 1037 UNTS 151 (adopted 16 November 1972, entered into force 17 December 1975) (World Heritage Convention).
Convention on Access to Information, Public Participation in Decision-Making and Access to Justice in Environmental Matters 2161 UNTS 447 (Aarhus; adopted 25 June 1998, entered into force 30 October 2001).

Convention on Biological Diversity, 1760 UNTS 79 (signed 5 June 1992, entered into force 29 December 1993).

Convention on Biological Diversity, Subsidiary Body on Scientific, Technical and Technological Advice, Marine Coastal Biodiversity: Review, Further Elaboration and Refinement of the Programme of Work, *Study of the Relationship between the Convention on Biological Diversity and the United Nations Convention on the Law of the Sea with Regard to the Conservation and Sustainable Use of Genetic Resources on the Deep Seabed*, UN Doc. UNEP/CBDSTTA/8/INF/3 Rev.1 (22 February 2003), para 39, 11 (SBSTTA Study).

Convention on Long Range Transboundary Air Pollution 1302 UNTS 217 (adopted 13 November 1979, entered into force 16 March 1983) (LRTAP) includes protocols on sulphur compounds (1985, 1994), nitrogen oxides (1988) and volatile organic compounds (1991). The Vienna Convention (1985) is followed by the Montreal Protocol (1987) and subsequent revisions in London (1990), Copenhagen (1992) and Vienna (1995).

Convention on the Conservation of Antarctic Marine Living Resources, 1329 UNTS 48 (signed 20 May 1980, entered into force 7 April 1982).

Criddle, Evan J. and Evan Fox-Decent, 'A Fiduciary Theory of Jus Cogens' (2009) 34 *The Yale Journal of International Law* 331–387.

Christoff, Peter, 'Ecological Citizens and Democracy', in Mark J. Smith (ed.), *Thinking Through the Environment: A Reader* (Routledge, London 1999).

Crouch, C., *Postdemocrazia* (Roma/Bari edn, Laterza, 2003); *Post-Democracy* (Oxford University Press, Oxford 2004).

Crutzen, Paul and Eugene Stoermer, The 'Anthropocene' (2000) 41 *Global Change Newsletter* 17–18.

Curtin, Deane, *Chinnagounder's Challenge: The Question of Ecological Citizenship* (Indiana University Press, Bloomington, IN 2001).

D'Amato, Anthony and Sudir K. Chopra, 'Whales: their Emerging Right to Life' (1991) 85 *AJIL* 21.

Dahrendorf, Ralf, 'The Changing Quality of Citizenship', in Bart van Steenbergen (ed.), *The Condition of Citizenship* (SAGE, London 1994).

De Angelis, Massimo, *The Beginning of History: Value Struggles and Global Capital* (Pluto, London 2007).

Declaration of the United Nations Conference on the Human Environment (Stockholm), UN Doc. A/CONF/48/14/REVI (1972) (Stockholm Declaration).

Declaration on Permanent Sovereignty over Natural Resources, GA Res 1803 (XVII) (1962).

Deneen, Patrick J., *Democratic Faith* (Princeton University Press, Princeton, NJ 2005).

Desai, Bharat, *International Environmental Governance: Towards UNEPO* (Brill Nijhoff, Leiden 2014).
Development and International Co-operation: Environment, A/42/427 (1987) Annex ('Our Common Future').
Deveney, Patrick, 'Title, Jus Publicum, and the Public Trust: An Historical Analysis' (1976) 1 *Sea Grant Law Journal* 12.
Division for Ocean Affairs and the Law of the Sea, Office of Legal Affairs, United Nations, *The Law of the Sea: Concept of the Common Heritage of Mankind: Legislative History of Article 133 to 150 and 311(6) of the United Nations Convention on the Law of the Sea* (United Nations, 1996).
Dobson, Andrew, *Citizenship and the Environment* (Oxford University Press, Oxford 2003).
Dobson, Andrew, 'Ecological Citizenship: A Defence' (2006) 15 (3) *Environmental Politics* 447.
Dodds, Felix, Michael Strauss and Maurice F. Strong, *Only One Earth: The Long Road via Rio to Sustainable Development* (Routledge, New York 2012).
Dower, N., 'The Earth Charter and Global Citizenship: A Way Forward', in Peter Blaze Corcoran (ed.), *The Earth Charter in Action: Toward a Sustainable Development* (Royal Tropical Institute, Amsterdam 2005).
Dower, N. and J. Williams (eds), *Global Citizenship: A Critical Reader* (Edinburgh University Press, Edinburgh 2002).
Dunn, John (ed.), *Democracy: The Unfinished Journey* (Oxford University Press, Oxford 1993).
Durner, Wolfgang, 'Internationales Umweltverwaltungsrecht', in Christoph Möllers et al. (eds), *Internationales Verwaltungsrecht: Eine Analyse anhand von Referenzgebieten* (Mohr Siebeck, Tuebingen 2007).
Dyer, Adair, 'International Recognition and Adaptation of Trusts: the Influence of the Hague Convention' (1999) *Vanderbilt Journal of Transnational Law* 989.
Dyer-Witheford, Nick, 'Commonism', *Turbulence* (2007): 1. http://turbulence.org.uk/turbulence-1/commonism/.
Eckersley, Robin, 'Deliberative Democracy, Ecological Representation, and Risk: Towards a Democracy of the Affected', in Graham Smith (ed.), *Democratic Innovation, Deliberation, Representation and Association* (Routledge, London 2000).
Edwards, Michael, 'Global Civil Society and Community Exchanges: A Different Form of Movement' (2001) 13 *Environment and Urbanization* 145.
Engel, J. Ronald, 'The Earth Charter as a New Covenant for Democracy', in Peter Miller and Laura Westra (eds), *Just Ecological Integrity: The*

Ethics of Maintaining Planetary Life (Rowman & Littlefield, Lanham, MD 2002).

Engel, J. Ronald, 'Contesting Democracy', in J. Ronald Engel, Laura Westra and Klaus Bosselmann (eds), *Democracy, Ecological Integrity and International Law* (Cambridge Scholars Publishing, Newcastle Upon Tyne 2010).

Engel, J. Ronald, 'The Earth Charter as a New Covenant for Democracy', in Klaus Bosselmann and J. Ronald Engel (eds), *The Earth Charter: A Framework for Global Governance* (KIT Publishing, Leiden 2010).

Ethiopia v South Africa, Liberia v South Africa (South West Africa cases), Second Phase, Judgement, *ICJ Rep* (1966).

Everdeen, N., *The Natural Alien: Humankind and the Environment*, 2nd edn (University of Toronto Press, Toronto 1993).

Experts Group on Environmental Law, 'Proposals for Strengthening the Legal and Institutional Framework', in R.D. Munro and J.G. Lammers (eds), *Environmental Protection and Sustainable Development: Legal Principles and Recommendations* (Graham & Trotman/M. Nijhoff, London/Boston 1987).

Finn, P., 'The Forgotten "Trust": The People and the State', in M. Cope (ed.), *Equity: Issues and Trends* (The Federation Press, Leichhardt, NSW, Australia 1995).

Fisher, Douglas, *Legal Reasoning in Environmental Law: A Study of Structure, Form and Language* (Edward Elgar Publishing, Cheltenham, UK/Northampton, MA 2013).

Flader, Susan, 'Aldo Leopold and Environmental Citizenship' (1999) 87 *Transactions of the Wisconsin Academy of Science, Arts and Letters* 23.

Fox-Decent, Evan, *Sovereignty's Promise: The State as a Fiduciary* (Oxford University Press, Oxford 2012).

Francioni, Francesco, 'International Common Goods: An Epilogue', in Frederico Lenzerini and Ana Filipa Vrdoljak (eds) *International Law for Common Goods: Normative Perspectives on Human Rights, Vulture and Nature* (Hart Publishing, Oxford 2014).

Frankel, T., 'Fiduciary Law' (1983) 71 *California Law Review* 795.

Funke, Björn M., 'The Precautionary Principle', in Klaus Bosselmann and J. Ronald Engel (eds), *The Earth Charter: A Framework for Global Governance* (KIT Publishing, Leiden 2010).

Gambetta, D.G., 'Can We Trust Trust?', in D.G. Gambetta (ed.), *Trust* (Basil Blackwell, New York 1988).

Gans, Chaim, *The Limits of Nationalism* (Cambridge University Press, Cambridge 2003).

Gehring, Thomas and Isabel Plocher, 'Making an Administrative Trustee Agent Accountable: Reason-based Decision Making within the Kyoto

Protocol's Clean Development Mechanism' (2009) 53 *International Studies Quarterly* 669.

General Agreement on Tariffs and Trade (Apr. 15, 1994), *Marrakesh Agreement Establishing the World Trade Organization*, Annex 1A, *The Legal Texts: The Results of the Uruguay Round of Multilateral Trade Negotiations* 17 (1999), 1867 U.N.T.S. 187, 33 I.L.M. 1153 (1994).

Goldman, Michael, 'Introduction: The Political Resurgence of the Commons', in Michael Goldman (ed.), *Privatizing Nature: Political Struggles for the Global Commons* (Rutgers University Press, New Brunswick, NJ 1998).

Goldstein, Judith and Richard Steinberg, 'Negotiate or Litigate? Effects of WTO Judicial Delegation on US Trade Politics' (Winter 2008) 71 (1) *Law and Contemporary Problems* 257.

Göpel, Maja, *Guarding Our Future: How to Include Future Generations in Policy Making* (World Future Council, Hamburg 2010).

Gordon, H. Scott, 'The Economic Theory of a Common-Property Resource: The Fishery' (1954) 62 (2) *Journal of Political Economy* 124–142.

Gordon, Ruth E., 'Some Legal Problems with Trusteeship' (1995) 28 *Cornell Int'l L. J.* 301.

Goulet, Dennis, 'The Ethics of Power and the Power of Ethics', in Dennis Goulet, *The Cruel Choice: A New Concept in the Theory of Development* (University Press of America, Lanham, MD 1985).

Griffith, William B., 'Trusteeship: A Practical Option for Realizing Our Obligations to Future Generations?', in Andrew Light and Avner De-Shalit (eds), *Moral and Political Reasoning in Environmental Practice* (The MIT Press, Cambridge, MA 2003).

Grober, Ulrich, *Sustainability: A Cultural History* (Green Books, Cambridge 2012).

Groom, A.J.R. and P. Taylor (eds), *The United Nations at the Millennium: The Principal Organs* (A&C Black, London 2000).

Gutmann, Amy and Dennis Thompson, *Democracy and Disagreement* (Belknap Press, Cambridge, MA 1990).

Habermas, Jürgen, *Between Facts and Norms: Contributions to a Discourse Theory of Law and Democracy* (The MIT Press, Cambridge, MA 1998).

Habermas, Jürgen, 'Citizenship and National Identity', in Bart van Steenbergen (ed.), *Condition of Citizenship* (SAGE, London 1994).

Habermas, Jürgen, 'Towards a Cosmopolitan Europe' (2003) 14 *Journal of Democracy* 86.

Habermas, Jürgen, 'Wahrheitstheorien', in Helmut Fahrenbach (ed.), *Wirklichkeit und Reflexion* (Neske, Pfullingen 1973).

Hammarskjöld, D. and K. Falkman (eds), *To Speak for the World:*

Speeches and Statements by Dag Hammarskjold, Secretary-General of the United Nations 1953–1961 (Atlantis, Stockholm 2005).

Hardin, Garrett, 'The Tragedy of the Commons' (1968) 162 *Science* 1243–1248.

Hassan, Parvee, 'Earth Charter: An Ethical Lodestar and Moral Force', in Peter Blaze Corcoran (ed.), *The Earth Charter in Action: Toward a Sustainable Development* (KIT Publishers, Leiden 2005).

Hayward, Tim, *Political Theory and Ecological Values* (Polity Press, Cambridge 1998).

Hayward, Tim, 'Constitutional Environmental Rights: A Case for Political Analysis', in Andrew Light and Avner De-Shalit (eds), *Moral and Political Reasoning in Environmental Practice* (The MIT Press, Cambridge, MA 2003).

Heap, John A. and Martin Holdgate, 'The Antarctic Treaty System as an Environmental Mechanism: An Approach to Environmental Issues', in Polar Research Board, *Antarctic Treaty System: An Assessment* (National Academy Press, Washington, DC 1986).

Heidegger, Martin, *Der Ursprung des Kunstwerk* (first published 1950; Reclam, Ditzinger 1960).

Heinrichs, Johannes, 'A Model of Value-Based Democracy as Condition of Ecological Sustainability', in J. Ronald Engel, Laura Westra, and Klaus Bosselmann (eds), *Democracy, Ecological Integrity and International Law* (Cambridge Scholars Publishing, Newcastle Upon Tyne 2010).

Held, David, *Global Transformations: Politics, Economics and Culture* (Stanford University Press, Stanford, CA 1999).

Held, David, *Models of Democracy*, 3rd edn (Stanford University Press, Stanford, CA 2006).

Held, David, 'Liberty in the Age of Cosmopolitanism', in Yongjune Park (ed.), *Re-evaluation of Values: (A) Journey in Search of Core Values* (Mull Publishing, Seoul 2010).

Helfrich, Silke, *Commons: The Network of Life and Creativity* (Henrich Böll Stiftung, Berlin 2008).

Helfrich, Silke and David Bollier (eds), *Self-sustaining Abundance: The Commons, Beyond Market and State* (Henrich Böll Stiftung, Rheinberg 2012).

Helfrich, Silke and Jörg Haas, *The Commons: A New Narrative for Our Time* (Henrich Böll Stiftung, Berlin 2009).

Hess, Charlotte, 'Mapping the Commons', paper presented at 'Governing Shared Resources: Connecting Local Experience to Global Challenges', the 12th Biennial Conference of the International Association for the Study of the Commons, University of Gloucestershire, Cheltenham, UK, 14–18 July 2008.

Hess, Charlotte and Elinor Ostrom (eds), *Understanding Knowledge as a Commons: From Theory to Practice* (The MIT Press, Cambridge, MA 2007).

Higgins, Polly, *Eradicating Ecocide: Laws and Governance to Stop the Destruction of the Planet* (Shepheard-Walwyn, London 2010).

Hilary, John (ed.), *The Transatlantic Trade and Investment Partnership (TTIP): A Charter for Deregulation, an Attack on Jobs, an End to Democracy* (Rosa Luxemburg Stiftung, Brussels 2014).

Hobley, Anthony, 'Creating a Global Carbon Market', in Paul Q. Watchman (ed.), *Climate Change: A Guide to Carbon Law and Policy* (Globe Business Publishing, London 2008).

Honoré, Tony, 'On Fitting Trusts Into Civil Law Jurisdictions', *University of Oxford Legal Research Paper Series*, Paper No. 27/2008 (September 2008).

Horn, Laura, 'Rio+20 United Nations Conference on Sustainable Development: Is this the Future We Want?' (2013) 91 (1) *MqJICEL* 18.

'Human Impact Report: Climate Change – The Anatomy of a Silent Crisis' (Global Humanitarian Forum, 2009).

Intergovernmental Panel on Climate Change, *Fourth Assessment Report: Climate Change* (IPCC, 2007).

International Convention for the Regulation of Whaling, 62 Stat. 1716, 161 UNTS 74 (signed 2 December 1946, entered into force 10 November 1948).

International Covenant on Civil and Political Rights 999 UNTS 171 (adopted 16 December 1966, entered into force 23 March 1976).

International Status of South-West Africa (Advisory Opinion) [1950] ICJ Rep 128. Separate Opinion of Judge McNair, 149.

International Treaty on Plant Genetic Resources for Food and Agriculture 2400 UNTS 303 (adopted 3 November 2001, entered into force 29 June 2004).

Irbinati, Nadia and Mark E. Warren, 'The Concept of Representation in Contemporary Democratic Theory' (2008) *Annual Review of Political Science* 387.

IUCN Commission on Environmental Law and World Conservation Union, in cooperation with the International Council of Environmental Law, 'Draft International Covenant on Environment and Development, 2nd edn' (IUCN, 2000).

Jackson, J., 'Sovereignty-Modern: A New Approach to an Outdated Concept' (2003) 97 (4) *American Journal of International Law* 782.

Jackson, T., *Prosperity Without Growth? The Transition towards a Sustainable Economy* (Sustainable Development Commission, London 2009).

Johnston, J., 'Who Cares about the Commons?' (2003) 14 (4) *Capitalism, Nature, Socialism* 1–41.

Jonas, Hans, *The Imperative of Responsibility: In Search of an Ethics for the Technological Age* (University of Chicago Press, Chicago 1984).

Kaldor, M., H. Anheir and M. Glasius, *Global Civil Society 2003/4* (SAGE, London 2003).

Kaul, Inge, 'Meeting Global Challenges: Assessing Governance Readiness', in Hertie School of Governance (ed.), *Governance Report 2013* (Oxford University Press, Oxford 2013).

Kaul, Inge, I. Grunberg and M.A. Stern (eds), *Global Public Goods: International Cooperation in the 21st Century* (Oxford University Press, Oxford 1999).

Kelsey, Jane, *The FIRE Economy* (Bridget Williams, Wellington 2015).

Kelsey, Jane, *Serving Whose Interests? The Political Economy of Trade in Services Agreements* (Routledge, New York 2008).

Kelsey, Jane (ed.), *No Ordinary Deal: Unmasking the Transpacific Partnership Free Trade Agreement* (Allen and Unwin, Sydney 2010).

Kim, Rakhyun and Klaus Bosselmann, 'International Environmental Law in the Anthropocene: Towards a Purposive System of Multilateral Environmental Agreements' (2013) 2 *Transnational Environmental Law* 285.

Kim, Rakhyun and Klaus Bosselmann, 'Operationalizing Sustainable Development: Ecological Integrity as a *Grundnorm* of International Law' (2015) 24 (2) *Review of European, Comparative and International Environmental Law*.

Kiss, Alexandre and Dinah Shelton, *International Environmental Law*, 2nd edn (Transnational Publishers, New York 2000).

Klein, Naomi, *This Changes Everything: Capitalism vs the Climate* (Simon & Schuster, New York 2014).

Kotzé, Louis, *International Environmental Governance: Law and Regulation for the 21st Century* (Edward Elgar Publishing, Cheltenham, UK/ Northampton, MA 2012).

Kyoto Protocol to the Framework Convention on Climate Change 2303 *UNTS* 148 (adopted 11 December 1997, entered into force 16 February 2005).

Lafuente, Antonio, *The Four Realms of the Commons* (Henrich Böll Stiftung, Berlin 2008).

Lakoff, George, *Don't Think of an Elephant! Know Your Values and Frame the Debate* (Chelsea Green Publishing, White River Junction, VT 2004).

Lal, R., 'Soil Carbon Sequestrian Impacts on Global Climate Change and Food Security' (2004) 304 (5677) *Science* 1623.

League of Nations, *Covenant of the League of Nations* 225 Parry 195; 1 Hudson 1; 112 BFSP 13; 13 AJIL Supp. 128 (1919).

Leahy, Stephen, 'Peak Soil: The Silent Global Crisis' (2008) 23 (1) *Earth Island Journal* 58.

Lefeber, Rene, *Transboundary Environmental Interference and the Origin of State Liability* (Kluwer Law International, The Hague 1996).

Leib, Ethan J., David L. Ponet and Michael Serota, 'A Fiduciary Theory of Judging' (2013) 101 *California Law Review* 699.

Leopold, Aldo, *The Essential Aldo Leopold*, edited by Curt Meine and Richard Knight (University of Wisconsin Press, Madison, WI 1999).

Lerch, Achim, *The Tragedy of the 'Tragedy of the Commons'* (Henrich Böll Stiftung, Berlin 2008).

Levi, Isaac, *The Covenant of Reason: Rationality and the Commitments of Thought* (Cambridge University Press, Cambridge 1997).

Liu, Jian, 'Trust Funds as Mechanisms for Sustainable Development', in Michael Bothe and Peter H. Sand (eds), *Environmental Policy: From Regulation to Economic Instruments* (Martinus Nijohoff, Dordrecht 2002).

Locke, J., *Two Treatises on Government* (Cambridge University Press, Cambridge 1988).

Lucy, William N.R., and Catherine Mitchell, 'Replacing Private Property: The Case for Stewardship' (1996) 55 (3) *Cambridge Law Journal* 566–600.

Luhmann, Niklas, *Ecological Communication* (Chicago University Press, Chicago 1986).

Luhmann, Niklas, *Social Systems* (Stanford University Press, Stanford, CA 1995).

Lupoi, Maurizio, 'The Civil Law Trust' (1999) *Vanderbilt Journal of Transnational Law* 967.

MacPherson, C.B., *The Political Theory of Possessive Individualism* (Clarendon Press, Oxford 1962).

Majone, Giandomenico, 'Two Logics of Delegation: Agency and Fiduciary Relations in EU Governance' (2001) 2 *European Union Politics* 103.

Malone, Linda A. and Scott Pasternack, *Defending the Environment: Civil Society Strategies to Enforce International Environmental Law* (Island Press, Washington, DC 2006).

Manin, Bernard, 'On Legitimacy and Political Deliberation' (1987) 15 *Political Theory* 351.

Manno, Jack P., 'Haudenosaunee Great Law of Peace: A Model for Global Environmental Governance', in J. Ronald Engel, Laura Westra, Klaus Bosselmann (eds), *Democracy, Ecological Integrity and International Law* (Cambridge Scholars Publishing, Newcastle Upon Tyne 2010).

Marrakesh Agreement Establishing the World Trade Organization, Apr. 15, 1994, *The Legal Texts: The Results of the Uruguay Round of Multilateral Trade Negotiations* 4 (1999), 1867 U.N.T.S. 154, 33 I.L.M. 1144 (1994).

McGoldrick, Will, Donald Feaver and Andrew Maver, 'Fiduciary Duty and Climate Governance: Challenges for International Diplomacy and Law', in Ken Coghill, Charles Sampford and Tim Smith (eds), *Fiduciary Duty and the Atmospheric Trust* (Ashgate, Farnham 2012).
McKay, Peter A., 'DOW Is Off 7, 401.24 Points from its Record High in '07', *The Wall Street Journal* (3 March 2009).
McMurtry, J., 'The Life-Ground, the Civil Commons and the Corporate Male Gang' (2001) *Canadian Journal of Development Studies* XXII.
Meine, Curt, *Aldo Leopold: His Life and Work* (University of Wisconsin Press, Madison, WI 1988).
Melnyk, Andriy Y., 'United Nations Trusteeship System', in R Wolfrum (ed.), *The Max Planck Encyclopedia of Public International Law* (Oxford University Press, Oxford 2013).
Merternskoetter, Paul, 'National Courts as Trustees of Humanity?' (2013) Global Trust Working Paper Series 04/2013.
Mill, John Stewart, *Considerations on Representative Government* (first published 1861).
Mische, Patricia, 'National Sovereignty and Environmental Law', in Simone Bilderbeck (ed.), *Biodiversity and International Law* (Netherlands National Committee for the IUCN, 1992).
The Montreal Protocol on Substances that Deplete the Ozone Layer (adopted 16 September 1987, entered into force 1 January 1989).
Murillo, Jimena, 'Common Concern of Humankind and Its Implications in International Environmental Law' (2008) *Macquarie Journal of International & Comparative Environmental Law* 5.
Najam, Adil, 'The Case against a New International Environmental Organization' (2003) 9 *Global Governance* 367.
Najam, A., M. Papa and N. Taiyab, *Global Environmental Governance: A Reform Agenda* (International Institute for Sustainable Development, Winnipeg, Canada 2006).
Nanda, V.P. and W. Ris Jr., 'The Public Trust Doctrine: A Viable Approach to International Environmental Protection' (1976) 5 *Ecology LQ* 291.
Nash, Roderick, 'Limits of American Liberalism', in Thomas Tanner (ed.), *Aldo Leopold: The Man and His Legacy* (Soil Conservation Society of America, Ankeny 1987).
Nasr, Seyyed Hossein, 'Islam and the Environmental Crisis', in Steven C. Rockerfeller and John C. Elder (eds), *Spirit and Nature: Why the Environment is a Religious Issue* (Beacon Press, Boston 1992).
Nearing, M.A., F.F. Pruski and M.R. O' Neal, 'Expected Climate Change Impacts on Soil Erosion Rates: A Review' (2004) 59 *Journal of Soil and Water Conservation* 45.

Newell, Peter, 'A World Environment Organisation: The Wrong Solution to the Wrong Problem' (2002) 25 *The World Economy* 659.

New Zealand Ministry for the Environment, 'Key facts about climate change' (1 November 2010).

Neyer, Jürgen and Michael Schröter, 'Deliberative Europe and the Rejected Constitution', in Erik Eriksen, Christian Joerges and Florian Rödl (eds), *Law and Democracy in the Post-National-Union* (Arena-Report, Oslo 2006).

Nicholson, Graham, 'The Common Heritage of Mankind and Mining: An Analysis of the Law as to the High Seas, Outer Space, the Antarctic and World Heritage' (2002) *New Zealand Journal of Environmental Law* 6.

Nozick, Robert, *Anarchy, State, and Utopia* (Basic Books, New York 1974).

Oberthür, Sebastian and Thomas Gehring, 'Reforming International Environmental Governance: An Institutionalist Critique of the Proposal for a World Environment Organisation' (2004) 4 *International Environmental Agreements: Politics, Law and Economics* 359.

Olson, Mancur, *The Logic of Collective Action: Public Goods and the Theory of Groups* (Harvard University Press, Cambridge, MA 1965).

Oreskes, Naomi, 'Beyond the Ivory Tower: The Scientific Consensus on Climate Change' (2004) 306 (5702) *Science* 22.

Ostrom, Elinor, *Governing a Commons from a Citizen's Perspective* (Henrich Böll Stiftung, Berlin 2008).

Ostrom, Elinor, *Governing the Commons: The Evolution of Institutions for Collective Action* (Cambridge University Press, Cambridge 1990).

Ostrom, Elinor, Roy Gardner, and James Walker, *Rules, Games, and Common-Pool Resources* (University of Michigan Press, Ann Arbor 1994).

Pachauri, R.K. and A. Reisinger (eds), 'Climate Change 2007: Synthesis Report. Contribution of Working Groups I, II and III to the Fourth Assessment Report of the Intergovernmental Panel on Climate Change' (Intergovernmental Panel on Climate Change, 2007).

Palmer, Deputy Prime Minister Geoffrey, quoted in (January–March 1989) 39 (2) *New Zealand External Relations Review* 9–11.

Pardo, Arvid, 'New Horizons in Ocean Science and Law', in E. Borgese (ed.), *Pacem in Maribus* (Dodd, Mead & Co., New York 1972).

Parkin, Sara, *Positive Deviant: A 21st Century Revolution* (Earthscan, London 2010).

Perritt, Henry, 'Structures and Standards for Political Trusteeships' (2004) 8 *University of California Los Angeles Journal of International Law and Foreign Affairs* 391.

Plant, Glen, 'Institutional and Legal Responses to Global Warming', in Robin Churchill and David Freestone (eds), *International Law and*

Global Climate Change (Graham & Trotman/M. Nijhoff, London/Boston 1991).

Pogge, Thomas, 'Cosmopolitanism and Sovereignty' (1992) 103 *Ethics* 48.

Polanyi, Karl, *The Great Transformation: The Political and Economic Origin of Our Time* (Beacon Press, Boston 1990).

Prager, Ellen J., with Sylvia A. Earle, *The Oceans* (McGraw-Hill, New York 2000): ix.

Rawls, John, *A Theory of Justice*, 2nd edn (Harvard University Press, Cambridge, MA 1999).

Raz, Joseph, 'Human Rights in the Emerging World Order' (2010) 31 (1) *TLT* 42.

Redgwell, Catherine, 'Reforming the United Nations Trusteeship Council', in W. Bradnee Chambers and Jessica F. Green (eds), *Reforming International Environmental Governance: From Institutional Limits to Innovative Reforms* (United Nations University Press, Tokyo 2005).

Redgwell, Catherine, *Intergenerational Trusts and Environmental Protection* (Manchester University Press, Manchester 1999).

Reisman, W., 'Sovereignty and Human Rights in Contemporary International Law' (1990) 84 (4) *American Journal of International Law* 866.

Report of the Secretary-General, Intergenerational Solidarity and the Needs of Future Generations. UN Doc. A/68/100 (2013).

Report of the Secretary-General, Renewing the United Nations: A Programme for Reform, UN Doc. A/51/950 (1997).

Resolution of the United Nations General Assembly, The Future We Want, UN Doc. A/RES/66/288, Annex (2012).

Review of the Role of the Trusteeship Council, 87th Plenary Meeting, A/50/142, 11 December 1995.

Richardson, Benjamin, 'Trends in North America and Europe', in Klaus Bosselmann, David Grinlinton and Prue Taylor (eds), *Environmental Law for a Sustainable Society*, 2nd edn (NZCEL Monograph Series 2013).

'Riots Rock Greece as Thousands Take to the Streets', *Huffington Post* (3 November 2010).

Roche, Maurice, *Rethinking Citizenship: Welfare, Ideology and Change in Modern Society* (Polity Press, Cambridge 1992).

Rockström, Johan, Will Steffen, Kevin Noone, Asa Persson, F. Stuart Chapin III, Eric F. Lambin, et al., 'A Safe Operating Space for Humanity' (2006) 461 *Nature* 472.

Roggema, Rob, *Adaptation to Climate Change: A Spatial Challenge* (Springer, Berlin 2009).

Root, Terry L., J.T. Price, K.R. Hall, S.H. Schneider, C. Rosenzweig and

J.A. Pounds, 'Fingerprints of Global Warming on Wild Animals and Plants' (2005) 421 *Nature* 57–60.
Rose, Carol M., 'Joseph Sax and the Idea of the Public Trust' (1998) 25 *Ecology LQ* 351.
Rousseau, Jean-Jacques, *Discours sur l'origine et les fondements de l'inégalité parmi les hommes* (first published 1755).
Rowe, Jonathan, 'The Hidden Commons', *YES!* (30 June 2001).
Sachs, Wolfgang, *Planet Dialectics; Explorations in Environment and Development* (Zed Books, London 1992).
Sachs, Wolfgang, Tilman Santarius and Patrick Carniller, *Fair Future: Resource Conflicts, Security and Global Justice: A Report of the Wuppertal Institute for Climate and Energy* (Zed Books, London 2005).
Sand, Peter H., 'Sovereignty Bounded: Public Trusteeship for Common Pool Resources' (2004) 4 *Global Environmental Politics* 47.
Sand, Peter H., 'The Evolution of Transnational Environmental Law: Four Cases in Historical Perspective' (2012) 1 *Transnational Environmental Law* 183.
Sand, Peter H., 'The Rise of Public Trusteeship in International Law' (2013) Global Trust Working Paper Series 04/2013, 21.
Sand, Peter H., 'The Concept of Public Trusteeship in the Transboundary Governance of Biodiversity', in Louis Kotzé and Thilo Marauhn (eds), *Transboundary Governance of Biodiversity* (Brill, Leiden 2014).
Santos, Boaventura de Sousa, 'Beyond Abyssal Thinking: From Global Lines to Ecologies of Knowledge' (29 June 2007) *Eurozine*.
Sax, Joseph, 'The Public Trust Doctrine in Natural Resources Law' (1970) 68 *Michigan Law Review* 471.
Scherhorn, Gerhard, 'Transforming Global Resources into Commons', in David Bollier and Silke Helfrich (eds), *The Wealth of the Commons: A World Beyond Market and State* (Levellers Press, Amherst, MA 2014).
Schiller, Friedrich, *Über naive und sentimentalische Dichtung* (Reclam, Ditzinger 1978).
Schmitt, Carl, *The Crisis of Parliamentary Democracy* (The MIT Press, Cambridge, MA 1988; original publication 1923, 2nd edn 1926).
Scholte, Jan Aaart, 'Civil Society and Democracy in Global Governance' (January 2011) CSGR Working Paper 65/01, 21.
Schrijver, Nico, 'International Organization for Environmental Security' (1989) 20 *Bulletin of Peace Proposals* 2.
Schröter, Michael W., 'Lebensmittelrechtliche Vorsorge als Rechtsprinzip – nationale, europäische und welthandelsrechtliche Aspekte', ZERP-Diskussionspapier 4 (University of Bremen, Bremen 2002).
Schröter, Michael W., 'Liberalism and Sustainability: Two Colliding Principles?', in Laura Westra, Klaus Bosselmann and Colin

Soskolne (eds), *Globalisation and Ecological Integrity in Science and International Law* (Cambridge Scholars Publishing, Newcastle Upon Tyne 2011).
Schweitzer, Albert, *Ehrfurcht vor dem Leben' in Kultur und Ethik* (Beck, Munich 1923).
Science and Environmental Health Network and International Human Rights Clinic at Harvard Law School, *Models for Protecting the Environment for Future Generations* (October 2008).
Sealy, L.S., 'Fiduciary Relationships' (1962) 20 *Cambridge Law Journal* 69.
Secretariat of the Convention on Biological Diversity, *Global Biodiversity Outlook 3* (Montreal, 2010).
Shackelford, Scott J., 'The Tragedy of the Common Heritage of Mankind' (2008) 27 *Stanford Environmental Law Journal* 101–120.
Shiva, Vandana, *Monocultures of the Mind: Perspectives on Biodiversity and Biotechnology* (Zed Books, London 1993).
Shiva, Vandana, 'The Greening of the Global Reach', in Wolfgang Sachs (ed.), *Global Ecology: A New Arena of Political Conflict* (Zed Books, London 1993).
Shiva, Vandana, *Biopiracy: The Plunder of Nature and Knowledge* (South End Press, Cambridge, MA 1996).
Siefkes, Christian, *The Commons of the Future: Building Blocks for a Commons-based Society* (Henrich Böll Stiftung, Berlin 2008).
Skinner, Quentin, *States and Citizens: History, Theory, and Prospects* (Cambridge University Press, Cambridge 2003).
Skolimowski, H., *Eco-Philosophy* (Boyars, London 1981).
Smith, Graham, *Deliberative Democracy and the Environment* (Routledge, London 2003).
Sohn, Louis B., 'The Stockholm Declaration on the Human Environment' (1973) 14 *Harv. Int'l L. J.* 423.
Solomon, S., D. Qin, Z. Manning, M. Chen, M. Marquis, K.B. Averyt, M. Tignor and H.L. Miller (eds), *Climate Change 2007: The Physical Science Basis Contribution of Working Group to the Fourth Assessment Report of the Intergovernmental Panel on Climate Change* (Cambridge University Press, Cambridge 2007).
Soroos, Marvin S., 'The Evolution of Global Commons', in Ho-Won Jeong (ed.), *Global Environmental Policies: Institutions and Procedures* (Palgrave, New York 2001).
Soroos, Marvin S., 'Global Institutions and the Environment: An Evolutionary Perspective', in Regina S. Axelrod, Stacy D. VanDeveer and David Leonard Downie (eds), *The Global Environment: Institutions, Law, and Policy*, 3rd edn (CQ Press, Thousand Oaks, CA 2011).
Stahn, Carsten, *The Law and Practice of International Territorial*

Administration: Versailles to Iraq and Beyond (Cambridge University Press, Cambridge 2008).

'State of the World Forests' (Food and Agriculture Organization of the United States, 2007).

Stec, Stephen, 'Humanitarian Limits to Sovereignty: Common Concern and Common Heritage Approaches to Natural Resources and the Environment' (2010) 12 *International Community Law Review* 361.

Steenbergen, Bart van, 'Towards a Global Ecological Citizen', in Bart van Steenbergen (ed.), *Condition of Citizenship* (SAGE, London 1994).

Steinberg, Richard, 'Judicial Lawmaking at the WTO: Discursive, Constitutional, and Political Constraints' (2004) 92 (2) *Am. J. Int'l L.* 247.

Stoddart, Hannah (ed.), *A Pocket Guide to Sustainable Development Governance*, 1st edn (Stakeholder Forum, Common Wealth Secretariat 2011).

Stone, Christopher D., 'Should Trees Have Standing? Towards Legal Rights for Natural Objects' (1972) 45 *California Law Review* 450.

Stone, Christopher D., 'Defending the Global Commons', in Philippe Sands (ed.), *Greening International Law* (Earthscan, London 1993).

Stone, Christopher D., *The Gnat is Older than Man: Global Environment and Human Agenda* (Princeton University Press, Princeton, NJ 1993).

Stone Sweet, Alec and Thomas L. Brunell, 'Trustee Courts and the Judicialization of International Regimes: The Politics of Majoritarian Activism in the European Convention on Human Rights, the European Union and the World Trade Organization' (Spring 2013) 1 *Journal of Law and Courts* 60.

Strange, S., 'The Declining Authority of States', in D. Held and A. McGrew (eds), *The Global Transformations Reader: An Introduction to the Globalization Debate*, 2nd edn (Polity Press, Cambridge 2003).

Suzuki, David, *David Suzuki: The Autobiography* (Greystone Books, Vancouver 2007).

Suzuki, David, *The Legacy* (Allen & Unwin Publishing, London 2010).

Suzuki, David, Amanda McConnell and Adrienne Mason, *The Sacred Balance: Rediscovering Our Place in Nature* (Allen & Unwin Publishing, London 1997).

Taylor, C., 'Atomism', in *Philosophical Papers Volume 2: Philosophy and the Human Sciences* (Cambridge University Press, Cambridge 1985).

Taylor, Prue, *An Ecological Approach to International Law: Responding to the Challenges of Climate Change* (Routledge, London 1998).

Taylor, Prue, 'From Environmental to Ecological Human Rights: A New Dynamic in International Law' (1998) 10 *The Georgetown International Environmental Law Review* 2.

Taylor, Prue, 'The Imperative of Responsibility in a Legal Context: Reconciling Responsibilities with Rights', in Laura Westra, Klaus Bosselmann and Richard Westra (eds), *Reconciling Human Existence with Ecological Integrity* (Earthscan, London 2008).

Taylor, Prue, 'Common Heritage of Mankind Principle', in Klaus Bosselmann, Daniel Fogel and J.B. Ruhl (eds), *The Encyclopedia of Sustainability, Vol. 3: The Law and Politics of Sustainability* (Berkshire Publishing, Great Barrington, MA 2011).

Taylor, Prue, 'The Future of the Common Heritage of Mankind: Intersections with the Public Trust Doctrine', in Laura Westra, Prue Taylor and Agnes Michelot (eds), *Confronting Ecological and Economic Collapse* (Routledge, Abingdon 2013).

Taylor, Prue and Lucy Stroud, *Common Heritage of Mankind: A Bibliography of Legal Writing* (Fondation de Malte, Valletta, Malta 2013).

Teubner, Günther, *Recht als Autopoetisches System* (Suhrkamp, Frankfurt 1989).

Thomson, J., 'State Sovereignty in International Relations: Bridging the Gap between Theory and Empirical Research' (1995) 39 (2) *International Studies Quarterly* 213.

Toynbee, Arnold Joseph, *A Study of History: Reconsiderations*, Vol. 12 (Oxford University Press, Oxford 1961).

Tunks, Andrea, 'Tangata Whenua Ethics and Climate Change' (1997) 1 *N.Z. J. Envtl L.* 67.

Turner, Bryan S. (ed.), *Handbook of Citizenship Studies* (SAGE, London 2002).

Turnipseed, Mary, Michael Blumm, Duncan Currie, Kristina Gjerde, Stephen Roady, Peter Sand, et al., *Operationalizing Ubiquitous Stewardship Mandates in Ocean Law and Policy with the Public Trust Doctrine or Using the Public Trust Doctrine to Achieve Ocean Stewardship* (2013, unpublished).

Turnipseed, Mary, Michael C. Blumm, Duncan E.J. Currie, Kristina M. Gjerde, Peter Sand, Mary C. Wood, et al., 'Using the Public Trust Doctrine to Achieve Ocean Stewardship', in Christina Voigt (ed.), *The Rule of Law for Nature* (Cambridge University Press, Cambridge 2013).

Tyler, Tom, *Why People Obey the Law* (Princeton University Press, Princeton, NJ 2006).

Underhill, A. and D.J. Hayton, *Underhill & Hayton: The Law Relating to Trusts and Trustees*, 15th edn (Butterworths, London 1995).

Understanding on Rules and Procedures Governing the Settlement of Disputes, Marrakesh Agreement Establishing the World Trade Organization, Annex 2, *The Legal Texts: The Results of the Uruguay*

Round of Multilateral Trade Negotiations 354 (1999), 1869 U.N.T.S. 401, 33 I.L.M. 1226 (1994).

United Nations Convention on the Law of the Sea 1833 UNTS 3 (adopted 10 December 1982, entered into force 16 November 1994).

United Nations Educational, Scientific and Cultural Organization, 'Declaration on the Responsibilities of Current Generations towards Future Generations', adopted 12 November 1997 (Records of the General Conference, 29th Session, Vol. 1, Paris, 1998).

United Nations Environmental Programme (UNEP) Finance Initiative, Biodiversity and Ecosystem Service Work Stream, 'Demystifying Materiality: Hardwiring Biodiversity and Ecosystem Services into Finance' (CEO Briefing, October 2010).

United Nations Framework Convention on Climate Change 1771 UNTS 107 (adopted 9 May 1992, entered into force 21 March 1994).

UN Secretary-General, *An Agenda for Peace, Preventive Diplomacy, Peacemaking and Peace-Keeping*, Report of the Secretary-General, delivered to the Security Council (17 June 1992).

United States–Safeguard Measures on Imports of Fresh, Chilled or Frozen Lamb Meat from New Zealand and Australia AB-2001–1, WT/DS177,178/AB/R (01–2194) (adopted by WTO Dispute Settlement Body, 16 May 2001).

Universal Declaration of Human Rights (UDHR) GA Res 217 A(III) (adopted 10 December 1948).

US National Research Council, Board on Science and Technology for International Development, *Conserving Biodiversity: A Research Agenda for Development Agencies* (National Academy Press, Washington, DC 1992).

Vavilov, Nicolai I., *Origin and Geography of Cultivated Plants* (Cambridge University Press, Cambridge 1992).

Viikari, Lotta, *From Manganese Modules to Lunar Regolith: A Comparative Legal Study of the Utilization of Natural Resources in the Deep Sea Bed and Outer Space* (University of Lapland, Lapland 2002).

Vilela, Mirian and Peter Blaze Corcoran, 'History and Provenance of the Earth Charter: Building Consensus on Shared Values', in Peter Blaze Corcoran (ed.), *The Earth Charter in Action: Toward a Sustainable Development* (Royal Tropical Institute, Amsterdam 2005).

Viñuales, Jorge E., 'Managing Abidance by Standards for the Protection of the Environment', in Antonio Cassesse (ed.), *Realizing Utopia: The Future of International Law* (Oxford University Press, Oxford 2012).

Vogler, John, *The Global Commons: Environmental and Technological Governance*, 2nd edn (Wiley, New York 2000).

Walton, John G., *The Concept of Trusteeship in International Environmental Law* (unpublished LLM thesis, University of Auckland).
Ward, Halina, *Committing to the Future We Want: A High Commissioner for Future Generations at Rio+20*, Discussion Paper (Foundation for Democracy and Sustainable Development, World Future Council, March 2012).
Ward, Halina, 'One World: Democracy and Sustainable Development' (Presentation to Salzburg Global Seminar Boar Weekend, Salzburg, June 2009).
Watchman, Paul Q., 'Introduction', in Paul Q. Watchman (ed.), *Climate Change: A Guide to Carbon Law and Policy* (Globe Business Publishing, London 2008).
Weeramantry, C.G., *Law in Crisis: Bridges of Understanding* (Capemoss, London 1975).
Weeramantry, C.G., 'Foreword', in M.C. Segger and A. Khalfan (eds), *Sustainable Development and Law: Principles, Practices, and Prospects* (Oxford University Press, Oxford 2004).
Weiss, Edith Brown, 'The Planetary Trust: Conservation and Intergenerational Equity' (1984) 11 *Ecology LQ* 495.
Weiss, Edith Brown, *In Fairness to Future Generations: International Law, Common Patrimony, and Intergenerational Equity* (The United Nations University, Tokyo, Japan and Transnational Pub., New York 1989).
Weiss, Edith Brown, 'The Coming Water Crisis: A Common Concern of Humankind' (2012) 1 (1) *Transnational Environmental Law* 153.
Weston, Burns H. and David Bollier, *Green Governance: Ecological Survival, Human Rights, and the Law of the Commons* (Cambridge University Press, Cambridge 2014).
Westra, Laura, 'Future Policy Paths for Ecological Integrity', in Laura Westra, Klaus Bosselmann and Richard Westra (eds), *Reconciling Human Existence with Ecological Integrity: Science, Ethics, Economics and Law* (Earthscan, London 2008).
Westra, Laura, *Human Rights: The Commons and the Collective* (UBC Press, Vancouver, BC, Canada 2011).
Westra, Laura, *The Supranational Corporation: Beyond the Multinationals* (Brill, Leiden 2013).
Westra, Laura, *Revolt against Authority* (Brill, Leiden 2014).
Wheatley, Steven, *The Democratic Legitimacy of International Law* (Hart Publishing, Oxford 2010).
White, Jr, Lynn Townsend, 'The Historical Roots of Our Ecological Crisis' (1967) 155 *Science* 3767.
WHO, *World Health Report 2000: Health Systems, Improving Performance* (World Health Organization, Geneva 2000).

WHO Framework Convention on Tobacco Control 2302 UNTS 166 (adopted 21 May 2003).

WHO Revision of the International Health Regulations, WHA Res. 58.3, World Health Assembly, 58th Ass. (23 May 2005).

Wilde, Ralph, 'Trusteeship Council', in Thomas G. Weiss and Sam Daws (eds), *Oxford Handbook on the United Nations* (Oxford University Press, Oxford 2007).

Willson, Carolyn L., 'Changing the Charter: The United Nations Prepares for the Twenty-First Century' (1996) *American Journal of International Law* 90.

Wilson, Edward O., *Biophilia* (Harvard University Press, Cambridge, MA 1984).

Wilson, Sarah, *Todd & Wilson's Textbook on Trusts*, 9th edn (Oxford University Press, Oxford 2009).

Wise, Carla A., 'Green all the Lawyers', Interview of Mary C. Wood, *Utne Magazine*, September–October 2008.

Wood, Mary C., 'Nature's Trust: A Legal, Political and Moral Frame for Global Warming' (2007) 34 *Environmental Affairs* 577.

Wood, Mary C., 'Atmospheric Trust Litigation', in W.H. Rogers and M. Robinson-Dorn (eds), *Climate Change Reader* (Carolina Academic Press, Durham, NC 2011).

Wood, Mary C., *Nature's Trust: Environmental Law for a New Ecological Age* (Carolina University Press, Durham, NC 2013).

Woollaston, Philip, quoted in (October–December 1987) 37 (3) *New Zealand Foreign Affairs Review* 47.

World Commission on Environment and Development, *Our Common Future*, 'Brundtland Report' (Oxford University Press, Oxford/New York 1987).

WWF, *Living Planet Report 2010* (WWF, 2010).

Young, Michael D. and Bonnie J. McCay, 'Building Equity, Stewardship, and Resilience into Market Based Property Rights Systems', in Susan Hanna and Mohan Munasinghe (eds), *Property Rights and the Environment: Social and Ecological Issues* (Beijer International Institute of Ecological Economics/The World Bank, Washington, DC 1995).

Zaum, Dominik, *The Sovereignty Paradox* (Oxford University Press, Oxford 2007).

WEBSITES

http://www.alec.org/about-alec/

http://www.earthcharterinaction.org/content/pages/Read-the-Charter.html

http://www.futurejustice.org

http://www.gfmer.ch/TMCAM/WHO_Minelli/Index.htm
http://www.globalcommonstrust.org
http://globalvillages.ning.com/
http://www.icecoalition.com
http://www.iucn.org/what/tpas/biodiversity/
http://www.mfe.govt.nz/issues/climate/about/key-facts.html
http://www.onthecommons.org
http://turbulence.org.uk/turbulence-1/commonism
http://www.wwf.org.au/our_work/saving_the_natural_world/wildlife_and_habitats/australian_priority_species/whales/what_is_wwf_doing_to_protect_whales/whale_sanctuaries

Index